STAGING
the
RENAISSANCE

REINTERPRETATIONS OF ELIZABETHAN
AND JACOBEAN DRAMA

Edited by
DAVID SCOTT KASTAN and PETER STALLYBRASS

ROUTLEDGE

NEW YORK AND LONDON

Published in 1991 by

Routledge
An imprint of Routledge, Chapman and Hall, Inc.
29 West 35 Street
New York, NY 10001

Published in Great Britain by

Routledge
11 New Fetter Lane
London EC4P 4EE

Library of Congress Cataloging in Publication Data

Staging the Renaissance : essays on Elizabethan and Jacobean drama / edited by David Scott Kastan and Peter Stallybrass.
    p. cm.
  Includes bibliographical references and index.
  ISBN 0-415-90167-7.   ISBN 0-415-90166-9 (pbk.)
  1. English drama—17th century—History and criticism. 2. English drama—Early modern and Elizabethan, 1500–1600—History and criticism. 3. Theater—England—History—17th century. I. Kastan, David Scott. II. Stallybrass, Peter.
PR653.S7 1991
822'.309—dc20   91-26957

British Library Cataloguing in publication data also available

STAGING the RENAISSANCE

Contents

Part II   *The Plays*

Acknowledgments

The editors gratefully acknowledge the following publishers for their willingness to make materials available:

Catherine Belsey's "Alice Arden's Crime" is reprinted by permission of Routledge, Chapman and Hall from *The Subject of Tragedy* (1985), pp. 129–48.

Jonathan V. Crewe's "The Theater of the Idols: Theatrical and Anti-theatrical Discourse" is reprinted by permission of Johns Hopkins University Press from *Theatre Journal* 36 (1984): 321–44.

Jonathan Dollimore's "Subversion through Transgression" is reprinted by permission of Harvester Wheatsheaf and University of Chicago Press from *Radical Tragedy: Religion, Ideology and Power in the Drama of Shakespeare and his Contemporaries,* 2nd ed. (1989), pp. 109–19.

Sara Eaton's "Beatrice-Joanna and the Rhetoric of Love" is reprinted by permission of Johns Hopkins University Press from *Theatre Journal* 36 (1984): 371–82.

Jonathan Goldberg's "Sodomy and Society: The Case of Christopher Marlowe" appeared initially in *Southwest Review* 69 (1984): 371–78.

Stephen J. Greenblatt's "The Will to Absolute Play" is reprinted by permission of University of Chicago Press from *Renaissance Self-Fashioning* (1980), pp. 203–10.

Lisa Jardine's "Boy Actors, Female Roles, and Elizabethan Eroticism" is reprinted by permission of Harvester Wheatsheaf and Columbia University Press from *Still Harping on Daughters,* 2nd ed. (1989), pp. 9–33.

David Scott Kastan's "Workshop and/as Playhouse" is reprinted by permission of University of North Carolina Press from *Studies in Philology* 84 (1987): 324–37.

Peggy Knapp's "Ben Jonson and the Publicke Riot" is reprinted by permission from Johns Hopkins University Press from *ELH* 46 (1979): 577–94.

Ann Rosalind Jones's "Italians and Others" is reprinted by permission from Northwestern University Press from *Renaissance Drama* 18 (1987): 101–19.

Leah Marcus's "Pastimes and the Purging of Theater" is reprinted by permission of University of Chicago Press from *The Politics of Mirth: Jonson, Herrick, Milton, Marvell and the Defense of Old Holiday Pastimes* (1986), pp. 38–63.

Steven Mullaney's "Civic Rites, City Sites: The Place of the Stage" is reprinted by permission of University of Chicago Press from *The Place of the Stage* (1988), pp. 27–31, 47–55.

Karen Newman's "City Talk: Women and Commodification" is reprinted by the permission of Johns Hopkins University Press from *ELH* 57 (1989): 503–18.

Steven Orgel's "What is a Text?" is reprinted by permission of David Bergeron from *Research Opportunities in Renaissance Drama* 26 (1981): 3–6.

Annabel Patterson's "Censorship and Interpretation" is reprinted by permission of University of Wisconsin Press from *Censorship and Interpretation: The Conditions of Writing and Reading in Early Modern England* (1984), pp. 49–56.

Peter Stallybrass's "Reading the Body and the Jacobean Theater of Consumption" is reprinted by permission from Northwestern University Press from *Renaissance Drama* 18 (1987): 121–48.

Leonard Tennenhouse's "Playing and Power" is reprinted by permission of Routledge, Chapman and Hall from *Power on Display: The Politics of Shakespeare's Genres* (1986), pp. 102–12.

Frank Whigham's "Incest and Ideology" is reprinted by permission of the Modern Language Association from *PMLA* 100 (1985): 167–86.

1

Introduction:
Staging the Renaissance

David Scott Kastan and *Peter Stallybrass*

For thirty years, no new, wide-ranging anthology of essays on non-Shakespearean Renaissance drama has appeared to replace R. J. Kaufmann's *Elizabethan Drama* (1961) or Max Bluestone and Norman Rabkin's *Shakespeare's Contemporaries* (1962); yet during that time there has been a remarkable quantity of important new work in the field and, perhaps as crucially, a significant shift in the very ways in which the drama is conceived and approached. Tacitly accepting the dominance in literary studies of the New Criticism, Kaufmann wrote in the preface to his anthology that in the selected essays "the emphasis is on essentially critical rather than scholarly writing—on writing that sharpens vision and releases sympathy rather than that designed primarily to inform." For him Elizabethan drama is a "poetic drama," verbally rich and tonally complex, demanding sympathetic attention to a poetic texture that is immediately available. If his selection of essays reveals an attractive variety of critical interests, it is, he argues, because of the variousness of the drama "in its permissive and intricate attentions to all things men do to and for each other."[1] Particularly in the last decade, however, dramatic texts have been subjected to different kinds of scrutiny that make problematic considerably more than Kaufmann's unself-conscious use of "men" for the agents and objects of dramatic action. Returning in some sense to the historical interests of an even earlier scholarly age, recent criticism of the drama increasingly has insisted upon it not primarily as a "poetic" and individual art, but as a theatrical and collaborative activity, demanding a focus both on its discursive complexities and on the institutional conditions in which it was produced, demanding, that is, theoretical and historical commitments unnecessary and impossible for Kaufmann and his contemporaries.

Feminism, Marxism, poststructuralism, and psychoanalysis have productively transformed the ways in which we now conceive of texts and representation, while at the same time a renewed attention to historical specificity, necessitated precisely by the largely metaphoric if not metaphysical appeals to "History" of many of these theoretical initiatives, has emphasized the importance of the particular, and often contradictory, material determinants of the Renaissance stage. As criticism has moved away from the formalism of the 1950s and 1960s, it has had to recognize that dramatic texts are sites rather than the exclusive sources of meaning, places where audiences, readers, actors, writers (not to mention scribes and compositors) construct and contest meanings. And those meanings are in turn inflected by systems of patronage, censorship, and newly emergent market relations. In the English Renaissance theater, the text is structured by the multiple and complex collaborations that the theater demanded between patrons and players, playwrights and printers, playhouses and playgoers.

The essays in this volume attempt to register these collaborations, emphasizing the ways in which the theater is at once responsive to and constitutive of the social formations of Renaissance England. At the same time, these essays recognize that their historical grounding is not unproblematic. Inevitably we interpret history only from our necessarily partial—in both senses of the word—points of view, constructing the past from our present questioning. Yet, however conditioned and constrained, an understanding of the past is achieved in these essays that is something more than a mere projection of our own categories and concerns. All interpretations of the past may well be what Gramsci called "actual politics in the making," but the essays here avoid merely reproducing our own values and interests by refusing to collapse subject and object, by insisting on the historicity both of our object of study and of ourselves as observers, by insisting, that is, on history itself. What these essays offer, then, is not full, objective knowledge of a now past and completed history but an engaged reconstruction, necessarily mediated, provisional, and incomplete, of a history that is always in the making.

At one level, this collection is shaped by practical pedagogical concerns: most of the essays look at particular plays which regularly appear in courses on Tudor and Stuart drama. But the essays in the first section address more broadly the conditions of existence of the theater and theatrical scripts. They are in no sense intended as supplements to "close reading"; rather, they make explicit many of the presuppositions from which the essays in the second part begin. In particular, they attend to some of the most important "conditions of playing": the geographical and symbolic space of the theater; patronage and the staging of monarchical power; censorship; theatrical and anti-theatrical discourse; the heterogeneity of the theater's audience; the transvestism that marks English playing; the production of theatrical scripts; the (re)production of plays as literary property by modern editors. Yet although these introductory essays are in many ways complementary in their focus upon the various determinations weighing upon the drama, they also implicitly articulate contrasting and even contradictory perspectives. Did the theater stage the power of an aristocracy who controlled it through patronage and censorship or did it displace that power, giving it over into the hands of servants and vagrants? Were plays performed for the eye of power or for that of hodge-podge audiences, mixed in gender, class, and age? Did the transvestite acting tradition that produced an all-male stage reproduce a culture which was, as has recently been argued, "teleologically male"[2] or did it unsettle gender categories by producing them in/as masquerade? Are class distinctions reproduced and reinforced in the theater or are they unsettled by the fact that class positions can be mimed at all? Are all our notions of identity produced by anachronistic conceptions of literary property and the political individual?

The essays below give no single answer to these questions, but they all engage with the recent political and theoretical developments both inside and outside the academy from which these questions rise and which have reshaped Renaissance studies. Those developments have already been finely mapped in collections of essays on Shakespeare, such as Jonathan Dollimore and Alan Sinfield's *Political Shakespeare* (1985) and Jean Howard and Marion O'Connor's *Shakespeare Reproduced* (1987), anthologies that in their emphasis upon the contingency of the plays' values and social constructions reveal the tendentiousness of the recurring appeal to Shakespeare's timelessness and universality. But the attention to Shakespeare, inevitable and necessary given his canonical status and his position on educational syllabi, risks reinscribing the very centrality it would challenge and has perhaps obscured the more general shifts in recent analyses of Renaissance drama.

At the simplest level, the pressing political concerns of the last three decades have brought new plays to our attention. As gender has become a central category of analysis, largely due to the women's movement, the problematic construction of gender in the Renaissance has been traced in plays that were previously on the margins of academic courses (*Epicoene, Arden of Faversham, The Roaring Girl*) or, in the case of a play written by a woman (*The Tragedy of Mariam*), virtually unknown.[3] At the same time, these plays prevent too simple a correlation between gender and genre that may suggest itself (which would conceive of tragedy and history as privileged male spaces, comedy as the space of female rule and festive inversion). For whereas it is true that most of Shakespeare's tragedies (at least in their folio versions) are named after single male protagonists, tragedies with titles like *The Changeling, Women Beware Women, The White Devil, The Duchess of Malfi* suggest a different range of concerns, in which women are central or in which the very question of centrality is constituted as a problem. In *The White Devil,* for instance, the title page of the 1612 quarto affirms that the "tragedy" is that of "Paulo Giordano Ursini, Duke of Brachiano," thus reaffirming the hierarchies of gender and rank. But many readers (then as now) have found that "the Life and Death of Vittoria Corombona the famous Venetian Curtizan" provides the central scenes, while the fact that Vittoria's brother, the malcontent Flamineo, has twice as many lines as any other character, may suggest that the very notion of "central character" is inadequate in a play whose very title gives no clear point of reference (is "the white devil" of the title even a person rather than the church, the law, or the court?). What is certainly striking, though, is that the final deaths to be staged are those of a malcontent of uncertain position, a courtesan, and a black maid. Inversion of gender hierarchy here intertwines with inversion of class and racial hierarchies to dethrone the male aristocrat not only within the plot of the play but also within the generic norms of tragedy. The gendering of genre in many of these plays becomes a formal *problem* which opens up the contradictory ways in which genre constructs gender.

If recent feminist criticism has encouraged us to see gender as a constructed category, the gay and lesbian movements have interrogated the naturalness of sexual identity and helped us to see how sexuality is also a variable historical construction. We have seen as a result not only renewed attention to gender and sexuality as masquerade but also a concern with how a normalizing dominant ideology produces and is in turn challenged by that which it has defined as perverse.[4] As Jonathan Goldberg shows below, partly drawing upon Alan Bray's important book *Homosexuality in Renaissance England* (1982), there was no language of "homosexuality" (a late nineteenth-century term) as such (and therefore, incidentally, no language of "heterosexuality," this latter term being a back-formation from "homosexuality," only coined at the beginning of this century). The language of sodomy, though— a language of an *action* rather than an identity—was part of a larger discourse on "religious, political, and cosmic subversion." Yet it was precisely such subversions that Marlowe rehearsed upon the Elizabethan stage as "counterpositions."

Until recently in Britain and America, there has been considerably less attention to questions of race and ethnicity (unlike in Latin America where there has long been a major debate around Shakespeare's *Tem-*

pest[5]). But the publication of Ania Loomba's *Gender, Race, Renaissance Drama* (1989), for example, demonstrates how an analysis of colonialism and imperialism is crucial to understanding a drama which staged its new-found lands both as conquest and as interrogation of the master's voice.[6] There has also been increasing recognition of the dominant role which Ireland played in the attempt to forge an English national identity, and of the ways in which the Irish presented active resistance to that identity. As Ann Jones shows below, the Irish appear as a demonized reference point even in a play like *The White Devil* which is set in Italy. More generally, in writing of places like Venice and Malta, dramatists were able in displaced form to examine the meetings of, and conflicts between, cultures, between European and African, Italian and Turk, Italian and English, Christian and Jew. If this attention to exoticized Others was in part a staging of marks of difference which would affirm, by negation, an emergent national identity, those very marks exercised a peculiar fascination which threatened both the centrality and the stability of that identity.

What we have been suggesting here is that identity—gendered, sexed, classed, racialized—has been increasingly seen by critics as an historical *production* rather than as an essential given. This view, challenging the familiar Burkhardtian notion of the Renaissance as the founding moment of individual autonomy, has, of course, been most powerfully developed by Stephen Greenblatt in *Renaissance Self-Fashioning* (1980) and *Shakespearean Negotiations* (1988). In the earlier book, Greenblatt described how he set out to write about the way in which Renaissance writers fashioned themselves:

> But as my work progressed, I perceived that fashioning oneself and being fashioned by cultural institutions—family, religion, state— were inseparably intertwined. In all my texts and documents, there were, so far as I could tell, no moments of pure, unfettered subjectivity; indeed, the human subject itself began to seem remarkably unfree, the ideological product of the relations of power in a particular society. (256)

Greenblatt's view of the cultural production of subjectivity has at times, as his critics have argued, depended upon a monolithic notion of power as an all-embracing system that produces subversion only the more effectively to contain it. In such a view, the staging of the Moor, the Jew, the masterless woman, the transvestite, the malcontent are the necessary supports for the development of the state's hegemonic powers. The theater itself, then, becomes an agent of the absolutist state, reproducing its strategies and celebrating and confirming its power.

Such a position is elaborated most fully in Leonard Tennenhouse's influential book, *Power on Display* (1986), which powerfully explores the process by which power is produced and legitimated on the Renaissance stage.

The account of the stage as fully dominated and determined by the demands and desires of the court is, however, in some tension both with the cultural vision of many European Marxists and North American cultural critics, who, in different ways, recognize that the process of cultural domination can never be total.[7] Alan Sinfield, for instance, emphasizes the extent to which the elite was composed of conflicting class fractions, while Jonathan Dollimore has brilliantly argued that the theater itself provided a radical challenge to dominant religious, political, and sexual orthodoxies.[8] Indeed, many recent critics have argued against any unitary conception of domination, demanding a subtle understanding of the hegemonic process, in which the elite can be seen as both fractured in itself (along lines of gender, for instance) and, at the same time, as challenged by counter-hegemonic forces (e.g. the urban bourgeoisie or radical religious sects). Ideological fissures and social disjunctions are inevitable and are precisely what permit the possibility of challenge and change. Though his work has usually been taken as demonstrating the dominant culture's ability successfully to contain any subversive threat, Greenblatt himself has always recognized both the contingency of power and the pressures that resist and disperse it. Even in *Renaissance Self-Fashioning,* he recognizes "that self-fashioning occurs at the point of encounter between an authority and an alien, that what is produced in this encounter partakes of both the authority and the alien that is marked for attack, and hence that any achieved identity always contains within itself the signs of its own subversion or loss" (9). Here, the notion of containment seems to suggest less a fixed state than a local maneuver, liable within the contingencies of the political process to disintegration and reformulation. And in his recent *Shakespearean Negotiations,* Greenblatt insists that "the stage was not part of a single coherent, totalizing system" (19) but rather served as a fertile medium through which cultural meanings and values were shaped, transmitted, challenged, and changed.

Greenblatt's refusal of a rigidly functionalist understanding of the operation of the stage parallels much recent writing on the Renaissance theater that has argued against any view of the stage either as being safely contained by power or actually constituent of it and that has argued, indeed, against the very model of subversion and containment as an effective analytic concept.[9] While this now familiar binary has undoubtedly generated much fine work, suggesting the extent to which the theater was itself a powerful agent in the production of the social formation, it tends to assume cultural production as homogeneous, a process in which elite and popular cultural forms endlessly reproduce each other, and it tends to view all dissonance as permitted, even produced, by the dominant order as the necessary irritant which sustains it. Many of the essays collected here, however, actively resist any such totalized understanding of social practices, emphasizing difference rather than dominance, contradiction rather than containment. Cultures should, we would maintain, be seen less as bounded wholes than as articulations of uneven temporalities and contradictory discursive practices.

Steven Mullaney, for instance, in *The Place of the Stage* (1988) has suggested the complex interaction between center and margins in the theater's spatial location. He argues that the theater, expelled to the margins of the city, reinscribed the languages of power and subordination in the space previously occupied by the leprosarium but now rubbing sides with bear pits, brothels, and the criminal subculture. The tropes of a dominant ideology (reified by E. M. W. Tillyard as "the Elizabethan World Picture"[10]) were thus quite literally dis-placed, moved to the margins where they were held up to the scrutiny of shopkeeper and lady, apprentice and aristocrat alike. Located in the Liberties, the theater was both part and not part of the city, which no doubt was appropriate for the home of a commercial acting company that was both dependent and not dependent upon its aristocratic patrons; and the actors themselves, deemed rogues, vagabonds, and beggars by the 1572 Poor Act, were formally members of aristocratic households, the members of the King's Men even entitled to call themselves gentlemen. These contradictions of the theater were the inescapable conditions of playing and suggest that the spectacle of rule was not merely reproduced in its representations but dislocated and redistributed.

The very modes of representation of the commercial theater, indeed, produced ideological dissonance. Popular staging practices, as Robert Weimann has finely argued, regularly shift the action between an upstage *locus* and a downstage *plataea* and thus continually displace the dominant aristocratic ideology, submitting its postures and assumptions to the interrogation of clowns and commoners.[11] On stage and in the audience, the playhouse thus registered and rehearsed a variety of social and linguistic conventions; diverse accents and dialects, styles and values, sounded, intermingled, and clashed; the polyphony challenging the homogenizing and unifying pressure of the theater of state. In presenting the spectacle of power, the commercial theater with its multiple and often contradictory voices revealed the fantasy of univocality *as* a fantasy, while it simultaneously exposed the heterogeneity that it would anxiously deny.

There was, of course, one univocality in the commercial theater which was more than a fantasy; all the parts on the stage were played by males. As Stephen Orgel has elsewhere argued, however, there was nothing necessary or inevitable about the absence of women from the stage.[12] Throughout Europe, women were performers, and there was no English law forbidding them to act. Indeed, female actors could be seen when continental troupes visited England. Yet if women were absent from the stage, they were not absent from the audience, as Jean Howard discusses below. While the boy actor performed femininity upon the stage, women were part of the spectacle of the audience, and were denounced as such by anti-theatrical writers. Yet women were not only part of the spectacle, but themselves spectators, and therefore, as Howard argues, able to reverse the direction of the gaze. At the same time, on the stage a "single" gender was split into multiple sexualized roles, and gender was treated as itself a masquerade, a teetering performance.

Indeed, one of the ideological contradictions that the Elizabethan theater staged was between a rigidly hierarchical model of gender, in which male ruled female (as the head ruled the foot, the monarch the commoner, the human the animal), and a model in which any clear sexual differentiation was impossible. The transvestism of the theater drew attention to the instability of gender categories, but that instability was already inscribed within what was still the dominant Galenic medical discourse. According to the Galenic view, the only genital distinction between men and women was one of heat—the heat which caused the female vagina to "pop out" into the morphologically identical male penis. Or, as Ambroise Paré, perhaps the greatest Renaissance surgeon, put it, the genitals of men and women differ "onely in situation and use. For that which man hath apparent without, that women have hid within."[13] We even have to reconsider menstruation in a world where it was believed that men as well as women should have their periods—hence the medical significance of purgation or letting blood through incision, cupping, or leeching.

In Galenic discourse, then, there was no stable biological divide between male and female. Not only was conception a mingling of male and female seed, but the maintenance of gender differentiation required the most minute and vigilant attention so as to preserve the heat of the male and the coldness of the female. Gender was manifestly a *production,* in which sexual difference was constructed and transformed. But this production was made visible upon the stage, where the mark of sexual difference was a question of clothes—clothes which could be, and were, changed for other clothes in a dizzying series of metamorphoses. Clothes, the most regulated symbols of gender in the Renaissance, became malleable props upon the stage.

If clothes were the visible supports of gender identity, they were also the crucial markers of class status. At least eight proclamations were issued in Tudor England in order to prevent "the confusion . . . of degrees" that results "where the meanest are as richly apparelled as their betters."[14] Regularly protest was heard against the "mingle-mangle," as Stubbes called it, produced by a social transvestism, "so that it is verie hard to knowe who is noble, who is worshipful, who is a gentleman, who is not."[15] Regulation of dress was necessary to mark and secure social difference, testifying to a deep anxiety about the "unmeasurable disorder" that cross-dressing might bring about. The state strove to prohibit it, acutely aware that dressing across the naturalized class as well as gender boundaries threatened the carefully constructed hierarchical order of early modern England. But the transgressive cross-dressing on the streets of London was of course the very essence of the English Renaissance theater.[16] Anti-theatrical tracts shrilly protested the fluidity of social identity on the stage. Gosson finds it equally objectionable that in the theater a boy would "put one the attyre, the gesture, the passions" of a woman and that "a meane person" would "take upon him the title of a Prince with counterfeit port and traine."[17] The categories of class and gender seem notably constructed and mutable when, as in the theater, they are seen to be dependent upon the shape-shifting of actors. Acting itself threatens to reveal the artificial and arbitrary nature of social being.

The stage thus presented classed and gendered identity as problematic rather than given and fixed (as the naturalizing ideology of degree would have it), but it also exposed and troubled the very concept of autonomous individual identity, a notion that itself was increasingly articulated within the emergent domain of authorship. The theater, however, the very place in which writing emerged as a profession in Renaissance England, in fact complicated the idea of individual authorship and agency. In what sense *was* a dramatist an author? Title pages of Renaissance plays suggest that, if the author was increasingly worthy of mention, his presence was often secondary to the name of an acting company and even to the publisher. Ben Jonson was famous for his attempts to raise the status of dramatists above patron and audience alike, and in the publication of two of his quartos, *Volpone* (1607) and *The Case is Altered* (1609), the plays' titles are subordinated to the author: "BEN: IONSON/ his Volpone," "BEN IONSON/ His Case is Alter'd." But the history of the latter title page suggests how limited was the author's control of his own status. For *The Case is*

Altered was given three title pages in a single year. Only on the first, printed for William Barrenger, is Jonson given such preeminence. When, immediately after that publication, Barrenger went into partnership with Bartholomew Sutton, a new title page was added, testifying to the relationship but completely erasing the name of Ben Jonson. In a third title page, Jonson's name returned but, no doubt for economic reasons, crowded into the middle of the previous title page in unceremonious and ungainly fashion. Such title pages remind us that the ownership of plays was entirely controlled by theatrical companies and members of the Stationers' Company. These institutions could, of course, mobilize a dramatist's name as itself a publicity device. If the conditions of the printhouse and playhouse inevitably work to decenter and deconstruct the author, dispersing him in the collaborations of book and play production, he is often reconstructed in the book*shop,* constructed by and for commerce. We need to recognize the extraordinary labor through which modern editors have repeated this pattern, suppressing the collaborative conditions of Renaissance drama so as to create the Jonson canon, the Webster canon, and so on, in imitation of the equally problematic Shakespeare canon that had begun to be formed in the early seventeenth century.[18]

The attempt to separate out author from author in the collaborations of printhouse and playhouse, to attribute this passage to Shakespeare and that to Fletcher, this to Jonson and that to Dekker, this to Middleton and that to Rowley (to say nothing of the insistence that the dramatic text registers only the dramatist's intentions rather than interventions of the theater company), has been part of the larger project by which post-Renaissance cultural institutions have tried to elevate "art" above the contaminations of the market place and to construct a purified domain of the individual author that would be prior to the social relations of cultural production. But in the case of Renaissance dramatic texts, as Stephen Orgel notes below, the assumption that "the authority of a text derives from the author is almost never true." The early quarto titles declare the extent to which a play was inescapably

> a collaborative process, with the author by no means at the center of the collaboration. The company commissioned the play, usually stipulated the subject, often provided the plot, often parcelled it out, scene by scene, to several playwrights. The text thus produced was a working model, which the company then revised as seemed appropriate. The author had little or no say in these revisions: the text belonged to the company, and the authority represented by the text— I am talking about the *performing* text—is that of the company, the owners, not that of the playwright, the author.

And if the performing text was controlled by the companies, the published text was controlled by the Stationers' Company. Our point here is not in any sense to reduce the significance of these texts but merely to suggest the extent to which they were multiply determined, radical collaborations that can be recognized as such only as we explore the actual conditions of theatrical and textual production.[19]

As recent critics have begun to reinvestigate those conditions and reinstate them into the critical discourse surrounding the drama, they have also discovered some of the inadequacies of our traditional critical terms. The notion of "character," for instance, which was dethroned but not dismantled by New Criticism, ignores the textual processes of naming, unnaming, and renaming, which are characteristic of Renaissance play-texts, although not of the "cleaned-up" modern editions which we now habitually use in the classroom. As Random Cloud argues below, even those lists of *dramatis personae* which are now universally affixed to the beginnings of a play were rarely to be found at the beginning of Renaissance quartos and folios. Such lists give us, ready-made, the "individual characters" from whose "minds" the speeches that follow are presumed to flow. But, for example, as Cloud notes, the person whom modern editions of *All's Well that Ends Well* confidently introduce as "Countess of Rossillion, mother to Bertram" has no textual existence as such in Shakespeare's first folio. In the folio, there are five different speech tags—Mother, Countess, Old Countess, Lady, and Old Lady—for what we take to be a single role. Each title suggests not a fixed essence but a social *relation:* in terms of the family, in terms of political hierarchy, in terms of age, in terms of gender. There is no single "substance" ("the individual") in which these "accidents" inhere. The "accidents" (contingencies, occasions, conflicting roles) *are* the substance.

Most of the essays collected here similarly, if somewhat less literally, displace the unified individual, emphasizing, rather, the shifting and contradictory relations of power and desire which form (and transform) the person. They thus characteristically dwell upon the local and the contingent rather than the "essential" and the "timeless." This is both because they are concerned to defamiliarize that too-often fetishized object of study, the Renaissance, and because, in showing the processes by which identity is formed, they explore the ways in which identities are themselves part of a political process in which the very extent to which we are formed suggests the radical possibilities for transformation. The essays of this collection make those possibilities manifest and urgent, demonstrating powerfully that it was rarely essences and centralities which the drama of the English Renaissance most powerfully staged, but inversions, perversions, the local maneuvers of dressing up and of masquerade, the violent or ingenious word or device in which a whole order of things trembles and fractures.

Notes

1. *Elizabethan Drama: Modern Essays in Criticism,* ed. R. J. Kaufmann (New York: Oxford University Press, 1961). See also *Shakespeare's Contemporaries,* ed. Max Bluestone and Norman Rabkin, 1962; 2nd ed. (Englewood Cliffs, New Jersey: Prentice Hall, 1970).

2. Stephen Greenblatt, *Shakespearean Negotiations: The Circulation of Social Energy in Renaissance England* (Berkeley: University of California Press, 1988), 88.

3. Most of the impressive early feminist work was on Shakespeare. See, for instance, *The Woman's Part: Feminist Criticism of Shakespeare,* ed. Carolyn Ruth Swift Lenz, Gayle Greene, and Carol Thomas Neely (Urbana: University of Illinois Press, 1980) and Coppélia Kahn, *Man's Estate: Masculine Identity in Shakespeare* (Berkeley: University of California Press, 1981). Recent work that addresses the drama more generally includes Lisa Jardine, *Still Harping on Daughters: Women and Drama in the Age of Shakespeare* (Brighton: Harvester, 1983); Linda Woodbridge, *Women and the English Renaissance* (Urbana: University of Illinois Press, 1984); Dympna Callaghan, *Woman and Gender in Renaissance Tragedy: A Study of King Lear, Othello, The Duchess of Malfi, and The White Devil* (Atlantic Highlands, NJ: Humanities Press, 1989); and Mary Beth Rose, *The Expense of Spirit: Love and Sexuality in English Renaissance Drama* (Ithaca: Cornell University Press, 1988).

4. See Jonathan Dollimore's "Subjectivity, Sexuality, and Transgression: The Jacobean Connection," *Renaissance Drama* n.s. 17 (1986): 53–81; and his "The Cultural Politics of Perversion: Augustine, Shakespeare, Freud, Foucault," *Genders* 8 (1990): 1–16.

5. For an account, see Roberto Fernández Retamar, "Caliban: Notes Towards a Discussion of Culture in Our America," trans. Lynn Garafola, David McMurray, and Robert Márquez, *The Massachusetts Review* 15, 1–2 (1974): 7–72.

6. Ania Loomba, *Gender, Race, Renaissance Drama* (Manchester: Manchester University Press, 1989). See also Eldred Jones, *Othello's Countrymen: The African in English Renaissance Drama* (London: Oxford University Press, 1965); and, more recently, Anthony G. Barthelmy, *Black Face, Malignant Race: The Representation of Blacks in English Drama from Shakespeare to Southerne* (Baton Rouge: Louisiana State University Press, 1987); Karen Newman's essay, " 'And wash the Ethiop white': Femininity and the Monstrous in *Othello,*" in *Shakespeare Reproduced: The Text in History and Ideology,* ed. Jean Howard and Marion O'Connor (London: Methuen, 1987): 143–162; Martin Orkin, "*Othello* and the 'plain face' of Racism," *Shakespeare Quarterly* 38 (1987): 166–188.

7. See, for example, Catherine Belsey, *The Subject of Tragedy* (London and New York: Methuen, 1985); Jonathan Dollimore, *Radical Tragedy: Religion and Ideology in the Drama of Shakespeare and His Contemporaries* (Brighton: Harvester, 1983); Franco Moretti, "The Great Eclipse: Tragic Form as the Deconsecration of Sovereignty," in *Signs Taken for Wonders: Essays in the Sociology of Literary Forms* (London: Verso, 1983); Alan Sinfield, *Literature in Protestant England 1560–1660* (Beckenham: Croom Helm, 1983); Michael D. Bristol, *Carnival and Theater: Plebeian Culture and the Structure of Authority in Renaissance England*

(London and New York: Methuen, 1985); Walter Cohen, *Drama of a Nation: Public Theater in Renaissance England and Spain* (Ithaca and London: Cornell University Press, 1985); Jean E. Howard, "The New Historicism in Renaissance Studies," *English Literary Renaissance* 16 (1986): 13–43; Louis Montrose, "The Purpose of Playing: Reflections on a Shakespearean Anthropology," *Helios* n.s. 7 (1980): 51–74; " 'The Place of a Brother' in *As You Like It*: Social Process and Comic Form," *Shakespeare Quarterly* 32 (1981): 28–54; and "Renaissance Literary Studies and the Subject of History," *English Literary Renaissance* 16 (1986): 5–12; Phyllis Rackin, *Stages of History: Shakespeare's English Chronicles* (Ithaca and London: Cornell University Press, 1990); Don E. Wayne, "Power, Politics, and the Shakespearean Text: Recent Criticism in England and the United States," in *Shakespeare Reproduced: The Text in History and Ideology*, ed. Jean E. Howard and Marion F. O'Connor (New York and London: Methuen, 1987), 47–67 and "Drama and Society in the Age of Jonson: *An Alternative View*," *Renaissance Drama* 13 (1982): 103–130.

8. Alan Sinfield, "Power and Ideology: An Outline Theory and Sidney's *Arcadia*," *ELH* 52 (1985): 259–277; Jonathan Dollimore, *Radical Tragedy, passim.*

9. For a recent challenge to the pervasive binary of subversion and containment, see Theodore B. Leinwand, "Negotiation and New Historicism," *PMLA* 105 (1990): 477–490.

10. E. M. W. Tillyard, *The Elizabethan World Picture* (London: Chatto & Windus, 1943). For a recent critique of Tillyard, effectively remobilizing intellectual history, see Rebecca W. Bushnell's *Tragedies of Tyrants: Political Thought and Theater in the English Renaissance* (Ithaca and London: Cornell University Press, 1990).

11. Robert Weimann, *Shakespeare and the Popular Tradition in the Theater: Studies in the Social Dimension of Dramatic Form and Function*, ed. Robert Schwarz (Baltimore and London: Johns Hopkins University Press, 1978), esp. 237–245.

12. Stephen Orgel, "Nobody's Perfect: Or Why Did the English Stage Take Boys for Women?," *SAQ* 88 (1989): 7–30; see also Jardine, *Still Harping*, 9–36 and Phyllis Rackin, "Androgeny, Mimesis, and the Marriage of the Boy Heroine on the English Renaissance Stage," *PMLA* 102 (1987): 29–41.

13. Ambroise Paré, *The Workes*, trans. T. Johnson (London, 1634), 128. See more generally on medical theories of gender difference in the Renaissance, Tom Laqueur's important essay, "Orgasm, Generation, and the Politics of Reproductive Biology," *Representations* 14 (1986): 1–41.

14. *Tudor Royal Proclamations*, ed. Paul L. Hughes and James F. Larkin (New Haven: Yale University Press, 1969), vol. 3, 175.

15. *Phillip Stubbes's Anatomy of the Abuses in England in Shakespere's Youth, A.D. 1583*, ed. F. J. Furnivall (London: New Shakespeare Society, 1879), 41, 33.

16. See Stephen Orgel, "Making Greatness Familiar," in *The Power of Forms in the English Renaissance*, ed. Stephen Greenblatt (Norman, Oklahoma: Pilgrim Books, 1982), 41–48.

17. Stephen Gosson, *Plays Confuted in Five Acts* (London, 1579), sig. G7.

18. Margreta de Grazia, *Shakespeare Verbatim* (Oxford and New York: Oxford University Press, 1991).

19. On theatrical conditions, see, for instance, Scott McMillin, *The Elizabethan Theater and the Book of Sir Thomas More* (Ithaca and London: Cornell University Press, 1987) and Andrew Gurr, *Playgoing in Shakespeare's London* (Cambridge:

Cambridge University Press, 1987); on textual production, see the fine work of Joseph Loewenstein, "The Script in the Marketplace," *Representations* 12 (1985): 101–114, and of Peter W. M. Blayney, *The Texts of King Lear and their Origins: Nicholas Okes and the First Quarto* (Cambridge: Cambridge University Press, 1982).

Part I

The Conditions of Playing

2

Civic Rites, City Sites:
The Place of the Stage

Steven Mullaney

I

On July 21, 1557, two men were conveyed out of London and ferried across the Thames to a hospital located on the outskirts of Southwark.[1] It was known as the Lock: a place of incarceration but also, as the name suggests, a *site de passage,* a place where the new inmates could live out their lives in peace if not in comfort, fed and tended by the Warden of the hospital, the Guider, whose duty it was to oversee the passage of God's afflicted as they made their way from this life to the next. The men remain nameless, but their anonymity can hardly obscure the significance that attaches to them. They were the last recorded lepers of early modern London and its environs.

We do not know how long the two survived in their new abode; we do know that at the time of their ritual seclusion ten lazar-houses or leprosariums still stood outside the city walls, situated in every direction and serving to mark the extreme verge of the suburbs known as London's Liberties. We also know that, as leprosy performed its slow withdrawal from European populations and as leprosariums came to house a more heterogeneous collection of the ill, homeless, or otherwise disadvantaged, their prominence on the horizon of the city's concern was rapidly waning. In early modern London, however, that prominence was also being eclipsed by new cultural phenomena that were taking the place of customary forms of marginal spectacle and display, displacing tradition and transforming or troping the significance of London's Liberties. Overshadowing all other forms of the new, both from the vantage point of literary history and from the perspective of the city itself, were the popular playhouses of Elizabethan London.

It was in 1576, nearly twenty years after leprosy performed its last and finally triumphal procession, that James Burbage, a joiner by trade, made his own excursion beyond the city walls to erect a playhouse in the Liberty of Holywell, to the north of London. The Shoreditch Theatre was either the first or the second permanent playhouse constructed in Europe since late antiquity, but much to London's well-documented discomfort it did not remain unique for long. By the turn of the century the city was ringed with playhouses to the north and the south, posted strategically outside its jurisdiction and beyond the powers of civic containment or control. They were "houses of purpose built," as John Stockwood complained in 1578, ". . . and that without the Liberties, as who woulde say, 'There, let them saye what they will say, we wil play."[2] Although contemporaneous sources are notoriously silent about the construction of the popular theaters, the work of Chambers, Bentley, Wickham, and others has with considerable success glossed the first clause of Stockwood's complaint; better than ever before, we now know what it meant that these were "houses of purpose built," expressly designed for theatrical performance.[3] What has remained largely unaddressed by such research, however, is precisely that aspect of the playhouses which their antagonists found not only noteworthy but also outrageous. What mattered to Elizabethans was neither the facilities nor the design of the theaters but, as O.L. Brownstein has recently reminded us, their location.[4] What Stockwood finds distinctive and scandalous, even to the point of an audacious and unruly eloquence, is not the architecture but the place of the stage, its marginal yet commanding situation on the threshold of early modern London.

It is the place of the stage, the cultural and ideological significance of its pronounced marginality, that concerns me here. I begin by juxtaposing lazar-house and playhouse not to suggest a simple analogy or homology between such distinct cultural phenomena, but rather to bring into view a cultural and geopolitical domain—the Liberties themselves—and to examine the traditions of marginal ritual, spectacle, and license which had for centuries defined and been maintained in that domain, and which in a crucial sense prepared the ground for the Elizabethan popular stage, albeit in a sense that London itself was less than happy with. Such an examination, concerned as it is with the social definition of space—with the recreation of place as significant space, the translation of physical topography into a cultural topology—must begin with the recognition that the late Medieval and Renaissance city was shaped not by the dictates of urban planning and population control but by the varied rites of initiation, celebration, and exclusion through which a ceremonial social order defined, maintained, and manifested itself, in time and in space. It must begin, that is to say, with the recognition that customary approaches to early modern ritual and ceremony, however astute in themselves, have failed to grasp both the strategic function and the context of civic ritual in the pre-modern city.

Focusing primarily on those rituals and ceremonies organized around central figures of authority—Elizabeth's pre-coronation passage, annual Lord Mayor's processions—we have tended to view them as initiatory rites of passage, vehicles by which figures of power were conveyed to their proper place in the social hierarchy, their passage into prominence at once negotiated and celebrated by ritual means. Such a perspective is not false, but it is misleading. It removes civic ritual from its urban context, obscuring the degree to which that context—the landscape of the urban community itself—was not merely the setting for civic ritual but also its most lasting record, a topographical text being simultaneously composed and interpreted by means of ritual process. Any city could be described, regardless of its time and place, as a projection of cultural values and beliefs—as a casting of ideals and ideologies into concrete form, an inscription of cultural practices and contradictions in the very landscape of community. As the recent work of Natalie Davis and others has suggested, however, our talk of civic space and cultural inscription means something altogether different when it refers not to the constructs of the modern age but to those of a more ritually oriented and maintained society.[5] Public ritual and ceremony did not merely take place in the late Medieval and Renaissance city. Instead they provided the vehicles with which a community could chart, in its actual topography, the limits and coherence of its authority, the vehicles by which the urban landscape was itself articulated and defined, the civic terrain shaped and translated into significant space. In the varied ceremonies and festivities conducted throughout the year in sixteenth-century London, both within and without the confines of its ancient Roman wall, the city's image of itself was at once dramatized and, through repetitive performance and mnemonic association, inscribed in the physical body of the community itself. When a Lord Mayor's Pageant achieved its plotted course through the city the ceremony itself was at an end, but the concerns of the community thus celebrated and conveyed were not exhausted by their ritual progress. Rather, such concerns were set in context, transcribed into a language of monuments and commonplaces. When ceremony ceased, the city remained: a trace, a record, a living memory of the cultural performances it both witnessed and served to embody. The pre-modern or ceremonial city was a dramatic and symbolic work in its own right, a social production of space, an *oeuvre* (as Henri Lefebvre has rightly characterized it)[6] composed and rehearsed over the years by artisanal classes and sovereign powers, for whom meaning was always a public event, culture an "acted document,"[7] and power a manifest thing, to be conspicuously bodied forth in the urban land-scape.

In the case of sixteenth-century London, my own reading of the resulting "rhetoric" of civic space is heavily indebted to John Stow's *Survay*—not only for the information it provides, but also and more crucially for the method with which it is composed. Motivated by social changes and an unprecedented population explosion that were making the cultural landscape of London increasingly unrecognizable to its own citizens, Stow describes the *Survay* as a "Discovery" of London, and it is precisely that: an archaeology of the city, a systematic uncovering of its various lines and sites of significance. The *Survay* is organized not as an analysis of London, however, but as a walk through it—a peripatetic representation of London, in which the city serves as its own map, an open book for those (like Stow) who know how to read it. With Stow we move from place to place in the city, inquiring at each site as to the significance of the place, the images it holds, the events it has witnessed, the customs and rituals that have left their mnemonic traces on its streets and conduits. Stow's passage through the city amounts to an attentive transcription of the memory traces impressed upon the civic landscape by time and ceremonial circum-stance; indeed, London acts for its surveyor as a vast memory system, an extensive and monumental memory-theater. But if Stow's London is a memory-theater, where images of the past adhere to particular places and can be retrieved or recreated by the sort of topical and ambulatory inquiry that structures the *Survay*, it is also a city; like the artificial memory-theaters described by Frances Yates, it is a symbolic and even a rhetorical device, but it is also an inhabited one. Its common places were actual sites, visited and frequented by the citizens of Lon-don, and at the same time they served as commonplaces in the rhetorical sense of the word: as *topoi* or *loci communes*, sites of potential mean-ing, open and available to various figures and uses, even capable—as rhetorical topoi often are—of antithetical or ambivalent significance.

Stow devotes over half his *Survay* to the area outside the walls of the city, and in so doing he reminds us that the definition provided by London's wall and the natural barrier of the Thames was more equivo-cal than the city's clear outline at first suggests. From our vantage point, it is easy to be taken in by the walls of the Medieval or Renais-sance city—to regard them, as even Fernand Braudel does in his other-wise inspired overview of early modern towns,[8] as sheer, antithetical boundaries defining inside against outside, what is native and integral to the community against what is foreign and alien to it. In a manner necessary to its symbolic economy, however, the walled city was not a binary but a tertiary construct. Within the city walls, the ideals,

aspirations, and mystifications of community were staged in an extensive repertory of civic rituals and cultural performances; the margins
of the city served as a more ambivalent staging ground, as a place
where the contradictions of the community—its incontinent hopes,
fears, and desires—were prominently and dramatically set on stage.
Between city and country stood "an uncertain and somewhat irregular
territory"[9] where the powers of city, state, and church often came
together (to maintain, for example, a hospital or lazar-house) but did
not hold full sway. London's Liberties, extending up to a mile from
the city proper, were a part of the city yet set apart from it; they were
free or "at liberty" from manorial rule or obligation to the crown, but
they were also outside the jurisdiction of the Lord Mayor. They formed
a transitional zone between the city and the country, various powers
and their limits, this life and the next. It was here that citizens retired
to pursue pastimes without a proper place within the community,
and their retreat was a heterogeneous one: alongside gaming houses,
marketplaces, taverns, bear-baiting arenas, and brothels stood (before
their dissolution) monasteries, sites of execution, and, at the extreme
verge of the Liberties, the ten lazar-houses that ringed the city by the
end of the sixteenth century.

What unites such distinct phenomena is a pronounced cultural ambivalence; they do not fit into the binary, either/or classifications of the
social order, but they were not, as a result, fully excluded from that
order. A place was made for them on the margins of the ordered, and
they in turn served to define that place, the Liberties, as a domain of
cultural ambivalence and excess. Leprosy is hardly the only marginal
figure, but it is an extreme and thus illuminating instance.

II

The sudden rise of leprosariums throughout Europe in the eleventh
and twelfth centuries (Queen Maud founded London's first in 1118)
signaled a fundamental shift in the cultural significance of the disease.
Medieval Biblical commentary conflated Lazarus the beggar with Lazarus of Bethany, raised from the dead in a prefiguration of the final
resurrection. The leper became a lazar: long regarded as a mortifying
spectacle,[10] a figure of the living dead to be banished from the community in relatively straightforward rites of exclusion, he now became a
figure of sacred pollution, no longer a mere memento mori but a
monumental reminder that resurrection awaited even the most ravaged
of bodies. Once free (or condemned) to wander, the lazar was now
bound fast to the horizon of community. His ritual seclusion began
with what would be his last confession and a mass for the dead;

removed from the ecclesiastical community, he was also stripped of all marital and lineal rights, then led outside the city gates where he was declared dead to the world but alive to God.[11] The lazar-house stood by not to quarantine his disease—visitors were received, even prostitutes from neighboring brothels; inmates were allowed out to shop for food, and summarily turned out of doors if found in violation of the monastic rules of the house—but rather to make manifest his anomalous status and to situate it in a margin of transition between one world and the next.

The twelfth century also marks a period of urban renaissance throughout Europe, when many new towns were founded and many old ones were transformed along lines that would remain stable until the late Renaissance. According to Braudel, the walled medieval town becomes the norm at this time.[12] The lazar-houses framed the city: they hedged it in and placed it in context, with a result that could best be described as a form of dramatic irony. The arc described by the lazar-houses echoed the more substantial enclosure of London's walls, but the echo was a parodic one, a monumental reminder that to declare a province of authority was also to declare its limits. An organization, a community, or a culture are bound together by their acts of definition, but the bind is an inescapably double one, defining at the same time the limitations of organization, community, or culture. Anomalous and ambiguous, uncontained by either the categories or the powers that be, leprosy stood in the Liberties as a constant reminder of such limits: a marginal gloss on the ambivalence that circumscribes any will to contain.

The Liberties were social and civic margins, and they also served as margins in a textual sense: as places reserved for a "variety of sences" (as the translators of the 1611 Bible described their own margins) and for divergent points of view—for commentary upon and even contradiction of the main body of their text, which in this instance means the body politic itself. Inside the ceremonial city, ritual and spectacle were organized around central figures of authority, emblems of cultural coherence. The figures we encounter outside the city walls are liminal ones, and the dramaturgy of the margins was a liminal breed of cultural performance, a performance of the threshold, by which the horizon of community was made visible, the limits of definition, containment, and control made manifest. In his *Survay*,[13] Stow describes a graveyard located outside the city walls where unknown foreigners were brought when they died, nameless and unmourned, to be buried in a communal cemetery aptly known as No Man's Land (II, 81). The epithet could easily be applied to the Liberties as a whole. What escaped classification within the social structure of the city was lodged outside the physical embodiment of society. As we follow Stow around the city's perimeter we encounter a heterogeneous collection of the outcast and the anomalous, lodged outside the order they had in a sense already exceeded.

In close proximity to scaffolds of execution stood hospitals, originally monastic and later maintained by the city; they served not so much to cure the sick or prevent contagion as to provide a place set apart for those whose ailments had already, like the crimes of the condemned, dissociated them from the social body. The juxtaposition of scaffold and hospital displays a certain decorum: both served as sites of passage, where those who were neither living nor dead but embarked on a journey between the two states could be accommodated and displayed, according to their kind. Stow provides an example of such accommodation when he pauses to comment on Wapping-in-the-Woze. It was "the usuall place of execution," Stow writes, "for the hanging of Pirates & Sea Rovers, at the low water marke there to remaine, till three tides had overflowed them" (II, 70–71). The condemned thieves were not so much hung as staked out in a realm where land and sea held equal claim, a tidal zone between the powers of human and divine authority. Even in death the power of the community over their bodies ebbed slowly, making them serve as ambiguous signs of power, emblems of both the manifest efficacy of the reigning social structure and of the frontier beyond which human authority did not extend.

To view such a spectacle merely as a display of efficacious power would be to ignore half the scene being composed. In an age of conspicuous expenditure, when a family fortune could be exhausted in single display of ostentatious mourning,[14] rituals of power and authority were paradoxical affairs. Whenever power or prestige was at stake, Renaissance authority achieved the full apogee of its assertion, its most extreme manifestation, at its own expense—when most conspicuously expended or consumed. Ceremonies of power were ceremonies of loss as well, and in the margins of the city such ceremonies amounted to ritual demarcations of the limits of social and political authority. Marginal spectacle conformed to an ambivalent dynamic, whether it took the shape of public execution, the ritual seclusion and display of leprosy, or the more benign manifestations of civic incontinence represented by the brothels and gaming houses of the Liberties.

When it did not exile or execute them, early modern power licensed those things it could neither contain nor control. London's stews and other marginal pleasures, the libidinal economy of the "licentious liberties" (to employ Henry VIII's phrase), were one of the results. Although less formally maintained than the other cultural phenomena manifested in the Liberties, license also bears the seeds of its own contradiction. It refers at once to what is permitted and to what transgresses the bounds of permission. License shades into licentiousness without even the trace of a seam. "Like changeable silk," as even Lord Chesterfield was forced to admit, "we can easily see there are two different colors, but we cannot easily discover where the one ends, and the other begins."[15] Like the word, the act of licensing is two-sided and ambidextrous. A license is a token of the agent who grants it, and so can serve its bearer as an emblem or imprimatur of authority. Once issued, however, a license leaves the control as well as the hands of the licensing agent. With a license, one can take license or liberties; issuing a license is at once an assertion of authority, and a declaration of its limits.

To choose to display one's limits or to acknowledge them after the fact—to participate, as the powers of city, church, and state traditionally did, in the staging of their own incontinence—does not reduce the margin of ambiguity that circumscribes and to an extent subverts authority. But a certain power, albeit a paradoxical one—a power grounded in its own limits and contradictions—is thus maintained and manifested. "Spectacle," according to Guy de Bord, "is the existing order's uninterrupted discourse about itself. It is the diplomatic representation of hierarchic society to itself, where all other expression is banned."[16] Even the license of the Liberties implied the authority of those institutions which implicitly or explicitly licensed it; however ambivalent, the implication was of use and profit, serving to assert an image of authority even at its limits, its verge or vanishing point. It was quite another matter, however, when the reigning hierarchy of London found the spectacle of its own vulnerability and limits thrust upon it, as it did in the latter half of the sixteenth century.

III

When they gazed out over their Liberties in the sixteenth century, what the city fathers saw was a discomfiting and anamorphic scene. Traditional forms of marginal spectacle and license were being overlaid with the new, making the community the victim of its own ritually inscribed and maintained contradictions. The civic and social structure I have been tracing here had been remarkably stable for centuries, but only because that structure had made room for what it could not contain, had included all that exceeded the strict bounds of binary or antithetical definition. The city thus conceived was a perpetual stasis machine, its stability powered by the incontinence and instability it so rigorously hedged itself with and gave way to. In the latter half of the sixteenth century, however, the Liberties were taking liberty, and London was a captive audience to the unfolding social drama. The cast was of course a large one, ranging from victims of enclosure and foreign tradesmen to outlaws, Puritans, and players, but it was the latter who were erecting a viable and highly visible institution of their own on the grounds of the city's well-maintained contradictions. They added their own voice to the existing order's previously uninterrupted discourse about itself: "There, let them saye what they will say, we wil play." Like the lazar-houses, playhouses soon ringed the city in a parodic echo of its containment; they were not comfortably fixed emblems of anomaly and ambivalence, however, but "Houses of Proteus,"[17] places where social categories were merged or violated, selves reshaped and recreated, on stage and off. Like the plague, which would come to be inseparable from popular drama in the cultural imagination, a player was difficult to identify and impossible to put down, and his theatricality was equally contagious. As one Lord Mayor complained, masterless men and vagabonds gathered at theaters "to recreate themselves:"[18] to learn a new role, strike a new strategem or disguise, profit at playing and pleasure. From the city's point of view, the playhouses were the source of all the ills pestering London, and in a sense the city fathers were right—but only insofar as those playhouses were a full manifestation of the "incontinent rule" that had always reigned in the Liberties. Born of the contradiction between Court license and city prohibition, popular drama emerged as a cultural institution only by materially embodying that contradiction: by dislocating itself from the strict confines of the existing social order and taking up a place on the margins of society. When popular drama moved out into the Liberties, it appropriated a civic structure of spectacularly maintained contradictions, and converted that structure to its own ends, translating its cultural situation into a liberty that was at once moral, ideological, and topological—a liberty or freedom to experiment with a wide range of available perspectives on its own times, and on the historical conditions of its own possibility.

Notes

1. For London's last lepers and a valuable survey of the city's lazar-houses, see Marjorie B. Honeybourne, "The Leper Hospitals of the London area," *London and Middlesex Archaeological Society Transactions* 21 (1963), 3–61.

2. *A Sermon Preached at Paules Crosse* . . . (London, 1578), 134.

3. The most useful single study of the playhouses is Glynne Wickham, *Early English Stages, 1300–1600,* 3 vols. (London: Routledge & Kegan Paul, 1963); see also Walter C. Hodges, *The Globe Restored* (London: Oxford Univ. Press, 1968), and

A New Companion to Shakespeare Studies, ed. K. Muir and S. Schoenbaum (Cambridge: Cambridge Univ. Press, 1971).

4. O. L. Brownstein, "A Record of London Inn-Playhouses from 1565 to 1590," *Shakespeare Quarterly* 22 (1971), 23.

5. On the shaping of an ideological terrain by ritual practice, see Natalie Z. Davis, "The Social and the Body Sacred in Sixteenth-Century Lyons," *Past and Present* 90 (1981), 40–71; André Leroi-Gourhan, *Le geste et la parole* (Paris: A. Michel 1965), II: 138–205; Henri Lefebvre, *Le droit et la ville* (Paris: Anthropos, 1968); Paul Clavel, *Espace et pouvoir* (Paris: Presses universitaires de France, 1978); Charles Phythian-Adams, "Ceremony and the Citizen: The Communal Year at Coventry, 1450–1550," in *The Early Modern Town,* ed. Peter Clark (New York: Longman, 1976), 106–128; Joseph Rykwert, *The Idea of a Town: The Anthropology of Urban Form in Rome, Italy, and the Ancient World* (Princeton: Princeton Univ. Press, 1976); and Robert J. Thornton, *Space, Time, and Culture Among the Iraqw of Tanzania* (New York: Academic Press, 1980), 9–20.

6. Henri Lefebvre, *Le droit et la ville* (Paris: Presses universitaires de France, 1978), 53.

7. For the phrase and an admirable discussion of culture as symbolic action, see Clifford Geertz, "Thick Description: Toward an Interpretive Theory of Culture," in *The Interpretation of Cultures* (New York: Basic Books, 1973), 3–32.

8. Fernand Braudel, *Capitalism and Material Life,* tr. M. Kochan (New York: Harper and Row, 1973), 382.

9. Virginia Gildersleeve, *Government Regulations of the Elizabethan Drama* (1908; rpt. New York: Burt Franklin, 1961), 140.

10. *Patrologiae cursus completus, series graeca,* ed. J. P. Migne (Paris: Seu Petit-Montrouge, 1841–64), 36: 579.

11. For the interpretive conflation, and a well-informed inquiry into the cultural significance of leprosy, see Peter Richards, The Medieval Leper and His Northern Heirs (Totowa, New Jersey: Rowman and Littlefield, 1977), 5–56.

12. Braudel, *Capitalism,* 397–98.

13. Quotations from Stow are from the two-volume edition edited by C. L. Kingsford (Oxford, 1909).

14. See Lawrence Stone, "The Anatomy of the Elizabethan Aristocracy," *The Economic History Review* 18 (1948), 12–13.

15. Cited by Tony Tanner, "License and Licencing: To the Presse or to the Spunge," *The Journal of the History of Ideas* 38 (1977), 5.

16. Guy de Bord, *Society of the Spectacle* (Detroit: Black and Red, 1977), 24.

17. For the Protean player, and an excellent study of the dialectical relationship between Elizabethan drama and culture, see Louis Adrian Montrose, "The Purpose of Playing: Reflections on a Shakespearean Anthropology," *Helios* n.s. 7 (1980), 51–74.

18. "The Remembrancia," in *Dramatic Records of the City of London,* ed. E. K. Chambers (London: The Malone Society, 1907), I: 77.

3

Playing and Power

Leonard Tennenhouse

I

Elizabeth Tudor knew the power of display. She also knew how to display her power as queen. This is not to say that even so powerful a monarch as she could determine the conditions for effectively displaying political power. Upon her accession, if not well before, Elizabeth found herself thoroughly inscribed within a system of political meaning. Marie Axton explains:

> for the purposes of the law it was found necessary by 1561 to endow the Queen with two bodies: a *body natural* and a *body politic*. (This body politic should not be confused with the old metaphor of the realm as a great body composed of many men with the king as a head. The ideas are related but distinct.) The body politic was supposed to be *contained within the natural body of the Queen.* When lawyers spoke of this body politic they referred to a specific quality: the essence of *corporate perpetuity*. The Queen's natural body was subject to infancy, error, and old age; her body politic . . . was held to be unerring and immortal.[1] (emphasis mine)

The "lawyers," as Axton observes, "were unable or unwilling to separate state and monarch."[2] Elizabeth also insisted upon identifying her body with England on grounds she embodied the mystical power of the blood. Her natural body both contained and stood for this power. It did so at a moment when England was ready to understand power in nationalist terms and Elizabeth was bent on displaying her power accordingly. Her sexual features figured into a representation of the monarch's body and redefined the concept of the body politic in certain characteristically Elizabethan ways. At the same time, I will insist, the monarch's sexuality was always just that, the *monarch's* sexuality.[3] As such, the features of Elizabeth's body natural were always already components of a political figure which made the physical vigor and autonomy of the monarch one and the same thing as the condition of England. The English form of patriarchy distributed power according to a principle whereby a female could legitimately and fully embody the power of the patriarch. Those powers were in her and nowhere else so long as she sat on the throne. They were no less patriarchal for being embodied as a female, and the female was no less female for possessing patriarchal powers. In being patriarchal, we must conclude, the form of state power was not understood as male in any biological sense, for Elizabeth was certainly represented and treated as a female. The idea of a female patriarch appears to have posed no contradiction in terms of Elizabethan culture. This chapter pursues several implications of this iconic notion of the queen's body by way of considering the conditions for political display.

First, I shall cite one or two examples to suggest how far a Tudor monarch could go in maintaining his or her iconographic status. Accounts of the debate on the Act of Supremacy reveal that some members of Parliament felt that to name a woman Supreme Head of the Church was more than most Catholics and many Protestants would tolerate. Although her brother and father had assumed the title of "Supreme Head" of the Church of England, Elizabeth agreed to revise the title she bore to "Supreme Governor." This was just one of many occasions where she allowed her image to be sexed. But when sexuality was used in any way to compromise her patriarchal prerogatives, the queen reacted in an entirely different manner. In 1576, for instance, the recently appointed Archbishop Grindal wrote her to request that "you would not use to pronounce so resolutely and preemptorily, *quasi ex auctoritate,* as ye may do in civil and extern matters. . . ."[4] The queen immediately sequestered Grindal and would have removed him entirely from his post, had he not "forstalled the arrangements . . . by dying, still in office."[5] Where she would tolerate minor changes in title, then, she would brook absolutely no challenge to the power inherent in her blood. By the same token, upon assuming the throne, she renewed the practice initiated by her father and continued by her brother which installed the royal coat of arms over the chancel arch of the churches of England. Her coat of arms thus replaced the religious images which had been condemned in the iconoclastic reform of the English Church. "Honor toward this royal emblem, if not civic veneration," writes John Phillips, "was now demanded from Englishmen. . . ."[6] As the church came to house the secular emblems of state, the queen's sexual body acquired the power of a religious image. Bishop Jewel, for one, referred to her as "the only nurse and mother of the church."[7] Elizabeth treated sex as her particular signature upon the body politic which in no way changed the essential nature of its power.[8]

The identification of the queen's sexual body with the political body was no less absolute than the iconic bonding of the political body to the sacred authority of the Church. Roy Strong discusses the royal coat of arms as but "one of a series of material objects which were universally regarded as emanations of royal power. In this way, he continues, "the royal arms erected in churches as manifestations of the royal governorship of the *Ecclesia Anglia* become 'portraits' of the Queen."[9] Strong includes this emblem with the paintings and engravings that represented her natural body. Among these portraits, I would like to take special notice of the Ditchley portrait that shows Elizabeth standing upon the map of England, as well as a Dutch engraving of 1598 which, in similar fashion, portrays her body enclosing Europe against the Pope and the power of Spain. Such portraits as these made explicit, in Peter Stallybrass's words, "the conjunction of imperial virgin and cartographic image to constitute together the terrain of Elizabethan nationalism."[10] Even when the bond between her body and the body politic was not represented in territorial terms, however, this bond was still apparent in portraits where the surface of her body was ornamented with the power and wealth of the state. That Elizabeth wanted her subjects to know they were admiring England's power in gazing upon her image is apparent in her response to the industry which sprang up for the purpose of representing the queen. In 1563 a proclamation was drafted calling for one painter to have access to the queen "to take the natural representation of her majesty," and "to prohibit all manner of other persons to draw, paint, grave, or portray her majesty's personage or visage. . . ."[11] Though apparently never enforced, this proclamation "was designed to counter the production of debased images of the Queen."[12] Along with others drafted during her reign, this measure suggests that it was not royal vanity that made her fret over "deform'd" images and counterfeit portraiture but her awareness of the queen's image as a kind of political coin whose iconic value had to be protected.

There is evidence to suggest that Elizabeth's loyal subjects were not the only ones to accept the iconic nature of her representation. Her enemies apparently believed that because her image "partook in some mysterious way of the nature of the sitter it was also potentially dangerous." Strong bases this speculation, as he explains, on the fact that "Throughout the reign efforts were made to dispose of the Queen by stabbing, burning, or otherwise destroying her image."[13] Burghley was sufficiently worried about such attacks on the queen's image to treat them as dangerous offenses. But the way in which an assault on Elizabeth's personal iconography constituted an assault on the body politic itself is explained still more clearly by an incident in *Richard II*. Bullingbroke declares he is executing Bushy and Green for the crimes of "disfiguring" the king. Such an act of treason evidently extends to assaults on any member of the aristocracy if it extends to the signs and symbols of royal blood. Thus Bullingbroke charges the pair with "disparking" his own lands, defacing his coat of arms, and razing his imprese, "leaving me no sign," he says, "Save men's opinion and my living blood / To show the world I am a gentleman" (III.i.25–7).

In a system where the power of the monarch was immanent in the official symbols of the state, the natural body of the monarch was bound by the same poetics of display. That Elizabeth knew the power of such display is evident in her willingness to help finance and stage a passage through London the day before her coronation.[14] Unlike the more important pageants which had been financed for her sister by foreign communities in London, Elizabeth excluded from the passage either the support or the participation of "any foreign person."[15] This point was emphasized in the account of the passage that was published almost immediately afterwards. Her pageant therefore provided an exclusively English context for displaying her power. This well-known description of her passage through London to Westminster the day before her coronation suggests the degree to which the signs and symbols of power were all understood in reference to her body:

> if a man shoulde say well, he could not better tearme the Citie of London that time, than a stage wherein was shewed the wonderful spectacle, of a noble hearted Princesse toward her most loving People, and the People's exceding comfort in beholding so worthy a Soveraigne, and hearing so Prince like a voice, which could not but have set the enemie on fyre, since the verture is in the enemie always commended, much more could not but enflame her naturall, obedient, and most loving People, whose weale leaneth onely uppon her Grace and her Government.[16]

The staging of this official passage, like that of a royal progress, not only brought forth the queen's body and displayed it in the context of her considerable entourage. It also called forth elaborate pageants, tributes, opulent shows of all kinds in response to the queen's appearance. These to be witnessed by large numbers of people. To speak of the queen's body in such terms is not to speak of the desiring subject or the object of desire she has become in historical narratives written in the nineteenth and twentieth centuries. To the contrary, the aesthetic performances centered in the figure of the queen were entirely political, as they aimed at identifying the monarch's body with English power in all its manifestations.[17]

II

Displaying the monarch's body was so essential to maintaining the power of state that the aesthetics of such displays shaped the theater which grew up during Elizabeth's reign. On 16 May 1559, she imposed a "temporary inhibition of plays," and her Privy Council assumed jurisdiction over all theatrical performances. While her brother had also imposed a temporary restraint on the production of plays during periods of social unrest, no other Tudor monarch maintained such tight control over the plays and players as Elizabeth.[18] By 1572 only barons or personages of higher degree were allowed the privilege of maintaining "minstrels or players of interludes." This legislation was amended, but not changed substantially, in 1576, in 1584–5, and again in 1597–8.[19] It would appear that only members of the peerage could be trusted with so powerful a political medium. After the mid-1570s, the very existence of the elaborate machinery of playhouses, acting companies, and censorship procedures was obviously associated with the political interests of the queen. Ann Jennalie Cook suggests that "the entire rationale for the existence of dramatic companies was that they provided essential recreation for the sovereign. In theory, she continues, "public performances merely provided an opportunity for rehearsal and perfection of plays before they were presented at Court."[20] I simply want to take this notion more literally than Cook does. Her research shows a theater audience largely composed of the so-called privileged playgoers who identified their interests with those of the queen.[21] But it was as much, if not more, the treatment of the aristocratic body on stage as it was the constitution of the audience, I will argue, that made the public theater and the Inns of Court drama resemble other displays of state power. It is easy for us to imagine how, for such an audience, the staging of chronicle history and even tragedy made openly political statements. Though perhaps not so obvious to a modern reader of Renaissance literature, the romantic comedies and Petrarchan lyrics were bound by the same imperative to identify the queen's body with that of the state. More than any other monarch, we should recall, Elizabeth regulated the sexual relations of her court. In such an environment as this, a drama was never more political than when it turned on the body of an aristocratic woman.

I will use the much abused play *Titus Andronicus* to make my point. As thoroughly unnatural as its staging of sexual relations seems today.

Titus plays on the whole notion of the state as the body of an aristocratic female. Titus's daughter is raped and disfigured in the second
act of the play. Shakespeare's stage directions suggest he brings her on
stage after the rape mainly in order to call attention to her mutilated
condition. The sheer spectacle of a woman, herself dismembered, carrying her father's amputated hand in her mouth has not earned this
play a particularly high place in a canon based on lofty ideas and good
taste. The mutilation of Lavinia's body has been written off as one
of the exuberant excesses of an immature playwright or else as the
corrupting influence of another poet.[22] But I would like to consider
these sensational features as part of a political iconography which
Shakespeare understood as well as anyone else, one which he felt
obliged to use as well as free to exploit for his own dramatic purposes.
With this purpose in mind we might understand the otherwise outrageous scene in which Titus receives his own hand along with the
heads of his two sons from Saturninus, the emperor. Seeing the human
members which have been severed from himself, Titus issues this mem-
orably gruesome command,

> Come, brother, take a head,
> And in this hand the other will I bear;
> And, Lavinia, thou shalt be employed;
> Bear thou my hand, sweet wench, between thy teeth.
> (III.i.279–82)

To tell her father she has been raped as well as mutilated, Lavinia has
to rifle through a volume of Ovid with her handless arms until she
finds the account of Philomel. Shakespeare's stage direction reads, "*She
takes the staff in her mouth, and guides it with her stumps, and writes*"
(s.d., IV.i.76).

What is important in this—as in the other scenes where Lavinia's
body appears as synecdoche and emblem of the disorder of things—is
that Shakespeare has us see the rape of Lavinia as the definitive instance
of dismemberment. I write this knowing it defies the logic inherent in
the figure of rape. We are accustomed to think of rape as a boundary
violation where the outsider forcibly penetrates some sacred cultural
territory—the sanctuary of the home or the enclosure of the individual,
if not the autonomy of the aristocratic community—and calls these
concepts into question. But Shakespeare uses rape for this purpose
neither in *Titus Andronicus* nor in *The Rape of Lucrece*. He does not
allow us to name rape as the crime when we find rape reinscribed upon
Lavinia's body as the crime of dismemberment. Indeed amputation
displaces penetration as Lavinia's stumps point back to the story of

Philomel in order to make the fact of rape known. What Shakespeare does stage, then, is the fact of dismemberment as a highly self-conscious revision of his classical materials. I would like to suggest that this peculiar turning of rape into dismemberment is a singularly Elizabethan move. The mutilation of Lavinia's body simply restates her father's murder of his own son, the decapitation of her two brothers, her father's self-inflicted amputation, his dicing up of the emperor's step-sons for their mother's consumption, and all the slicing, dicing, chopping, and lopping that heaps bodies upon the stage in *Titus Andronicus*. Lavinia's body restates and interprets this seemingly gratuitous carnage in a way that must have been clear to an Elizabethan audience in as much as her body was that of a daughter of the popular candidate for emperor of Rome, the first choice of wife for the emperor of Rome, and the betrothed of the emperor's younger brother. That as such she stands for the entire aristocratic body is made clear when Marcus Andronicus, inspired by the pile of bodies heaped at the banquet table, enjoins the citizens of Rome, "Let me teach you how to knit again / . . . These broken limbs into one body (V.iii.70–2).

Dismemberment entails the loss of members. Thus the initial gesture of penetration does not seem to matter so much in Shakespeare's version of the Philomel story as the condition of Lavinia's body which both conceals and points to the initial act of penetration. Rather than make Lavinia serve as the object of illicit lust, Shakespeare uses her body as the site for political rivalry among various families with competing claims to power over Rome. For one of them to possess Lavinia is for that family to display power over the rest—nothing more nor less than that. By the same token, to wound Lavinia is to wound oneself, as if dismembering her body were dismembering a body of which one were a part, thus to cut oneself off from that body. To make certain we see this distinction between an earlier meaning of rape and his own, Shakespeare has Lavinia destroyed by the remaining hand of her father, but not because her rape has stained his blood. Before killing her, Titus asks the emperor for clarification on precisely this point:

> Was it well done of rash Virginius
> To slay his daughter with his own right hand,
> Because she was enforc'd, stain'd, and deflow'r'd?
> (V.iii.36–8)

Saturninus answers that Virginius was right to slay Virginia, but not for the reason Titus gives, not because she was "deflow'r'd" (Virginia was not), but rather, the emperor says, "Because the girl should not survive her shame, / And by her presence still renew his sorrows" (lines

41–2). Titus's farewell to Lavinia repeats the distinction between her "shame" and his "sorrow" which transforms the concepts of dishonor and pollution usually associated with rape into quite a different order of transgression: "Die, die, Lavinia, and thy shame with thee, / And with thy shame thy father's sorrow die" (lines 46–7). The play proves that the murder of his daughter is a self-inflicted wound on Titus's part. Like any claim on Lavinia's body that leads to its mutilation, this blow brings death to all those competing for power over Rome.

But Shakespeare's *The Rape of Lucrece* makes this theme of self-slaughter still more explicit. While her rape at the hands of Tarquin is reported rather than dramatically represented, the penetration of Lucrece's body by her own dagger repeats the rape in figurative terms which merit elaborate display. This display effectively translates penetration into dismemberment. It is Lucrece's mutilated body to which the poem draws our eyes, as Lucrece's father throws himself ". . . on her self-slaughtered body," and "from the purple fountain Brutus drew / The murd'rous knife" (1733–5). Not her penetration by the knife but its withdrawal, we should note, releases the flow of blood which transforms the female body into a grotesquely disfigured object. Shakespeare takes this occasion to render the female in emblematic terms which resemble the Ditchley portrait in its bonding of the cartographic image to the sexual body of the monarch. Here—in the rape of Lucrece—the female body displays such violation in terms that suggest it is the aristocratic body imaged forth as, for example, in the Ditchley portrait. It is the body figured as the state which has been ravaged:

> and, as it [the knife] left the place,
> Her blood, in poor revenge, held it in chase;
>
> And bubbling from her breast, it doth divide
> In two slow rivers, that the crimson blood
> Circles her body in on every side,
> Who like a late-sack'd island vastly stood
> Bare and unpeopled in this fearful flood.
> (1735–41)

Shakespeare's use of the terms "late-sack'd" and "unpeopled" together with a phrase like "self-slaughtered" is worth noting. By describing the mutilated woman in such apparently self-contradictory terms, he not only equates the health of the aristocratic body with that of the state, or island, he also specifies the nature of the threat to the nation's well-being. Lucrece is only *like* a "late-sack'd island" whose territory has been invaded and devastated by forces from without. She has actually been destroyed from within. The last scene of *Titus* makes the same turn on the whole notion of rape as the figure for an alien invasion. Upon encountering the heap of carnage on the stage, Aemilius asks Lucius, the new emperor:

> Tell us what Sinon hath bewitch'd our ears,
> Or who hath brought the fatal engine in
> That gives our Troy, our Rome, the civil wound.
> (V.iii.85–7)

Again, rape has become the penetration of a political body, in this case, by "the fatal engine" of the Greeks. In equating rape with civic disorder, however, once again Shakespeare couples seemingly contradictory terms. He identifies Rome's fate with Troy's in such a manner as to equate Lavinia's rape with the wounding of the body politic. But then he adds a peculiarly Elizabethan twist and has Aemilius call the mutilated body of the state, Rome's "shameful execution on herself" (V.iii.76).

The same use of this material occurs in *The Rape of Lucrece* where Shakespeare compares Tarquin to Sinon (lines 1520–68), the Greek who convinced the Trojans they should accept the gift which bore lethal invaders in its belly. He also has Brutus address Lucrece's husband in terms that attribute the victim's "wretchedness" as much to her suicide as to Tarquin's initial assault on her body: "Thy wretched wife mistook the matter so, / To slay herself that should have slain her foe" (1826–7). In both cases Shakespeare changes his sources to stress the element of self-destruction rather than the kingdom's suffering at the hand of an invader. In her study of Salutati's *Declamatio Lucretiae*, Stephanie Jed explains the politics inherent in the Lucrece story as it was taken up by Salutati. It became part of the Humanist project reshaping classical materials into a Florentine historiography during the fifteenth century in Italy. Particularly important to my argument is the relationship Jed draws between the figure of rape and the nationalist strategies which represent the birth and justification of state power as an act of self-purification and enclosure in the face of foreign penetration. In the Italian version of the story, as Jed explains it, rape is clearly a crime of pollution.[23] It finds an antidote in Lucrece's suicide and the Tarquins' expulsion, which cuts off the polluting members and strengthens Rome.

When he equates rape with dismemberment, then, Shakespeare is revising the whole ethos of the sources for stories of rape as well as those about Lucrece in order to make them English. Almost every editor has been willing to write off this peculiar behavior of the figure of rape in *Titus Andronicus* as a lapse on Shakespeare's part. In the notes to one edition of *Titus,* Frank Kermode is frankly puzzled by Shakespeare's use of the story of Virginius, a father in Livy's account, who slew his daughter in order to prevent her body from becoming the site of family dishonor. Kermode writes, "This Roman centurion killed his daughter to *prevent* her rape. Either the dramatist has got the story wrong or he is failing to convey the idea that Titus has a better case for killing Lavinia than Virginius had for killing his daughter."[24] Critics rarely muster the boldness to chastise Shakespeare in this way for the careless use of his source materials. Thus we must sit up and take note when so fine a critic as Kermode feels perfectly comfortable in doing this. Kermode obviously feels he is on stable cultural ground when he holds Shakespeare to a logic of rape. Kermode's thinking on sexual matters is obviously locked into the notion that penetration is the essential element of rape, as such it is conceptually the opposite of dismemberment, or the figure of castration. According to this more modern politics of the body, it can make no sense to equate rape with dismemberment because political power is never figured out in female form: the female body represents the absence of power. Page duBois makes this point more eloquently in an essay on *Coriolanus* where she contrasts the Freudian reading of Rome as a masculine site of power to the Rome one encounters in Shakespeare's *Coriolanus.* The power of Shakespearean Rome in that play is not only female—duBois argues convincingly that Shakespeare has inscribed Coriolanus's body with females features—but it is also dismembered. Coriolanus is cut off from mother, from Rome, and ultimately from himself, in a sequence that identifies these acts of mutilation as one and the same.[25] As duBois's critique of Freud also suggests, Shakespeare's way of sexing power points less to some sexual problem or to a lapse of craftsmanship in the poet than it does to his thinking within a poetics of sexuality that radically differs from our own. To understand the degree to which Renaissance sexuality has to be figured out as a different political formation, we might turn to another Renaissance revision of the classical text.

Shakespeare was not the only one to modify Livy's story of Virginius for the Elizabethan stage. Some twenty-five years before *Titus Androni-cus,* a hybrid moral interlude with Senecan features was written under the title of *Appius and Virginia.* In this early Elizabethan play, Virginius claims he would rather commit suicide than see his daughter deflowered by Appius, but then Virginia corrects her father's suicidal inclinations by giving him this lesson in the logic of Livy's text: "If I be once spotted, / My name and kindred then forth wilbe blotted; / And if thou my father should die for my cause / The world would accompt me as gilty in cause" (vii.794–7).[26] There is a reason why the early Elizabethan Virginius does not have his politics of rape quite right; his deviation from the classical model allows the author of this interlude to draw the equation between her rape and his death, neither of which occurs in the classical story. To be sure, this is not so clear a statement of Elizabethan ideology as the heaping of bodies upon the stage for which the mutilated body of the woman stands as both cause and emblem, but it is an Elizabethan use of the female body nonetheless. It identifies the power of the state with the state of the female body and sees the danger to the state arising from the competition of rivalrous forces within the aristocratic body rather than from that body's penetration by forces from without. Besides, the very name Virginia could in no way have been a matter of personal choice for an Elizabethan author. To use it was to invoke the official iconography of state, which constituted a political gesture whether one's use of the virgin was faithful to Livy's account or not. And should the audience not understand this from the start, the Tudor interlude informs them outright that Virginia is not only "A virgin pure" but also "a quene in life" (v.478). These changes in classical stories of rape were obviously made for an age which thought of state power as female. Under such circumstances, these representations—perhaps any representation—of the aristocratic female provided the substance of a political iconography which enhanced the power of the Elizabethan state.

Notes

1. Marie Axton, *The Queen's Two Bodies: Drama and the Elizabethan Succession* (London: Royal Historical Society, 1977), p. 12.

2. *The Queen's Two Bodies,* p. 12.

3. I am employing Foucault's notion of sexuality in *The History of Sexuality,* trans. Robert Hurley (New York: Pantheon, 1978). Thus the queen's sexuality is not only historically different from the forms it takes in our culture but hers is also different from other forms in her own culture.

4. Claire Cross, "Churchmen and royal supremacy," in *Church and Society in England: Henry VIII to James I,* eds. Felicity Heal and Rosemary O'Day (London: Macmillan, 1977), p. 27.

5. Patrick Collinson, "The downfall of Archbishop Grindal and its place in Elizabethan political and ecclesiastical history," in *The English Commonwealth 1547–1640: Essays in Politics and Society* (New York: Barnes and Noble, 1979), p. 53.

6. John Phillips, *The Reformation of Images: Destruction of Art in England 1535–1660* (Berkeley: Univ. of California Press, 1973), p. 119.

7. Quoted in Francis Yates, *Queen Elizabeth as Astrea: The Imperial Theme in the Sixteenth Century* (London: Routledge & Kegan Paul, 1975), p. 78.

8. She of course could also be treated as the Amazon queen when the occasion permitted as Winifred Schleiner has shown, "Divina virago: Queen Elizabeth as

an Amazon," in *Studies in Philology*, 75 (1978), 163–80. See also Louis Adrian Montrose, " 'Shaping fantasies': figurations of gender and power in Elizabethan culture," in *Representations*, 1 (1983), 76–8.

9. Roy C. Strong, *Portraits of Queen Elizabeth I* (Oxford: Clarendon, 1963), p. 39.

10. Peter Stallybrass, " 'Wee feaste in our Defense': Patrician Carnival in Early Modern England and Robert Herrick's 'Hesperides.' " *English Literary Renaissance* 16 (1986): 234–52.

11. *Tudor Royal Proclamations: The Later Tudors 1553–1587*, eds. Paul L. Hughes and James F. Larkin (New Haven: Yale Univ. Press, 1969), II, 240.

12. *Portraits of Queen Elizabeth I*, p. 5.

13. *Portraits of Queen Elizabeth I*, p. 40.

14. David M. Bergeron, "Elizabeth's coronation entry (1559): new manuscript evidence," in *English Literary Renaissance*, 8 (1978), 3–8; and his *English Civic Pageantry, 1558–1642* (Columbia: Univ. of South Carolina Press, 1971), pp. 12–23.

15. For accounts of the pageants for Edward and Mary, see Sydney Anglo, *Spectacle, Pageantry and Early Tudor Policy* (Oxford: Clarendon, 1969), pp. 280–343. Mary had allowed foreign companies to underwrite many of the costs of her pageant, and Edward, Reformation prince though he may have been, had the papal representative in his train.

16. (Anon.) *The Quenes Maiesties Passage through the Citie of London to Westminster the Day before her Coronation* (New Haven: Yale Univ. Press, 1960), pp. 28–9.

17. On the politics of such aesthetic display in addition to Bergeron's discussion, see Jonathan Goldberg, *James I and the Politics of Literature: Jonson, Shakespeare, Donne, and Their Contemporaries* (Baltimore: Johns Hopkins Univ. Press, 1983), pp. 28–30; and Mark Breitenberg, " 'The Hole matter opened': iconic representation and interpretation in *The Queen's Majesty's Passage*," in *Criticism*, 28 (1986).

18. Glynne Wickham, *Early English Stages 1300–1600* (London: Routledge & Kegan Paul, 1963), II.i.75–90.

19. For the documents, see E. K. Chambers, *The Elizabethan Stage* (Oxford: Clarendon, 1951), IV, 269–71, 324.

20. Ann Jennalie Cook, *The Privileged Playgoers of Shakespeare's London 1576–1642* (Princeton: Princeton Univ. Press, 1981), p. 100. See, for example, Privy Council Minutes 25 February 1592 and 19 February 1598 in *The Elizabethan Stage*, IV, 307–8 and 325.

21. Martin Butler, in *Theater and Crisis 1632–1642* (Cambridge: Cambridge Univ. Press, 1984), pp. 293–306, takes issue with Cook's representation of the audience. Hers, he notes, while offering a useful corrective to Harbage's idealization of the lower classes, makes the audience too homogeneous a group of privileged playgoers. For my purposes the important point is less the exact socio-economic makeup of the audience and more the representations of the signs and symbols of state authority the stage mounted.

22. T. S. Eliot, for example, called *Titus* "One of the stupidest and most uninspired plays ever written," in "Seneca in Elizabethan translation," *Selected Essays* (New York: Harcourt Brace, 1932), p. 67. For a brief summary of other examples of the low esteem in which *Titus* has been held, see Nicholas Brooke, *Shakespeare's Early Tragedies* (London: Methuen, 1968), pp. 13–15.

23. Stephanie Jed, "Salutati's *Declamatio Lucretiae*," paper presented to the Renaissance Society of America, 1985.

24. *The Riverside Shakespeare*, ed. G. Blakemore Evans (Boston: Houghton Mifflin, 1972), p. 1049, note to V.iii.36.

25. Page duBois, "A disturbance of syntax at the gates of Rome," *Stanford Literature Review* 2 (1985): 185–208.

26. *Tudor Interludes*, ed. Peter Happe (Harmondsworth: Penguin, 1972). Citations of the text are to this edition.

4

Censorship and Interpretation

Annabel Patterson

The principles of the hermeneutics of censorship can perhaps be clarified by turning to a famous case: Ben Jonson's *Sejanus*. Jonson, as his editors have pointed out, had a long history of trouble with the authorities. He was at various times, and not only in his rambunctious youth, subjected to various degrees of harassment for his work in the public theater:

> Imprisoned for his share in *The Isle of Dogs,* 1597, cited before Lord Chief Justice Popham for *Poetaster,* 1601; summoned before the Privy Council ... for *Sejanus,* 1603; imprisoned for his share in *Eastward Ho,* 1605; "accused" for *The Devil Is an Ass,* 1616; examined by the Privy Council for alleged verses of his on Buckingham's death [an event connected, as we shall see, to the reception history of *Sejanus*]; and cited before the Court of High Commission for *The Magnetic Lady,* 1632.[1]

In addition, there is evidence that throughout his life Jonson meditated on these facts, and incorporated them into a political and social theory of literature, a poetics of censorship. In his *Epigrammes* he complained frequently about different aspects of Jacobean censorship. No. 44 attacks a personal enemy who "cryes out, my verses libells are; / And threatens the starre-chamber, and the barre." The subject of No. 59, "On Spies," needs no comment. No. 68, "On Playwright," deals, in a powerfully squeezed form, with repression of the public theater:

> Play-wright convict of publike wrongs to men,
> Takes private beatings, and begins againe.
> Two kindes of valour he doth shew, at ones;
> Active in's braine, and passive in his bones.
>
> (8:49)

Jonson's interrogation of the tension between private opinion and public behavior caused him late in life to re-collect his previously unpublished poems of both the Jacobean and Caroline eras, and to transform them in the process into a new literary form. If we read *Underwood,* a posthumously published volume, in the sequence that Jonson provided, we can discover in it a lyric narrative, a sociopolitical autobiography. And at approximately the same stage in his development, Jonson inserted into *Timber,* a collection of a different kind, a reflection on a long life of insecurity, of being misunderstood:

> I have been accus'd to the Lords, to the King; and by great ones. ...They objected, making of verses to me, when I could object to most of them, their not being able to reade them, but as worthy of scorne. Nay, they would offer to urge mine owne Writings against me; but by pieces, (which was an excellent way of malice) as if any mans Context, might not seeme dangerous, and offensive, if that which was knit, to what went before, were defrauded of his beginning; or that things, by themselves utter'd, might not seeme subject to Calumnie, which read entire, would appeare most free. (8:604–5)

He thereby articulated another central principle of the hermeneutics of censorship, that interpretations could be radically different depending on what one selected as the context of the utterance.

This issue is raised, in reverse, by *Sejanus,* a play which becomes more "dangerous," in the sense that Jonson used that word in *Timber,* the more widely it is contextualized. In 1603 Jonson was accused of writing treason in *Sejanus;* but no records survive of the specifics of the charge, of what form the treason was supposed to have taken. Modern critics have assumed either that he was suspected of alluding to the fall of Essex two years earlier, as the most obvious recent case of an ambitious favorite who came to grief, in which case the offense would have been to imply that Elizabeth had been a Tiberius; or that he was responding positively to the moment of James's accession by advising moderation and a liberal climate for the expression of political opinion.[2] At any rate, whatever exceptions were taken to the text or the timing of the 1603 *Sejanus* as actually performed (and we of course have no knowledge of what was actually spoken on the stage), Jonson was apparently able to answer them to his accusers' satisfaction. No further action was taken against him at that time.

But he then, in 1605, proceeded to publish a text of the play, a text that seems designed to provoke the same kind of curiosity as that aroused by Hayward's *Life and Reign of King Henry IV,* while at the same time giving Jonson better protection. The very fact that his plot is

drawn from Roman and not from English history suggested a scholarly
enterprise, rather than a topical one. But the particular section of
Roman history selected, and indeed the reputation of Tacitus, the
historian upon whom Jonson primarily depended, would have indicated to his audience that his motives were not entirely archeological.[3]

Jonson's preface both stresses his loyalty to the crown and his scholarly dependence on historical sources. In his preliminary address to the
readers of the play, he asserts that the use of classical reference and
quotation is not for show, but to prove his "integrity in the story
[history]" and to protect himself from "those common torturers, that
bring all wit to the rack." He even cites editions and page references
to facilitate a check on his sources. His own responsibility for the text
is thereby minimized. On the other hand, some of the commendatory
verses reminded the original reader that the play was ambiguous, and
had had problems of reception previously. Hugh Holland closed his
sonnet by alluding to Jonson's arrest, but in language derived from the
play:

> Ne of such crimes accuse him, which I dare
> By all his Muses sweare, be none of his.
> The Men are not, some Faults may be these Times.

Another contributor, identified merely as "Friend" ("φιλος"), made
his poem a riddle on the problem of understanding:

> Thy Poeme (pardon mee) is meere deceat.
> Yet such deceate, as thou that doest beguile,
> Art juster farre than they who use no wile:
> And they who are deceaved by this feat
> More wise, then such who can eschewe thy cheat.
> For thou hast given each parte so just a stile,
> That Men suppose the Action now on file;
> (And Men suppose, who are of best conceat.)
> Yet some there be, that are not moov'd hereby,
> And others are so quick, that they will spy
> Where later Times are in some speech enweav'd;
> ....
> [Those] are so dull, they cannot be deceav'd,
> These so unjust, they will deceave themselves.[4]

The seventeenth-century reader was encouraged, as Carleton by Chamberlain, to see what he could find; but at the same time he was warned
that most readings are either oversimple or oversubtle. Close study of
the text is required; but that there is a "right" interpretation cannot

be guaranteed. (It is typical of the conditions under which the modern reader must operate that these verses have been effaced from the text they were intended to introduce, either by complete omission, in texts designed for students, or, as in Herford and Simpson's edition of Jonson's works, by being banished to a separate volume.)

More important, the play actually dramatizes the hermeneutics of censorship. In a central scene, the historian Cremutius Cordus is tried in the Senate for an "oblique" attack on Tiberius in his annals, on the grounds that he has implied "parallels," or rather contrasts, between present tyranny and the old republican era. The charge seems patently unjust, and Cordus's famous speech of defense, translated entirely from Tacitus, disclaims any such intention. The effect, according to Jonas Barish in his edition of the play, was to provide a symbolic statement of the nature and function of *Sejanus,* and to disclaim any topical intention there also, on the grounds that history is, or should be, nonpartisan, a neutral mediator of fact.

What Barish did not perceive, however, is that the disclaimer, as extended to Jonson, must be disingenuous. The play speaks, it is true, to a climate of excessive, even perverse, interpretive ability by the government and its agents.[5] As another of Sejanus's victims puts it:

> . . . our writings are,
> By any envious instruments (that dare
> Apply them . . . made to speake
> What they will have.
>
> (4:423)

But this same character also delivers a comment on the indictment of Cordus, and the public burning of his annals, that leads in another direction. Still following Tacitus closely, he remarks that "the punishment / of wit doth make [its] authority increase":

> Nor doe they ought, that use this crueltie
> Of interdiction, and this rage of burning;
> But purchase to themselves rebuke, and shame,
> And to the writers an eternall name.
>
> (4:408)[6]

Now, this was already one of the loci classici for discussions of freedom of speech, or of intellectual freedom in a broader sense. Sir Francis Bacon had alluded to it in a pamphlet intended to advise Elizabeth on how to handle the theological pamphlet wars of the 1580s.[7] Milton would apply it in 1644, when he turned the whole force of his classical eloquence against the licensing act of the Long Parliament; and Jonson is here clearly using Tacitus to deliver a warning to the instruments of censorship in his own day. The very survival of Cordus's story, in fact, proves his point about the inefficacy of censorship, while the fate of Sejanus argues its unwisdom.

Jonson's play, therefore, allows Cordus to protest a political climate of overdetermination, and to argue the wisdom of rulers who permit historians their natural and necessary privileges. Augustus set the example by allowing Livy such eulogies of Pompey "as oft Augustus called him a Pompeian: / Yet this hurt not their friendship" (4:406). But Jonson's position must be more complex, as his perspective is longer. To *retell* Tacitus's historical account of Cordus's historiography in 1605 is itself both a historiographical and a historical act, one which inevitably provokes John Chamberlain's question, "Why such a storie shold come out at this time?" Men of "best conceat" would "suppose the Action now on file," and Jonson's emphasis on censorship would encourage such curiosity and indeed sanction it. Suspicious readers need not identify themselves with Sejanus or Tiberius. As suppression ensures the survival of censored texts, so it justifies authorial suppressions, or obliquities. As Jonson explained in *Timber, or Discoveries,* those jottings that blend politics with poetics, only a candid government deserves a transparent culture:

> The mercifull Prince is safe in love, not feare. Hee needs no Emissaries, spies, Intelligencers, to intrap true Subjects. Hee feares no Libels, no Treasons. His people speake, what they thinke; and talke openly, what they doe in secret. They have nothing in their brests, that they need a Cipher for. (8:600)

Jonson's interest in Tacitus was not, however, restricted to the story of Sejanus, or solely explicable by the temporary need for a cipher. Nor was the "meaning" for him of Tacitus, as a name and model, restricted to the confrontation between Sejanus and Cordus, a confrontation in which the rights and wrongs of the issue were expressed in chiaroscuro. The lighting in which Tacitus appeared in European writers and readers in the sixteenth and seventeenth centuries was in general far more diffused, if not confusing. The picture of Tacitus as a republican thinker and champion of free speech was certainly available. In 1656, for example, as Orest Ranum has shown in his study of French historiography in the age of absolutism, Racine could compile a commonplace book of excerpts from the *Annals* which gave special emphasis to the thematization of cultural repression, to the relationship between political life and literary creativity, of which a vital historiography was a central aspect; and when he came to the *moralitas* by which Tacitus had summed up the trial of Cordus, "punitis ingeniis gliscit auctoritas," Racine added his own gloss, "livres défendus."[8] But for other readers, Tacitus was far less transparent; indeed his text became a celebrated instance of difficulty and obscurity, qualities to be valued or devalued according to the reader's frame of reference. For Sir Richard Baker, one of the bright young men associated with the circle of John Donne at the beginning of the seventeenth century, obscurity had its own attraction. The darkness of Tacitus

> is pleasing to whosoever by labouring about it, findes out the true meaning; for then he counts it an issue of his owne braine, and taking occasion from these sentences to goe further than the thing he reads, and that without being deceived, he takes the like pleasure as men are wont to take from hearing metaphors, finding the meaning of him that useth them.[9]

Such thinking is surely connected to the interpretive challenges with which Jonson surrounded his first major essay into the transmission of Taciteanism.

And beyond such epistemological darkness lay the more sinister reputation that the historian had acquired in some quarters, the "black Taciteanism" that resulted from his influence on Machiavelli and Guicciardini as historians, or more generally from his association with a cynical view of politics, so different from the republican idealism of Livy, so readily associated with those elements in any state that were malcontent, even seditious. There is reason to believe that all these views of Tacitus were in some complicated way present in Jonson's consciousness, and at different stages of his experience arranged themselves in different patterns of preference. In order to give a balanced account of how the hermeneutics of censorship developed in this most complex of authors, we need to follow this pattern a little further.

At some comparatively early stage in his development, Jonson wrote (and published in the 1616 folio) a poem on the subject of Sir Henry Savile's translation of Tacitus.[10] The epigram did not appear in the 1591 edition of Savile's translation, or in any subsequent edition, despite its formal resemblance to a commendatory poem. Its theme is unquestionably similar to that of *Sejanus*, in that Jonson praises Savile especially for his honesty as a translator, which in turn reflects the honesty of the original; and he urges Savile, now that Roman history has been treated with such fidelity, to turn his talents to the service of a national historiography "We need a man," Jonson wrote:

> . . . can speake of the intents,
> The councells, actions, orders, and events
> Of state, and censure them: we need his pen
> Can write the things, the causes, and the men.
> But most we need his faith (and all have you)
> That dares nor write things false, nor hide things true.
>
> (8:62)

These lines were themselves a translation of the great definition of *historia* in Cicero's *De oratore* (II.xv.62–63).

In 1605 Jonson, as we have seen, presented his own exemplum of the true Tacitean historian in the figure of Tacitus's Cordus; but he also did something else rather peculiar. He reworked his definition of the true historian from that presumably earlier epigram, and had it delivered, ironically, by Sejanus, as the very grounds of his attack on Cordus. Cordus is described as a "writing fellow" who

> . . . doth taxe the present state,
> Censures the men, the actions, leaves no tricke,
> No practice unexamin'd, paralels
> The times, the governments, a profest champion,
> For the old libertie.
>
> (4:385)

Now in 1616, when Jonson remarked to Drummond of Hawthornden that "Tacitus wrott the secrets of the Councill and Senate," he also confided an English political secret, that the prefatory epistle to Savile's translation of Tacitus, signed A. B., was really written by the earl of Essex (1:142). This is one of the best indications that we have that the original *Sejanus* was in some way connected to the Essex conspiracy. As F. J. Levy has shown, the activists and malcontents who surrounded Essex at the turn of the century were known to be reading Tacitus;[11] and Jonson, if we are to judge from his cautious apology for Essex in *Cynthia's Revels,* was one of them. Such facts make it difficult to accept the notion that four years later Jonson was so impressed by the heinousness of Essex's crime, so convinced of the country's hegemonic needs, that he transformed the earl from Actaeon into Sejanus, and had him cruelly dismembered after all. Yet we can tell that he changed his mind about Tacitus. Sometime before 1616 he had written a sardonic little poem called *The New Crie,* attacking the amateur politicians of London. "The councells, projects, practices they know, / And what each prince doth for intelligence owe," he sneered, parodying for the second time his definition of the Tacitean historian, who "can speake of the intents, / The councells, actions, orders, and events / Of state, and censure them." The men of the new cry have, moreover, the same authority for their disruptive behavior as had Essex, as had Jonson himself. They "carry in their pockets Tacitus,"

> And talke reserv'd, lock'd up, and full of feare,
> Nay, aske you, how the day goes, in your eare.
> Keep a starre-chamber sentence close, twelve days:
> And whisper what a Proclamation sayes.
> ....
> They all get Porta, for the sundrie wayes
> To write in cypher, and the severall keyes.
>
> (8:59)

And, most significantly "all forbidden bookes they get." In this poem, perhaps because Jonson had been deeply shocked by the implications of the Gunpowder Plot in 1605, in which he himself was marginally implicated, obliquity has reassumed its dishonest meaning. Fear is now the obsession not of the censor but of the censurer; Tacitus has become a model of subversion; the noble defense of freedom of speech has vanished in the dislike of "forbidden bookes"; "what a Proclamation sayes" has acquired the form of a taboo. Whatever Jonson had originally meant by *Sejanus* in 1603, what it meant to him in 1605 could not, it seems, have remained untouched and unchanged by the writing of this poem. Yet it is typical of his own brand of honesty that it appears *along with Sejanus* and the praise of Savile's Tacitus in the 1616 folio, as part of the record, a record of ambiguity and interpretive difficulty, in which texts and historical events are equally resistant to simple, settled meanings.

Notes

1. C. H. Herford, P. Simpson, and E. Simpson, eds., Ben Jonson, *Works,* 11 vols. (Oxford: Clarendon Press, 1925–52), 11:253.

2. See Jonas Barish, ed., *Sejanus His Fall* (New Haven: Yale Univ. Press, 1965), pp. 16–17; and Herford and Simpson, *Works,* 1:36–37.

3. Jonathan Goldberg, *James I and the Politics of Literature* (Baltimore: The Johns Hopkins University Press, 1983) argues that "Roman" drama in this period was primarily the result of James's own preference for seeing himself in imperial terms. This causes certain problems of chronology, since the English interest in Roman history as a source of plot, theme, metaphor, and even ideology neither began nor ended with the reign of James; witness Shakespeare's *Elizabethan* Roman plays, the liminal status of the 1603 *Sejanus,* the tendentious use of Lucan during the civil war, or Marvell's use of Suetonius as a metaphor for the cultural climate of the 1670s. The point could be more safely made in more general terms: as English intellectuals tried to come to terms with different styles of monarchical absolutism,

they constantly returned, for a frame of reference, to the most relevant sections of the history of imperial Rome.

4. Jonson, *Works*, 11:314, 316–17. On these poems, see also Norbert Platz, " 'By Oblique Glance of His Licentious Pen,' " in *Recent Research on Ben Jonson* (Salzburg: Institut für Englische Sprache und Literatur, 1978), pp. 72–76.

5. This is the argument used by David Bevington, *Tudor Drama and Politics* (Cambridge: Harvard University Press, 1968), pp. 8–25, to *limit* the scope of topical reading.

6. Tacitus, *Annals*, IV, 34.

7. Francis Bacon, *A Wise and Moderate Discourse, concerning Church-affairs* (1641), p. 11. Though first printed posthumously as a comment on the Smectymnuan controversy, Bacon's pamphlet was written in 1589 with reference to the Admonition controversy.

8. Orest Ranum, *Artisans of Glory: Writers and Historical Thought in Seventeenth-Century France* (Chapel Hill, N.C.: University of North Carolina Press, 1980), pp. 282–91.

9. Richard Baker, trans., Vergilio Malvezzi, *Discourses upon Cornelius Tacitus*, Preface; cited by Alfred Alvarez, *The School of Donne* (London: Chatto & Windus, 1961), p. 40.

10. Henry Savile, *The Ende of Nero and Beginning of Galba. Fower Bookes of the Histories of Cornelius Tacitus* (Oxford, 1591).

11. F. J. Levy, *Tudor Historical Thought* (San Marino, California: Huntington Library, 1967), pp. 251, 261–62. For the ambiguous reputation of Tacitus in England, see also M. F. Tenney, "Tacitus in the Politics of Early Stuart England," *Classical Journal* 37 (1941): 151–63; and Edwin B. Benjamin, "Milton and Tacitus," *Milton Studies* 4 (1972): 117–40.

5

The Theater of the Idols: Theatrical and Anti-theatrical Discourse

Jonathan V. Crewe

No less than Shakespeare and Jonson, Marlowe began writing plays in the wake of the anti-theatrical campaign initiated in 1579 by Stephen Gosson and pursued by succeeding pamphleteers.[1] With *Tamburlaine*, Part 1, Marlowe thus began his dramatic career in a cultural and political milieu preconditioned by anti-theatricalism. While it might be suggested that Marlowe's drama, like that of his major successors, constitutes a *response* to this anti-theatricalism—a simultaneous exploitation and defense of the theatrical medium[2]—it is also possible to see both dramatists and anti-theatricalists as participants by 1587 in an anxious cultural discourse of theater in which questions of chronological priority (of "attack" and "response") are not of paramount importance. This will be my assumption in considering the implicit dialogue between Marlowe and the anti-theatrical pamphleteer William Rankins, author of *A Mirrour of Monsters*, both of whom come on the scene in 1587.[3]

For both Marlowe and Rankins, the thing at issue is simple but fundamental: what is to be inferred from the nature and above all the magnitude of theatrical images?[4] What does the proliferation and also the scale of such images imply about the culture in which they are produced? In the case of Rankins, the answer looks easy: *all* theatrical phenomena, being "monstrous," are culturally alien and hence profoundly threatening.

This shocked response may reveal something of the sheer novelty and magnitude of staged spectacle in the Elizabethan public theater, and may help to explain why, in Rankins's pamphlet, it is as if the threat of the monstrous has suddenly become acute.[5] Moreover, while monstrousness might seem to belong properly to the biological sphere, for Rankins it exists also in the ideological and sociopolitical spheres—

indeed, it is this derivative or analogical "monstrousness" rather than the primary biological phenomenon that concerns Rankins.[6]

In Rankins's mind, monstrousness comes to be identified not only with moral transgression and even with demonic possession (anxieties that fuel much Jacobean anti-theatricalism, not to mention *Dr. Faustus*) but also with insupportable transgression of class and cultural boundaries. To Rankins, the result of such transgressions is the appearance in both the social and theatrical spheres of new and alien *personae*, threatening constitutive cultural definitions of the human. Refusing to acknowledge that *a priori* lawful images and definitions of the human subject (of "man") might be negotiable within Christian culture and/ or within the Elizabethan political world, Rankins perceives only an explosive threat to those definitions. This perception of the monstrous is not, however, confined to Rankins's pamphlet or to anti-theatricalists, but is also embodied, as the Marlowe concordance shows, in *Tamburlaine 1* and *2* and *The Jew of Malta*—the Marlowe plays in which, almost exclusively, that terminology appears. To various characters in these plays, both protagonists look monstrous in ways that Rankins would have understood. The accusation is vitiated when it is made by the plays' losers—the Soldan in *Tamburlaine* or Calymath in *The Jew of Malta*—yet the charge has been repeated in modern criticism, where the insupportable, often "inhuman," scandalousness of Marlovian protagonists continues to be found upsetting. Where does Marlowe stand vis-à-vis Rankins (or vis-à-vis modern critics) on the question of the monstrous?

Even if it could be assumed that Marlowe identifies himself with his protagonists, thus flouting the accusation that they *are* monstrous, the poetics of Elizabethan drama would inhibit his capacity to idealize these figures. The conception of the dramatic protagonist as a negative exemplum is too powerfully entrenched in the sixteenth century for any simple reversal to be probable either at the level of poetic theory or of audience response. (However inclined the audience might be to succumb to the theatrical magnetism of Marlowe's protagonists, not only they but the audience get "punished" by their deaths.) For Marlowe fully to legitimize his monsters would require him to overthrow (upset) practically all dominant cultural presuppositions of the sixteenth century as well as purge the resulting anxieties. It is scarcely conceivable that even Marlowe could have imagined or desired that full-scale "emancipation." It might thus be accurate to say that while Rankins tries to preclude the monstrous, or at least contain the threat it represents, Marlowe aggressively renegotiates its relationship to assumed norms.

One manifest feature of *Tamburlaine* is the protagonist's movement

from an outside to an inside position—from the role of outlaw to that
of lawgiver. Tamburlaine's potential *normativeness* is thus embodied
in the structure of the play and also perceived, even if not consistently
so, by those around him. Cosroe asks: "What stature wields he, and
what personage?", to which Menaphon replies:

> Of stature tall, and straightly fashioned,
> Like his desire, lift vpwards and diuine,
> So large of lims, his ioints so strongly knit,
> Such breadth of shoulders as might mainely beare
> Olde *Atlas* burthen, twixt his manly pitch,
> A pearle more worth, then all the worlde is plaste:
> Wherein by curious soueraintie of Art,
> Are fixt his piercing instruments of sight:
> Whose fiery cyrcles beare encompassed,
> A heauen of heauenly bodies in their Spheares:
> That guides his steps and actions to the throne,
> Where honor sits inuested royally;
> Pale of complexion: wrought in him with passion,
> Thirsting with souereignty and loue of armes.[7]

The Tamburlaine pictured here acquires an astounding yet paradoxically ideal or definitive magnitude. Menaphon's points of reference—
Hercules/Atlas, the geocentric cosmos, ideal monarchy—are all obviously lawful and even culturally authoritative. In making Tamburlaine
definitively embody this set of images, Menaphon already "centers"
him. Menaphon's simultaneous hyperbolic magnification and cultural
normalization of Tamburlaine are facilitated by the blank verse medium, in which a principle of interminable cumulativeness, hence of
inflation without end, coexists with a metrical rule that bids to become
(as in fact it does) the norm for English dramatic verse. The medium
itself, then, may seem to side with Menaphon's attempt and even to
exceed it, enabling Tamburlaine to continue where Menaphon leaves
off. Although Menaphon's picture will be completed—framed—by his
own attempted closure, the lack of any internal mechanism of arrest
(e.g., the terminal rhyming couplet) means that the boundaries of
Menaphon's representation, which is also an attempted containment
of Tamburlaine, can be ruptured. In suggesting, moreover, that Tamburlaine's "likeness" is not established with reference to any external
paradigm, but only with reference to his *own* desire, Menaphon's
representation embodies a principle of change and expansion that will
rupture it.

This is exactly what happens when Tamburlaine, paradoxically redefining the norm, situates himself in an "imperfect" cosmos in which he is "alwaies moouing as the restless Spheares" (II.vi.876). Then again, resisting Cosroe's attempt to legitimize his own rule despite being a usurper, Tamburlaine justifies further rebellion by reminding Cosroe that "the thirst of raigne and sweetnes of a crowne, / . . . causde the eldest sonne of heauenly *Ops,* / To thrust his doting father from his chaire" (II.ii.863–865). Usurpation and patricide thus get enunciated as the universal rule instead of remaining the possibly secret truth that fictions of legitimacy belie. In short, the issue of Tamburlaine's cultural egregiousness or definitiveness is continuously negotiated within the play, and in being so, seemingly brings within the realm of the negotiable most of the constitutive categories of Elizabethan cultural and political order. Subject to this negotiation will also be the place of the player in that adjustable order.

In relation to Rankins's *Mirrour,* it does not really matter how substantial a critique of the protagonist Marlowe may consciously embody in *Tamburlaine* 1 and 2—how, for example, Tamburlaine may be shown not to live up to the limitless promise of the blank verse medium—nor does it really matter whether the effect of Marlowe's play would really—given the particular audience—have been to unleash or exorcise the demonic protagonist. The point is that Tamburlaine becomes thinkable as the embodiment of the culture's true destiny. A Tamburlaine "uplifted" by unrepressed desire, by imaginative opportunism rather than preconception, and by his (and his maker's) seemingly guiltless embrace of self-magnifying artifice can appear to be no monster but rather the figure in which the human form divine again manifests itself after a degrading interregnum. This possibility is emphasized by Tamburlaine's participation in an "authentic" (i.e., erotic rather than chastely alienated or abject) relation to the gods: "About [his shoulders] hangs a knot of Amber heire / . . . On which the breath of heauen delights to play" (II.i.477–479). Marlowe makes the "Scythian"—i.e., the conventionally barbarous in Elizabethan terms—not merely oppose but paradoxically represent cultural norms, thus reestablishing a "lost" or eclipsed scale of perfection.

To Rankins, however, such a rationale would presumably have been insufficient to change the authoritative dispensation under which theatrical "monstrousness" is at once foreseen and prohibited. Rankins grounds his argument in St. Paul's canonical pronouncement (reinforced by authoritative voices including that of Augustine in *The City of God*) against forms of degenerative idolatry. In the light of these pronouncements, theater can be construed as nothing more nor less than the scene of a pagan cult, in which men become not gods but beasts:

When they [the pagan gentiles] counted them selves wyse, they became fooles: and turned the glorie of the immortall God, unto an
image, made not only after the similtude of mortal man, but also of
birdes, and foure footed beastes, and of crepyng beastes. Wherefore
God gave them up to uncleaneness, through the lustes of their owne
heartes, to defyle their owne bodies among themselves. Whiche
chaunged his trueth for a lye, and worshipped and served the creature,
more then the creator, which is to be praysed forever.[8]

While other anti-theatrical writers (and Marlowe as playwright) pick
up on the themes of homosexuality and sophisticated "vice" also
treated by Paul in this letter, Rankins confines himself largely to the
monstrous deformation and idolatrous transformation of the Christian
man to which the theater supposedly lends itself. For Rankins, the
departure from a culturally inscribed Christian image and scale of
perfection not only represents a gross moral lapse but also portends
cultural apostasy. The players are accused, among other things, of
"[taking] vpon them the persons of Heathen men, imagining themselves
(to vaineglory in the wrath of God) to be the men whose persons they
present, wherein, by calling on *Mahomet,* by swearing by the Temples
of Idolatry, dedicate the Idols, by calling upon *Iupiter, Mars, Venus,*
& other such petty Gods, they doo most wickedly robbe God of his
honour, and blaspheme the vertue of his heauenly power" (F.22).
    While Rankins denies any power of real transformation to the imagi-
native metamorphoses enacted by the players, he also reveals a contradictory anxiety about the players' tendency to forget themselves and
become what they act, possibly communicating their self-delusion to
their audiences. The pamphlet's subtitle refers to "the *infectious* sight
of Playes," and it seems that, in spite of its assumed powerlessness
to alter the facts, the theater may nevertheless facilitate profoundly
threatening cultural and individual metamorphoses as well as unprecedented boundary-crossings. The cultural apostasy Rankins fears may
be possible, in his terms, only as a lapse into common delusion, but
the threatened universality of that lapse carries it beyond the realm of
absurdity and into one of horror.[9]
    If the authoritative source and some of the cultural determinants of
Rankins's argument are now apparent, and if they seem to authorize
a decisive anti-theatricalism, they do not render his own situation
uncomplicated or perhaps even make it differ in the last resort from
Marlowe's. Rankins identifies the players (as distinct from the images
they project) with the material theater, the image of which is inscribed
on their own bodies: "men doo then transforme that glorious image
of Christ into the brutish shape of a rude beast, when the temple of

our bodies whiche should be consecrate vnto him, is made a stage
of stinking stuffe, a den for theeues, and an habitation for insatiate
monsters" (F.2). The distinction between playhouse and player and
subsequently between player and audience (body politic) is abolished,
leaving theater, which also is characterized as a labyrinth, to stand in
simple, traditional opposition to the temple. This feat of reduction does
not, however, liberate Rankins from the world of images. On the
contrary, the specular trope of his own *Mirrour* tends to multiply
rather than limit the "monstrousness" he contemplates, and ultimately
to confine his perception *within* a theater of monstrous images—a
specular labyrinth. The encompassing both of the culture and of the self
by "monstrousness" thus becomes undeniable, and the anti-theatrical
argument tends to succumb hysterically to the revelation of its own
impossibility both in principle and sociocultural practice.

Moreover, to Rankins the theater remains a scene of scandalous play,
not of dramatic representation. His anti-theatricalism characteristically
seizes on the players and the playhouse rather than specific plays or
dramatic genres, as if theatrical representations are either transparent
or immaterial. No particular form of drama—or, as Puttenham might
say, of dramatic poem—can alter the nature of theater or mitigate its
harmfulness. Yet one characteristic form taken by that play, as we
discover elsewhere in his pamphlet, is masking or masquerading. Ran-
kin's pamphlet includes a creaky allegory of contemporary English life
as theater, in which he witnesses the opulently performed marriage of
Pride and Lust.[10] The images that are purportedly those of carnal
"luxury" evoke the self-display not just of players, however, but of the
queen—of the queen *as* player. The *courtly* masque thus becomes the
form in which theatrical "monstrousness" decisively manifests itself,
while the distinction between court and theater dissolves:

> [Luxuria] rising from hir bed of Securitie, hanged with Curtins of
> Carelesnes, with valances of Vanitie, she dressed hir head with such
> costly Calles, Earings, Jewels, Periwigs & Pearls, as if for varietie of
> attire, she had a store house of trumperie. Nor was there any thing
> left vndone, but that which should be doone, Amongst the rest to
> make hir seeme more amiable to hir best beloued shee painted hir
> faire face with spots of shadowed modestie. (F.4)

Not only are the queen and her favorites figures within rather than
outside the theater, but their masquerade will transform the commoners into a theatrical audience and the kingdom itself into a pagan
theater—the scene of a truly popular romantic cult—in which a mysterious conjunction has occurred between extreme forms of narcissistic

display and widespread devotion.[11] Luxuria, says Rankins, "striueth to rule in the hearts of most men" (F.4); the success with which it does so is a function of the theater's spectacular rather than specular powers.

Despite its possible utility in the context of factional politics, then, Rankins's strategy of denial seems more quixotic, frustrated, or paradoxically ineffectual as a means of defense than Marlowe's problematic acceptance. The mounting hysteria of the Puritan attack on theater (culminating in Prynne's *Histriomastix*) as well as the eventual failure of the Puritan anti-theatrical policy may imply no more than an inept politics. Yet they may also suggest a doomed refusal to acknowledge what is culturally constitutive or historically accomplished at a level beyond the reach of political cures. Although Rankins fictionally projects a non-theatrical self conceived in the image of Christ as the basis of his radical anti-theatricalism, the Pride he stigmatizes as monstrous does not appear in his text under its common medieval name of Superbia, connoting inward swelling or tumidity, but rather under the name of Fastus (spelled "Faustus" on more than one occasion!), a condition of external deportment involving both lofty disdain and a certain "fastidious" distancing. The shift suggests that the inwardness of the moral or "carnal" condition of pride has given way to a corresponding external condition belonging to the theater, where "Fastus" personified exists only in a relation between player and beholder.[12] The substance of the self, capable of being infected by evil but also of being healed, dissolves in the Elizabethan theatrical world of magnified appearances, allowing no purchase to the argument Rankins tries to articulate.

Notes

1. Stephen Gosson, *The Schoole of Abuse* and *Short Apologie of the Schoole of Abuse* (1579), *Playes Confuted in Five Actions* (1582); Henry Denham, *A Second and Third Blast of Retrait from Playes and Theatres* (1580); Phillip Stubbes, *Anatomie of Abuses* (1583).

2. Insofar as the anti-theatrical campaign can be regarded as a cause, its unwanted effect is to empower and give substance to the institution it attacks. Counterintuitively, what we call major Elizabethan drama emerges after that campaign, not the other way around.

3. William Rankins, *A Mirrour of Monsters* (1587); repr. ed. Arthur Freeman (New York: Garland Publishing, 1973).

4. "Enormities," implying both excessive magnitude and moral transgression, is one of Rankins's terms. It also becomes a term in the Puritan anti-theatrical lexicon, to which Jonson responds in *Bartholomew Fair*. While farcically defusing some of the dread attendant upon theatrical "enormity" as well as "idolatry," Jonson does not fully exorcise the demon, which reappears in the guise of a bodily excess.

5. Rankins commands sabbatarian legislation and other unspecified if draconian measures against theatrical "abuses," yet the situation Rankins represents already seems to call for the final Puritan solution of closing the theaters.

6. The moral and biological sense remain interlocked at the time Rankins writes in England, and the connection is strongly reaffirmed in apocalyptic diatribes like Stephen Bateman's *The Doome Warning all Men to Judgement* (1581). In it, the course of human history is reinterpreted under the aspect of the "prodigious." A principled separation of biological and moral monstrousness only begins to be effected, notably in France by Ambroise Paré, at about the time Marlowe and Rankins are writing.

7. *The Works of Christopher Marlowe*, ed. C. F. Tucker Brooke (Oxford: The Clarendon Press, 1969): II.i.460–74. Line numbers throughout are Brooke's through-line numbers.

8. This passage from the Geneva Bible is cited by Clarke Hulse in *Elizabethan Metamorphic Verse* (Princeton: Princeton University Press, 1982): 101. Hulse notes that the particular form of anti-theatricality implicit in this letter arises from Paul's confrontation with the practices of a sophisticated hellenistic paganism. In the next paragraph, Paul deals with the "unnatural" practices of homosexuality and gender-reversal, thus authorizing another version of Elizabethan anti-theatricalism and setting the stage for Marlowe's erotic poems as well as *Edward II*. It is not, however, along this particular axis of hebraism and hellenism that Rankins and Marlowe situate themselves in 1587; the issue remains that of an idolatrous gigantism and adoration of false images.

9. For Rankins, but not for him alone, the threatening prospect of a popular conjunction, facilitated by theatrical abuses, also arises between the revived paganism of the classical world and a new Muslim paganism, with which Marlowe does indeed flirt in *Tamburlaine, Part 2*.

10. Rankins's conjunction of Pride and Lust, although traditional, would be somewhat misplaced in relation to Marlowe's work. The pride of Tamburlaine is inseparable from a marked asceticism, a "pale" sublimation of desire, that is dramatized for example in his relations with Zenocrate. Even in Rankins's pamphlet, sexuality *per se* tends to be associated with the *comic* behavior of theatrical spectators engaged in amorous intrigues, while Luxuria (lust personified) resolves itself into narcissistic display and self-absorption. In doing so, it may mark the historic shift in the meaning of "luxury" from lustfulness to opulence. Rankins's "mirror of princes" text may also allow him, in common with other Protestant militants, to warn against the queen's marriage to the Duc d'Alençon, a major source of anxiety in 1579.

11. It is no doubt background of this kind that informs Milton's *Eikonoklastes* among other documents of the Puritan revolution. Rankins explicitly acknowledges (also unsuccessfully tries to explain away) the fact that the theater enjoys royal and ecclesiastical protection: "But some . . . may object . . . that I . . . alledge more than I dare auouche, to speake against them that are priueleged by a Prince, naye more sworne seruants to the annointed" (F.2). Both the theatricality of court life and the access to the court of upstart players and playwrights could only confirm the worst Puritan suspicions.

12. By making the theater into the scene of a pagan cult, Rankins traps himself in the archaic doubleness of the sacred as antithetically but *simultaneously* elevated and filthy; rarefied and polluted. "Fastidiousness" establishes both the conjunction and the separation, while also theatricalizing and politicizing the sacred.

6

Boy Actors, Female Roles, and Elizabethan Eroticism

Lisa Jardine

Every schoolchild knows that there were no women actors on the Elizabethan stage; the female parts were taken by young male actors. But every schoolchild also learns that this fact is of little consequence for the twentieth-century reader of Shakespeare's plays. Because the taking of female parts by boys was universal and commonplace, we are told, it was accepted as "verisimilitude" by the Elizabethan audience, who simply disregarded it, as we would disregard the creaking of stage scenery and accept the backcloth forest as "real" for the duration of the play.[1]

Conventional or no, the taking of female parts by boy players actually occasioned a good deal of contemporary comment, and created considerable moral uneasiness, even amongst those who patronized and supported the theaters. Amongst those who opposed them, transvestism on stage was a main plank in the anti-stage polemic. "The appareil of wemen is a great provocation of men to lust and leacherie," wrote Dr. John Rainoldes, a leading Oxford divine (quoting the Bishop of Paris), in *Th' Overthrow of Stage-Playes* (Middleburgh, 1599). And he continues with an unhealthy interest which infuses the entire pamphlet: "A womans garment beeing put on a man doeth vehemently touch and moue him with the remembrance and imagination of a woman; and the imagination of a thing desirable doth stir up the desire."[2]

According to Rainoldes, and the authorities with whose independent testimony he lards his polemic, the wearing of female dress by boy players "is an occasion of wantonnes and lust."[3] Sexuality, misdirected towards the boy masquerading in female dress, is "stirred" by attire and gesture; male prostitution and perverted sexual activity is the inevitable accompaniment of female impersonation.

There is, of course, a hysterical edge to Rainoldes's argument which we should not necessarily consider appropriate to less commitedly anti-stage members of the Elizabethan public. (Possibly the fact that the pamphlet was printed abroad indicates that it was exceptionally vitriolic, and recognized as likely to provoke.) Nevertheless, I begin with the extreme position to draw the reader's attention to the lively possibilities available for sexually ambiguous play on "female parts" in Elizabethan and Jacobean drama, and in comedy in particular. In support of a widespread sense of possibility for gratuitous titillation in drawing attention to the role-playing of the boy player, there is a curious poem by Thomas Randolph (himself a minor dramatist), entitled "On a maide of honour seene by a schollar in Sommerset Garden":

> As once in blacke I disrespected walkt,
> Where glittering courtiers in their Tissues stalkt,
> I cast by chaunce my melancholy eye
> Upon a woman (as I thought) past by.
> But when I viewed her ruffe, and beaver reard
> As if *Priapus*-like she would have feard
> The ravenous *Harpyes* from the clustred grape,
> Then I began much to mistrust her shape;
> When viewing curiously, away she slipt,
> And in the fount her whited hand she dipt,
> The angry water as if wrong'd thereby,
> Ranne murmuring thence a second touch to fly,
> At which away she stalkes, and as she goes
> She viewes the situation of each rose;
> And having higher rays'd her gowne, she gaz'd
> Upon her crimson stocking which amaz'd
> Blusht at her open impudence, and sent
> Reflection to her cheeke, for punishment.
> As thus I stood the Gardiner chaunce to passe,
> My friend (quoth I) what is this stately lasse?
> A maide of honour Sir, said he, and goes
> Leaving a riddle, was enough to pose
> The crafty *Oedipus*, for I could see
> Nor mayde, nor honour, sure noe honesty.[4]

The poem is a riddle, to which the answer is (like the riddle posed to Oedipus), "a man": the "maide of honour" is "nor mayde" (not female), "nor honour" (not courtly), "sure noe honesty" (certainly not chaste) because "she" is a boy player "transvestied"—a travesty of a woman. Somerset House was used for play performances before Charles I and his queen throughout the 1630s, and we might even conjecture that the occasion for Randolph's poem was twelfth night, 1634, when the queen arranged for the King's Company to perform

Fletcher's *The Faithful Shepherdess* for Charles, which "the King's Players acted in the Robes she and her Ladies acted their Pastoral in the last year."[5] What more decadent than a boy dressed as a woman in the very clothes worn by an actual "maid of honour" to the queen on a previous occasion?

Whether or not there was an actual performance corresponding to the subject of Randolph's verse, it is clearly meant to be erotic (and was omitted from Randolph's published poems in 1638). Priapus is the god of fertility associated with the penis; the Harpies (whom the maid of honour outdoes in predatoriness) were hideous birds with women's faces who preyed on the blind prophet Phineus: in Henry Peacham's Emblem Book *Minerva Britanna* (London, 1612), they represent "extortionists and sycophants" ("In repetundos, et adulatores").[6] Randolph's Harpy-like predator threatens with her sexuality (Priapus), reinforced by her ruff (frequently seen by contemporary moralists as a symbol of sexual licence)[7] and her erect "beaver" (a hat, also alluded to as unseemly for its ambiguous use by men and women, and its "cocky" assertiveness). His/her crimson stockings and the ornamental "roses" on her fancy shoes confirm her "impudence," that is, lack of modesty, immodest boldness. The upshot is, just as Rainoldes predicted, that the dour scholar's interest is translated from curiosity into unhealthy erotic interest in the play-boy.

There is another poem by Randolph which supports this suggestion that the boy player is liable to be regarded with erotic interest which hovers somewhere between the heterosexual and the homosexual around his female attire. This poem is also couched as a riddle: Why does the elderly Lesbia pay through the nose to keep young Histrio, the boy actor, in a manner more fitting for a courtier? Having run through a description of Histrio's extravagances—elaborate dress, gambling, horse-racing—he reaches his facetious conclusion:

> Then this I can no better reason tell;
> 'Tis 'cause he playes the womans part so well.
> I see old Madams are not only toyle;
> No tilth so fruitfull as a barren soyle
> Ah poore day labourers, how I pitty you
> That shrinke, and sweat to live with much adoe!
> When had you wit to understand the right,
> 'Twere better wages to have work'd by night.[8]

Histrio is Lesbia's kept lover, her paid sexual partner. She is prepared to support his wildest extravagances because he is so good in bed: he "playes the womans part so well"—lewdly, he brings her adeptly to sexual climax. The boy player is by trade a "player of women's parts"; he acts the female roles on stage. And this femaleness is invoked in his sexual relations with his aging mistress in her name—she is Lesbia, the ancient lesbian lover (whence of course the term derives), so that her young partner is androgynous, female in persona but male in his sexuality. The source of his good fortune with Lesbia is actually (so Randolph implies) that he so ably satisfies her sexual demands (lasciviousness and excess being implied by the fact that she is "barren soil"—procreation is not the intention). Histrio "playes the womans part so well" offstage as well as on.

The ordinary playgoer does not keep constantly in his or her mind the cross-dressing implications of "boys in women's parts," but it is nevertheless available to the dramatist as a reference point for dramatic irony, or more serious *double entendre*. This *double entendre* adds sexual innuendo, I think, when "playing the woman's part" is invoked on the stage. In Shakespeare's *Cymbeline,* Posthumus, persuaded that his wife Imogen has been unfaithful, rails against womankind in general:

> Is there no way for men to be, but women
> Must be half-workers? We are all bastards . . .
> Me of my lawful pleasure she restrain'd,
> And pray'd me oft forebearance; did it with
> A pudency so rosy, the sweet view on't
> Might well have warm'd old Saturn; and I thought her
> As chaste as unsunn'd snow. O, all the devils!
> This yellow Iachimo in an hour—was't not?
> Or less!—at first? Perchance he spoke not, but,
> Like a full-acorn'd boar, a German one,
> Cried "O!" and mounted; found no opposition
> But what he look'd for should oppose and she
> Should from encounter guard. Could I find out
> The woman's part in me! For there's no motion
> That tends to vice in man but I affirm
> It is the woman's part.[9]

In his rage at Imogen's imputed promiscuousness Posthumus dwells with disturbing explicitness on his wife's sexual behavior. Her modest reluctance in the face of his husbandly sexual demands was doubly culpable in its counterfeiting. It is to be contrasted with the "Cried 'O!' and mounted" of her sex with Iachimo. And in the progressively obsessive sequence of associations which leads Posthumus from initial outburst to out-and-out abuse of all women, the transition from the "mounting" to the catalogue of vicious qualities which are "feminine" is surely made by way of Randolph's pun (the commonplace *double entendre*) on "the woman's part." Iachimo encounters no opposition to his assault save the physical obstruction of the female pudenda— "the women's part," that which Imogen "Should from encounter guard." On this bawdy sense is quickly superimposed that of "peculiarly female characteristic." Posthumus attributes vice in mankind in general to those human characteristics which are specific to the female. And this sense again, in a speech on the stage, of a female character indeed acted by a boy, modifies into play-*acting* the woman's part: vice is symbolically represented by the exaggeratedly female posturings of the boy who "takes the woman's part":

> It is the woman's part. Be it lying, note it,
> The woman's; flattering, hers; deceiving, hers;
> Lust and rank thoughts, hers, hers; revenges, hers;
> Ambitions, covetings, change of prides, disdain;
> Nice longing, slanders, mutability,
> All faults that man may name, nay, that hell knows,
> Why hers, in part or all.[10]

The punning which provides a titillating wittiness in Randolph's poem infuses Posthumus's rant with distorted sexual obsession. All that is potentially evil and disruptive about sexuality is to be associated with female roles—women's parts.

If we turn now to the female figures in Shakespeare's comedies, traditionally portrayed as healthily asexual heroines in Royal Shakespeare Company productions, we find them, I believe, strongly recalling the cross-dressing themes to which I have drawn attention. My contention is that these figures are sexually enticing *qua* transvestied boys, and that the plays encourage the audience to view them as such. The audience is invited to remark the "pretty folly," the blush, the downcast shameful glance of the boy player whose "woman's part" requires that he portray female qualities, but in *male* dress. The flavor of this "unhealthy" interest is to be found in the stylized scene in *The Merchant of Venice* in which Jessica elopes with her lover Lorenzo:

> *Jessica*   I am glad 'tis night, you do not look on me,
>   For I am much asham'd of my exchange;
>   But love is blind, and lovers cannot see
>   The pretty follies that themselves commit,
>   For, if they could, Cupid himself would blush
>   To see me thus transformed to a boy.

> Lorenzo   Descend, for you must be my torchbearer.
> Jessica   What! must I hold a candle to my shames?
>   They in themselves, good sooth, are too too light.
>   Why, 'tis an office of discovery, love,
>   And I should be obscur'd.
> Lorenzo   So are you, sweet,
>   Even in the lovely garnish of a boy.[11]

As it is also when the noble Portia herself describes how she will appear when she dons male dress to follow her husband secretly on his journey:

> Portia   When we are both accoutred like young men,
>   I'll prove the prettier fellow of the two,
>   And wear my dagger with the braver grace,
>   And speak between the change of man and boy
>   With a reed voice; and turn two mincing steps
>   Into a manly stride; and speak of frays
>   Like a fine bragging youth; and tell quaint lies,
>   How honourable ladies sought my love,
>   Which I denying, they fell sick and died—
>   I could not do withal. Then I'll repent,
>   And wish, for all that, that I had not kill'd them.
>   And twenty of these puny lies I'll tell,
>   That men shall swear I have discontinued school
>   Above a twelvemonth.[12]

Are the "mincing steps" Portia will turn into a "manly stride" the ambiguous stage manners of a "womanish boy"?[13] When she brags how she "could not do withal," when ladies passionately loved her, does she brag in her male persona, for which the ladies fell (she had no inclination to take them up on their passion, or, even, there were too many to cope with)? Or does she play on her hidden female sex— she had no means of consummating such a relationship?[14] Is Jessica coy because dressed as a boy her love for Lorenzo is titillating (serving torchbearer, boy-lover), or because she blushes to show her legs in breeches? In other words, the *double entendres* of these speeches by blushing heroines (played by boys) as they adopt male dress to follow their male lovers are both compatible with the heterosexual plot, and evocative of the bisexual image of the "wanton female boy." When Julia, in *The Two Gentlemen of Verona*, prepares to adopt her male disguise, she alludes directly to "effeminacy" of boy's dress, and its seductive allure:

> Lucetta   But in what habit will you go along?
> Julia   Not like a woman, for I would prevent
>   The loose encounters of lascivious men;

	Gentle Lucetta, fit me with such weeds As may beseem some well-reputed page.
Lucetta	Why then, your ladyship must cut your hair.
Julia	No girl; I'll knit it up in silken strings With twenty odd-conceited true-love knots— To be fantastic may become a youth Of greater time than I shall show to be.
Lucetta	What fashion, madam, shall I make your breeches?
Julia	That fits as well as "Tell me, good my lord, What compass will you wear your farthingale." Why ev'n what fashion thou best likes, Lucetta.
Lucetta	You must needs have them with a codpiece, madam.
Julia	Out, out, Lucetta, that will be ill-favour'd.
Lucetta	A round hose, madam, now's not worth a pin, Unless you have a codpiece to stick pins on.[15]

If Julia were really concerned to appear as a "well-reputed page" to avoid the "loose encounters of lascivious men," she would not purpose to adopt a hair-style "knit up in silken strings / With twenty odd-conceited true-love knots": a style inveighed against as decadent and immoral by stage polemicists and dress reformers. Nor would she and Lucetta launch into a discussion of comparative breeches fashion which focuses on ornamental covering for the genitals—another favorite target for the moral indignation of contemporary pamphleteers.[16]

At the focus of attention in all these passages is the alluring "beardless boy." It does not matter that the coy seductiveness of the boy player is for plot purposes being appreciated by a woman (as in Viola's "Make me a willow cabin at your gate" speech before Olivia in *Twelfth Night*,[17] or in Venus's uncontrolledly lascivious pursuit of Adonis in *Venus and Adonis*). "Playing the woman's part"—male effeminacy— is an act for a male audience's appreciation. When the noble ladies of the drama dress their pages in women's dress in an idle moment, they draw attention to his availability as an object of *male* erotic attention:

Boy	It will get . . . me a perfect deale of ill will at the mansion you wot of, whose ladie is the argument of it: where now I am the welcom'st thing vnder a man that comes there.
Clerimont	I thinke, and aboue a man too, if the truth were rack'd out of you.
Boy	No faith, I'll confesse before, sir. The gentlewomen play with me, and throw me o' the bed; and carry me in to my lady; and shee kisses me with her oil'd face; and puts a perruke o' my head; and askes me an' I will weare her gowne; and I say, no: and then she hits me a blow o' the eare, and calls me innocent, and lets me goe.[18]

The page confirms the lewd innuendo of his being "the welcom'st thing vnder a man," even as he protests that he doesn't play sexual games with his mistress and her gentlewomen.

I think this must influence our reading of the dramatically powerful scenes in the drama in which cross-dressed girls appear (boy/girl/boy). At the height of the action in *The Two Gentlemen of Verona*, for instance, Julia, disguised as a boy, describes her abandoned mistress (that is, in fact, Julia herself) to Silvia, now ardently pursued by Julia's fickle ex-lover:

> *Julia*   I thank you, madam, that you tender her.
> Poor gentlewoman, my master wrongs her much.
> *Silvia*   Dost thou know her?
> *Julia*   Almost as well as I do know myself.
> To think upon her woes, I do protest
> That I have wept a hundred several times. . . .
> *Silvia*   Is she not passing fair?
> *Julia*   She hath been fairer, madam, than she is. . . .
> *Silvia*   How tall was she?
> *Julia*   About my stature; for at Pentecost,
> When all our pageants of delight were play'd,
> Our youth got me to play the woman's part,
> And I was trimm'd in Madam Julia's gown;
> Which served me as fit, by all men's judgments,
> As if the garment had been made for me;
> Therefore I know she is about my height.
> And at that time I made her weep agood,
> For I did play a lamentable part.
> Madam, 'twas Ariadne passioning
> For Theseus' perjury and unjust flight;
> Which I so lively acted with my tears
> That my poor mistress, moved therewithal,
> Wept bitterly; and would I might be dead
> If I in thought felt not her very sorrow.
> *Silvia*   She is beholding to thee, gentle youth.
> Alas, poor lady, desolate and left!
> I weep myself, to think upon thy words.[19]

A recent critic has drawn particular attention to this scene in which "Julia disguised as a page, invents for her rival . . . a story that describes her apparent male self playing 'the woman's part' in the clothes of her real female self":[20]

> The layers insulating this story from reality enable [Julia] to reveal herself through her disguise, to express her deep grief at being aban-

doned, and to engender a sympathetic response from her onstage and offstage audience. . . . Julia, by playing male and female, actor and audience, herself and not herself, shares with Silvia grief at male betrayal and female abandonment.[21]

Everything that I have been saying suggests that we should be extremely wary of such a reading, which imputes peculiarly female insight to Julia, or to Silvia via Julia's masquerade. Julia is indeed, at this point in the play, "herself and not herself"; but the play in this scene is largely on her *maleness,* as a means of projecting strong and theatrical feelings for the benefit of her "onstage and offstage audience." Silvia's exclamation of deep sympathy—"Alas, poor lady, desolate and left!"—refers in the first instance to Ariadne's story, which stimulates and enhances a sense of "grief" in general (as Lucrece's perusal of the tapestry of the weeping Hecuba underscores and generalizes her despair in *The Rape of Lucrece*).[22] Both Julia then (supposedly) and Silvia now weep at the *proverbially* lamentable tale of Ariadne on Naxos. This is theatrical representation—not "real" (female) feeling, as Hamlet is all too aware when he weeps at the player's "lamentable" rendering of Aeneas' set speech recounting Hecuba's grief at the death of Priam, in *Hamlet.*[23]

Hamlet's reaction ("What's Hecuba to him or he to Hecuba, / That he should weep for her?") is that it is ironic that a mere player can weep real tears "but in a fiction, in a dream of passion" (tears which in their turn stimulate Hamlet's own). Real grief is harder to face up to, to understand, to feel. So Julia, Silvia, and their audience react with strong feelings of grief to a representation of pathos *with which they have nothing to do.* It is intrinsically "pathetic," engendering pathos, stimulating grief. "I weep myself to think upon thy words," says Silvia. The weeping is not *qua* woman, but *qua* audience, responding to a culturally familiar emblem of abandonment. The "layers insulating this story from reality" reveal nothing about "real" womanly feelings: on the contrary, they code "admirable grief" in the stereotype representation of the "weeping woman strong in suffering."[24] The boy player armed with his arsenal of female characteristics and mannerisms mimes out the acceptable form of heroic womanhood prostrate with grief. The player's and "Sebastian's" (alias Julia's) and Silvia's emotion is *womanish* because uncontrolled by "manly" restraint.

Notes

1. J. Kott, "Shakespeare's bitter Arcadia," in *Shakespeare Our Contemporary* (London: Methuen, 1965, 1972 edn), pp. 191–236, does point to the importance of cross-dressing in the comedies, but not in a way which I find very useful. For an

attempt to make more constructive critical use of the girl/boy disguise, see N. K. Hayles, "Sexual disguise in *As You Like It* and *Twelfth Night*," *Shakespeare Survey*, 32 (1979), pp. 63–72. On acting conventions in general in the period, see most recently A. Gurr, *The Shakespearean Stage 1574–1642* (Cambridge: Cambridge Univ. Press, 1980).

2. J. Rainoldes, *Th' Overthrow of Stage-Plays* (Middleburgh, 1599), p. 97. On the anti-stage polemic, especially its use of cross-dressing as a basic ground for attack, see K. Young, "An Elizabethan defense of the stage," *Shakespeare Studies by Members of the Department of English of the University of Wisconsin* (Madison: Univ. of Wisconsin Press, 1916), pp. 103–24, and "William Gager's defense of the academic stage," *Transactions of the Wisconsin Academy of Sciences, Arts and Letters* XVIII (1916), pp. 593–638; J. W. Binns, "Women or transvestites on the Elizabethan stage? An Oxford controversy," *The Sixteenth-Century Journal*, V (1974), pp. 95–120; A. F. Kinney, *Markets of Bawdrie: The Dramatic Criticism of Stephen Gosson* (Salzburg: Institut für Englische Sprache und Literatur, 1974).

3. Rainoldes, *op. cit.*, p. 97.

4. BL, Add. MS 11811, in H. Gardner (ed.), *The Metaphysical Poets* (Harmondsworth: Penguin Books, 1957). My thanks are due to Dr. J. C. Barrell of King's College, Cambridge, who first drew my attention to this poem.

5. G. E. Bentley, *The Jacobean and Caroline Stage*, 7 vols. (Oxford: Clarendon Press, 1941–68), I, 39.

6. Scholar Press Facsimile, 1969, p. 115.

7. See Lisa Jardine, *Still Harping on Daughters* (Brighton: Harvester Press, 1983), p. 14.

8. W. C. Hazlitt (ed.), *Poetical and Dramatic Works of Thomas Randolph*, 2 vols. (London: Reeves and Turner, 1875), II.540.

9. *Cymbeline* II.v.1–22.

10. *Ibid.*, II.v.22–8. Compare *As You Like It* III.ii.374–88.

11. *The Merchant of Venice* II.vi.34–45.

12. III.v.63–76.

13. For explicit reference to the "reed voice" of the boy player, see *Hamlet* II.ii.416.

14. "Withal" has just this ambiguity in the period: it has the sense both of "therewith" and "moreover," "in addition": "I couldn't do anything with it" (I couldn't perform), and "I couldn't cope with it."

15. *The Two Gentlemen of Verona* II.vii.39–56.

16. See Jardine, *Still Harping*, p. 148.

17. I.v.250.

18. Ben Jonson, *Epicoene, or The Silent Woman*, I.i.6–18, in C. H. Herford and P. Simpson (eds.), *Works* (Oxford: Clarendon Press, 1937), V, 165.

19. IV.iv.136–71.

20. Carolyn Ruth Swift Lenz, Gayle Greene, and Carol Thomas Neely, *The Woman's*

Part: Feminist Criticism of Shakespeare (Urbana: University of Illinois Press, 1980), p. 13.

21. *Ibid.*

22. See Jardine, *Still Harping,* p. 192.

23. *Hamlet* II.ii.513.

24. See Jardine, *Still Harping,* p. 181.

7

Women as Spectators, Spectacles, and Paying Customers

Jean E. Howard

In the "Documents of Control" section of *The Elizabethan Stage*, E. K. Chambers records a 1574 Act of the Common Council of London which represents an attempt to restrain and regulate public playing within the Liberties.[1] The reasons cited for such restraint are numerous and familiar: the gathering together of playgoers in inns and yards spreads the plague; it creates opportunities for illicit sexual encounters; and it provides the occasion for the dissemination, from the stage, of "unchaste, uncomelye, and unshamefaste speeches and doynges."[2] The document is long, and it contains little that would surprise anyone familiar with Renaissance polemic against the public stage or with the numerous petitions sent by the City to the Queen and her Council urging the restraint of playing during the next thirty years. What particularly interested me, however, was the way the document concludes, which is thus:

> ... this Act (otherwise than towchinge the publishinge of unchaste, sedycious, and unmete matters:) shall not extend to anie plaies, Enterludes, Comodies, Tragidies, or shewes to be played or shewed in the pryvate hous, dwellinge, or lodginge of anie nobleman, Citizen, or gentleman, which shall or will then have the same thear so played or shewed in his presence for the festyvitie of anie marriage, Assemblye of ffrendes, or otherlyke cawse withowte publique or Commen Collection of money of the Auditorie or behoulders theareof, reservinge alwaie to the Lorde Maior and Aldermen for the tyme beinge the Judgement and construction Accordinge to equitie what shalbe Counted suche a playenge or shewing in a pryvate place, anie things in this Acte to the Contrarie notwithstanding. (p. 276)

What is striking to me here is the absolutely clear demarcation between the dangers of public playing, involving the "Commen Collection of money of the Auditorie," and the acceptability of playing within a "pryvate hous, dwellinge, or lodginge" where presumably no money was collected and where the audience had therefore not been transformed by a commercial transaction from guests to customers. As was to be true in a number of anti-theatrical tracts and petitions from the City, what is specified here as objectionable about certain kinds of theatrical activity is less the matter or content of plays *per se,* and more the practices surrounding public playing: specifically, the removal of the scene of playing from the controlled space of the nobleman's house to a public venue; the dailiness of public playing versus its occasional use, for example, as part of a wedding festivity; the transformation of those who attend the play from guests or clients of a great man or wealthy citizen to paying customers; and, implicitly, the transformation of dramatists from straightforward servants of the nobility to something more akin to artisan entrepreneurs. In short, in this document public playing is presented as altering social relations by the emergent material practices attendant upon play production and attendance, quite apart from any consideration of the ideological import of the fictions enacted on the stage.

Another document written a few years later, when amphitheater playhouses were an established fact, underscores a similar point. In *The Schoole of Abuse,* 1579, Stephen Gosson, drawing on Ovid and classical attacks on the theater, rehearses a number of objections to the public theater that were to become standard tropes of English antitheatrical polemic: theater teaches immorality; it allures the senses rather than improves the mind; it encourages flouting of the sumptuary laws; it serves as a meeting place for whores and their customers.[3] While Gosson certainly raises objections to the *content* of plays, he too is keenly alert to the disruptive potential embedded in the very activity of going to a play. It provides occasion, for example, for the conspicuous display of ornate attire and for the promiscuous mixing together of social groups. The money that allowed an upstart crow to ape the clothes of his betters and to display them at the theater also allowed him to purchase a seat in the galleries. While the public theaters were hierarchically designed to reflect older status categories (common men in the pit; gentlemen in the galleries; lords on the very top), in actuality one's place at the public theater was determined less by one's rank than by one's ability or willingness to pay for choice or less choice places. Money thus stratified the audience in ways at least potentially at odds with older modes of stratification, a fact with which Ben Jonson was still ruefully coming to terms several decades later when in the preface to *Bartholomew Fair* he satirically enjoins various members of the audience at the Hope Theater to offer criticism of his play strictly in proportion to the amount of money they had laid out at the theater door.

> It is further agreed that every person here have his or their free-will of censure, to like or dislike at their own charge, the author having now departed with his right: it shall be lawful for any man to judge his six pen'orth, his twelve pen'orth, so to his eighteen pence, two shillings, half a crown, to the value of his place; provided always his place get not above his wit. And if he pay for half a dozen, he may censure for all them too, so that he will undertake that they shall be silent. He shall put in for censures here as they do for lots at the lottery; marry, if he drop but sixpence at the door, and will censure a crown's worth, it is thought there is no conscience or justice in that.[4] (Induction, 76–86)

At court, as Jonson's epilogue to the same play suggests, he can count on a spectator, the king, whose judgments are absolute and whose position is fixed, unaffected by the fluidity of market relations. In the public theater things are different. Much to Jonson's dismay, his art has become rather too much like a Bartholomew Fair commodity liable to judgment by those who can and will pay to see it, whatever their rank, education, and taste.

I wish to suggest that in such a context the ideological consequences of playgoing might be quite different for different social groups. Gosson indirectly broaches this issue in what is for me the most interesting part of his tract, namely, the concluding epistle, which is addressed to "the Gentlewomen, Citizens of London," a category of playgoer apparently significant enough to warrant Gosson's specific attention.[5] From Andrew Gurr's important study, *Playgoing in Shakespeare's London,* we now know that women were in the public theater in significant numbers and that the women who attended the theater were neither simply courtesans nor aristocratic ladies; many seem to have been citizens' wives, part of that emergent group, "the middling sort," whom Gosson most explicitly addresses.[6] The presence of such women at the theater clearly worries Gosson, and he voices his worries in a typically paternalistic form: i.e., as a concern for woman's safety and good reputation. What Gosson argues is that the safest place for woman to be is at home, busy with household management, with neighborhood gossips, and, for recreation, with books. As he says, "The best councel I can give you, is to keepe home, and shun all occasion of ill speech."[7] The dangerous place for woman to be is the theater. The interesting question is why.

Ostensibly, the threat is to woman's sexual purity. In the body of his tract Gosson argues that the theater is a place for sexual assignations; it is a "market of bawdrie."[8] Various wantons and paramours, knaves and queens "Cheapen the merchandise in that place, which they pay for elsewhere as they can agree."[9] Presumably, any woman—and not just a prostitute—could fall prey to passion if inflamed by the allegedly lewd behavior of the actors or by the amorous addresses of her male companions at the theater. Yet in his concluding epistle, Gosson dwells less on the possibility that the gentlewoman citizen may go off to sleep with a fellow playgoer and more on the danger posed to her by being gazed at by many men in the public space of the theater. As Gosson says:

> Thought is free; you can forbidd no man, that vieweth you, to noute you and that noateth you, to judge you, for entring to places of suspition.[10]

The threat is not so much to woman's bodily purity, as to her reputation. In Gosson's account the female playgoer is symbolically whored by the gaze of many men, each woman a potential Cressida in the camp of the Greeks, vulnerable, alone, and open to whatever imputations men might cast upon her. She becomes what we might call the object of promiscuous gazing. Gosson presents the situation entirely paternalistically. For the "good" of women he warns them to stay at home, to shut themselves away from all dangers, and to find pleasure in reading or in the gossip of other women.

Yet who is endangered, really, by women's theatergoing? The intensity of Gosson's scrutiny of the woman playgoer indicates to me that her presence in the theater may have been felt to threaten more than her own purity, that in some way it put her "into circulation" in the public world of Elizabethan England in ways threatening to the larger patriarchal economy within which her circulation was in theory a highly structured process involving her passage from the house and surveillance of the father to the house and surveillance of the husband. This process was more complicated and class specific than I am indicating here, and it is also true that men, at least in the elite classes, often had their marriage choices determined by the father and were in no absolute sense free agents. But it was as the privileged sex that men circulated through the structures of Elizabethan society, and it was they to whom women were by and large accountable, and not vice versa. The threat the theater seems to hold for Gosson in regard to ordinary gentlewomen is that in that public space such women have become unanchored from the structures of surveillance and control "normal" to the culture and useful in securing the boundary between "good women" and "whores." Not literally passed, like Cressida, from hand to hand, lip to lip, the female spectator passes instead from eye to eye, her value as the exclusive possession of one man cheapened, put at risk, by the gazing of many eyes. To whom, in such a context, does woman belong? Are her meaning and value fixed, or fluctuating? How does one classify a woman who is not literally a whore and yet who is not, as good women were supposed to be, at home? To handle the ambiguity, the potential blurring of ideological categories, Gosson would send the gentlewoman citizen out of the theater and back to her house, husband, father, books, and gossips, where such questions admit of easier answers.

Yet I suspect the threat to the patriarchal order is even more complex than I have so far indicated. By drawing on the Cressida analogy, I have seemed to assent to Gosson's most fundamental premise, namely, that women in the theater were simply objects of scrutiny and desire, and that in that position they were in danger of being read as whores or otherwise becoming commodities outside the control of one man. But what if one reads the situation less within the horizons of masculinist ideology and asks whether women might have been empowered, and not simply victimized, by their novel position within the theater? In the theatrical economy of gazes, could men have done all the looking, held all the power? Joel Steinberg could not bear the thought that Hedda Nussbaum was looking at him, and he beat her eyes until artificial tearducts had to be inserted in one of them. Is it possible that in the theater women were licensed to look—and in a larger sense to judge what they saw and to exercise autonomy—in ways that problematized women's status as object within patriarchy? I have no definitive answer to my own question yet, but what I tentatively suggest is that Gosson's prescriptive rhetoric may be a response, not only to a fear *for* woman, but also to a fear *of* woman, as she takes up a place in an institution which, as Steven Mullaney has argued, existed at least symbolically on the margins of authorized culture, opening space for the transformation, as much as the simple reproduction, of that culture.[11] At the theater door, money changed hands in a way which enabled women access to the pleasure and privilege of gazing, certainly at the stage, and probably at the audience as well. They were therefore, as Jonson ruefully acknowledges, among those authorized to exercise their sixpence worth, or their penny's worth, of judgment. Whether or not they were accompanied by husbands or fathers, women at the theater were not "at home," but in public, where they could become objects of desire, certainly, but also desiring subjects, stimulated to want what was on display at the theater, which must have been, not just sexual opportunity, but all the trappings of a commodifying culture worn upon the very backs of those attending the theater and making it increasingly difficult to discern "who one really was" in terms of the categories of a status system based on fixed and unchanging social hierarchies. As Jean-Christophe Agnew has argued, the Renaissance stage made the liquidity of social relations in a commercializing culture its theme.[12] I would simply argue that the practice of playgoing may have embodied that liquidity, not simply thematized it. For Gosson good wives who took up a place at the public theater were dangerously out of their true and appropriate place, and he clearly meant to return them to that proper place by threatening those who remained in the place of danger with the name of whore. The question is, when is a person out of her place *in* danger and when is she *a* danger to those whom, by her new placement, she is displacing?

I am suggesting that in the public theater, where men and women alike were both spectacles and spectators, desired and desiring, I doubt that only women's chastity or women's reputations were at risk, despite Gosson's polemic to that effect. Even when this theater, through its fictions, invited women to take up the subordinate positions masculine ideology defined as proper for them, the very practice of playgoing put women in positions potentially unsettling to patriarchal control. To be part of urban public life as spectator, consumer, and judge moved the gentlewoman citizen outside of that domestic enclosure to which Gosson would return her. While it does no good to exaggerate the powers of women in such a situation, I think the anti-theatrical polemicists were right to worry about female theatergoing, though not only for the reasons they were able to articulate. Reading Gosson, I wonder about the unsaid of his text. Focusing on the danger *to* women, did he not also feel endangered *by* them? In short, was Gosson's unspoken fear that the practice of female theatergoing, the entry of the middle-class woman into the house of Proteus, was part of a larger process of cultural change altering social relations within urban London and putting pressure on the gender positions and definitions upon which masculine dominance rested?

Notes

1. A much longer version of this essay entitled "Scripts and/versus Playhouses: Ideological Production and the Renaissance Public Stage" appeared in *Renaissance Drama* 20 (1989), 31–49.

2. E.K. Chambers, *The Elizabethan Stage*, 4 vols. (Oxford: The Clarendon Press, 1923), Vol. IV, pp. 273–74.

3. Stephen Gosson, *The Schoole of Abuse* (1579; Rpt. New York: Garland Publishing Company, 1973).

4. Ben Jonson, *Bartholomew Fair*, ed. Eugene M. Waith (New Haven: Yale Univ. Press, 1963), pp. 30–31.

5. S.P. Zitner in "Gosson, Ovid, and the Elizabethan Audience," *Shakespeare Quarterly* 9 (1958), 206–08, explores the extent to which Gosson's account of the Elizabethan playgoing audience in the body of *The Schoole of Abuse* draws upon passages in Ovid's *Art of Love*. He concludes that Gosson's descriptions should not be taken as an unmediated eyewitness report of Elizabethan theatergoing. Gosson's debt to Ovid, as well as his polemical intentions, must be taken into account before one accepts his treatise as description of objective fact. In this essay I am more interested in the concluding epistle to the gentlewomen of London than in the body of the tract. More importantly, however, I assume that all of Gosson's tract is ideological and interested, rather than dispassionately objective. I am concerned with why Gosson and his fellow anti-theatricalists circulated certain narratives (whatever their source) about women at the theater; and I wish to offer a counter-account of what the middle-class woman's presence in that cultural space may have signified in terms of changing social relations in early modern England.

6. Andrew Gurr, *Playgoing in Shakespeare's London* (Cambridge: Cambridge Univ. Press, 1987), esp. pp. 56–60.

7. Stephen Gosson, *The Schoole of Abuse*, Sig. F4.

8. *Ibid.*, Sig. C2.

9. *Ibid.*, Sig. C2.

10. *Ibid.*, Sig. F2.

11. Steven Mullaney, *The Place of the Stage: License, Play, and Power in Renaissance England* (Chicago: Univ. of Chicago Press, 1988), esp. pp. 26–59.

12. Jean-Christophe Agnew, *Worlds Apart: The Market and The Theater in Anglo-American Thought, 1550–1750* (Cambridge: Cambridge Univ. Press, 1986), esp. pp. 111–14.

8

Sodomy and Society:
The Case of Christopher Marlowe

Jonathan Goldberg

Within a few days of his mysterious death, a document appeared labeling Marlowe as an atheist and a homosexual. Signed by Richard Baines, the note lists some nineteen charges said to represent Marlowe's opinions "Concerning his Damnable Judgment of Religion, and scorn of gods word."[1] At first glance, the list can appear rather random in its organization, a series of opinions on the truth of the gospels occasionally intermixed with more overtly political utterances and, towards the end, pausing for one moment to insert a bit of sexual bravura: "That all they that love not Tobacco & Boies were fooles." I would like to suggest, however, that this document, arranged to fit the preconceptions of the authorities to whom Baines was reporting, reveals the constitution of homosexuality within the social text. Although the document is usually referred to as the Baines libel, it speaks a discursive truth.

To place this document within the social discourses that give it its voice, I rely on Alan Bray's brilliant book, *Homosexuality in Renaissance England.*[2] Bray argues that there were no discrete terms for homosexual behavior in the period; *sodomy* always was embedded in other discourses, those delineating anti-social behavior—sedition, demonism, atheism. In *sodomy* English society saw its shadow: the word expressed sheer negation, an absence capable of taking root in anyone, and necessarily to be rooted out. In homosexuality so construed and so entangled with religious, political, and cosmic subversion, the most fundamental malaises of Elizabethan society were given expression. These are the contexts voiced in the Baines libel. There was, Bray argues, no recognition of homosexuality *per se,* no terms to identify a homosexual except within a seditious behavior that knew no limits. For homosexual acts were not localized in Elizabethan society; homosexual persons were not identified. Rather, sodomy was disseminated throughout society, invisible so long as homosexual acts failed to connect with the much more visible signs of social disruption represented by unorthodox religious or social positions.

What was Marlowe's place in Elizabethan society? What made him a likely object of Baines's accusations? These are the questions raised by the conjunction of the libel and the argument Bray makes about the social invisibility of the sodomite. They are not easy questions to answer. The facts of Marlowe's life, and, particularly, of his death, do not easily reveal themselves. Here is what the standard biographies report:

On 18 May 1593, the Privy Council issued a warrant for Marlowe's arrest; two days later he presented himself and agreed to remain in London until he was called again. Some two weeks later, on 30 May 1593, Marlowe spent the entire day in the house of one Eleanor Bull in the company of three male companions. They talked, dined, strolled in the garden; after dinner, a dispute arose, and, in the course of the argument, Marlowe received a wound in the eye from which he died instantly. On 1 June, he was buried. On 2 June, a copy of Baines's allegations against Marlowe was made and sent to the queen.

This narrative is full of questions. We do not know why the Privy Council ordered Marlowe's arrest—it may as easily have been to secure his testimony against someone as to charge him with criminal activity. We certainly do not know that allegations of treason, blasphemy, atheism, or sodomy were involved. Nor do we know whether the fact that Marlowe had not been recalled before the Privy Council by 30 May means that the case, whatever it was, had been dropped, or whether it was still pending. We do not know if the Baines document was related to the case, nor if it bears some connection to Marlowe's death. Its date of composition cannot be determined. We do not even know whether Eleanor Bull's establishment was a public tavern or a private house.

We do know, however, that the three men with whom Marlowe spent his last day had all served in various capacities as government spies, and that Marlowe's murderer, Ingram Friser, was released after a month's imprisonment. Records show Friser transacting business on the day of his release for Sir Thomas Walsingham, a close relative of Sir Francis Walsingham, Queen Elizabeth's Secretary of State and head of her secret service. Marlowe spent eight hours in the company of these men because he shared their social connections; he, too, had been patronized by Sir Thomas; he, too, had been employed as a government spy. One of these men had acted as a double agent, securing the crucial evidence for the conviction of Mary Queen of Scots. Marlowe, however, had a place with such accomplished double agents, men whose business it was to voice what society regarded as inexorably opposed to it. He is reported to have traveled in France, and there to have presented himself as a Catholic sympathizer. As a government agent, Marlowe was given an identity that was, at one and the same time, a counter-identity. What Elizabethan society called Other, it also employed in its service. The Baines libel records this voice—the voice, that is, of Marlowe's rebellion against his society which is also the rebellion which his society employed him to voice. The Baines libel, in short, speaks from the position of a socially sanctioned *double agency*, and speaks in the recognition that such a position permits. What adds full impact and eeriness to this is the strong likelihood that this identity constituted as an Otherness was in fact Marlowe's *real* identity. There is, of course, no way to say simply what a real identity is in such a construction. But what I would suggest is that it locates a place for a homosexual identity in Elizabethan society.

The Baines document will clarify what I mean.

The first four allegations are directed against religion, undermining the priority of Christian belief by insisting on the radical historicity of religion and its political uses. Moses is called a juggler, the wandering in the wilderness a way of founding "everlasting superstition . . . in the hartes of the people," Adam a latecomer in human history. In short, "the first beginning of Religion was only to keep men in awe," the fourth allegation reads. Machiavelli might be speaking. Yet, in placing these opinions in Marlowe's mouth, Marlowe is allowed to bring to its ultimate destination an impulse which also stands as a cornerstone of normative Renaissance culture and political conservatism, the humanist's desire for authentic history which had led to such accomplishments as labeling the Donation of Constantine a forgery or to the production of an authoritative biblical text. Humanistic philology, in performing such activities, had not been operating in a pure or apolitical fashion; the scholarly work served emerging states and reforming churches; political sinecures were the scholar's reward. In the libellous accusation, an arm of the state is turned back against it; the state's use of religion is affirmed as a scandal. The alleged opinions, in brief, recognize the subversive potential in an apparatus of state power.

The next set of allegations also concerns religion, but the emphasis now lies on the Bible as fiction. Christ is read as a bastard, his mother as a whore, and his father as a carpenter; and thus his crucifixion as evidence that "the Jewes . . . best knew him and whence he Came." Marlowe is said to have regarded Catholicism as a "good Religion," thanks to its elaborate ceremonies; "all Protestantes are Hypocriticall asses." The logic of these accusations is thus revealed. Reading the Bible literally, as a good Protestant, the Marlowe of Baines's text realizes that only Catholic mystification can save the text from its gross palpability. Marlowe turns Protestant hermeneutics on its head, and Catholicism emerges as a "good Religion" merely because it embraces the fictions of ceremony rather than indulging in the Protestant hypocrisy which pretends to a literalism that it will not see through. Once again we could describe the voice assigned to Marlowe here as the articulation of a founding cultural antithesis. The perception that society itself is a matrix of fictions, and that one of its strongest fictional components involves the denial of its fictionality, describes, too, the double agency that generates Marlowe's identity. These allegations, in fact, seize hold of such possibilities when Marlowe is reported to have said "That if he were to write a new Religion, he would undertake both a more Excellent and Admirable methode," adding "that all the new testament is filthily written."

It is at this point that the allegation of sodomy is made, coming after charges that Christ knew the whorish woman of Samaria dishonestly and was "bedfellow" of John the Evangelist, "that he used him as the sinners of Sodoma." The sexual irregularity of Christ's behavior represents a full literalization of the incarnation; it also authorizes Marlowe's praise of the love of boys and tobacco. Baines's Marlowe coopts the Bible through a misreading rooted in the demystifying historicity of earlier claims. Once again, the radical reading arises from a possibility offered to Protestant readers. Once again, then, mainstream habits of thought and central tenets of Elizabethan culture produce their own subversion.

Soon after Marlowe's death, his fellow playwright and sometime roommate, Thomas Kyd, was charged with atheism; in response, he insisted that Marlowe, not he, held irregular opinions. In one of two letters written in his own defense, Kyd produced a list, briefer than Baines's, of Marlowe's beliefs. This time, Marlowe is said to have called St. Paul a juggler; Kyd claims that Marlowe told him that to write in imitation of St. Paul could only lead to bad poetry. What is striking in Kyd's allegations is that it opens with the charge of Christ's sodomy: "He would report St. John to be our savior Christes *Alexis* . . . that is that Christ did love him with an extraordinary love." The allusion, of course, is to Virgil's second eclogue, Corydon's lament about the unforthcoming Alexis. The overt homosexuality of the Virgilian text coupled with the demystification of the Bible once again arises from a central habit of Renaissance thought, the conjunction of classicism and Christianity.

Perhaps what needs further glossing is the coupling of the love of boys with tobacco. Tobacco has a particular historical valency that ought not to be overlooked; colonizing activities were directed to its importation, and support of tobacco could be taken as a sign of patriotism. Early in the Baines allegation, the juggling of Moses had been compared invidiously to the talents of "one Heriots being Sir W Raleighs man"; Raleigh and Heriot, in fact, were often suspected of atheistical beliefs; but Raleigh was also the queen's instrument in exploring the virgin territories of the new world, and Heriot, serving as a government spokesman, had written an account of Virginia praising the importation of tobacco. Once more, sodomy has been placed in a context in which official government positions and their accompanying malaise both speak.

Indeed, the Baines document moves from sodomy to its most explicit political allegations, questioning St. Paul's (and by extension, Luther's and the Elizabethan state's) prescriptions about obedience to magistrates, and including the bizarre claim in which Baines's Marlowe says he has as much right to mint coins as the queen—asserting, too, that he had learned the art from "one poole," a fellow prisoner in Newgate. Marlowe *had* spent time in Newgate, charged as an accomplice to a murder, and one Poole was in fact the double agent who had deceived Mary Queen of Scots, and with whom Marlowe spent his final day. The bizarre declaration has other connections as well, for it translates into the public realm the earlier assertions about Marlowe's power as a writer of fictions; these coins are the counterfeit representations upon which political economy rests, and which Marlowe claims to have seen through and to be able to better. Such claims hold the key, too, to the final pair of allegations with which the Baines document ends. "That the Angell Gabriell was Baud to the holy ghost, because he brought the salutation to Mary" and "that on[e] Ric Cholmley hath Confessed that he was perswaded to Marloe's Reasons to become an Atheist." Seemingly unrelated, the final charges point to the insidious powers of persuasion upon which authority—and authoring—rest.

This final point leads, of course, to the aspect of Marlowe that I might have been expected to have started with, his identity as an author. Although that is never explicitly charged against him in Baines's note, the spectre of the theater lurks behind his text. It is there, for instance, in the word *juggler,* which includes in its range of associations con man, cheap entertainer, magician, trickster, storyteller, conjurer, actor, and dramatist, as Stephen Greenblatt has noted.[3] The conjunction of boys and tobacco also summons up the theater, with its boy actors and profligate audience, the object of puritanical horror and government legislation. Even false coins might call up a phrase from Sir Philip Sidney's *Defence* which defines poetry as "a representing, counterfeiting, or figuring forth."[4] The demystifications in the document, in short, authorize its voice, lending it the authority writers and monarchs shared, not necessarily very comfortably. For the document, we might say, *legitimizes* Marlowe, but much as the theater was legitimated, at once placed and policed, censored and yet situated in the "liberties," on the border of the city, allowed a certain sphere of freedom to represent what might not be said within the city's confines, to give the illusion of autonomous and full discourse.[5] The theater was at once marginalized and supported by the government; when James I came to the throne of England, he took the theaters under his patronage. Elizabeth had said, in 1586, that "princes are set on stages in the sight and view of all the world," and James repeated her remark in his treatise on kingship, the *Basilikon Doron*.[6] In it, he also listed crimes that were treasonous and warranted death. Among them was sodomy. James, of course, was notorious for his overtly homosexual behavior. Yet, his treatise does not simply dissimulate; rather, it shows that sodomy was so fully politicized that no king could possibly apply the term to himself. Marlowe's theatrical milieu, as hospitable to homosexuality as any institution in the period can be said to have been (boy actors were regularly suspected of being what they counterfeited) is the place, in short, where the counter-voices of the culture were acted out.

The theater was permitted to rehearse the dark side of Elizabethan culture; it was a recreative spot where sedition could wear the face of play, where authors could make assertions as potent as monarchs'. In the theater, kings were the puppets of writers; greatness was mimed; atheists, rebels, magicians, and sodomites could be publicly displayed. And nowhere, of course, more strikingly than in Marlowe's heroes, the sodomitical Edward II, for instance, the Jew of Malta, Faustus and Tamburlaine. Marlowe's identity in his culture comes from his rehearsal of these counter-positions, and the words of Richard Baines, government spy, report how Marlowe, a fellow spy, acquired a counter-identity at once countenanced and denounced by his society. Like the heroes he created, Marlowe lived and died in the impossible project—as author, government spy, and sodomite—of the marginalized, negativized existence permitted him. Marlowe and his heroes, Stephen Greenblatt says, live lives in the recognition of the void, in the realization (I mean that both ways) that rebellion never manages to find its own space, but always acts in the space that society has created for it. To play there is to be nowhere and to recognize that the solidity of social discourse carries with it, as its support and as its own undermining, the very negations in which such play can occur. When Marlowe's audience assembled to see *The Jew of Malta,* they were greeted by a prologue spoken by Machiavelli, telling them, "I count religion but a childish toy/ And hold there is no sin but ignorance."[7] Baines's note ascribes to

Marlowe the rhetoric of his inventions. Marlowe is charged with *being* what he and his society allowed existence only as *negations* and *fictions*. Marlowe was not just playing.

That negativized identity has repercussions that stretch into our own time, however great the historical differences between the place of homosexuality in Renaissance society and ours. In the years between Marlowe and us, homosexuality has fastened upon what society has rejected as the place in which an antithetical discourse and a claim for social placement could be made. At the turn of this century, as the example of Oscar Wilde suggests, it was, in part, in *theatricality* that such claims were made. And it was also in theatricality that, at first, Wilde was saved. It was because he was charged with *posing* as a "somdomite" (not with being one) that he filed his libel suit; when he ultimately was convicted, he maintained that it was for writing a beautiful letter, a prose poem like one of Shakespeare's sonnets to his young man. The authenticity of inauthenticity was the ground upon which Wilde met his society. The history of homosexuality in the past 100 years has been of its emergence in the sphere of otherness to which it has been confined, its foundation in a discursive sphere in which it attempts to lay claims to a radically threatening otherness. Yet, it is always menaced and vulnerable, and whether we can ever find an authenticity that is not capable of being absorbed by, and crushed by, the society in which we exist, is the question raised, it seems to me, by the case of Christopher Marlowe.

Notes

1. A facsimile and transcription appear on pp. 308–9 of A.D. Wraight, *In Search of Christopher Marlowe* (N.Y.: Vanguard Press, 1965). An up to date summary of information about Baines can be found in C.B. Kuriyama, "Marlowe's Nemesis: The Identity of Richard Baines," in Kenneth Friedenreich, Roma Gill, and Constance B. Kuriyama, ed., *"A Poet and a filthy Play-maker": New Essays on Christopher Marlowe* (N.Y.: AMS Press, 1988), pp. 343–60.

2. London: Gay Men's Press, 1982. Bray's book remains the best treatment of its subject; however, there are some problematic aspects to its theory and practice that have become clearer to me since I wrote this essay. It was pp. 83–90 of Eve Kosofsky Sedgwick's *Between Men: English Literature and Male Homosocial Desire* (N.Y.: Columbia University Press, 1985) that first alerted me to areas of his work that needed scrutiny, and I have continued this critique, while continuing to rely on Bray's work, in "Colin to Hobbinol: Spenser's Familiar Letters," *South Atlantic Quarterly* 88 (1989): 107–26, esp. pp. 111–14.

3. See "Invisible Bullets: Renaissance Authority and Its Subversion," *Glyph* 8 (1981): 40–61, esp. pp. 42ff., which consider the Baines and Kyd allegations. (The essay appears in a final form in Stephen Greenblatt, *Shakespearean Negotiations* [Berkeley and Los Angeles: University of California Press, 1988]). This is perhaps the

appropriate place to note my indebtedness throughout this essay to Greenblatt's work, not least to his treatment of Marlowe in *Renaissance Self-Fashioning* (Chicago: University of Chicago Press, 1980).

4. *A Defence of Poetry,* ed. J.A. Van Dorsten (Oxford: Oxford University Press, 1966), p. 25.

5. Cf. Steven Mullaney, *The Place of the Stage* (Chicago: University of Chicago Press, 1988), pp. 1–59.

6. For further discussion, see my *James I and the Politics of Literature* (Baltimore: Johns Hopkins University Press, 1983; Stanford: Stanford University Press, 1989), pp. 113–16.

7. *The Complete Plays of Christopher Marlowe,* ed. Irving Ribner (Indianapolis and New York: Odyssey Press, 1963), p. 179.

9

What is a Text?

Stephen Orgel

Modern scientific bibliography began with the assumption that certain basic textual questions were capable of correct answers: that by developing rules of evidence and refining techniques of description and comparison the relation of editions of a work to each other and to the author's manuscript could be understood, and that an accurate text could thereby be produced. Behind these assumptions lies an even more basic one: that the correct text is the author's final manuscript, which is sometimes (though usually not in Renaissance bibliographical practice) interpreted to mean the last printed edition published during the author's lifetime.

We assume, in short, that the authority of a text derives from the author. Self-evident as it may appear, I suggest that this proposition is not true: in the case of Renaissance dramatic texts it is almost never true, and in the case of non-dramatic texts it is true rather less often than we think.

What scientific bibliography has taught us more clearly than anything else is that at the heart of our texts lies a hard core of uncertainty. I want to consider the implications of this not so much for editorial practice as for our whole notion of the nature of the materials we are dealing with—the structuralist's question "what is a text?" has a particular force when it is applied to the texts of Renaissance plays. The two works that bear most directly on my subject are E. A. J. Honigmann's *The Stability of Shakespeare's Text* (1965) and G. E. Bentley's *The Profession of Dramatist in Shakespeare's Time* (1971), books whose implications seem to me far more radical and far-reaching than has generally been recognized.

I shall start with the second of these books. Bentley makes it clear how much the creation of a play was a collaborative process, with the author by no means at the center of the collaboration. The company commissioned the play, usually stipulated the subject, often provided the plot, often parceled it out, scene by scene, to several playwrights. The text thus produced was a working model, which the company then revised as seemed appropriate. The author had little or no say in these revisions: the text belonged to the company, and the authority represented by the text—I am talking now about the *performing* text—is that of the company, the owners, not that of the playwright, the author. This means that if it is a performing text we are dealing with, it is a mistake to think that in our editorial work what we are doing is getting back to an author's original manuscript: the very notion of "the author's original manuscript" is in such cases a figment.

Shakespeare might seem to be an exception, since he was not simply the playwright but also an actor and shareholder in the company—he was literally his own boss. But I do not think he is an exception: I think he was simply in on more parts of the collaboration. I shall return to this and to its implications in a few moments, but first I want to clarify it with a contrasting example. Ben Jonson provides an excellent control for our notions of Renaissance dramatic texts. Jonson makes a large point out of insisting that the printed versions of his plays are substantially different from the versions that were staged. He complains of the actors' cuts—other playwrights (including Shakespeare) report interpolations or revisions, with varying degrees of resentment. *Sejanus* constitutes what we might think of as a classic example for our purposes. The play was first written in collaboration with another playwright; that was the version the actors performed. But in preparing the play for publication, Jonson *took control* of the text: he replaced his collaborator's scenes with ones of his own, and added a good deal of new material, largely historical documentation. He is lavish in praise of his collaborator, but he also (pointedly I would think) doesn't mention his name, and since there are no other records, we can only speculate about who he was. Jonson here has succeeded in *suppressing* the theatrical production, and has replaced it with an independent, printed text, which he consistently refers to, moreover, not as a play but as a poem.

This example is, in Jonson's canon, extreme but not uncharacteristic. Why does he rewrite his plays for publication? Precisely because he hasn't sufficient *authority* in the theatrical versions. The only way for Jonson to assert his authority over the text was to alter it and publish it: the authority, that is, lies in the publication.

But even here, we would have to say that the author is a curiously shadowy figure. Let's move away from drama for a moment, to a situation where the issues might seem to be more clear-cut: the work of professional poets. For the Elizabethan age Spenser is the prime example, and yet Spenser continually asserts that the *authority* of his text derives not from his genius but from the poem's subject and patron, the queen. Our tendency is to dismiss this claim as flattery. Flattery it may be, but it cannot be dismissed on that account. As Jonathan Goldberg's book on Spenser, *Endlesse Worke (1981),* quite brilliantly demonstrates, the question of authority in Spenser's text is both crucial and profoundly problematic. Similarly, when Ben Jonson says in *The Masque of Blackness* that he "apted" his invention to the commands of Queen Anne, he is distinguishing the *invention* of the text from its *authority.* Spenser and Jonson are the first writers in English to declare their status as professional poets—"laureate poets," in Richard Helgerson's excellent term—and it is therefore very important for them to locate the *authority* of their texts. They both locate it not in themselves, but in their patrons. (Jonson is a more ambiguous case than Spenser, but ambiguous here only means that he wants it both ways.)

It may seem that I am now working with a notion of authority that no longer involves what we ordinarily mean by it when we use it in relation to literature—that the text represents the poet's mind, voice, intentions (though we tend to be wary about the last of these), and that when we write about, say, *The Faerie Queene,* we are writing about Spenser. It would be perverse to argue that this is not true, but that is precisely what I am arguing. Let's take another analogy: Michael Baxandall, in *Painting and Experience in 15th Century Italy,* discusses the documents relating to one of Filippo Lippi's commissions. Not only is the contract for the painting quite detailed about what is to be included, but a correspondence survives from which it is clear that Lippi sent sketches to the patron for instructions about the composition and colors. Here is another example, from my own work: I was always puzzled about why Inigo Jones regularly did his costume designs in a brown or grey wash, and indicated the colors with annotations— wouldn't it have made more sense simply to do the paintings in color, so that both masquers and dressmakers could actually see what the costume was going to look like?—out of several hundred surviving drawings, there are only seven in which the color of the costume appears. The answer became clear when I got a look at the notes and letters accompanying the drawings: Jones would do his designs, and then submit them to the Queen. The Queen chose the colors, and made whatever alterations in the design that she wished.

Now: when we write about a Lippi painting or an Inigo Jones drawing, are we really writing about Lippi or Jones? Aren't we, at the very least, writing about a complex collaboration in which the question of authority bears precisely on our notions of the nature of the artist's invention?

Let's return to literature and drama. I said that the only way for
Jonson to assert his authority over his texts was to publish them, and
for Jonson this was a genuinely effective strategy. For most writers,
however, the situation was quite different. The authority of the published text was, for the most part, that of the publisher: he owned it;
the author's rights in the work ended with his sale of the manuscript.
The publisher was fully entitled to alter the manuscript if he saw fit—
the manuscript was his. In this respect the publisher was precisely
analogous to the theatrical company or to the recipient of a verse
epistle or a manuscript poem—or, to carry the analogy further, into
an area where the situation has remained largely unchanged since the
Renaissance, precisely analogous to the owner of a painting. Once the
painting has been sold, we do not believe that the artist has any further
rights in it. The owner may cut it down to fit a particular place in his
house or a frame he happens to like, may have it repainted to suit his
taste, may even (as Lady Churchill recently did with Graham Sutherland's very famous portrait of her husband) destroy it, and we do not
acknowledge that the artist has any say in the matter. In this last case,
I'd think the question of authority in the work was especially critical:
to believers in the autonomy of the artist, the painting was a Sutherland;
but to Sir Winston, the painting was a version of himself, and he didn't
like it. The authority in this case belonged to the subject/patron—just
as Spenser says it does in *The Faerie Queene*.

Let's return now to a text. We have two versions of the first sonnet
of *Astrophil & Stella*. The 1590 quarto version reads as follows:
"Loving in truth and fain in verse my love to show,/ That the dear she
might take some pleasure of my pain. . . ." The Countess of Pembroke's
folio version reads: ". . . That she (dear she) might take some pleasure
of my pain." How shall we interpret this variation? Is Q's printer
misreading the manuscript? It seems unlikely—those parentheses
would be difficult to miss. Is the Countess then revising? She claims to
be printing authentic texts, from her brother's own papers—does the
concept of authenticity perhaps involve making improvements? Or was
"she (dear she)" in the original manuscript, and did it seem too irregular
or advanced for Q's editor, and did *he* improve it? Or were there,
perhaps, as in the case of so many Donne poems, two (or more) versions
of this sonnet, both Sidney's, both final, both authentic? The reason it
is a mistake to believe we can answer this question isn't merely that
we cannot in fact do so; it is that it places an anachronistic emphasis
on the author.

Now let's return to Shakespeare. E. A. J. Honigmann, in *The Stability
of Shakespeare's Texts,* shows quite persuasively that the notion of
final or complete versions assumed by virtually all modern editors of

Shakespeare is inconsistent with everything we know not only about Renaissance theatrical practice, but about the way writers in fact work. Poets are always rewriting, and there is no reason to think that many of the confusions in Shakespeare's texts don't involve second thoughts, or amalgams of quite separate versions of a play. I'd want to go a great deal further than this, but the idea of the basic instability of the text seems to me an absolutely essential one.

I have argued that most literature in the period, and virtually all theatrical literature, must be seen as basically collaborative in nature, and I have said that Shakespeare can be distinguished from most other playwrights only because he was in on more parts of the collaboration. Editors who get this far usually want to go on to argue that Shakespeare's company wouldn't have presumed to alter Shakespeare's text—the play was, after all, written by the boss. I would argue, on the contrary, that all this means is that Shakespeare would have been in on the revisions. Or *might* have been: think about the text of *Macbeth*. We believe the opening scenes have been truncated, we know the witches' songs are by Middleton, and the Hecate scene and a later passage seem also to be non-Shakespearean interpolations for a court performance: if all this is true, where is Shakespeare's authority? If the changes were made after Shakespeare's retirement or death, why did the company think that was the right text to include in the folio? I suggest that the case of *Macbeth* is only an extreme example of the normal procedure. The text we have was considered the best (or "correct") text of the play at the time the folio was prepared. And if we think of the texts of Marlowe's *Dr. Faustus,* we shall see an even more extreme example, in which the author has become a curiously imprecise, intermittent, and shifting figure, even on the title-page. He is referred to in the 1604 first quarto as "Ch. Marl.," and in the 1616 quarto as "Ch. Marklin."

To summarize, then: when we make our editions, of Shakespeare or any other dramatist, we are *not* "getting back to the author's original text." We know nothing about Shakespeare's original text. We might know something about it if, say, a set of Shakespeare's working notes or rough drafts ever turned up, or if we ever found the text that Shakespeare presented to the company as their working copy. But if we did find such a manuscript, that would be something different from the play—just as different as the printed text of *Sejanus* is from Jonson's play. It is a difference in the opposite direction, but I would argue that the degree of difference is probably about the same.

10

"The very names of the Persons": Editing and the Invention of Dramatick Character

Random Cloud

In his Preface to the 1723 edition of "The Works of M[R] *William Shakespeare*" Alexander Pope seems to have intended praise:

> every single character in Shakespear is as much an Individual, as those in Life itself; it is as impossible to find any two alike; . . . had all the Speeches been printed without the very names of the Persons, I believe one might have apply'd them with certainty to every speaker.

The editor's confidence that one could supply a whole corpus' worth of missing speech tags (!) must reflect his conception of the distinct in-dividuality (hence the distinct unity) of each of this playwright's dramatic characters. He *is* onto something, of course, for lifelike characterizations (in the major roles, if not in "every single character") is one of Shakspere's most conspicuous achievements.

But Pope is also quite offtrack. However unified the interpretation of a Shakspearean role can be made to seem in performance or in modern editions, the very names of the Persons in the earliest Shakespear texts very frequently vary. (That you don't know *what* the hell I am talking about shows how poped your Shakespeare is.) In order to contradict the editor it is not even necessary that we deny his critical premise, of Shakesper's appeal to Life itself; one merely has to read the evidence of the earliest quartos and folios. So, if you like: *when it comes to the very names of the Persons, every single character in Shakespear is as Dividual as those in Life itself.*

Pope's fantasy about speech tags is scarcely innocent. In openly praising Shakespeare's artistic coherence, he secretly congratulates his own reductive editing; for Pope played fast and loose with the evidence

Ro. Would I were fleepe and peace fo fweet to reft
The grey eyde morne fmiles on the frowning night,
Checkring the Eafterne Clouds with ftreaks of light,
And darkneffe fleckted like a drunkard reeles,
From forth daies pathway,made by *Tytans* wheeles.
Hence will I to my ghoftly Friers clofe cell,
His helpe to craue,and my deare hap to tell.

Exit.

Enter Frier alone with a basket. (night,
Fri. The grey-eyed morne fmiles on the frowning
Checking the Eafterne clowdes with ftreaks of light:
And fleckeld darkneffe like a drunkard reeles,
From forth daies path,and *Titans* burning wheeles:
Now ere the fun aduance his burning eie,

of Shakspear's text, suppressing the artistic variation of names that contradicts the editorial notion of unity.

With how much certainty would Pope's imagined restorer cope with this crux in the 1599 quarto of *Romeo and Juliet*, if its speech tags were actually removed—here, where essentially the same four lines are assigned not only to a young man passionately in love for the first time, but also to an old and mortified friar? That Shakespeare assigned this speech to such very different roles suggests that its duplicated words have little to express of the Personal experiences of either of them. Isn't it better to say that precisely *because* they are repeated, these four lines have an *im*Personal expression; that the speech primarily tells time (a function discharged elsewhere in this play by an *im*personal Chorus); or that it creates an ambiance verbally, as the modern stage does with lighting; or that it serves to close or open a scene in a *play:* that it is *dramatically* or *scenically* functional, and not unmediatedly *mimetic* or redolent of the *personal* character of Life itself?

Or consider this passage in the 1623 folio *All's Well*.

Cou. You haue difcharg'd this honeftlie, keepe it to your felfe, manie likelihoods inform'd mee of this before, which hung fo tottring in the ballance, that I could neither beleeue nor mifdoubt : praie you leaue mee, ftall this in your bofome, and I thanke you for your honeft care : I will fpeake with you further anon. *Exit Steward.*

Enter Hellen.

> *Old.Cou.* Euen ſo it vvas vvith me when I was yong:
> If euer vve are natures, theſe are ours,this thorne
> Doth to our Roſe of youth righlie belong
> Our bloud to vs, this to our blood is borne,
> It is the ſhow, and ſeale of natures truth,
> Where loues ſtrong paſſion is impreſt in youth,
> By our remembrances of daies forgon,
> Such were our faults, or then we thought them none,
> Her eie is ſicke on't, I obſerue her now.

Although there are two speech tags here, there is only one speech and only one speaker, to whom, as we read along, Shakspeare gives a new name in the very midst of his speech. Now, once an actress intones the words of Shakespeare's dialogue, they become her own, as it were, in the service of the role she performs. The residual variant speech tags, however, remain behind in Shakespere's "voice"; for surely they are all his vocatives. To whom else can we ascribe his naming? Certainly to no one *in* the fiction.

Surely they are all Shakspeare's vocatives.

What caused Shakespear to rename the role during the speech, I don't know either. But playing with names, as Samuel Johnson so sympathetically observed, was Shakespeare's "fertile Cleopatra." In fact, during the course of the play the author used five different speech tags for this one role:

Mother, Countess, Old Countess, Lady, and *Old Lady.*

One of the simplest explanations for the repeated and augmented speech tag is that it marks a seam in the layering of composition. The second part of the speech could easily have been scripted first, or, if it came second, it may have been written at some remove from the first part. The ideal unity we read *into* such a text runs up against a fragmentation or a multiplicity that we actually read. It is a problem of interpretation whether such supposed traces of construction are to be swept under the rug in production, as if they were mere noise, or whether they are to be attended to as message—as discontinuities in tone, or in action, or in what interests me most here, in dividual characterization.

Understandably, an actress of this role is liable to be focused (in a way Pope would understand intuitively) on her own *character;* she may most readily come to conceive an individual identity (especially before rehearsals) from the inside out, as it were—from reading all the dialogue assigned to her, as if she is centered in what she says. So, let's imagine for contrast how a director might view the overall flow of *action* during this speech, and from that outward perspective counsel the actress. The director may feel that the Stewart's exit and Hellen's entrance mark a pause or turning of the action which will orient the audience to new themes and new relationships, in the course of which the audience's perception of this role will be reassessed. (As she is about to initiate talk about the new themes of youth and age, it should be easy for actress and director to talk each other's language, though they come from different directions.)

Suppose, for the ease of argument, that the director wants the audience to see the young woman's entrance slightly before the Countess does. From our point of view, Helen's entrance onto a silent stage occupied only by the Countess would, without a word's yet being spoken, offer us an emblem of *Youth vs. Age;* we would perceive the Countess now not solely from her own perspective (built up from the dialogue she has spoken, or from that she is about to speak), but rather relatively, ironically, and from the outside. In this silent moment she would be re-perceived by the audience as an *Old* countess—not because she *is* old (though she is), but because with Hellen beside her she suddenly *looks* old.

Now, this moment of silence is nevertheless textual (though you won't find it in modern editions. Its text is that of the new speech tag, which states, in the author's voice, that the speaker of the dialogue to follow is *Old.* When the silence ends, the first line of her resumed speech discovers, as I said, that age is a theme there too: "it vvas . . . when I was yong." But age and youth are, crucially, not the only themes. The rest of the Old Countess's first line, "Euen so . . . vvith me," can be read as affirming that the two women are alike in their capacity for love, and this theme is not directly about age. The redundancy of the new tag and the dialogue it ushers in is thus *selective* redundancy; and selective redundancy between such internal textual categories as tag and dialogue externalizes itself as *interpretation.* (And whose interpretation, do you suppose?)

Later in the play Shakespeare switches to *Old Lady* as the tag for this role, again during conversation with Hellen. (She is "*Old,*" by the way, only when Hellen is present.) If, in the speech we have been analyzing, Shakespeare had switched to the *Old Lady* tag after Hellen's entrance, might we not have felt that the thematic redundancy of tag and dialogue was now less about age than about *Being Female?* Do you see why I say that selective redundancy is interpretive? Or imagine this: elsewhere Shakespeare tags Hellen as "*La.*" Suppose Shakspeare called them both "Ladies" here. In addition to the *Female* theme, might we not detect that of *Gentility?*

Here are the lines that immediately follow the passage already photoquoted.

> *Hell.* What is your pleafure Madam ?
> *Ol.Cou.* You know *Hellen* I am a mother to you.
> *Hell.* Mine honorable Miftris.
> *Ol.Cou.* Nay a mother, why not a mother? when I
>   fed a mother
> Me thought you faw a ferpent, what's in mother,
> That you ftart at it ? I fay I am your mother,

At the start of the play Shakespeare's stage-tag name for the Countess was *Mother.* Suppose Shakespeare had reverted to this tag at the entrance of Hellen. Would not such a redundancy direct our attention to the *Maternal-Filial* dynamic of the encounter, which is strongly borne out in these later lines, rather than to the theme of *Age vs. Youth?*

Of course, an actress can convey her age and be simultaneously womanly and motherly and ladylike. My fancied substitutions from among Shakespeer's other variant speech tags are intended to show merely that each of his options for naming this character could be redundant of *some*thing in the dialogue, but not of everything; his specific choices of tag do interpret dialogue through selective emphasis. It is helpful to remember that no one speaks in Shakespeare's plays without being summoned by a name for each speech. Each time he summoned a character, Shakespeare was free to rename her, and he was just the author to exploit that freedom. He is thus, thank God, unpredictable. Pope's nomenclature for Shakespeare's characters is highly predictable; Shakespeare's is not. So I'll put it to you. When you read Shakespeare do you want to read Shakespeare? or do you want to read Pope?

March 5, 1834

Coler: *Shakespeare's intellectual action is wholly unlike that of Ben Jonson or Beaumont and Fletcher. The latter see the totality of a sentence or passage, and then project it entire. Shakespeare goes on creating, and evolving B out of A, and C out of B, and so on, just as a serpent moves, which makes a fulcrum of its own body, and seems for ever twisting and untwisting its own strength.*

My remarks suggest that the identity of dramatic character need not be an internal affair; it can be relational and interactive—an interaction no less between one role and another on stage, than between a role and its scriptor. Such an approach also suggests the inherently social nature of drama and theater, and argues for a competing primacy to the one that Pope celebrated—of action and confrontation, as in the struggle between hero and antagonist. Not only is it not philosophically necessary to ascribe a primary or a transcendent unity to the notion of individual, isolated character that so obsesses modern history, but also the text and Shakespeare's nomenclutter resists such appropriation.

No one can say how Ed Pope would have assigned the tags for this speech in *All's Well* if, as he fantasized, they were stripped away from the original evidence. However, his actual edition cuts out the Countess's "*Old*"—and voilà, by *reductio editionis,* a Shakespearean Individual.

> *Count.* You have difcharg'd this honeftly, keep it to your felf; many likelihoods inform'd me of this before, which hung fo tottering in the ballance, that I could neither believe nor mifdoubt: pray you leave me, ftall this in your bofom, and I thank you for your honeft care; I will fpeak with you further anon.
>
> 6   [*Exit Steward.*

SCENE

All's well that Ends well.

SCENE VII.

Enter Helena.

Count. Ev'n fo it was with me when I was young;
    If we are nature's, thefe are ours: this thorn
Doth to our rofe of youth rightly belong,
    Our blood to us, this to our blood is born;
It is the fhow and feal of nature's truth,
Where love's ftrong paffion is impreft in youth;
By our remembrances of days foregone,
Such were our faults, or then we thought them none.
Her eye is fick on't, I obferve her now.

Curiously, Pope repeats the tag "*Count.*," but this is not because he is conserving this rare example of Shakespeare's multiple naming. Rather, Pope himself had a neo-classy notion of scene divisions. For him an entrance or exit during a speech initiated a new editorial scene, and the first speech of such a new scene required an editorial speech tag—even if there is no interruption of the flow of speech. Thus, Pope would have had a tag here even if Shakespear hadn't. Although Pope idealized the unity of character, we can surmise that this now-unpopular editorial practice tended to atomize Shakespearian action, a sin comparable to the editorial structuring of the action into acts, which is still much in vogue, though there is no basis for it in many Shakesper's early publications. In any case, we certainly may edit the quotation with which this paper opened:

> Pop: *Had all the speeches been printed with* Shakespear'*s very names of the Persons, I believe an Editor may apply his own names with certainty to every speaker.*

Pope was only the second "editor" of Shakespeare, as we have come to use that term. The first was Rowe, whose edition appeared in 1709, almost two decades before Pope's, who closely followed Rowe's lead in renaming characters. Prior to them, and the age of Shakespeare Editing which they initiated, stretched a century and more, back to the quarto editions of Shakespeare's individual works, which began appearing before his death, and to the collected editions in folio, which came out after. During that century, these quartos and folios were frequently reprinted, one printing often serving uncritically as copy for the next, the compositors modernizing graphic features and punctuation, for example, as they went. Compositors would attempt to correct what seemed to be obvious mistakes, but, human nature being what it is, would also create new errors. And so this pre-Editorial era of transmission evidences a gradual corruption and naive sophistication of Shakespeare's texts. Perhaps the simplest way to characterize this period is to say that Shakespeare's text was drifting.

Such a process can be tolerated at first by wary and ingenious readers, but it must inevitably have a break-point, when the textual errors become so grossly compounded that average readers can no longer understand the text, or when the text deviates so considerably from whatever early versions may have survived, that collation of them produces a list of variants longer than the original work. But such cumulative drift of the reprinted texts in the 17th century can scarcely account in itself for the birth of Editing. True, the fourth folio at the end of this period has its sorry moments textually, but Renaissance readers did not expect the kind of accuracy in printed books that we do. 17th-century readers must have been astute at detecting error and double-guessing authorial intent behind the frequent, palpable errors. In any event, Shakespeare at this time was merely a good read. Luckily, he had died before he had become the Bard, whose every word was sacred. (He had to wait for Editing to be so canonized.) I suggest, therefore, that the impetus for Editing lay outside the internal problems posed by the drifting texts, just as I suggest that the impetus for continued Editing in the 20th century lies outside the internal problems of the text. The urge to edit stemmed from the profound transformation of English culture in the 18th century, which was typified by its fascination with Taste, Propriety, and Criticism as preceptors to art. The age had its positive sides, no doubt, but its stuffiness can be measured by the passionate reaction to it (to look ahead) in Romanticism, just as much as in the freedom and wildness (to look back) of the Elizabethan texts that it sought to discipline, tidy, and regulate.

A corollary of the editorial reform of speech tags is the creation of editorial dramatis-personae lists. No Shakespeare text published before his death has such a list, and only a handful exist in the folio tradition after his death. Why editors should inflict dramatis-personae lists on plays, and not novellae-personae lists on novels or sonnetae-personae lists on sonnet sequences, is not clear to me. For the most part, editors act, they do not explain. It is not that such lists are not helpful to a reader who wants such intro-textual Aids, but that they take the conservative form they do in edition after edition, when there are a thousand different ways to help a reader, is strange. The crucial thing to observe is that the dramatis-personae list has insinuated itself between the title page and the opening of Act 1, Scene 1. These editorial lists have now become as sacrosanct as the very body of Shakespeare's playtext.

It was decades ago that the battle was joined to check the critical tendency to count Lady MacBeth's children—to project the Girlhood of Shakespeare's Heroines, to use Mary Cowden Clarke's telling phrase. But can such a battle really be won as long as dramatis-personae lists continue to infiltrate Shakespeare's text? These lists imply that characters are solid entities,

The Countess

that pre-exist their functions in the play, rather than illusions

now *Mother* now *Old Countess* now *Lady* . . .

built up out of the simultitudinous dynamic of *all* the ingredients of dramatic art, of which character is only a part.

Edition after edition suggests that editors do not read Shakespeare's text afresh to compile such lists. No, they read and crib them from other editors, in a tradition that stems from Pope's appropriation of Rowe. Both their editions were published by the astute Tonson, who claimed his copyright, I understand, not in *Shakespeare's,* but in his *editors'* words. (Do you $mell a fault?) But ever since Tonson's rights ran out, it seems always to be the same originally arbitrary, now-traditional list—the same peckering order, men above women, gentle above common—and only so much info, and of such and such a slant. Lear is *King,* but not a Father, or a Fool. Albany is *Husband to Goneril;* but she is *Lear's Daughter,* not Albany's Wife—or Edmund's Lover, or her Sisters' Rival, or a Suicide. Duke Frederick is *the Usurper of Duke Senior's dominions;* the latter *lives in banishment.* MacBeth, however, is merely *a General in the King's army.* It doesn't say where *he* lives; nor does it say he is a King-Killer. Bertram is *Count of Rossillion,* not an Egotistical Snob; yet Parolles is his *Parasitical Follower.* Julius Caesar is, comfortingly, plain Julius Caesar. But Marc Antony is one of the *Triumvirs*—a position he achieved after Caesar's death, even though at this early point in the unfolding of the action of the play—I mean this early point in the unfolding of the *dramatis-personae list*—Caesar is evidently not dead yet. At least not very dead.

Obviously the dramatis-personae lists' perspectives on Shakespeare's characters are as crock-eyed as those in a cubist painting. Of such stuff is Editorial Unity made. . . .

Part II

The Plays

11

"Tragedies naturally performed": Kyd's Representation of Violence

THE SPANISH TRAGEDY (c. 1587)

James Shapiro

According to Stephen Greenblatt's by now familiar formulation, there "is subversion, no end of subversion [in Elizabethan drama], only not for us." Nor, seemingly, for the Elizabethans either, since for Greenblatt subversion is always and necessarily contained: the "apparent production of subversion" is "the very condition of [royal] power."[1] It is a depressing conclusion, especially for those who want to see the theater as an agent of social change. Perhaps the vicious cycle of "subversion contained" is not quite as grim as Greenblatt would have us believe: he himself acknowledges that plays like *King Lear* strain this process to "the breaking point,"[2] while other new historicists, working backwards from the political and social dislocations that followed the closing of the theaters in 1642, have located the source of these revolutionary impulses in the earlier drama.

Nevertheless, both those who would argue for containment and those who insist that the drama is ultimately subversive tend to speak of *state power* and (to an even greater extent) *theatrical representation* as stable, fixed entities. Invariably, these critics "demonize" the absolutist state while "valorizing" the transgressive theater that would seek to challenge it. Evidence suggests, however, that the Elizabethan theater's relationship to political and judicial authority was more complex than either subverting or confirming state power; the theater's boundaries as a judicial institution were especially problematic. As a result of new historicism's totalizing view of antagonistic state and theater, the fluidity of the borders marking the respective domains of the theater and the state has generated little interest. Although scholars like Steven Mullaney have helped us identify "the place of the stage" geographically in Shakespeare's London,[3] its boundaries in relationship to competing sources of social and political authority in Elizabethan England remain largely uncharted.[4]

This essay examines the overlapping of authority that occurred at the site of one such boundary: staged violence. Since both the public theaters and the public authorities enacted high drama on scaffolds before crowds of spectators, it is easy to understand the need to keep these two kinds of performances distinct. Official forms of capital punishment were taboo in the theater no doubt because, as Foucault has argued, the scaffold of the state functioned not only as a "judicial" but also a "political" ritual in which a "momentarily injured sovereignty is reconstituted" and restored "by manifesting it at its most spectacular." Accordingly, the "public execution did not [merely] reestablish justice; it reactivated power." For the Renaissance ruler, then, the "ceremony of the public torture and execution displayed for all to see the power relation that gave his force to the law."[5] To permit the theater to imitate state spectacle could undermine the terrible power of officially sanctioned violence by showing it often enough to make it familiar or by resituating it within ethically and politically ambiguous contexts.

Consequently, though Tudor and Stuart drama was an extraordinarily bloody affair, playwrights steered clear of trespassing on this royal prerogative: characters are stabbed or poisoned, have their throats slit, or are shot while hanging chained from the upper stage, but only on the rarest occasions do we see them hanged from a noose, decapitated, or tied to a stake and then burned, or punished in the other ways carefully prescribed by the state.[6] We can search the canons of Marlowe, Shakespeare, Jonson, Webster, and others in vain for instances where characters are put to death the same way that convicted felons were in Elizabethan England.[7]

Thomas Kyd's *The Spanish Tragedy* (c. 1587)[8] stands as a striking exception. Its audience watches as Pedringano is tried, condemned, and "turned off" by a hangman, and witnesses as well the preparations for the torture and execution of Alexandro, who is bound "to the stake" onstage and prepared to be burned to death. It would also seem to offer the paradigmatic example of how drama can be a powerful agent of social change: the staging of Hieronimo's play results in the death of a royal heir and destroys the political accommodation between Spain and Portugal. Yet Hieronimo's court spectacle only attains this power when it oversteps the bounds of what we would ordinarily consider theater. The lines separating official and theatrical violence are blurred, as Kyd's play insistently seeks out representational no-man's-land, testing the boundaries between the prerogatives of the state and those of the theater. In so doing the play raises the possibility that it is not the opposition between state and theater, but their potential confusion and indistinguishability, that makes theater powerful and (to the political authorities) dangerous.

In exploring this possibility, this essay questions whether the terms and categories of thought that dominate current historicist and materialist discourse (e.g., "opposition," "containment," "subversion," "resistance,") are simply too inflexible, or themselves too ideologically bound (however "retheorized") to admit the possibility that the changes that may occur in individuals or societies through the mediation of theater can be quite random, subject to all kinds of unexpected and unpredictable forces. Theater, this essay argues, can be "subversive," but it is usually so in ways that are unforeseen by author, censor, or functionalist historicist.[9] Hieronimo's old play, "long forgot" (4.1.80), only becomes subversive within the context of a situation unimaginable when Hieronimo first wrote it; so too does Kyd's *The Spanish Tragedy:* in its afterlife upon the Jacobean and Caroline stages it was identified with the transgressive behavior of Englishwomen in ways unimaginable at the time of its composition. It is theater's unpredictability, then, that makes it so dangerous and at the same time so difficult to suppress or censor effectively.

The Privy Council knew exactly what subversive writing it was looking for in the spring of 1593: someone had posted a "lewd and vyle ticket or placarde" inciting London's apprentices "to attempt some vyolence" upon the city's foreign workers.[10] In the course of the investigation Kyd's lodgings were searched and atheistical tracts were found in his possession. Atheism was a capital offense. Kyd desperately maintained that the tracts were Marlowe's and had been accidentally shuffled among his papers when they had shared chambers two years before. He was imprisoned in Bridewell, where he was tortured by strappado.[11] In his written confession addressed to Sir Thomas Puckering, Kyd protested that

> [I]f I knewe eny whom I co[u]ld justlie accuse of that damnable offence to the awefull Ma[jes]tie of god or of that other mutinous sedition tow[a]rd the state I wo[u]ld as willinglie reveale them as I wo[u]ld request yo[u]r L[ordshi]ps better thoughtes of me that never have offended you.[12]

Life, cruelly, was imitating art: five years before, Kyd had written a comparable declaration in *The Spanish Tragedy,* when Alexandro, falsely accused of treason, protests that he is innocent:

> But this, O this, torments my labouring soul,
> That thus I die suspected of a sin,
> Whereof, as heavens have known my secret thoughts,
> So am I free from this suggestion.
>
> (3.1.43–4)

The Viceroy's response—"No more, I say! to the tortures!" (3.1.47)—was apparently echoed by the Bridewell authorities. In Kyd's play Alexandro was spared from torture at the last moment. Kyd himself was not so lucky. He wrote shortly after his release of "bitter times and privie broken passions"[13] and was dead by the following August. In one of the darker ironies of the period, a playwright who explored so insightfully the workings of state violence had become, through unforeseen circumstances, its victim. It is likely that even as Kyd suffered in prison his play was being performed to admiring spectators.[14]

The same authorities who had so rigorously suppressed materials "lately published by some disordered and factious persons in and about the cittie of London"[15] nonetheless allowed a different kind of writing, Kyd's *Spanish Tragedy,* to circulate freely throughout England, both in print and on stage. Unlike atheistical tracts or racist placards, Kyd's play did not contain lines or passages whose potential subversiveness could be easily identified. Kyd and his fellow playwrights were careful enough to avoid writing that would lead to violent social disturbances. When they did not, the Master of the Revels was responsible for identifying and censoring such passages. But neither he nor the Bishop of London and Archbishop of Canterbury (who censored printed texts) were equipped to deal with the kind of subversion that occurred when the boundary between the domains of theater and the state was transgressed.

The action of Kyd's play repeatedly returns to the site of this contested boundary. The appearance of Alexandro, tied "to the stake" (SD 3.1.49), provides an intimation, though not a fully realized example, of state violence enacted onstage. The most obvious example is Pedringano's lengthy trial and public execution in Act 3, scene 6, which conforms closely in its outward features to the spectacle of public execution with which Londoners would have been familiar.[16] Pedringano enters "bound" to the "court," is asked to "[c]onfess [his] folly and repent [his] fault," and does so: "First I confess, nor fear I death therefore,/I am the man 'twas I slew Serberine" (3.6.29–30). As Foucault observes, such a confession "for satisfaction of the world" (3.6.25) was a crucial part of the ceremony of state execution, as was the condemned individual's relationship with the executioner, also elaborated upon in this scene.[17] Pedringano even partakes of the obligatory prayers and address to the spectators who have come to witness his execution. He asks the hangman to "request this good company to pray with me" (3.6.84), before reversing himself: "now I remember me, let them alone till some other time, for now I have no great need" (3.6.86–87). Hieronimo, as Knight Marshall overseeing this ceremony, is appalled to see "a wretch so impudent." He exits, ordering that the execution take place. The stage direction indicates that Pedringano's hanging occurs in full view, as the hangman "*turns him off*" (SD 3.6.104).

Yet the execution fails both judicially and politically. The judicial failure is underscored when the hangman, having learned of Lorenzo's role in Horatio's murder, approaches Hieronimo, admits that "we have done [Pedringano] wrong," and asks that the Knight Marshall stand between him and "the gallows" (3.7.26). It fails politically because Pedringano thinks that he is only playing his part in Lorenzo's plot, in which disaster will be averted with the reading of the King's pardon. For him the execution is just good theater. As a result, the representation of state violence undermines the authority of the state, since the symbolic meaning of a public execution, that which gives it sufficient integrity to reinscribe and reactivate the power of the sovereign, never occurs. Rather than confirming state justice, Pedringano's death merely parodies and demystifies it, as it parodically recalls the unceremonious execution (and perhaps even token disembowelment) of Horatio, who had been hanged from an arbor, then stabbed, in Act 2, scene 4.

Pedringano's mistaken belief that his execution is merely theater points to something particularly disturbing about theatrical representations of violence: neither the actor to be executed nor the spectators who witness the execution can be entirely sure that the violence is not real. We tend to speak of theater as a place where violence is merely represented, but it is well to remember that the Elizabethan stage doubled as a site of actual violent spectacle. Bear and bull baiting, for example, alternated with play production at the Hope Theater, while fencing was popular at others. Around the time of the first production of Kyd's play there was even a notorious incident in which spectators were accidently killed: Philip Gawdy writes in a letter to his father on 16 November 1587 that:

> My L[ord] Admyrall his men and players having a devyse in ther playe to tye one of their fellowes to a poste and so to shoote him to deathe, having borrowed their callyvers one of the players handes swerved his peece being charged with bullett missed the fellowe he aymed at and killed a chyld, and a woman great with chyld forthwith, and hurt an other man in the head very soore.[18]

The state might resort to what Greenblatt (borrowing from Thomas Hariot) refers to as "invisible bullets"[19]; the actors fired real ones. It is also worth remarking that the theaters were identified as a place for violent riots, and that they were situated nearby—and perhaps in the minds of Londoners identified with—the other sites of theatrical violence: London's prisons. Even more remarkably, the theaters served not only as sites of theatrical executions, but, on occasion, a place where individuals were put to death. Stow reports in his *Annales* (1615) that around the time of the earliest production of *The Spanish Tragedy* hangings took place at the Theatre. W. Gunter, a foreign priest, was hung "at the Theater" on August 28, 1588, and on October 1, of that same year, another priest, William Hartley, was also executed "nigh the Theator."[20]

Elizabethans were aware that the practice of using the playhouse for public executions had a predecent in the theater of ancient Rome. Thomas Heywood, for example, in his *Apology for Actors* (written c. 1607), describes the Roman practice of executing capital offenders in the theater. Heywood substantiates his account by citing a passage from Kyd's *Spanish Tragedy:*

> It was the manner of their Emperours, in those dayes in their publicke Tragedies to choose out the fittest amongst such, as for capital offences were condemned to dye, and imploy them in such parts as were to be kil'd in the Tragedy, who of themselves would make suit rather so to dye with resolution, and by the hands of such princely Actors, then otherwise to suffer a shamefull & most detestable end. *And these were Tragedies naturally performed.* And such Caius Caligula, Claudius Nero, Vitellius, Domitianus, Comodus, & other Emperours of Rome, upon their festivals and holy daies of greatest consecration, used to act. Therefore M. Kid in the *Spanish* Tragedy, upon occasion presenting it selfe, thus writes.
>
> > Why Nero thought it no disparagement,
> > And Kings and Emperours have tane delight,
> > To make experience of their wits in playes.[21]
> > [4.1.87–89]

In Foucault's terms, the actions of these "princely Actors" displays, without the mediation of a public executioner, "the dissymmetry between the subject who has dared to violate the law and the all-powerful sovereign who displays his strength.[22] Such action would have placed an Elizabethan ruler in a double bind, since, as scholars like Stephen Orgel, Jonathan Goldberg, and Stephen Greenblatt have urged, royal power was manifested theatrically;[23] the sovereign had a considerable interest in not being represented in the public theater.

Heywood's quotation from *The Spanish Tragedy* is taken from a scene in which precisely this issue is at stake. When Hieronimo invites the Portuguese prince to perform in his play, Balthazar is shocked at the very idea—"What, would you have us play a tragedy?" (4.1.86). He knows that princes do not act in tragedies for good reason: since rulers are *de facto* actors, a prince would only expose the foundations of his power by performing onstage. Although he wishes to humor Hieronimo, Balthazar knows that the stage is potentially subversive in that it can easily collapse carefully circumscribed social roles by confusing two kinds of performances.[24] Notably, in the example Heywood offers, the tyrants, the victims, and the audiences were all aware that this was tragedy "naturally performed"; there is no pretence or deception. The question that remains is what distinguishes these executions from official ones, except that these take place in the theater (or, for that matter, what distinguishes this production from another, except that the actor is killed)?

The possibility of theatrical performances in which people were actually killed onstage without their (or the audience's) knowledge was seized upon by the anti-theatrical writers, who warned that the kind of bloody spectacle supervised by Hieronimo was one of the dark secrets of the Elizabethan stage. I.G., the author of *A Refutation of the Apology for Actors* (1615), insinuates that Elizabethan actors took advantage of this confusion of theater and real life to kill unwitting actors onstage in front of unwitting spectators. Responding to Heywood's "memorable example of Julius Caesar, that slew his own servant whiles he acted *Hercules furens* on the Stage," I.G. finds in the same anecdote evidence against the players:

> Which example indeed greatly doth make against their Playes. *For it's not unlikely but a Player might doe the like now, as often they have done.* And then what a lamentable project would there be for the Spectators to behold: As many times it happens when their supposed nocent persons are falsely hanged, and divers of them ready to be strangld.[25]

I.G. conflates a number of disturbing scenarios. The first is one in which, like Heywood's "princely Actors," a ruler acting in a play kills a subject. The story of Julius Caesar killing his servant differs from the ones quoted above in that Caesar's actions were not premeditated, nor were they intended as a display and confirmation of royal power. Rather, Caesar, caught up in the part he was playing, forgot that he was only acting. I.G. then implies that this is a common danger of theatrical practice—that it is not unlikely that a player may forget himself, or, he then suggests more cynically, that players may capitalize on the audience's inability to distinguish between a real and a fake onstage murder, permitting actors to hang their victims "falsely." After all, given the sophistication of Elizabethan stagecraft, how can we be sure that, in Hieronimo's ambiguous phrase, the "wondrous plausible" (4.1.85) violence is merely represented?

All this might be dismissed as the fantasy or nightmare of an empowered theater out of control, appropriating the prerogative of the state by taking justice into its own hands. But according to an account by Will Kempe, the famous comic actor for Lord Strange's Men and subsequently the Chamberlain's Men, the public theater did on occasion usurp the state's role in punishing criminals. Kempe recounts in his travelogue, *Kempe's Nine Daies Wonder* (1600), that while passing through Burnt-wood, on market day,

> two Cut-purses were taken, that with other two of their companions followed mee from London (as many better disposed persons did:) but these two dy-doppers gave out when they were apprehended, that they had laid wagers and betted about my journey. Whereupon the Officers bringing them to my Inne, I justly denied their acquaintance, saving that I remembered one of them to be a noted Cut-purse, *such a one as we tye to a poast on our stage, for all people to wonder at, when at a play, they are taken pilfring.*[26]

Apparently, cutpurses caught in the act in the public theater were haled onstage, and tied to one of the posts of the stage. What makes all this even more confusing is that cutpurses are busily playing a role, masquerading as members of an audience and preying on their unsuspecting fellows. They are unmasked by revealing their true identity onstage, where, like criminals, they are forced to perform a different kind of role. Just as the state freely appropriates theatricality, so too (at least in such instances) the theater took upon itself the prerogative of the state, and in a kind of publicly authorized theatrical display, acted very much as the state did.

What would have happened to our conception of theatrical representation, one is tempted to ask, if a cutpurse had been caught and dragged onstage at that moment in a production of *The Spanish Tragedy* when Pedringano was bound to "the stake" (or, for that matter, during the anonymous Admiral's Men's play of 1587, when the actor about to be shot at is tied to the stage post)? Would the actor have been cut down and the cutpurse put up in his place? Has that stage post taken on the symbolic identity as the site of a criminal's punishment (and in a regular production, when an actor rather than a cutpurse was tied to it, would it have retained that symbolic force)? What distinguishes the punishment of an actor playing a criminal from the punishment of a criminal brought onstage and turned into a kind of actor? For that matter, when actors punish cutpurses onstage, is it still theater? Theater within theater? A state within theater?[27]

Kyd's exploration of the potential indistinguishability of theatrical and state violence reaches its climax in the denouement of *The Spanish Tragedy*. In his role as Knight Marshal, Hieronimo is called upon to fulfill a double function: both to "punish such as do transgress" (3.6.12) within the verge of the court, and to provide royal entertainment. In Act 4, scene 4, these roles coincide in the "tragedy" in which Hieronimo is both "Author and actor" (4.4.147). Kyd fully exploits in this scene the representational no-man's-land between official and theatrical violence. The result is a drama that serves as an immediate and unqualified agent of social change: Hieronimo's entertainment results in the death of Lorenzo, nephew to the King of Spain (and his apparent heir), as well as Balthazar, son and heir to the Viceroy of Portugal.[28] Hieronimo achieves justice by inverting the practice of "kings and emperors" like Nero who "have ta'en delight/To make experience [i.e., trial] of their wits in plays" (4.1.88–89).

Hieronimo's revenge drama depends upon a blurring of representational boundaries. Not only the onstage audience, comprising the "Spanish King, [the] Viceroy, the Duke of Castile, and their train" (4.4.1 SD), but the audience in the London theater is unaware that the murders they witness in the play are "permanent." Hieronimo triumphantly explains that their expectations are misplaced:

> Haply you think, but bootless are your thoughts,
> That this is fabulously counterfeit,
> And that we do as all tragedians do:
> To die today, for fashioning our scene,
> The death of Ajax, or some Roman peer,
> And in a minute starting up again,
> Revive to please tomorrow's audience.
> No, princes.
>
> (4.4.76–83)

Drama is empowered, but only when Hieronimo's play becomes more than imitation of action. A play written in another time and place turns out to be politically transgressive by accident. Hieronimo had "by chance" (4.1.78) written it in his university days at Toledo, when he was "young" and "plied [himself] to fruitless poetry" (4.1.71–72). The playbook, "long forgot," was, he says, "found this other day" (4.1.80). There may be an additional level of irony at work here, if in fact the subject of Hieronimo's play—the tragedy of *Soliman and Perseda*—was taken from an extant play of that title attributed to Kyd himself.

Kyd goes to considerable lengths to show that it is not the words by themselves which are transgressive; in fact, for no apparent reason Hieronimo insists that his play be spoken in sundry languages, which Balthazar fears will be "a mere confusion,/ And hardly shall . . . be understood" (4.1.180–1). It is not what Jerzy Limon has called "dangerous matter"[29] that is politically subversive, but the theatrical use to which those words and actions could be put. The anxieties of Elizabethan anti-theatrical writers were not entirely misplaced.

The Spanish Tragedy's own transgressive potential, like that of Hieronimo's revived play, would be realized in a historical moment unimaginable at the time of its composition, when Kyd's play became identified as a site of female resistance to patriarchal constraints. This identification first appears in Richard Braithwait's conduct book, *The English Gentlewoman* (1631), in the chapter on female "behaviour," where Braithwait holds up for "reproofe" those women who "give too easy raines to liberty" (53). He offers as an example a woman who was so enamored of the theater, which she frequented regularly, that on her deathbed she still cried out for Kyd's play. Going to the theater both to see and be seen

> is her daily taske, till death enter the Stage and play his part; whom shee entertaines with such unpreparednesse, as her *extreme act* presents objects of infinite unhappinesse: "As it sometimes fared with a Gentlewoman of our owne Nation, who so fairly bestowed the expence of her best houres upon the Stage, as being surprized by sicknesse, even unto death, she became so deafe to such as admonished her of her end, as shee clozed her *dying scene* with a vehement calling on *Hieronimo*." (53–54)

The anonymous (and probably fictitious) Englishwoman's obsessive attendance at the theater has so stripped her of reason that she dies confusing life with theater, calling not on her Maker but "on Hieronimo."

Braithwait's anecdote clearly appealed to the anti-theatricalist William Prynne, who offered an embellished version of the story in his

Histriomastix (1633). In Prynne's account the woman dies crying out "*Hieronimo, Hieronimo;* O let me see *Hieronimo* acted" (556). Prynne tries to make the story more plausible by insisting that Braithwait, his source, was "then present at her departure" (556). A decade later, when Braithwait "revised, corrected, and enlarged" *The English Gentlewoman* (1641), he retells the story in greater detail, and changes the ending to make her transgression even more shocking. Here, the woman "who so daily bestowed the expence of her best houres upon the Stage" (199) thinks, in her maddened state, that she actually *is* Hieronimo:

> when her Physician was to minister a Receipt unto her, which hee had prepared to allay the extremity of that agonizing fit wherewith shee was then assailed, putting aside the Receipt with her hand, as if shee rejected it, in the very height and heate of her distemper, with an active resolution used these words unto her Doctor: ["]Thankes good Horatio, take it for thy paines.["] (299)

In this version her actions are made to seem even more horrifying, as the dying woman's reflexive theatricality condemns her soul: she turns her deathbed into theater, projecting onto her physician the role of Horatio, retaining for herself Hieronimo's (or is this the dying Hamlet speaking?). Her soul is lost even as she loses her own identity by assuming that of the male actor's, and reverses (and mirrors) *The Spanish Tragedy's* blurring of theatrical and real death.

The various versions of the anecdote suggest that Kyd's play, having entered the cultural vocabulary, becomes the means of expressing transgressive social attitudes: the play becomes the symbol of a dying woman's refusal to conform to cultural norms, even as the public theater, in Braithwait's account, becomes one of the few places where a woman could transgress the constraints placed on where she can go and what she can do. It may well be that Kyd's Belimperia provides a model for Braithwait's transgressive Englishwoman: only in the theater, after all, in her role as Perseda, was Belimperia sufficiently empowered and "able" (4.4.65) to revenge the wrongs done to her.[30] Kyd's great insight, though one that he did not live to see realized (if, indeed, he really saw it at all), was that theater's most serious threat to rival cultural practices and institutions derives from its unactivated potential, making dormant transgressive possibilities difficult to predict and even more difficult to control. As more archival material on theatrical practice becomes available in projects like the Records of Early English Drama (evidence that will no doubt qualify the largely anecdotal history that characterizes my own and many other historicist studies) the complex relationship between theater and state in Elizabethan culture will have to be rewritten. At this juncture the best that can be said is that there is no end of subversion, even for us; it just may not be the subversion we had been looking for.[31]

Notes

1. *Shakespearean Negotiations* (Berkeley: Univ. of California Press, 1988), p. 65.

2. Greenblatt, *Shakespearean Negotiations*, p. 65.

3. *The Place of the Stage: License, Play, and Power in Renaissance England* (Chicago: Univ. of Chicago Press, 1988).

4. There are some important recent exceptions: see *The Violence of Representation*, ed. Nancy Armstrong and Leonard Tennenhouse (New York and London: Routledge, 1989), especially Peter Stallybrass, " 'Drunk with the Cup of Liberty': Robin Hood, the carnivalesque, and the rhetoric of violence in early modern England" (pp. 45–76); and Leonard Tennenhouse, "Violence done to women on the Renaissance stage" (pp. 77–97). Also see Pieter Spierenburg, *The Spectacle of Suffering* (Cambridge: Cambridge Univ. Press, 1984); J.A. Sharpe, " 'Last Dying Speeches': Religion, Ideology and Public Execution in Seventeenth Century England," *Past and Present* 107 (1985), 144–67; David Nicholls, "The Theatre of Martyrdom in the French Reformation," *Past and Present* 121 (1988), 49–73; and Samuel Y. Edgerton, Jr., *Pictures and Punishment: Art and Criminal Punishment during the Florentine Renaissance* (Ithaca and London: Cornell Univ. Press, 1985).

5. Michel Foucault, *Discipline and Punish: The Birth of the Prison*, trans. Alan Sheridan (New York: Pantheon Books, 1977), pp. 47–50.

6. J. H. Baker, "Criminal Courts and Procedure at Common Law, 1550–1800" in *Crimes in England, 1550–1800*, ed. J. S. Cockburn (Princeton: Princeton Univ. Press, 1977), provides a useful summary of official punishment of commoners in England. Until 1790 the judgment read to convicted male traitors and felons was as follows:

> You are to be drawn upon a hurdle to the place of execution, and there you are to be hanged by the neck, and being alive cut down, and your privy-members to be cut off, and your bowels to be taken out of your belly and there burned, you being alive; and your head to be cut off, and your body to be divided into four quarters, and that your head and quarters be disposed of where his majesty shall think fit. (p. 42)

Playgoers crossing the bridge to Southwark would pass under those heads on their way to and from the theaters. The judgment for male petty-traitors was to be "drawn and hanged," while capital felons like Pedringano were "to be hanged by [the] neck . . . until dead." See, too: John Bellamy, "To the gallows and after," in *The Tudor Law of Treason* (London: Routledge & Kegan Paul, 1979), pp. 182–227.

7. The Admiral's Men's stage property for a lost play—"i frame for the heading in Black Jone"—indicates that beheadings could be represented onstage (see E.K. Chambers, *The Elizabethan Stage*, 4 vols. [Oxford: Oxford Univ. Press, 1923], 3:97). In addition, an episode in Marlowe's *The Massacre at Paris* in which a dead man is hung "upon this tree" (line 493) suggests that there was some sort of

convention for hanging individuals onstage. There is the further possibility that Barabas's fate in Marlowe's *The Jew of Malta* (death by boiling in a cauldron) recalls the punishment for poisoning decreed by Henry VIII (though repealed in 1547). Barabas brags of poisoning wells (2.3.178) and subsequently poisons the nuns who have occupied his house. (For a brief account of this legislation, see Penry Williams, *The Tudor Regime* [Oxford: Oxford Univ. Press, 1979], p. 225). For a discussion of Marlowe and state violence see Karen Cunningham's "Renaissance Execution and Marlovian Elocution: The Drama of Death," *PMLA* 105.2 (1990), 209–22.

8. Quotations from the play are cited from Philip Edwards, ed., *The Spanish Tragedy*, The Revels Plays (Cambridge: Harvard Univ. Press, 1959).

9. Foucault (unlike many of his followers) is careful to acknowledge the unpredictable and improbable basis of much resistance: "there is a plurality of resistances, each of them a special case: resistances that are possible, necessary, improbable; others that are spontaneous, savage, solitary, concerted, rampant, or violent; still others that are quick to compromise, interested, or sacrificial." Foucault further urges that the search "for the headquarters that presides over" the "rationality" of power is misguided; "neither the caste which governs, nor the groups which control the state apparatus, nor those who make the most important economic decision direct the entire network of power that functions in a society." *The History of Sexuality*, Volume I: An Introduction, trans. Robert Hurley (New York: Vintage Books, 1980), pp. 95–96.

10. *Acts of the Privy Council*, ed. J. R. Dasent, n.s. 24, 1592–1593 (London: 1901), p. 187. The Council was aware of the potential danger of such writing: "oftentymes it doth fall out of suche lewde beginninges that further mischeife doth ensue" (187).

11. For an account of the modes of torture in Elizabethan England see John H. Langbein, *Torture and the Laws of Proof: Europe and England in the Ancien Régime* (Chicago: Univ. of Chicago Press, 1977), esp. pp. 73–90. That Kyd was not racked (as many have assumed) is made clear by Langbein's findings that after 1588 Bridewell replaced the Tower as the regular venue for torture; unlike the Tower, Bridewell was apparently not equipped with a rack. Under the Stuarts, the Tower regained its former prominence, and both rack and manacles were used in torture (84). Langbein also notes that the "reign of Elizabeth was the age when torture was most used in England" (82).

12. Quoted from the transcription of the letter provided in Arthur Freeman, *Thomas Kyd: Facts and Problems* (Oxford: Clarendon Press, 1967), p. 182. Sir Thomas Puckering had recently helped prosecute in the "Arraignment of Sir Richard Knightly, and other persons, in the Star-Chamber, for maintaining seditious Persons, Books, and Libels: 31 Eliz. Feb. 31, A.D. 1588." Knightly and fellow defendents were accused of publishing Puritan material described as "a most seditious and libellous pamphlet, *fit for a vice in a play*—and no other" (Howell, *State Trials* 1:1265 [italics mine]).

13. In his dedicatory epistle to the Countess of Sussex prefacing *Cornelia*, in F.S. Boas, ed., *The Works of Thomas Kyd* (Oxford: Clarendon Press, 1955), p. 102.

14. The play had a very strong run at Henslowe's Rose from the early months of 1592 through December–January 1593. The theaters were closed because of plague during the time of Kyd's imprisonment, but the players toured the provinces, and if we take Thomas Dekker's account of Ben Jonson's early career as an actor playing Hieronimo as indicative, Kyd's popular play was no doubt performed in

the countryside at this time (see Ben Jonson, *Works*, 12 vols., ed. C.H. Herford and Percy and Evelyn Simpson [Oxford: Clarendon Press, 1925–52], 1:13). *The Spanish Tragedy* may well hold the record for performances at different theaters: Michael Hattaway lists (in addition to the Rose) the Cross Keys Inn; the Theatre; Newington Butts; the Fortune; the Curtain; the Globe; and even Second Blackfriars; in addition to provincial and foreign tours (*Elizabethan Popular Theatre* [London: Routledge & Kegan Paul, 1982], p. 103). By 1633 the play had gone through eleven editions.

15. As quoted in Freeman, *Thomas Kyd*, p. 25.

16. Members of Kyd's audience could recently have witnessed the public executions of Anthony Babington and his co-conspirators for treason, in late September 1586. The account of their execution should give some idea of the spectacle of the scaffold:

> Ballard was first executed. He was cut down and bowelled with great cruelty while he was alive. . . . Savage broke the rope, and fell down from the gallows, and was presently seized on by the executioner, his privities cut off, and his bowells taken out while he was alive. Barnwell, Tichbourne, Tilney, and Abington were executed with equal cruelty.

The other executions took place the next day. Queen Elizabeth,

> being informed of the severity used in the Executions the day before, and detesting such cruelty, gave express orders that these should be used more favourably; and accordingly they were permitted to hang till they were quite dead, before they were cut down and bowelled. (Howell, *State Trials* 1:1158, 1160–61)

17. See Foucault, *Discipline and Punish*, esp. pp. 51–59.

18. Chambers, *The Elizabethan Stage*, 2:135.

19. See the chapter with that title in Greenblatt, *Shakespearean Negotiations*, pp. 21–65.

20. See Chambers, *Elizabethan Stage*, 2:396, n. 2. Also see: *A True Report of the Inditement, Arraignment, Conviction, Condemnation, and Execution of John Weldon, William Hartley, and Robert Sutton, who Suffred for High Treason* (1588); and "Unpublished Documents relating to the English Martyres, 1584–1603," ed. J.H. Pollen (Catholic Record Society, 5, 1908), p. 327.

21. Richard Perkinson, ed., Thomas Heywood, *An Apology for Actors* and I.G., *A Refutation of The Apology for Actors* (New York: Scholars' Facsimiles and Reprints, 1941), sig. E3ʳ, E3ᵛ [italics mine].

22. Foucault, *Discipline and Punish*, p. 49.

23. See Orgel, *The Illusion of Power: Political Theater in the English Renaissance* (Berkeley: Univ. of California Press, 1975); Goldberg, *James I and the Politics of Literature* (Baltimore: The Johns Hopkins Univ. Press, 1983); and Greenblatt, *Shakespearean Negotiations*, esp. pp. 63–65.

24. A Caroline parodic recollection of *The Spanish Tragedy* makes this point clearly. Thomas Rawlins's *The Rebellion* (1641) includes a scene in which a group of tailors (descendents of *A Midsummer Night's Dream*'s rude mechanicals) have rehearsed Kyd's play and prepare to entertain the king of Spain. The lead tailor, Vermine, like Shakespeare's Botton the Weaver, greedily wants to play all the parts, but will "Leave all to play the King," so that, as he declares in the real King's

presence, "I *Vermine* / The King will act before the King." The syntax is ambiguous: is there a pause after his name or does he introduce himself as "Vermine the King"? Is he a king who will act before the king, or is he to act the king before the King? Theater's capacity to confuse and elide social difference—a favorite subject of anti-theatrical tracts in the period—proved disturbing to a society that sought through institutional constraints to maintain these distinctions.

25. Perkinson, *A Refutation,* p. 28 [italics mine].

26. G.B. Harrison, ed., William Kempe, *Kempe's Nine Daies Wonder* (1600) (London: the Bodley Head, Ltd., 1923), p. 9 [italics mine].

27. Even after the closing of the theaters the slippery relationship between theatrical violence and political theatrics was recalled: "For when the Stage at *Westminster,* where the two Houses now Act, is once more restored back againe to *Black-Fryers,* they have hope they shall returne to their old harmlesse profession of killing Men in Tragedies without Man-slaughter" (from *Mercurius Anti-Britanicus* [11 August 1645], p. 20, rpt. in *The English Revolution III: Newsbooks I, Oxford Royalist,* Vol. 4, [London: Cornmarket Press, 1971], p. 322). I am indebted to William Sherman for this reference.

28. For an outstanding and groundbreaking discussion of the political implications of Hieronimo's play, see S. F. Johnson, "*The Spanish Tragedy,* or Babylon Revisited," in *Essays on Shakespeare and Elizabethan Drama in Honor of Hardin Craig,* ed. Richard Hosley (Columbia: Univ. of Missouri Press, 1962), pp. 23–36.

29. See Limon's *Dangerous Matter* (Cambridge: Cambridge Univ. Press, 1987).

30. Alternatively, Hieronimo's self-silencing may have offered itself as an appropriate model of resistance to dominant authority. For a discussion of silencing, subjectivity, and *The Spanish Tragedy,* see Catherine Belsey, *The Subject of Tragedy* (New York and London: Methuen, 1985), esp. pp. 75–78.

31. I am indebted to Jean Howard, David Scott Kastan, Stuart Kurland, William Sherman, Edward W. Tayler, and René Weis for their criticism of various drafts of this essay.

12

The Will to Absolute Play
THE JEW OF MALTA (1589)

Stephen J. Greenblatt

Marlowe's heroes fashion themselves not in loving submission to
an absolute authority but in self-conscious opposition: Tamburlaine
against hierarchy, Barabas against Christianity, Faustus against God,
Edward against the sanctified rites and responsibilities of kingship,
marriage, and manhood. And where identity in More, Tyndale, Wyatt,
and Spenser had been achieved through an attack upon something
perceived as alien and threatening, in Marlowe it is achieved through
a subversive identification with the alien. Marlowe's strategy of subversion is seen most clearly in *The Jew of Malta,* which, for this reason,
I propose to consider in some detail. For Marlowe, as for Shakespeare,
the figure of the Jew is useful as a powerful rhetorical device, an
embodiment for a Christian audience of all they loathe and fear, all that
appears stubbornly, irreducibly different. Introduced by Machiavel, the
stock type of demonic villainy, Barabas enters already trailing clouds
of ignominy, already a "marked case." But while never relinquishing
the anti-Semitic stereotype and the conventional motif of the villain-
undone-by-his villainy, Marlowe quickly suggests that the Jew is not
the exception to but rather the true representative of his society.
Though he begins with a paean to liquid assets, Barabas is not primarily
a usurer, set off by his hated occupation from the rest of the community,
but a great merchant, sending his argosies around the world exactly as
Shakespeare's much loved Antonio does. His pursuit of wealth does
not mark him out but rather establishes him—if anything, rather re-
spectably—in the midst of all the other forces in the play: the Turks
exacting tribute from the Christians, the Christians expropriating
money from the Jews, the convent profiting from these expropriations,
religious orders competing for wealthy converts, the prostitute plying
her trade and the blackmailer his. When the Governor of Malta asks
the Turkish "Bashaw," "What wind drives you thus into *Malta* road?,"

the latter replies with perfect frankness, "The wind that bloweth all the world besides, / Desire of gold" (3.1421–23). Barabas's own desire of gold, so eloquently voiced at the start and vividly enacted in the scene in which he hugs his money bags, is the glowing core of that passion which fires all the characters. To be sure, other values are expressed—love, faith, and honor—but as private values these are revealed to be hopelessly fragile, while as public values they are revealed to be mere screens for powerful economic forces. Thus, on the one hand, Abigail, Don Mathias, and the nuns are killed off with remarkable ease and, in effect, with the complicity of the laughing audience. (The audience at the Royal Shakespeare Company's brilliant 1964 production roared with delight when the poisoned nuns came tumbling out of the house.)[1] On the other hand, the public invocation of Christian ethics or knightly honor is always linked by Marlowe to baser motives. The knights concern themselves with Barabas's "inherent sin" only at the moment when they are about to preach him out of his possessions, while the decision to resist the "barbarous misbelieving *Turks*" facilitates all too easily the sale into slavery of a shipload of Turkish captives. The religious and political ideology that seems at first to govern Christian attitudes toward infidels in fact does nothing of the sort; this ideology is clearly subordinated to considerations of profit.

It is because of the primacy of money that Barabas, for all the contempt heaped upon him, is seen as the dominant spirit of the play, its most energetic and inventive force. A victim at the level of religion and political power, he is, in effect, emancipated at the level of civil society, emancipated in Marx's contemptuous sense of the word in his essay *On the Jewish Question:* "The Jew has emancipated himself in a Jewish manner, not only by acquiring the power of money, but also because *money* has become, through him and also part from him, a world power, while the practical Jewish spirit has become the practical spirit of the Christian nations. The Jews have emancipated themselves in so far as the Christians have become Jews."[2] Barabas's avarice, egotism, duplicity, and murderous cunning do not signal his exclusion from the world of Malta but his central place within it. His "Judaism" is, again in Marx's words, "a universal *antisocial* element of the *present time*" (34).

For neither Marlowe nor Marx does this recognition signal a turning away from Jew-baiting; if anything, Jew-baiting is intensified even as the hostility it excites is directed as well against Christian society. Thus Marlowe never discredits anti-Semitism, but he does discredit early in the play a "Christian" social concern that might otherwise have been used to counter a specifically Jewish antisocial element. When the

Governor of Malta seizes the wealth of the Jews on the grounds that it is "better one want for a common good, / Then many perish for a private man" (1.331–32), an audience at all familiar with the New Testament will hear in these words echoes not of Christ but of Caiaphas and, a few lines further on, of Pilate.[3] There are, to be sure, moments of social solidarity—as when the Jews gather around Barabas to comfort him or when Ferneze and Katherine together mourn the death of their sons—but they are brief and ineffectual. The true emblem of the society of the play is the slave market, where "Every one's price is written on his back" (2.764).[4] Here in the marketplace men are literally turned, in Marx's phrase, "into *alienable*, saleable objects, in thrall to egoistic need and huckstering" (39). And at this level of society, the religious and political barriers fall away: the Jew buys a Turk at the Christian slave market. Such is the triumph of civil society.

For Marlowe the dominant mode of perceiving the world, in a society hag-ridden by the power of money and given over to the slave market, is *contempt*, contempt aroused in the beholders of such a society and, as important, governing the behavior of those who bring it into being and function within it. This is Barabas's constant attitude, virtually his signature; his withering scorn lights not only on the Christian rulers of Malta ("thus slaves will learn," he sneers, when the defeated Governor is forced into submission [5.2150]), but on his daughter's suitor ("the slave looks like a hog's cheek new sing'd" [2.803]), his daughter ("An *Hebrew* born, and would become a Christian. / *Cazzo, diabolo*" [4.1527–28]), his slave Ithamore ("Thus every villain ambles after wealth / Although he ne'er be richer than in hope" [3.1354–55]), the Turks ("How the slave jeers at him," observes the Governor of Barabas greeting Calymath [5.2339]), the pimp, Pilia-Borza ("a shaggy, totter'd staring slave" [4.1858]), his fellow Jews ("See the simplicity of these base slaves" [1.448]), and even, when he has blundered by making the poison too weak, himself ("What a damn'd slave was I" [5.2025]). Barabas's frequent asides assure us that he is feeling contempt even when he is not openly expressing it, and the reiteration of the derogatory epithet *slave* firmly anchors this contempt in the structure of relations that governs the play. Barabas's liberality in bestowing this epithet—from the Governor to the pimp—reflects the extraordinary unity of the structure, its intricate series of mirror images: Pilia-Borza's extortion racket is repeated at the "national" level in the extortion of the Jewish community's wealth and at the international level in the Turkish extortion of the Christian tribute. The play depicts Renaissance international relations as a kind of glorified gangsterism, a vast "protection" racket.[5]

At all levels of society in Marlowe's play, behind each version of the racket (and making it possible) is violence or the threat of violence, and so here too Barabas's murderousness is presented as at once a characteristic of his accursed tribe and the expression of a universal phenomenon. This expression, to be sure, is extravagant—he is responsible, directly or indirectly, for the deaths of Mathias, Lodowick, Abigail, Pilia-Borza, Bellamira, Ithamore, Friar Jacamo, Friar Barnadine, and innumerable poisoned nuns and massacred soldiers—and, as we shall see, this extravagance helps to account for the fact that in the last analysis Barabas cannot be assimilated to his world. But if Marlowe ultimately veers away from so entirely sociological a conception, it is important to grasp the extent to which Barabas expresses in extreme, unmediated form the motives that have been partially disguised by the spiritual humbug of Christianity, indeed the extent to which Barabas is *brought into being* by the Christian society around him. His actions are always *responses* to the initiatives of others: not only is the plot of the whole play set in motion by the Governor's expropriation of his wealth, but each of Barabas's particular plots is a reaction to what he perceives as a provocation or a threat. Only his final strategem—the betrayal of the Turks—seems an exception, since the Jew is for once in power, but even this fatal blunder is a response to his perfectly sound perception that "*Malta* hates me, and in hating me / My life's in danger" (5.2131–32).

Barabas's apparent passivity sits strangely with his entire domination of the spirit of the play, and once again, we may turn to Marx for an explication of Marlowe's rhetorical strategy: "Judaism could not create a new world. It could only bring the new creations and conditions of the world within its own sphere of activity, because practical need, the spirit of which is self-interest, is always passive, cannot expand at will, but *finds* itself extended as a result of the continued development of society" (38). Though the Jew is identified here with the spirit of egotism and selfish need, his success is credited to the triumph of Christianity which "objectifies" and hence alienates all national, natural, moral, and theoretical relationships, dissolving "the human world into a world of atomistic, antagonistic individuals" (39). The concrete emblem of this alienation in Marlowe is the slave market; its ideological expression is the religious chauvinism that sees Jews as inherently sinful, Turks as barbarous misbelievers.

The Jew of Malta ends on a powerfully ironic note of this "spiritual egotism" (to use Marx's phrase) when the Governor celebrates the treacherous destruction of Barabas and the Turks by giving due praise "Neither to Fate nor Fortune, but to Heaven" (5.2410). (Once again, the Royal Shakespeare Company's audience guffawed at this bit of hypocritical sententiousness.) But we do not have to wait until the

closing moments of the play to witness the Christian practice of alienation. It is, as I have suggested, present throughout, and nowhere more
powerfully than in the figure of Barabas himself. For not only are
Barabas's actions called forth by Christian actions, but his identity
itself is to a great extent the product of the Christian conception of
a Jew's identity. This is not entirely the case: Marlowe invokes an
"indigenous" Judaism in the wicked parody of the materialism of Job
and in Barabas's repeated invocation of Hebraic exclusivism ("these
swine-eating Christians," etc.). Nevertheless Barabas's sense of himself,
his characteristic response to the world, and his self-presentation are
very largely constructed out of the materials of the dominant, Christian
culture. This is nowhere more evident than in his speech, which is
virtually composed of hard little aphorisms, cynical adages, worldly
maxims—all the neatly packaged nastiness of his society. Where Shylock is differentiated from the Christians even in his use of the common
language, Barabas is inscribed at the center of the society of the play,
a society whose speech is a tissue of aphorisms. Whole speeches are
little more than strings of sayings: maxims are exchanged, inverted,
employed as weapons; the characters enact and even deliberately
"stage" proverbs (with all of the manic energy of Breughel's "Nether-
landish Proverbs"). When Barabas, intent upon poisoning the nuns,
calls for the pot of rice porridge, Ithamore carries it to him along with
a ladle, explaining that since "the proverb says, he that eats with the
devil had need of a long spoon, I have brought you a ladle" (3.1360–
62).[6] And when Barabas and Ithamore together strangle Friar Barnadine, to whom Abigail has revealed their crimes in confession, the Jew
explains, "Blame not us but the proverb, Confess and be hang'd"
(4.1655).

Proverbs in *The Jew of Malta* are a kind of currency, the compressed
ideological wealth of society, the money of the mind. Their terseness
corresponds to that concentration of material wealth that Barabas
celebrates: "Infinite riches in a little room." Barabas's own store of
these ideological riches comprises the most cynical and self-serving
portion:

> Who is honor'd now but for his wealth?
> (1.151)

> Ego mihimet sum semper proximus
> (1.228)

> A reaching thought will search his deepest wits,
> And cast with cunning for the time to come.
> (1.455–56)

> . . . in extremity
> We ought to make bar of no policy.
>   (1.507–8)

>   . . . Religion
> Hides many mischiefs from suspicion.
>   (1.519–20)

> Now will I show my self to have more of the Serpent
> Than the Dove; that is, more knave than fool.
>   (2.797–98)

> Faith is not to be held with Heretics.
>   (1.1076)

> For he that liveth in Authority,
> And neither gets him friends, nor fills his bags,
> Lives like the Ass that *Æsop* speaketh of,
> That labors with a load of bread and wine,
> And leaves it off to snap on Thistle tops.
>   (5.2139–43)

> For so I live, perish may all the world.
>   (5.2292)

This is not the exotic language of the Jews but the product of the whole society, indeed, its most familiar and ordinary face. And as the essence of proverbs is their anonymity, the effect of their recurrent use by Barabas is to render him more and more typical, to *de-individualize* him. This is, of course, the opposite of the usual process. Most dramatic characters—Shylock is the appropriate example—accumulate identity in the course of their play; Barabas loses it. He is never again as distinct and unique an individual as he is in the first moments:

> Go tell 'em the Jew of *Malta* sent thee, man:
> Tush, who amongst 'em knows not *Barabas?*
>   (1.102–3)

Even his account of his past—killing sick people or poisoning wells—tends to make him more vague and unreal, accommodating him to an abstract, anti-Semitic fantasy of a Jew's past.

In this effacement of Barabas's identity, Marlowe reflects not only upon his culture's bad faith, its insistence upon the otherness of what is in fact its own essence, but also upon the tragic limitations of rebellion against this culture. Like all of Marlowe's heroes, Barabas defines himself by negating cherished values, but his identity is itself, as we have seen, a social construction, a fiction composed of the sleaziest materials in his culture.[7] If Marlowe questions the notion of literature as cautionary tale, if his very use of admonitory fictions subverts them, he cannot dismiss the immense power of the social system in which such fictions play their part. Indeed the attempts to challenge this system—Tamburlaine's world conquests, Barabas's Machiavellianism, Edward's homosexuality, and Faustus's skepticism—are subjected to relentless probing and exposed as unwitting tributes to that social construction of identity against which they struggle. For if the heart of Renaissance orthodoxy is a vast system of repetitions in which disciplinary paradigms are established and men gradually learn what to desire and what to fear, the Marlovian rebels and skeptics remain embedded within this orthodoxy: they simply reverse the paradigms and embrace what the society brands as evil. In so doing, they imagine themselves set in diametrical opposition to their society where in fact they have unwittingly accepted its crucial structural elements. For the crucial issue is not man's power to disobey, but the characteristic modes of desire and fear produced by a given society, and the rebellious heroes never depart from those modes. With their passionate insistence on will, Marlowe's protagonists anticipate the perception that human history is the product of men themselves, but they also anticipate the perception that this product is shaped, in Lukács phrase, by forces that arise from their relations with each other and which have escaped their control.[8] As Marx writes in a famous passage in *The Eighteenth Brumaire of Louis Bonaparte:* "Men make their own history, but they do not make it just as they please; they do not make it under circumstances chosen by themselves, but under circumstances directly found, given and transmitted from the past. The tradition of all the dead generations weighs like a nightmare on the brain of the living. And just when they seem engaged in revolutionising themselves and things, in creating something entirely new, precisely in such epochs of revolutionary crisis they anxiously conjure up the spirits of the past."[9]

Marlowe's protagonists rebel against orthodoxy, but they do not do so just as they please; their acts of negation not only conjure up the order they would destroy but seem at times to be themselves conjured up by that very order. *The Jew of Malta* continually demonstrates, as we have seen, how close Barabas is to the gentile world against which he is set; if this demonstration exposes the hypocrisy of that world, it cuts against the Jew as well, for his loathing must be repeatedly directed against a version of himself, until at the close he boils in the pot he has prepared for his enemy.

Notes

1. There is a discussion of this and other productions of Marlowe's play in James L. Smith, "*The Jew of Malta* in the Theatre," in *Christopher Marlowe,* ed. Brian Morris (London: Benn, 1968), pp. 1–23.

2. *On the Jewish Question* in Karl Marx, *Early Writings,* trans. and ed. T. B. Bottomore (New York: McGraw-Hill, 1963), p. 35. For a fuller exploration of the relation between Marx's essay and Marlowe's play, see Stephen J. Greenblatt, "Marlowe, Marx, and Anti-Semitism," *Critical Inquiry* 5 (1978), pp. 291–307.

3. G. K. Hunter, "The Theology of Marlowe's *The Jew of Malta,*" *Journal of the Warburg and Courtauld Institute* 27 (1964), p. 236.

4. Shylock attempts to make this a similarly central issue in the trial scene, but, as we might expect, the attempt fails (*Merchant of Venice,* 4.1.90–100).

5. For a modern confirmation of such a view, see Frederic C. Lane, *Venice and History* (Baltimore: Johns Hopkins University Press, 1966).

6. For the Jew as devil, see Joshua Trachtenberg, *The Devil and the Jews: The Medieval Conception of the Jew and Its Relation to Modern Anti-semitism* (New Haven: Yale University Press, 1943).

7. In a sense, Marlowe uses his hero-villains as satirist figures: he has them expose the viciousness of the world and then reveals the extent to which they are no different from what they attack. Recall Duke Senior to Jaques:

> Mos mischievous foul sin, in chiding sin,
> For thou thyself hast been a libertine,
> As sensual as the brutish sting itself;
> And all th'embossed sores and headed evils
> That thou with license of free foot hast caught,
> Wouldst thou disgorge into the general world.
> (*As You Like It,* 2.7.64–69)

8. See Georg Lukács, *History and Class Consciousness,* trans. Rodney Livingstone (Cambridge, Mass.: MIT Press, 1971), p. 15. The fountainhead of all modern speculation along these lines is Vico's *New Science.*

9. *Eighteenth Brumaire,* in *The Marx-Engels Reader,* ed. Robert C. Tucker (New York: Norton, 1972), p. 437.

13

Subversion through Transgression
DOCTOR FAUSTUS (c. 1592)

Jonathan Dollimore

One problem in particular has exercised critics of *Dr. Faustus:* its structure, inherited from the morality form, apparently negates what the play experientially affirms—the heroic aspiration of "Renaissance man." Behind this discrepancy some have discerned a tension between, on the one hand, the moral and theological imperatives of a severe Christian orthodoxy and, on the other, an affirmation of Faustus as "the epitome of Renaissance aspiration . . . all the divine discontent, the unwearied and unsatisfied striving after knowledge that marked the age in which Marlowe wrote" (Roma Gill, ed., *Dr. Faustus,* p. xix).

Critical opinion has tended to see the tension resolved one way or another—that is, to read the play as ultimately vindicating either Faustus or the morality structure. But such resolution is what *Dr. Faustus* as interrogative text[1] resists. It seems always to represent paradox— religious and tragic—as insecurely and provocatively ambiguous or, worse, as openly contradictory. Not surprisingly Max Bluestone, after surveying some eighty recent studies of *Dr. Faustus,* as well as the play itself, remains unconvinced of their more or less equally divided attempts to find in it an orthodox or heterodox principle of resolution. On the contrary: "conflict and contradiction inhere everywhere in the world of this play" (*"Libido Speculandi:* Doctrine and Dramaturgy in Contemporary Interpretations of Marlowe's *Dr. Faustus,"* p. 55). If this is correct then we might see it as an integral aspect of what *Dr. Faustus* is best understood as: not an affirmation of Divine Law, or conversely of Renaissance Man, but an exploration of subversion through transgression.

Limit and Transgression

Raymond Williams has observed how, in Victorian literature, individuals encounter limits of crucially different kinds. In *Felix Holt* there is the discovery of limits which, in the terms of the novel, are enabling: they vindicate a conservative identification of what it is to be human. In complete contrast *Jude the Obscure* shows its protagonist destroyed in the process—and ultimately because—of encountering limits. This is offered not as punishment for hubris but as "profoundly subversive of the limiting structure" ("Forms of English Fiction in 1848," p. 287). *Dr. Faustus*, I want to argue, falls into this second category: a discovery of limits that ostensibly forecloses subversive questioning in fact provokes it.[2]

What Erasmus had said many years before against Luther indicates the parameters of *Dr. Faustus*'s limiting structure:

> Suppose for a moment that it were true in a certain sense, as Augustine says somewhere, that "God works in us good and evil, and rewards his own good works in us, and punishes his evil works in us" . . . Who will be able to bring himself to love God with all his heart when He created hell seething with eternal torments in order to punish His own misdeeds in His victims as though He took delight in human torments? (*Renaissance Views of Man*, ed. S. Davies, p. 92)

But Faustus is not *identified* independently of this limiting structure and any attempt to interpret the play as Renaissance man breaking out of medieval chains always founders on this point: Faustus is constituted by the very limiting structure which he transgresses and his transgression is both despite and because of that fact.

Faustus is situated at the center of a violently divided universe. To the extent that conflict and contradiction are represented as actually of its essence, it appears to be Manichean; thus Faustus asks "where is the place that men call hell?," and Mephostophilis replies, "Within the bowels of these elements," adding:

> when all the world dissolves
> And every creature shall be purify'd,
> All places shall be hell that is not heaven.
> (v. 117, 120, 125–7)

If Greg is correct, and "purified" means "no longer mixed, but of one essence, either wholly good or wholly evil" (*Marlowe's Dr. Faustus*, Parallel Texts, p. 330), then the division suggested is indeed Manichean.[3] But more important than the question of precise origins is the fact that not only heaven and hell but God and Lucifer, the Good Angel and the Bad Angel, are polar opposites whose axes pass through and constitute human consciousness. Somewhat similarly, for Mephostophilis hell is not a place but a state of consciousness:

> Hell hath no limits, nor is circumscrib'd
> In one self place, but where we are is hell,
> And where hell is, there must we ever be.
> (v. 122–4)

From Faustus's point of view—one never free-ranging but always coterminous with his position—God and Lucifer seem equally responsible in his final destruction, two supreme agents of power deeply antagonistic to each other[4] yet temporarily co-operating in his demise. Faustus is indeed their subject, the site of their power struggle. For his part God is possessed of tyrannical power—"heavy wrath" (i. 71 and xix. 153), while at the beginning of scene xix Lucifer, Beelzebub, and Mephostophilis enter syndicate-like "To view the *subjects* of our monarchy." Earlier Faustus had asked why Lucifer wanted his soul; it will, replies Mephostophilis, "Enlarge his kingdom" (v. 40). In Faustus's final soliloquy both God and Lucifer are spatially located as the opposites which, *between them*, destroy him:

> O, I'll leap up to my God! Who pulls me down?
>
>   . . . see where God
> Stretcheth out his arm and bends his ireful brows
>
> My God, my God! Look not so fierce on me!
>
> Ugly hell, gape not! Come not, Lucifer.
> (xix. 145, 150–1, 187, 189)

Before this the representatives of God and Lucifer have bombarded Faustus with conflicting accounts of his identity, position, and destiny. Again, the question of whether in principle Faustus can repent, what is the point of no return, is less important than the fact that he is located on the axes of contradictions which cripple and finally destroy him.

By contrast, when, in Marlowe's earlier play, Tamburlaine speaks of the "four elements/Warring within our breasts for regiment" he is speaking of a dynamic conflict conducive to the will to power—one that "Doth teach us all to have aspiring minds" (*Part 1*. II. vii. 18–20)—not the stultifying contradiction which constitutes Faustus and his universe. On this point alone *Tamburlaine* presents a fascinating contrast with *Dr. Faustus*. With his indomitable will to power and warrior prowess, Tamburlaine really does approximate to the self-determining hero bent on transcendent autonomy—a kind of fantasy on Pico's theme of aspiring man. But like all fantasies this one excites as much by what it excludes as what it exaggerates. Indeed exclusion may be the basis not just of Tamburlaine as fantasy projection but *Tamburlaine* as transgressive text: it liberates from its Christian and ethical framework the humanist conception of man as essentially free, dynamic, and aspiring; more contentiously, this conception of man is not only liberated from a Christian framework but reestablished in open defiance of it. But however interpreted, the objective of Tamburlaine's aspiration is very different from Pico's; the secular power in which Tamburlaine revels is part of what Pico wants to transcend in the name of a more ultimate and legitimate power. Tamburlaine defies origin, Pico aspires to it:

> A certain sacred striving should seize the soul so that, not content with the indifferent and middling, we may pant after the highest and so (for we can if we want to) force our way up to it with all our might. Let us despise the terrestrial, be unafraid of the heavenly, and then, neglecting the things of the world, fly towards that court beyond the world nearest to God the Most High.
>
> (*On the Dignity of Man*, pp. 69–70)

With *Dr. Faustus* almost the reverse is true: transgression is born not of a liberating sense of freedom to deny or retrieve origin, nor from an excess of life breaking repressive bounds. It is rather a transgression rooted in an *impasse* of despair.

Even before he abjures God, Faustus expresses a sense of being isolated and trapped; an insecurity verging on despair pre-exists a damnation which, by a perverse act of free will, he "chooses." Arrogant he certainly is, but it is wrong to see Faustus at the outset as secure in the knowledge that existing forms of knowledge are inadequate. Rather, his search for a more complete knowledge is itself a search for security. For Faustus, "born, of parents base of stock," and now both socially and geographically displaced (Prologue, 11, 13–19), no teleological integration of identity, self-consciousness, and purpose obtains. In the opening scene he attempts to convince himself of the worth of several professions—divinity, medicine, law, and then divinity again—only to reject each in turn; in this he is almost schizoid:

> Having commenc'd, be a divine in show,
> Yet level at the end of every art,
> And live and die in Aristotle's works.
> Sweet Analytics, 'tis thou hast ravish'd me!

When all is done, divinity is best.

Philosophy is odious and obscure,
Both law and physic are for petty wits,
Divinity is basest of the three,
Unpleasant, harsh, contemptible, and vile.
(i. 3–6, 37, 105–8)

As he shakes free of spurious orthodoxy and the role of the conventional scholar, Faustus's insecurity intensifies. A determination to be "resolved" of all ambiguities, to be "resolute" and show fortitude (i. 32; iii. 14; v. 6; vi. 32, 64) is only a recurring struggle to escape agonized irresolution.

This initial desperation and insecurity, just as much as a subsequent fear of impending damnation, suggests why his search for knowledge so easily lapses into hedonistic recklessness and fatuous, self-forgetful "delight" (i. 52; v. 82; vi. 170; viii. 59–60). Wagner cannot comprehend this psychology of despair:

I think my master means to die shortly:
He has made his will and given me his wealth

I wonder what he means. If death were nigh,
He would not banquet and carouse and swill
Amongst the students.
(xviii. 1–2, 5–7)

Faustus knew from the outset what he would eventually incur. He willingly "surrenders up . . . his soul" for twenty-four years of "voluptuousness" in the knowledge that "eternal death" will be the result (iii. 90–4). At the end of the first scene he exits declaring, "This night I'll conjure though I die therefor." Later he reflects: "Long ere this I should have done the deed [i.e. suicide]/Had not sweet pleasure conquer'd deep despair" (vi. 24–5). This is a despairing hedonism rooted in the fatalism of his opening soliloquy: "If we say that we have no sin, we deceive ourselves, and there's no truth in us. Why, then, belike we must sin, and so consequently die" (i. 41–4). Half-serious, half-facetious, Faustus registers a sense of humankind as miscreated.

Tamburlaine's will to power leads to liberation through transgression. Faustus's pact with the devil, because an act of transgression without hope of liberation, is at once rebellious, masochistic, and despairing. The protestant God—"an arbitrary and wilful, omnipotent and universal tyrant" (Walzer, p. 151)—demanded of each subject that s/he submit personally and without mediation. The modes of power formerly incorporated in mediating institutions and practices now devolve on Him and, to some extent and unintentionally, on His subject: abject before God, the subject takes on a new importance in virtue of just this direct relation.[5] Further, although God is remote and inscrutable he is also intimately conceived: "The principal worship of God hath two parts. One is to yield subjection to him, the other to draw near to him and to cleave unto him" (Perkins, *An Instruction Touching Religious or Divine Worship*, p. 313). Such perhaps are the conditions for masochistic transgression: intimacy becomes the means of a defiance of power, the new-found importance of the subject the impetus of that defiance, the abjectness of the subject its self-sacrificial nature. (We may even see here the origins of subcultural transgression: the identity conferred upon the deviant by the dominant culture enables resistance as well as oppression.

Foucault has written: "limit and transgression depend on each other for whatever density of being they possess: a limit could not exist if it were absolutely uncrossable and, reciprocally, transgression would be pointless if it merely crossed a limit composed of illusions and shadows" (*Language, Counter-Memory, Practice,* p. 34). It is a phenomenon of which the anti-essentialist writers of the Renaissance were aware: "Superiority and inferiority, maistry and subjection, are joyntly tied unto a naturall kinde of envy and contestation; they must perpetually enter-spoile one another" (Montaigne, *Essays,* III. 153).

In the morality plays sins tended to involve blindness to the rightness of God's law, while repentance and redemption involved a renewed apprehension of it. In *Dr. Faustus* however sin is not the error of fallen judgment but a conscious and deliberate transgression of limit. It is a limit which, among other things, renders God remote and inscrutable yet subjects the individual to constant surveillance and correction; which holds the individual subject terrifyingly responsible for the fallen human condition while disallowing him or her any subjective power of redemption. Out of such conditions is born a mode of transgression identifiably protestant in origin: despairing yet defiant, masochistic yet willful. Faustus is abject yet his is an abjectness which is strangely inseparable from arrogance, which reproaches the authority which demands it, which is not so much subdued as incited by that same authority:

Faustus: I gave . . . my soul for my cunning.
All: God forbid!
Faustus: God forbade it indeed; but Faustus hath done it.

(xix. 61–4)

Mephostophilis well understands transgressive desire; it is why he does not deceive Faustus about the reality of hell. It suggests too why he

conceives of hell in the way he does; although his sense of it as a state
of being and consciousness can be seen as a powerful recuperation of
hell at a time when its material existence as a *place* of future punishment
was being questioned, it is also an arrogant appropriation of hell, an
incorporating of it into the consciousness of the subject.

A ritual pact advances a desire which cancels fear long enough to
pass the point of no return:

> Lo, Mephostophilis, for love of thee
> Faustus hath cut his arm, and with his proper blood
> Assures his soul to be great Lucifer's,
> Chief lord and regent of perpetual night.
> View here this blood that trickles from mine arm,
> And let it be propitious for my wish.
>
> (v. 54–8)

But his blood congeals, preventing him from signing the pact. Mephostophilis exits to fetch "fire to dissolve it." It is a simple yet brilliant
moment of dramatic suspense, one which invites us to dwell on the full
extent of the violation about to be enacted. Faustus finally signs but
only after the most daring blasphemy of all: "Now will I make an end
immediately/ . . . *Consummatum est:* this bill is ended" (v. 72–4).
In transgressing utterly and desperately God's law, he appropriates
Christianity's supreme image of masochistic sacrifice:[6] Christ dying on
the cross—and his dying words (cf. John xix. 30). Faustus is not
liberating himself, he is ending himself: "it is finished." Stephen
Greenblatt is surely right to find in Marlowe's work "a subversive
identification with the alien," one which "flaunts society's cherished
orthodoxies, embraces what the culture finds loathsome or frightening" (*Renaissance Self-Fashioning,* pp. 203, 220). But what is also
worth remarking about this particular moment is the way that a subversive identification with the alien is achieved and heightened through
travesty of one such cherished orthodoxy.

Power and the Unitary Soul

‾ For Augustine the conflict which man experiences is not (as the
Manichean heresy insisted) between two contrary souls or two contrary
substances—rather, one soul fluctuates between contrary wills. On
some occasions *Dr. Faustus* clearly assumes the Augustinian conception of the soul; on others—those expressive of or consonant with the
Manichean implications of universal conflict—it presents Faustus as
divided and, indeed, constituted by that division. The distinction which

Augustine makes between the will as opposed to the soul as the site of conflict and division may now seem to be semantic merely; in fact it was and remains of the utmost importance. For one thing, as *Dr. Faustus* makes clear, the unitary soul—unitary in the sense of being essentially indivisible and eternal—is the absolute precondition for the exercise of divine power:

> O, no end is limited to damned souls.
> Why wert thou not a creature wanting soul?
> Or why is this immortal that thou hast?
> Ah, Pythagoras' *metempsychosis,* were that true,
> This soul should fly from me and I be chang'd
> Unto some brutish beast: all beasts are happy,
> For when they die
> Their souls are soon dissolv'd in elements;
> But mine must live still to be plagu'd in hell.
>
> (xix. 171–9)

Further, the unitary soul—unitary now in the sense of being essentially incorruptible—figures even in those manifestations of Christianity which depict the human condition in the most pessimistic of terms and human freedom as thereby intensely problematic. The English Calvinist William Perkins indicates why, even for a theology as severe as his, this had to be so: if sin were a corruption of man's "substance" then not only could he not be immortal (and thereby subjected to the eternal torment which Faustus incurs), but Christ could not have taken on his nature.

Once sin or evil is allowed to penetrate to the core of God's subject (as opposed to being, say, an inextricable part of that subject's fallen *condition*) the most fundamental contradiction in Christian theology is reactivated: evil is of the essence of God's creation. This is of course only a more extreme instance of another familiar problem: how is evil possible in a world created by an omnipotent God? To put the blame on Adam only begs the further question: Why did God make Adam potentially evil? (Compare Nashe's impudent gloss: "Adam never fell till God made fools" [*The Unfortunate Traveller,* p. 269]).

Calvin, however, comes close to allowing what Perkins and Augustine felt it necessary to deny: evil and conflict do penetrate to the core of God's subject. For Calvin the soul is an essence, immortal and created by God. But to suggest that it partakes of *God's* essence is a "monstrous" blasphemy: "if the soul of man is a portion transmitted from the essence of God, the divine nature must not only be liable to passion and change, but also to ignorance, evil desires, infirmity, and

all kinds of vice" (*Institutes*, I. xv. 5). Given the implication that these
imperfections actually constitute the soul, it is not surprising that
"everyone feels that the soul itself is a receptacle for all kinds of
pollution." Elsewhere we are told that the soul, "teeming with . . .
seeds of vice . . . is altogether devoid of good" (I. xv; ii, iii). Here is yet
another stress point in protestantism and one which plays like *Dr.
Faustus* (and *Mustapha*) exploit: if human beings perpetuate disorder
it is because they have been created disordered.

The final chorus of the play tells us that Dr. Faustus involved himself
with "unlawful things" and thereby practiced "more than heavenly
power permits" (6, 8). It is a transgression which has revealed the
limiting structure of Faustus's universe for what it is, namely, "heavenly
power." Faustus has to be destroyed since in a very real sense the
credibility of that heavenly power depends upon it. And yet the punitive
intervention which validates divine power also compromises it: far
from justice, law, and authority being what legitimates power, it appears, by the end of the play, to be the other way around: power
establishes the limits of all those things.

It might be objected that the distinction between justice and power
is a modern one and, in Elizabethan England, even if entertained,
would be easily absorbed in one or another of the paradoxes which
constituted the Christian faith. And yet: if there is one thing that can
be said with certainty about this period it is that God in the form of
"mere arbitrary will omnipotent" could not "keep men in awe." We
can infer as much from many texts, one of which was Lawne's *Abridgement* of Calvin's *Institutes*, translated in 1587—around the time of the
writing of *Dr. Faustus*. The book presents and tries to answer, in
dialogue form, objections to Calvin's theology. On the question of
predestination the "Objector" contends that "to adjudge to destruction
whom he will, is more agreeable to the lust of a tyrant, than to the
lawful sentence of a judge." The "Reply" to this is as arbitrary and
tyrannical as the God which the Objector envisages as unsatisfactory:
"it is a point of bold wickedness even so much as to inquire the causes
of God's will" (p. 222; quoted from Sinfield, p. 171). It is an exchange
which addresses directly the question of whether a tyrannical God is
or is not grounds for discontent. Even more important perhaps is its
unintentional foregrounding of the fact that, as embodiment of naked
power alone, God could so easily be collapsed into those tyrants who,
we are repeatedly told by writers in this period, exploited Him as
ideological mystification of their own power. Not surprisingly, the
concept of "heavenly power" interrogated in *Dr. Faustus* was soon
to lose credibility, and it did so in part precisely because of such
interrogation.

Dr. Faustus is important for subsequent tragedy for these reasons and at least one other: in transgressing and demystifying the limiting structure of his world without there ever existing the possibility of his escaping it, Faustus can be seen as an important precursor of the malcontented protagonist of Jacobean tragedy. Only for the latter, the limiting structure comes to be primarily a socio-political one.

Lastly, if it is correct that censorship resulted in *Dr. Faustus* being one of the last plays of its kind—it being forbidden thereafter to interrogate religious issues so directly—we might expect the transgressive impulse in the later plays to take on different forms. This is in fact exactly what we do find; and one such form involves a strategy already referred to—the inscribing of a subversive discourse within an orthodox one, a vindication of the letter of an orthodoxy while subverting its spirit.

Notes

1. This concept, originating in a classification of Benveniste's, is developed by Catherine Belsey in *Critical Practice,* chapter 4.

2. Still important for this perspective is Nicholas Brooke's 1952 article, "The Moral Tragedy of Doctor Faustus."

3. The Manichean implications of protestantism are apparent from this assertion of Luther's: "Christians know there are two kingdoms in the world, which are bitterly opposed to each other. In one of them Satan reigns . . . He holds captive to his will all who are not snatched away from him by the Spirit of Christ . . . In the other Kingdom, Christ reigns, and his kingdom ceaselessly resists and makes war on the kingdom of Satan" (*Luther and Erasmus,* ed. Rupp, pp. 327–8; see also Peter Lake, *Moderate Puritans and the Elizabethan Church,* pp. 144–5). J. P. Brockbank, in a discussion of the Manichean background of *Dr. Faustus,* notes similarities between Faustus and the Manichean bishop of the same name mentioned by Augustine in the *Confessions*—himself an adherent of the Manichean faith for nine years; on Manicheanism generally, see also John Hick, *Evil and the God of Love,* chapter 3.

4. Cf. Walzer: "The imagery of warfare was constant in Calvin's writing"; specifically of course, warfare between God and Satan (*The Revolution of the Saints,* p. 65).

5. Cf. C. Burges, *The First Sermon* (1641): "A man once married to the Lord by covenant may without arrogancy say: this righteousness is my righteousness . . . this loving kindness, these mercies, this faithfulness, which I see in thee . . . is mine, for my comfort . . . direction, salvation, and what not" (p. 61; quoted from Conrad Russell, *Crisis of Parliaments,* p. 204).

6. Margaret Walters reminds us how Christian iconography came to glorify masochism, especially in its treatment of crucifixion. Adoration is transferred from aggressor to victim, the latter suffering in order to propitiate a vengeful, patriarchal God (*The Nude Male,* p. 10; see also pp. 72–5). Faustus's transgression becomes subversive in being submissive yet the reverse of propitiatory.

Works Cited

Belsey, Catherine. *Critical Practice*. London: Methuen, 1980.

Bluestone, Max. "*Libido Speculandi:* Doctrine and Dramaturgy in Contemporary Interpretations of Marlowe's *Doctor Faustus.*" *Reinterpretations of Elizabethan Drama*.
Ed. N. Rabkin. New York: Columbia University Press, 1969.

Brockbank, J. P. *Marlowe: Dr. Faustus*. London: Arnold, 1962.

Brooke, Nicholas. "The Moral Tragedy of Doctor Faustus." *Cambridge Journal* Aug.
1952:662–87.

Calvin, John. *Institutes*. Trans. Henry Beveridge. 2 vols. London: Clarke, 1949.

Davies, Stevie, ed. *Renaissance Views of Man*. Manchester: Manchester University Press,
1978.

Foucault, Michel. *Language, Counter-Memory, Practice*. Ithaca and New York: Cornell
University Press, 1977.

Greenblatt, Stephen. *Renaissance Self-Fashioning*. Chicago: University of Chicago Press,
1980.

Hick, John. *Evil and the God of Love*. Glasgow: Collins, The Fontana Library, 1968.

Lake, Peter. *Moderate Puritans and the Elizabethan Church*. Cambridge: Cambridge
University Press, 1982.

Lawne, William. *An Abridgement of the Institution of Christian Religion*. Trans. Christopher Fetherstone. Edinburgh, 1587.

Marlowe, Christopher. *Dr. Faustus 1604–16, Parallel Texts*. Ed. W. W. Greg. Oxford:
Clarendon, 1950.

———— *Dr. Faustus*. Ed. John Jump. London: Methuen, 1962.

———— *Dr. Faustus*. Ed. Roma Gill. London: Benn, 1965.

———— *Tamburlaine*. Ed. J. W. Harper. London: Benn, 1971.

Montaigne, Michel, *Essays*, trans. John Florio. 3 vols. London: Dent, 1965.

Nashe, Thomas. *The Unfortunate Traveller and other Works*. Ed. J. B. Steane. Harmondsworth: Penguin, 1972.

Perkins, William. *Works*. Ed. I. Breward. Abingdon: Sutton Courtenay, 1970.

Pico della Mirandola. *Oration: On the Dignity of Man*. In *Renaissance View of Man*.
Ed. Steve Davies, Manchester: Manchester University Press, 1978.

Rupp, E. Gordon, ed. *Luther and Erasmus: Free Will and Salvation*. London: SCM,
1969.

Russell, Conrad. *The Crisis of Parliaments*. London: Oxford University Press, 1971.

Sinfield, Alan. *Literature in Protestant England 1560–1660*. London: Croom Helm,
1972.

Walters, Margaret. *The Nude Male: A New Perspective*. New York and London:
Paddington Press, 1978.

Walzer, Michael. *The Revolution of the Saints: A Study in the Origins of Radical Politics*.
London: Weidenfeld and Nicolson, 1966.

Williams, Raymond. "Forms of English Fiction in 1848." *1848: The Sociology of
Literature*. Ed. F. Barker, Colchester: University of Essex, 1977.

14

Alice Arden's Crime
ARDEN OF FAVERSHAM (c. 1590)

Catherine Belsey

I

On Sunday 15 February 1551 Alice Arden of Faversham in Kent procured and witnessed the murder of her husband. She and most of her accomplices were arrested, tried, and executed. The goods of the murderers, worth a total of £184. 10s. 4½d., and certain jewels, were forfeit to the Faversham treasury. The city of Canterbury was paid 44 shillings for executing George Bradshaw, who was also present at the murder, and for burning Alice Arden alive.[1] At a time when all the evidence suggests that crimes of violence were by no means uncommon, Alice Arden's crime was cited, presented and re-presented, problematized and reproblematized, during a period of at least eighty years after it was committed. Holinshed, pausing in his account of the events which constitute the main material of the *Chronicles of England, Scotland and Ireland* to give a detailed analysis of the murder, explains that the case transgresses the normal boundaries between public and private:

> for the horribleness thereof, although otherwise it may seeme to be
> but a private matter, and therefore as it were impertinent to this
> historie, I have thought good to set it foorth somewhat at large.[2]

This "horribleness," which identifies Alice Arden's domestic crime as belonging to the public arena of history, is not, I want to argue, a matter of the physical details of the murder, or even of the degree of premeditation involved. On the contrary, the scandal lies in Alice Arden's challenge to the institution of marriage, itself publicly in crisis in the period. Marriage becomes in the sixteenth and seventeenth centuries the site of a paradoxical struggle to create a private realm and to take control of it in the interests of the public good. The crime coincides with the beginning of this contest. *Arden of Faversham*, which can probably be dated about 1590,[3] coincides with a major intensification of the debate about marriage, and permits its audience glimpses of what is at stake in the struggle.

II

There are a great many extant allusions to Alice Arden's crime.[4] It was recorded in the *Breviat Chronicle* for 1551, in the diary of Henry Machyn, a London merchant-tailor, and in Stow's *Annals of England* (1592, 1631) as well as in Holinshed's *Chronicles* (1577, 1587). Thomas Heywood gives it two lines in his 17-canto poem on the history of the world, *Troia Britannica* (1609), and John Taylor in *The Unnaturall Father* (1621, 1630) invokes it as an instance of God's vengeance on murderers. In addition to the play, which ran to four editions between 1592 and 1633,[5] "[The] complaint and lamentation of Mistresse Arden" was printed in ballad form, probably in 1633.

The official record of the murder was given in the Wardmote Book of Faversham, reprinted in Wine's Revels edition of the play, together with Holinshed's account and the ballad. According to the Wardmote Book, Arden was "heynously" and "shamefully" murdered, and the motive was Alice's intention to marry Mosby, a tailor whom she carnally kept in her own house and fed with delicate meats, with the full knowledge of her husband.[6] The value judgment established here is constant in all the accounts, and the word "shameful" defines the crime in the *Breviat Chronicle*,[7] in Holinshed,[8] on the title page of the first edition of the play, and again in the ballad.[9] What is contested in these re-presentations is not, on the whole, the morality of the murder, but its explanation, its meaning. Specific areas of the story are fore-grounded or reduced, with the effect of modifying the crime's significance. The low social status of Mosby, and Arden's complaisance, for instance, both intensify the disruption of matrimonial conventions, and these elements are variously either accounted for or played down. Arden's role in the story differs considerably from one narrative to another. My concern is not with the truth of the murder, not with an attempt to penetrate beyond the records to an inaccessible "real event," not to offer an "authoritative" interpretation of Alice Arden's crime. Rather, I want to examine the implications of the constant efforts at redefinition.

In Holinshed's analysis Arden was a gentleman, a tall and comely person, and Mosby "a blacke swart man." According to the marginal gloss in the second edition of the *Chronicles,* Alice's irrational preference is an instance of the radical difference between love and lust,[10] and her flagrant defiance of the marriage bond accountable in terms of human villainy: "Thus this wicked woman, with hir complices, most shamefullie murdered hir owne husband, who most entirelie loved hir all his life time."[11] But running through Holinshed's narrative is another account of the murder not wholly consistent with this view of Arden as innocent victim, which emphasizes God's vengeance on his greed for property. In this account Arden's avarice, repeatedly referred to in the story, is finally his undoing. His complaisance is a consequence of his covetousness: "bicause he would not offend hir, and so loose the benefit which he hoped to gaine at some of hir freends hands in bearing with hir lewdnesse, which he might have lost if he should have fallen out with hir: he was contented to winke at hir filthie disorder . . ."[12] After Arden's death, the field where the conspirators had placed his corpse miraculously showed the imprint of his body for two years afterward. This field was Arden's property, and in 1551 he had insisted that the St. Valentine's fair be held there, "so reaping all the gaines to himselfe, and bereaving the towne of that portion which was woont to come to the inhabitants." For this he was bitterly cursed by the people of Faversham.[13] The field itself had been "cruellie" and illegally wrestled from the wife of Richard Read, a sailor, and she too had cursed him, "wishing manie a vengeance to light upon him, and that all the world might woonder on him. Which was thought then to come to passe, when he was thus murdered, and laie in that field from midnight till the morning" on the day of the fair.[14] Again the marginal gloss spells out the moral implications: "God heareth the teares of the oppressed and taketh vengeance: note an example in Arden."[15] The murder is thus part of the providential scheme.

These two versions of Arden—as loving husband and as rapacious landlord—coexist equally uneasily in the play. Here the element of complaisance is much reduced: Arden has grounds for suspicion but not certainty. Mosby's baseness is a constant theme, and underlines Alice's irrationality. But what is new in the play is the parallel between Arden's dubious business deals and Alice's. A good part of the plot is taken up with Alice's negotiations with possible murderers. Michael is to carry out the crime in exchange for Susan Mosby. Clarke is to provide a poison, and subsequently a poisoned picture, in exchange for Susan Mosby. Greene gets £10 and a promise of £20 more, with land to follow, for his "plain dealing" in carrying out the murder (I, 517). Greene subcontracts the work to Black Will and Shakebag for £10. Finally, in desperation, Alice increases her offer to Black Will to £20, and £40 more when Arden is dead. They leave triumphantly with their gold when the work is completed (XIV, 249). Mosby, too, is part of this world of economic individualism, and there are indications that his motive is not love of Alice so much as desire to come by Arden's money (e.g., VIII, 11–44). He quarrels with Alice in terms of "credit," "advantages," "Fortune," and "wealth" (VIII, 80–92). If the play has any explanation to offer of Alice Arden's crime it is social and economic rather than providential. The event is primarily an instance of the breakdown of order—the rape of women and property—which follows when the exchange of contracts in a market economy supplants old loyalties, old obligations, old hierarchies.

But there are elements of the play which this reading leaves out of account. Some of the dialogue between Alice and Mosby invites a response which contradicts the play's explicit project, defined on the title page, of showing "the great malice and dissimulation of a wicked woman, [and] the unsatiable desire of filthie lust." In these speeches it is marriage which is identified as an impediment to true love, and images familiar from the poetry of the period seem to offer the audience a position of some sympathy with Alice's repudiation of the marriage bond:

> ALICE
> Why should he thrust his sickle in our corn,
> Or what hath he to do with thee, my love,
> Or govern me that am to rule myself?
> Forsooth, for credit sake, I must leave thee!
> Nay, he must leave to live that we may love,
> May live, may love; for what is life but love?
> And love shall last as long as life remains,
> And life shall end before my love depart.
> MOSBY
> Why, what's love, without true constancy?
> Like to a pillar built of many stones,
> Yet neither with good mortar well compact
> Nor cement to fasten it in the joints
> But that it shakes with every blast of wind
> And, being touched, straight falls unto the earth
> And buries all his haughty pride in dust.
> No, let our love be rocks of adamant,
> Which time nor place nor tempest can asunder.
> (X.83–99)

The natural and elemental images and the biblical echoes momentarily ennoble Alice's defiance of patriarchy. Early in the play Clarke makes explicit this other face of the crime:

> Let it suffice I know you love him well
> And fain would have your husband made away,
> Wherein, trust me, you show a noble mind,
> That rather than you'll live with him you hate
> You'll venture life and die with him you love.
>
> (I.267–271)

In these instances the play presents Alice Arden's challenge to the institution of marriage as an act of heroism. Alice rejects the metaphysics of presence which guarantees the social enforcement of permanent monogamy, in favor of a free sexuality, unauthorized within the play as a whole, but glimpsed at isolated moments:

> Sweet Mosby is the man that hath my heart;
> And he usurps it, having nought but this,
> That I am tied to him by marriage.
> Love is a god, and marriage is but words;
> And therefore Mosby's title is the best.
> Tush! Whether it be or no, he shall be mine
> In spite of him, of Hymen, and of rites.
>
> (I.98–104)

The ballad, almost certainly derived from the play, redefines the problem yet again. For the first time the woman is the unequivocal subject of the narrative, in contrast to the play, where the title indicates that it is Arden's tragedy rather than Alice's. The ballad reduces the story to two main elements—Alice's love and the series of contracts for the murder. These negotiations are recounted in all their detail within a text of only 192 lines. Arden's rapacity is ignored, and Holinshed's "blacke swart" Mosby becomes a man of "sugred tongue, good shape, and lovely looke" (1. 11). The ballad is a record of contracts made and broken for love. There is no explicit doubt of Alice's wickedness: her "secret dealings" come to light and are duly punished by her death (1. 167). At the same time, a curious formulation, perhaps a slip of the pen, picks up something of the element of ambivalence in the play: "And then by Justice we were straight condemn'd, / Each of us came unto a shameless end . . . " (ll. 165–166). "Shameless" here is unexpected—appropriate to their (impudent) behavior, perhaps, but not to their (disgraceful) execution. On a reading of the word in use during the fifteenth century, "shameless" could mean "free from disgrace" (OED, 3). Perhaps a parapraxis betrays the unconscious of the text, a world well lost for love, and Alice Arden heroic on the scaffold, exposing herself to death through death.

However that may be, these repeated reinterpretations of the events, reproblematizations of the murder, may be read as so many attempts to elicit a definitive meaning for Alice Arden's crime. In each case this definitive meaning remains elusive, in the sense that each text contains elements not accounted for in its over-all project. I want to argue that what is at stake in these contests for the meaning of the murder is marriage itself, but first I should like to draw attention to the prominence given to parallel cases in the period.

III

The existing historical evidence gives no reason to believe that there was a major outbreak of women murdering their husbands in the sixteenth century.[16] What it does suggest, however, is a widespread belief that they were likely to do so. The Essex county records for the Elizabethan period, for instance, reveal no convictions for this crime, but they list several cases of frightened husbands seeking the protection of the courts. In 1574 a Barnston man complained that his wife, "forgetting her duty and obedience as a wife, had sundry times maliciously attempted to bereave her husband of his life, so that he stand in great fear" both of her and of two men from Dunmow, her "adherents," who haunted his house at night.[17] In 1590 a man called Philpott complained that John Chandler, then living with his wife, had given his consent to Philpott's death, and Rowland Gryffyth deposed that he had been hired to carry out the murder.[18] The records of the ecclesiastical courts in the same county include two cases, both in 1597, of men who refused to live with their wives for fear that they would be murdered by them.[19]

When the crime was actually committed, it seems that notoriety instantly followed. In 1573 Anne Sanders (or Saunders) consented to the murder of her husband, a London merchant, by her lover, George Browne. The case rapidly became as widely known as the Arden murder. It was recorded by Arthur Golding in a pamphlet published in the same year and again in 1577; it was probably the subject of an anonymous pamphlet called "A Cruell murder donne in Kent" published in 1577;[20] the story was told by Holinshed and Stow again; and it was recounted by Antony Munday in *A View of Sundry Examples* (1580). Like the Arden case, the Sanders murder elicited a play, *A Warning for Fair Women* (probably ca. 1590) and a ballad, "The wofull lamentacion of mrs. Anne Saunders, which she wrote with her own hand, being prisoner in newgate. Justly condemned to death."[21] In the ballad Anne Sanders begs all women to be warned by her example; the play, unable to account in any other terms for so scandalous a crime, shows Anne, in an allegorical dumb show instigated by the Furies, suddenly torn between chastity and lust, then pledging herself to Browne in a ceremony which evokes the "sacrament prophane in mistery of wine" between Paridell and the adulterous Hellenore.[22]

In 1591 Mistress Page of Plymouth was executed with her lover and two other men for the murder of her husband. A ballad by Thomas Deloney appeared at once, recording "The Lamentation of Mr Pages Wife of Plimouth, who, being forc'd to wed him, consented to his Murder, for the love of G. Strangwidge."[23] Here the ambivalences implicit in the Arden narratives are foregrounded to produce a radical contradiction between sympathy and condemnation. The ballad gives a graphic account of the miseries of enforced marriage:

> My closen eies could not his sight abide;
> My tender youth did lothe his aged side:
> Scant could I taste the meate whereon he fed;
> My legges did lothe to lodge within his bed.
> (ll. 29–32)

At the same time,

> Methinkes the heavens crie vengeance for my fact,
> Methinkes the world condemns my monstrous act,
> Methinkes within my conscience tells me true,
> That for that deede hell fier is my due.
> (ll. 41–44)

In the circumstances it is particularly regrettable that *Page of Plymouth* by Jonson and Dekker, performed by the Admiral's Men in 1599, is now lost, as is *The History of Friar Francis,* produced, according to Henslowe's diary, in 1593/4, though not necessarily for the first time.[24] According to Heywood in 1612, when *The History of Friar Francis* was performed at King's Lynn it had the gratifying effect of inducing an apparently respectable woman in the audience to confess that seven years before she had poisoned her husband for love of a gentleman in precisely the same way as the protagonist of the play. Heywood is here writing in defense of the moral efficacy of stage plays, and it is worth noting that of the three instances he cites of the providential operation of the drama, two concern women murdering their husbands. In the second case it was the method of murder shown on the stage which caused "a woman of great gravity" to shriek loudly, and after several days of torment to confess that she had driven a nail into the temples of her husband twelve years before. She was duly tried, condemned, and burned.[25]

IV

According to John Taylor, writing in 1621, *"Arden of Feversham, and Page of Plimmouth,* both their Murders are fresh in memory, and the fearfull ends of their Wives and their Ayders in those bloudy actions will never be forgotten."[26] The prominence allotted to these cases, the suspicion which seems to have been prevalent in Essex in the period, and Heywood's instances of the salutory effects of stage plays in bringing such crimes to light, all point to a preoccupation with the possibility of women murdering their husbands which is not accounted for in any of the individual texts I have discussed. In *Arden of Faversham* Alice Arden defines her problem specifically in terms of the institutional regulation of sexuality by marriage:

> nothing could enforce me to the deed
> But Mosby's love. Might I without control
> Enjoy thee still, then Arden should not die;
> But, seeing I cannot, therefore let him die.
> (I. 273–276)

It is a contest for the control of sexuality in the period which throws marriage into crisis and precipitates the instability of the institution which is evident in crimes like Alice Arden's.

The history of marriage in the Middle Ages is a history of an effort to regulate sexuality by confining it within a framework of permanent monogamy. From the twelfth century onward the Church gradually extended its control over marriage, making efforts to contain instances of divorce and bigamy by urging with increasing insistence the public solemnization of matrimony after due reading of the banns on consecutive Sundays.[27] Since at the same time private marriage in the presence of witnesses was held to be valid and binding,[28] it was easy enough to produce just cause or impediment after the event. However, the banns were no guarantee against bigamy, since they were easily evaded by those who had anything to fear. In consequence, the process of taking control was slow and laborious, so that in 1540 it was still the case that bigamy was widespread, and that "no mariage coulde be so surely knytt and bounden but it shulde lye in either of the parties power and arbitre . . . to prove a precontracte a kynnerede an alliance or a carnall knowledge to defeate the same . . ."[29] Many of the cases which came before the ecclesiastical courts depended on such ingenuities, but Mi-

chael M. Sheehan finds, after investigating the late fourteenth-century
register of the consistory court of the Bishop of Ely, that there at least
"the court was primarily a body for the proof and defence of marriage
rather than an instrument of easy annulment."[30] The commitment of
the court to the stability of marriage above all other considerations
may be illustrated by one of the cases Sheehan cites. The marriage
between John Poynant and Joan Swan was annulled on the grounds of
the husband's impotence. Joan married again, and John took up with
Isabel Pybbel. When Isabel became pregnant John prepared to marry
her, but the court investigated the matter and found that, since John
was apparently not impotent after all, his marriage to Joan Swan
should be restored. John protested, claiming affinity within the forbidden degrees between Joan and Isabel, but the court was not impressed,
and the original marriage was eventually reinstated.[31]

The Anglican church took over on behalf of the sovereign this effort
to control the institution of marriage through the ecclesiastical courts,
but not without a struggle which generated a high degree of uncertainty
about the nature and permanence of marriage. The introduction of
registers of births, marriages, and deaths in 1538 was a move toward
population control, but at the same time the Reformation introduced
a liberalization of marriage which found a focus in a debate about
divorce that remained legally unresolved, apart from a brief interlude
during the Commonwealth, until the nineteenth century.[32]

The Catholic church had permitted separation *a mensa et thoro*
(from bed and board) for adultery, cruelty, apostasy, or heresy, and
divorce *a vinculo matrimonii* on the basis either of impotence or of a
prior impediment to valid marriage on grounds of consanguinity, affinity, or precontract. The act of 1540 attempted to abolish precontract
as grounds for divorce, but had no practical effect. Meanwhile, most
of the newly Protestant states had introduced divorce with remarriage
for the innocent party in cases of adultery and desertion. Similar legislation was urged in England, and was incorporated in the *Reformatio
Legum Ecclesiasticarum* of 1552. This was defeated in the House of
Commons, but the divorce provision had been sanctioned independently, when a commission under Cranmer had approved the remarriage of the divorced Northampton in 1548, a decision that was confirmed by Parliament in 1552. In practice, however, the ecclesiastical
courts largely refused to put the law into operation, and in consequence
the position of marriage remained extremely confused and controver-
sial for the rest of the century. The divorce debate reached a high point
in the 1590s, with the result that in the Canons of 1597 Convocation
declared all remarriage after divorce illegal. These were not sanctioned
by Elizabeth, but the principle was reiterated in the Canons of 1604

which were approved by James I, though without silencing the controversy.[33]

The importance of the divorce debate lies in its polarization of
conflicting definitions of marriage. Broadly, the Anglican position was
that marriage was indissoluble, that couples were joined by God for
the avoidance of fornication and the procreation of children, and
that there was no remedy but patience for marital disharmony and
discontent. The position of the radical Protestants is familiar from
Milton's divorce tracts, which carry the Puritan arguments to their
logical climax. Equally broadly, the Puritans held that marriage was a
civil covenant, a thing indifferent to salvation, that it depended on
consent, and that where this was lacking the couple could not be said
to be joined by God, and could therefore justly be put asunder. The
Reformers varied in the causes of divorce they were prepared to admit.
Only Milton gave real prominence to discord as a cause, while Henry
Smith, at the other extreme though still within the pro-divorce lobby,
recognized divorce for adultery but vigorously repudiated incompati-
bility as grounds:

> If they might bee separated for discorde, some would make a com-
> moditie of strife; but now they are not best to be contentious, for this
> law will hold their noses together, till weariness make them leave
> struggling, like two spaniels which are coupled in a chaine, at last
> they learne to goe together, because they may not goe asunder.[34]

Not all the Reformers were so optimistic about the couple learning
to go together. According to Martin Bucer, whose *De Regno Christi*
was addressed to Edward VI when the author was Professor of Divinity
at Cambridge, the Church's refusal to permit divorce compelled it to
tolerate "whordoms and adulteries, and worse things then these,"
"throwing men headlong into these evils."[35] "Neither," he argued,
"can God approve that to the violation of this holy league (which is
violated as soon as true affection ceases and is lost,) should be added
murder . . ."[36] John Rainolds, writing in 1597, insists that if divorce is
forbidden crimes like Alice Arden's are bound to follow: a husband
may be forced to live in permanent suspicion, or worse—

> And how can he choose but live still in feare & anguish of minde,
> least shee add drunckennesse to thirst, & murder to adultery: I meane
> least sher serve him as *Clytemnestra* did *Agamemnon, Livia* did
> *Drusus* as *Mrs. Arden* did her husband?[37]

V

There is some evidence for the bitterness of the struggle. John Dove, who preached a sermon against divorce in 1601, records that many people found his view offensive, "as unseasonable for the time, and unpleasing to the auditory."[38] Rainolds wrote his plea for divorce in 1597, but explains in a letter to Pye published in 1606 that the Archbishop of Canterbury at that time "thought it not meete to be printed: as containing dangerous doctrine." He urges Pye to cut out any references to him (Rainolds) in his own argument if he wants to get into print, especially since the Canons of 1604 have hardened the orthodox line.[39] Rainolds's own *Defence of the Judgment of the Reformed Churches* was published in 1609. The Archbishop's censorship seems to have been evenhanded, since at about the same time he also discouraged Edmund Bunny from publishing his case against divorce—in order to avoid controversy, on the grounds that he had already "staied" one of the contrary persuasion.[40] Bunny's book appeared in 1610. Later William Whately argued for divorce on grounds of desertion as well as adultery in books published in 1617 and 1624. Whately was brought before the Court of High Commission, and promptly reverted to the Anglican doctrine of the indissolubility of marriage.[41]

Even between the radicals there was considerable sectarianism on this issue. Milton, of course, encountered a good deal of controversy and was denounced by his fellow Puritans for his divorce pamphlets.[42] And at the very beginning of the debate an interesting piece of sleight of hand shows how delicate the whole issue must have been. In 1541 Miles Coverdale's translation of Bullinger's treatise on marriage was published as *The Christen State of Matrimonye*. Primarily a plea for marriage as a union of minds, and a corresponding repudiation of the Catholic doctrine of celibacy as a way of perfection, this included a chapter recommending divorce not only for adultery but also for "lyke and greater occasions."[43] *The Christen State of Matrimonye* was remarkably popular. Three new editions appeared within five years, and two more before the end of the century. Meanwhile, in 1542, there appeared *The Golden Boke of christen matrimonye* "newly set forth in English by Theodore Basille." "Theodore Basille" was Thomas Becon, and *The Golden Boke* was actually Coverdale's translation of Bullinger again, with four chapters silently omitted, including the one on divorce.

The contest for the meaning of marriage cannot be isolated from the political struggles which characterize the century between the Reformation and the English revolution. Both sides make explicit the parallel between the family and the state, marriage and the monarchy. "A house-holde is as it were a little common-wealth;"[44] "A Familie, is a naturall and simple Society of certaine persons, having mutual relationship one to another, under the private government of one."[45] At one extreme Milton argues for liberty within marriage as directly analogous to liberty in the commonwealth:

> He who marries, intends as little to conspire his own ruine, as he that swears Allegiance: and as a whole people is in proportion to an ill Government, so is one man to an ill mariage. If they against any authority, Covnant, or Statute, may by the soveraign edict of charity, save not only their lives, but honest liberties from unworthy bondage, as well may he against any private Covnant, which hee never enter'd to his mischief, redeem himself from unsupportable disturbances to honest peace, and just contentment.[46]

And if this position was not made explicit in the radical treatises before 1642, nonetheless it was identified by Anglican orthodoxy as implicit in the Puritan arguments. According to Bunny, divorce can lead only to "disorder."[47] Marriage cannot be dissolved at will any more than can the bond between master and servant, parent and child, "the Prince and the Subject." And for this reason, "the more heed should bee taken, that no such gap should be opened to any, as whereby the looser sort, when they should get their desire in this, should cast about to obtaine the like in other things also of greater consequence."[48] Dove, whose name entirely belies his political position, argues strenuously that,

> As when a servant runneth from his M. the chaine of bondage doth pursue him, and bring him back againe to his maister, so when a woman leaveth her husband, the lawe of Matrimony is as a chaine to draw her back againe to her husband . . . [49]

The libertines who believe in divorce pervert the scriptures for their own licentious ends, "Even as others will proove rebellion and high treason out of the scriptures, that the people are above their King."[50] The parallel between domestic patriarchy and authoritarian monarchy is a commonplace of the seventeenth century, and reaches its most notorious formulation, of course, in Robert Filmer's *Patriarcha*, written during the 1640s.[51]

Alice Arden, held in the chain of bondage which is marriage, in a period when liberty is glimpsed but not authorized, is caught up in a struggle larger than her chroniclers recognize. But it may be the political significance of Arden's assassination which causes Holinshed to identify Alice Arden's crime as marking the border between private and public, pamphlet and history.

VI

There is an indication in *Arden of Faversham* that in opting for Mosby in place of Arden, a freely chosen sexuality based on concord in place of the constraints of the institution of permanent marriage, Alice Arden may be committing herself to a form of power more deadly still, and less visible. Mosby's individualism is precisely that:

> Yet Mistress Arden lives; but she's myself,
> And holy church rites makes us two but one.
> But what for that I may not trust you, Alice?
> You have supplanted Arden for my sake
> And will extirpen me to plant another.
> 'Tis fearful sleeping in a serpent's bed,
> And I will cleanly rid my hands of her.
> But here she comes, and I must flatter her . . .
> (VIII.37–44)

The episode could be read as an allegory of the transition to the effective nuclear family, itself a mechanism of regulation more far-reaching but less visible than the repressive ecclesiastical courts. Arden's absolute rights over Alice are clear, and his threats are directed not against his wife but against the man who means to rob him of her, for which he

> Shall on the bed which he thinks to defile
> See his dissevered joints and sinews torn
> Whilst on the planchers pants his weary body,
> Smeared in the channels of his lustful blood.
> (I. 40–43)

This overt power and violence give way in Mosby's version of marriage to distrust and surveillance veiled by flattery; in an individualist society of "equals" authoritarian modes of control are replaced by reciprocal fear between partners within the social body. Further, flattery and death are the metaphorical destiny of the wife in the new family. Her standing improves (though always in subjection to her husband) but at the cost of new and more insidious forms of control.

Puritan marriage, founded on consent, is "appointed by God him-selfe, to be the fountaine and seminary of all other sorts and kinds of life, in the Common-wealth and in the Church."[52] To this end the family becomes quite explicitly an ideological apparatus, "a schoole wherein the first principles and grounds of government and subjection are learned: whereby men are fitted to greater matters in Church or Common-wealth."[53] In Puritan definitions of marriage and the family as "the Fountain and Seminary of good subjects,"[54] it is made very clear that "the holy and righteous government thereof, is a direct meane for the good ordering both of Church and Commonwealth; yea that the Lawes thereof beeing rightly informed, and religiously observed, are aveailable to prepare and dispose men to the keeping of order in other governments."[55] To ensure that the family becomes an adequate model and source of good government, the treatises recommend family prayers, grace before meals, keeping the sabbath, the education of the children and the servants, and the inculcation of the fundamental principles of law and order. The family, separated from the public realm of politics, nonetheless becomes a microcosm of it and, by practice and by precept, a training ground for the ready acceptance of the power relations established in the social body:

> For this first Societie is as it were the Schoole, wherein are taught and learned the principles of authoritie and subjection. And looke as the superior that faileth in his charge, will proove uncapable of publike imployment, so the inferiour, who is not framed to a course of Oeconomicall subjection, wil hardly undergoe the yoake of Civill obedience.[56]

The "liberalism" of the Reformers implies a constant scrutiny of marriage for "fitnes of mind and disposition,"[57] since harmony and concord are the precondition of a realm of hearth and home regulated from within. Vigilantly protected from sedition, and isolated from public and political affairs, the family is held in place in the social body as a model of the proper distribution of authority and submission, and thus the fountain and seminary of good subjects.

Read as a political event, Alice Arden's crime was a defiance of absolutism and, in common with the constant reproblematization of such crimes in the period, as well as the great numbers of "divorces" established in the sixteenth century without recourse to the civil or ecclesiastical authorities,[58] it constitutes evidence of the instability of central control at the time. Within a century of Arden's death the absolute power was to have been supplanted and Charles I executed in the name of the liberty of the people of England. The concomitant of this liberty was the construction of the affective nuclear family as an invisible mechanism of correction and control. The chain of bondage had given way to a net of power.

VII

The century following Alice Arden's crime was one of crisis—economic, ideological, and political. With hindsight it is possible to interpret many of the events of this period as elements in the social upheaval which found a focus in the civil war of the 1640s. On this reading of the period, the institution most evidently in crisis was the monarchy, but it is also apparent that challenges to authority and authoritarianism were delivered in a number of spheres, many of them more obviously remote from the institution of monarchy than the more explicitly analogous institution of the family. Clearly, such a reading of the history of this period, available to us retrospectively, was only partly accessible in the period itself, and it is this which accounts for the repeated attempts to define and redefine Alice Arden's crime, and which explains why it was so important and so impossible to furnish it with a final meaning. The assassination of Arden is never justified, but it is variously identified as a part of God's providential plan, as a tragedy, as the effect of social and economic change, or as an act of unauthorized heroism, a noble transgression of an absolute law. The re-presentations of the crime are (sometimes contradictory, never neutral) contributions to a discursive struggle for the meaning of resistance to absolutism. *Arden of Faversham* is one of the documents in this struggle, perhaps a relatively complex analysis, but by no means an isolated instance of the attempt to make sense of insurrection.

Meanwhile, the divorce debate, reaching a crisis in the decade which also produced three plays on the theme I have discussed, in the final years of Elizabeth's apparently successful efforts to hold at bay the pressures for social change, is the site of a discursive contest between distinct modes of social control. Its relevance to my argument is not simply that it provides a context for our understanding of the plays, but that it enables us to perceive more sharply what is at stake in this contest. Offering a promise of freedom from the "chain" (the recurring metaphor for authoritarianism) of marriage, the radical position on divorce leads in reality to a new mode of control, no longer centralized and overt, but internalized and invisible. The new family of the seventeenth century, still under "the government of one," remains a place in which power is exercised privately in the interests of public order. Alice Arden's bid for freedom, as the play implies, would have led, had it succeeded, to a new form of subjection, both for the woman within the family and for the family within the state. No text of the 1590s could formulate this point in these terms. Indeed, the explicit identification of the family as a mechanism of social control probably has its tentative beginnings in the nineteenth century. Nonetheless, Mosby's

threat that he will subject Alice to surveillance, flattery, and death
indicates a glimpse in this text of an issue which is more complex than
the simple opposition between authority and freedom, control and
consent.

Modern marriage, modern domestic patriarchy, and the modern
family as an ideological apparatus were produced in the struggles,
dispersed across a range of institutions and practices, of the sixteenth
and seventeenth centuries. In this sense the discursive history of Alice
Arden's crime is a significant part of the history of the present.

Notes

1. J. W. Ebsworth, ed., *The Roxburghe Ballads,* Vol. VIII, pt. 1 (Hertford, Eng.:
   Ballad Society, 1895), p. 48.

2. Printed in M. L. Wine, ed., *The Tragedy of Master Arden of Faversham,* The Revels
   Plays (London: Methuen 1973), p. 148. I have silently modernized all Renaissance
   typography. All references to the play are to this edition.

3. Wine argues for a date between 1588 and 1591, *ibid.,* p. xlv.

4. For details see Wine, *Tragedy of Master Arden,* pp. xxxvii–xxxviii.

5. *Ibid.,* p. xix–xxi.

6. *Ibid.,* pp. 160–161.

7. *Ibid.,* p. xxxvii.

8. *Ibid.,* p. 155.

9. *Ibid.,* p. 169.

10. *Ibid.,* p. 148.

11. *Ibid.,* p. 155.

12. *Ibid.,* p. 149.

13. *Ibid.,* p. 157.

14. *Ibid.,* p. 159.

15. *Ibid.*

16. See, e.g., F. G. Emmison, *Elizabethan Life: Disorder* (Chelmsford, Eng.: Essex
    County Council, 1970); C. S. Weiner, "Sex Roles and Crime in Late Elizabethan
    Hertfordshire," *Journal of Social History,* VIII (1975), 38–60. Weiner gives no
    instances at all. Emmison lists 131 cases of murder brought before the Essex county
    courts in the Elizabethan period. In three of these (or possibly two, if the case of
    the Great Wakering woman mentioned on p. 149 is the same as the one listed on
    p. 150), women were charged with poisoning their husbands. In each case the
    woman was acquitted, which implies (since acquittals, except in cases of employers
    murdering their servants, are rare) that the evidence must have been very slender.

17. Emmison, *Elizabethan Life: Disorder,* p. 162.

18. *Ibid.,* p. 199.

19. F. G. Emmison, *Elizabethan Life: Morals and the Church Courts* (Chelmsford,
    Eng.: Essex County Council, 1973), p. 162. Surprisingly, there were only two

instances of women protesting that they were similarly frightened of their husbands, and one of these had already been subject to marital violence.

20. Joseph H. Marshburn, "*A Cruell Murder Done in Kent* and Its Literary Manifestations," SP, XLVI (1949), 131–140.

21. Hyder Rollins, ed., *Old English Ballads 1553–1625* (Cambridge: Cambridge Univ. Press, 1920), pp. 340–348.

22. Charles Dale Cannon, ed., *A Warning for Fair Women* (The Hague: Mouton, 1975), II. 803–815 s.d. Cf. *The Faerie Queene,* III.ix.30. It is worth noting that, according to Golding's account. Anne Drurie, Browne's accomplice, must have been suspected of poisoning her own husband, since she denied the allegation on the scaffold (see Canon, p. 224).

23. F. O. Mann, ed., *The Works of Thomas Deloney* (Oxford: Clarendon Press, 1912), pp. 482–485. I am grateful to Margot Heinemann for drawing my attention to this ballad.

24. H. H. Adams, *English Domestic or Homiletic Tragedy. 1575–1642* (New York: Columbia Univ. Press, 1943), pp. 193–194.

25. Thomas Heywood, *An Apology for Actors* (London, 1612), sig. G 1^v–2^v.

26. John Taylor, *Works* (London, 1630), p. 140.

27. Michael M. Sheehan, "The Formation and Stability of Marriage in Fourteenth-Century England: Evidence of an Ely Register," MS XXXIII (1971), 228–263; G. E. Howard, *A History of Matrimonial Institutions,* 3 vols. (Chicago: Univ. of Chicago Press, 1904), I, 361.

28. Lawrence Stone, *The Family, Sex and Marriage in England, 1500–1800* (London: Weidenfeld and Nicolson, 1977), p. 31; Howard, *Matrimonal Institutions,* I, 336 ff.; Sheehan, "Formation and Stability of Marriage," p. 253.

29. Preamble to 32 Hen. VIII. ca. 38, cited by C. L. Powell, *English Domestic Relations 1487–1653* (New York: Columbia Univ. Press, 1917), p. 62.

30. Sheehan, "Formation and Stability of Marriage," p. 263.

31. *Ibid.,* p. 261.

32. The Cromwellian Marriage Act of 1653 placed the whole matter in the hands of the civil magistrates but gave no indication of the possible grounds for divorce. This legislation was not re-enacted after the Restoration (Powell, *English Domestic Relations,* pp. 99–100).

33. For an account of the legal position see Howard, *History of Matrimonial Institutions,* II, 76–85. Stone, *Family, Sex and Marriage,* pp. 37–41; Powell, *English Domestic Relations,* pp. 61–100; Ernest Sirluck, ed., *The Complete Prose Works of John Milton* (London: Oxford Univ. Press, 1959), II, 145–146.

34. Henry Smith, *A Preparative to Marriage* (London, 1591), p. 108.

35. Milton's translation, *Complete Prose Works,* ed. Sirluck, II, 447.

36. *Ibid.,* p. 470.

37. John Rainolds, *A Defence of the Judgment of the Reformed Churches* (London, 1609), p. 88.

38. John Dove, *Of Divorcement* (London, 1601), Preface.

39. Reproduced in John Howson, *Uxore dismissa propter Fornicationem aliam non licet superinducere* (Oxford, 1606).

40. Edmund Bunny, *Of Divorce for Adulterie and Marrying againe* (Oxford, 1610), Advertisement to the Reader.

41. William and Malleville Haller, "The Puritan Art of Love," *HLQ*, V (1941–1942), 235–272, 267–268.

42. Christopher Hill, *Milton and the English Revolution* (London: Faber, 1977), pp. 131–132.

43. H. Bullinger, *The Christen State of Matrimonye* (London, 1541), fol. lxxvii.

44. Robert Cleaver and John Dod, *A Godlie Forme of Householde Government* (London, 1612), p. 13. The first edition of this popular work appeared in 1598. Cf. William Gouge, *Of Domesticall Duties* (1622), pp. 16–17, cited by Haller, "Puritan Art of Love," p. 246.

45. William Perkins, *Christian Oeconomie, Works* (Cambridge, Eng., 1618), III, 669–700. *Christian Oeconomie* was written in Latin in 1590 and translated by Thomas Pickering in 1609.

46. Sirluck, *Complete Prose Works of Milton*, II, 229.

47. Bunny, *Of Divorce*, p. 161.

48. *Ibid.*, p. 52.

49. Dove, *Of Divorcement*, p. 33.

50. *Ibid.*, p. 51.

51. Gordon J. Schochet, *Patriarchalism in Political Thought* (New York: Basic Books, 1975).

52. Perkins, *Christian Oeconomie*, p. 671.

53. Gouge, *Of Domesticall Duties;* Haller, "Puritan Art of Love," p. 246.

54. Sirluck, *Complete Prose Works of Milton*, II, 447.

55. Pickering, in Perkins, *Christian Oeconomie*, Epistle Dedicatory.

56. *Ibid.*

57. Sirluck, *Complete Prose Works of Milton*, II, 605.

58. Powell, *English Domestic Relations*, pp. 61–62, 69–70.

15

Workshop and/as Playhouse
THE SHOEMAKER'S HOLIDAY (1599)

David Scott Kastan

"Nothing is proposed but mirth," Thomas Dekker assures his readers in the dedicatory epistle to *The Shoemaker's Holiday*. "I present you here with a merry conceited comedy," he says, a play that had recently been acted before the Queen, that ever enthusiastic though hypersensitive theatergoer, whose pleasure Dekker presents as evidence of the innocence of his offering: "the mirth and pleasant matter by her Highness graciously accepted, being indeed no way offensive."

Certainly critics have generally taken Dekker at his word. We are told again and again that the play is "indeed no way offensive," a triumph of middle-class vitality and generosity.[1] Its moral anomalies, if acknowledged at all, are subordinated to the genial energies of the exuberant Simon Eyre and his shoemakers. "In *The Shoemaker's Holiday*," writes Joel Kaplan, "faith is encouraged in the energy of a madcap lord of mirth who can wonderfully and magically revitalize a commonwealth."[2]

But, of course, anomalies do exist: class antagonisms between Lincoln and the Lord Mayor frame the action; Rafe comes back wounded from the war in France, while the aristocratic Lacy deserts yet is eventually knighted; and Eyre's fortune is made in a sharp business practice in which at very least he is guilty of impersonating a city official. But we are never asked to dwell on these discords. The romantic logic of the plot overwhelms the social and economic tensions that are revealed: Rafe and Jane are reunited, Lacy and Rose are wed, and class conflicts dissolve in the harmonies celebrated and confirmed in the Shrove Tuesday banquet in Leadenhall.

Though critics have often mistaken its vitality for verisimilitude, certainly the play cannot be understood as a realistic portrait of Elizabethan middle-class life. It is a realistic portrait only of Elizabethan middle-class dreams—a fantasy of class fulfillment that would erase the tensions and contradictions created by the nascent capitalism of the late sixteenth century. The comic form offers itself as an ideological resolution to the social problems the play engages. Social dislocations are rationalized and contained in a reassuring vision of coherence and community.

When, for example, Lacy enters disguised as Hans, looking for work as a shoemaker, Eyre dismisses him: "Let him pass, let him vanish! We have journeymen enow" (I.v.50–51). But the shoemakers themselves insist that he be taken on: "hire him, good master, that I may learn some gibble-gabble," says the irrepressible Firk, "twill make us work the faster" (I.v.47–49); and Hodge threatens to quit: "if such a man as he cannot find work, Hodge is not for you" (I.v.60–61). In the face of the wishes of his men Eyre relents: "By the Lord of Ludgate, I love my men as my life. . . . Hodge, if he want work I'll hire him" (I.v.69–71).

In reality, relations between English craftsmen and immigrant workers were hardly so supportive. Early in the century, antagonism toward alien workers erupted in the Evil May Day riots of 1517. Later, a formal complaint was registered in 1571 against immigrants, asserting that "the custome of the citty, and Acts of Councell in the citty are that no man being a stranger to the liberties of the city shall use by handicraftes within the cittie." The complaint asked that existing legislation be enforced to enjoin alien workers from practicing "any manuall trade within this kingdome except they were brought uppe seven yeares apprentices to the trade according to that statute," and added smugly, "which none or very fewe of them have beene."[3] In 1593, officers of the Cordwainers' Company undertook unauthorized "searches" of the precinct of St. Martin's le Grand, where foreign workers had established themselves. The inhabitants protested to Lord Burghley; "Burghley's lawyers," however, as Valerie Pearl writes, "upheld the right of the Livery Company to enter the liberty 'and search alone,' but they replied in diplomatic tones: it would be convenient for the officer of the liberty to accompany the 'search' and this could be obtained by writing to the Lord Mayor."[4] In 1593 and 1595 there was rioting as anxieties about foreign workers worsened in the face of the disastrously sharp rise in rents and food prices which left perhaps half the population of urban laborers, according to one estimate, living "in direst poverty and squalor, on the edge of destitution and starvation."[5] Such economic conditions were unlikely to breed enthusiasm for the "new come in" Dutch shoemakers, whose number by 1599, the year of Dekker's play, had swelled to 131, well over a quarter of the total number paying the required quarterage to the Cordwainers' Company, and about the same number as the Company's 152 yeomen.[6]

Dekker, however, idealizes the actual atomization of the culture in a fantasy of social cohesion and respect. He knew the realities of urban poverty (having himself been jailed for debt in 1598) and the increasing inability of the city or state to conceive effective schemes of relief.[7] The guild structure that once served to unite craftsmen in a fraternity devoted to the welfare and security of its membership became increasingly hierarchical and entrepreneurial, converting work from a system of solidarity to a system of exchange. In *The Seven Deadly Sins of London* (1606), Dekker complains that the guilds "that were ordained to be communities, had lost their first privilege, and were now turned monopolies,"[8] structures no longer of communal association but of commercial advantage.

Historical tensions that did exist are effectively erased by the play, though the erasure cannot go unnoticed by an audience in 1599 who lived the social formations that Dekker idealizes. If this is a fantasy it knows itself as such, and therefore cannot help reveal the contradictions it apparently would repress, transforming its discontinuities into a fiction of social and economic harmony. For example, Eyre makes his fortune by buying the cargo of a ship owner who "dares not show his head" (II.iii.17) in London. Eyre exploits the disadvantage of the shipowner to become a "huge gainer" (II.iii.21) in a triumph of capitalist enterprise which permits enormous profit and negligible risk. It is the dream of the Renaissance profiteer, like Sir Lionel Cranfield who, in 1607, wrote to Sir Arthur Ingram: "One rule I desire may be observed between you and me, which is that neither of us seek to advance our estate by the other's loss, but that we may join faithfully to raise our fortunes by such casualties as this stirring age shall afford."[9] Eyre raises his fortune by one such casualty.

The play, however, refuses to engage any moral concern that the episode might elicit. Eyre's social ambitions (clear in Deloney's *Gentle Craft*, where Eyre says: "Beleeue me, wife . . . I was studying how to make my selfe Lord Maior and thee a Lady"[10]) are here successfully deflected onto Margery. Even Eyre's appearance to the captain dressed as an alderman, with "a seal ring" and in "a guarded gown and a damask cassock" (II.iii.103–04), is presented not as cunning hypocrisy but as proleptic propriety: as Hodge says, "now you look like yourself, master" (II.iii.112).

Dekker's strategy of idealization becomes still clearer when we examine the purchase itself. Eyre obtains a cargo of "sugar, civet, almonds, cambric, and a towsand towsand tings" (II.iii.129–30), as the Dutch skipper says. These "tings," however, are precisely the luxuries that both English moralists and economists decried. The moralists were dismayed by "our present riot and luxury in diet and apparell,"[11] in the words of the Berkeley's historian, John Smyth; and the economists were disturbed by the outflow of capital, which might have revitalized the English economy, in the pursuit of unnecessary imports. Thus the Elizabethan merchant Gerrard de Malynes, in *The Canker of England's Commonwealth* (1601), lamented the "ouerbalancing of forraine commodities with our home commodities, which to supply or counteruaile draweth away our treasure and readie monie, to the great losse of the commonweale":

> our merchants, perceiuing a small gaine and sometimes none at all to be had vpon our home commodities, do buy and seek their gaines vpon forraine commodities . . . wherein although they may be gainers, yet the Realme generally beareth the losse, and they feed still vpon their mothers belly.[12]

"To export things of necessity," complained Thomas Fuller some forty years later, "and to bring in foreign needless toys, makes a rich merchant and a poor kingdom."[13]

Dekker's play, however, offers us a rich merchant and a rich kingdom, joyfully dispelling whatever fears might attach themselves to Eyre's speculation. Firk immediately domesticates the purchase, defusing the moralists' worry about luxury: "O sweet master! O sweet wares: prunes, almonds, sugar-candy, carrot-roots, turnips!" (II.iii.132–33). And the improbably "good copen" (II.iii.5), the extraordinary bargain that Eyre achieves, minimizes the expenditure of "readie monie" that mercantiles feared. Dekker's audience is left free to enjoy Eyre's success, untroubled by the anxieties that actual speculation in 1599 might be expected to arouse in a society increasingly aware of its economic instability and its heterogeneous elements and interests.

Dekker confronts the increasingly complex social and economic organization of pre-industrialized England but converts it into a comforting fiction of reciprocity and respect. Even the availability of the Dutch cargo is determined by an emotional rather than an economic bond: Hodge reports that the Dutch skipper, "for the love he bears to Hans, offers my master a bargain in the commodities" (II.iii.18–19). The skipper's "love" is presented as the necessary precondition of Eyre's profit. Significantly, Hammon's unsuitability for success in the comic world is finally revealed as he reverses the terms of this exchange, conceiving of profit as predominant over love: "here in fair gold / Is twenty pounds," he tells Rafe; "I'll give it for thy Jane" (V.ii.78–79). His offer literalizes Jane's fear that "many . . . make it even a very trade to woo" (IV.i.64). But Rafe, of course, refuses: "dost thou think a Shoemaker is so base to be a bawd to his own wife for commodity?" (V.ii.84–85).

The reconfirmation of Rafe and Jane's marriage asserts the power of love over hostile social and economic forces that threaten to divide and degrade, and their love is affecting precisely because it succeeds in the face of such powerful threats. The blocking action is not primarily the suit of Hammon but a society in which Jane can actually be lost in the burgeoning urban density of London and Rafe apparently killed—though in fact only wounded—in a war in which the poor serve unwillingly and anonymously. The report of an English victory in France announces that

> Twelve thousand of the Frenchmen that day died,
> Four thousand English, and no man of name
> But Captain Hyam and young Ardington.

"Two gallant gentlemen," laments Lincoln; "I knew them well" (II.iv.8–11). But four thousand Englishmen without name, like Rafe, lie dead in France unremarked.

Impressment and casualty reports would not be matters of indifference to the Rose Theatre audience in 1599. For three years, beginning in 1596, the number of impressed soldiers had begun to increase dramatically as the Irish situation worsened demanding reinforcements and reports reached England of renewed Spanish invasion plans.[14] By the summer of 1599 the fear of imminent Spanish attack grew acute. On August 1, John Chamberlain wrote from London to Dudley Carleton in Ostend:

> the alarme whereof begins to ringe in our eares here at home [is] as shrill as in your beseiged towne: for upon what groundes or goode intelligence I know not but we are all in a hurle as though the ennemie were at our doores. The Quenes shippes are all making redy, but this towne is commaunded to furnish 16 of theyre best ships to defend the river and 10000 men, whereof 6000 to be trayned presently and every man els to have his armes redy.[15]

But Rafe's safe return, after he has been reported dead, is a welcome fantasy of wish-fulfillment for a nation wearied and worried by war. Even his wound, if it testifies to the real dangers of combat, accommodates Dekker's strategy of idealization, for it serves to prove the ability of "the gentle craft" to protect and provide for its practitioners. "Now I want limbs to get wheron to feed," Rafe cries; but Hodge will have none of his self-pity: "Hast thou not hands, man? Thou shall never see

a shoemaker want bread, though he have three fingers on a hand"
(III.ii.78–80). Still able to function as a shoemaker, Rafe can make a
living and make a life in a community of concern, and when Jane is
found and recommits herself to him, her love confirms his place in the
comic world and the irrelevance of his wound.

The reaffirmation of Rafe and Jane's marriage redeems the alienation
of working-class lives, discharging the threats of social disintegration
and neutralizing the temptations of materialism. Denying Hammon's
suit, Jane turns to Rafe:

> Thou art my husband, and these humble weeds
> Makes thee more beautiful than all his wealth.
> Therefore I will but put off his attire,
> Returning it to the owner's hand.
>
> (V.ii.58–61)

But the play reveals an ambivalent fascination with money and property. The shoemakers insist that she not return what she has been given.
"Not a rag, Jane," declares Hodge: "The law's on our side: he that
sows in another man's ground forfeits his harvest" (V.ii.63–64). And
similarly, after Rafe indignantly rejects Hammon's offer of money for
Jane, Hammon presents it as a gift: "in lieu of that great wrong I
offered thy Jane / To Jane and thee I give that twenty pound" (V.ii.91–
92). Jane gets to keep the rich clothing Hammon gives her, and Rafe
gets the twenty pounds he rejects; improbably, choice in this world
does not involve loss.

Such denial is Dekker's characteristic strategy of "resolving" social
contradiction. On two other occasions money is offered in exchange
for the betrayal of loyalties: on each, integrity is powerfully asserted
but again no one is forced to suffer its consequences. At the beginning
of the play, Otley and his "brethren" give Lacy twenty pounds, nomi-
nally to "approve our loves / We bear unto my Lord, your uncle here"
(I.i.67–68); Lincoln, however, understands the real function of the gift:

> To approve your loves to me? No, subtlety!
> Nephew, that twenty pound he doth bestow
> For joy to rid you from his daughter Rose.
>
> (I.i.71–73)

Like Hammon's offer, also of "twenty pound," Otley's assumes that
emotions can be purchased or compensated in a commercial exchange.
But in the wish-fulfilling logic of the play, Otley's challenge to the
emotional authenticity of the relationship he opposes, like Hammon's,

turns a would-be purchase price into a gift; and Lacy, like Rafe, gets to keep the twenty pound (which he gives to Askew) and stay with the woman he loves.

Again, in Act IV, Otley tries to buy a betrayal, offering Firk an angel to tell him where Lacy, disguised as Hans, has gone. Firk replies indignantly:

> No point! Shall I betray my brother? No! Shall I prove
> Judas to Hans? No! Shall I cry treason to my
> corporation? No! I shall be firked and yerked then. But
> give me your money: your angel shall tell you.
> (IV.v.97–100)

Firk takes the money, but does not betray either his "brother" or his "corporation"; he sends Otley to St. Faith's Church where Hammon hopes to wed Jane: "Sir Roger Otley will find my fellow lame Ralph's wife going to marry a gentleman, and then he'll stop her instead of his daughter. O brave, there will be fine tickling sport!" (IV.v.151–54).

In both plots, economic relations would distort and degrade human relationships. Dekker, however, resolves the love plots happily, overcoming the threatened alienation that money would effect—but not by repudiating it in a romantic fantasy of emotional authenticity existing beyond the reach of, and validated by its opposition to, economic realities, but even more improbably: in a romantic fantasy of emotional authenticity that need not repudiate it, indeed that need not address the issue of alienation at all. This is a world in which characters may have their cake and eat it too: they are permitted both to express their integrity and to enjoy that with which they have been tempted.

If the wish-fulfilling operations of the text validate this moral sleight-of-hand, they perform a similar operation in social terms. The formal ratification of the two marriages apparently at once repudiates and recuperates a social stratification whose moral inadequacy is revealed by its hostility to love. The love of Rafe and Jane succeeds in the face of a world that restricts working-class freedom and assails its integrity, and Lacy and Rose overcome class antagonisms and deficiencies, triumphing over aristocratic condescension and bourgeois acquisitiveness. But both relationships finally confirm traditional social hierarchy; the marriage of Rafe and Jane ratifies working-class commonality, and, while the marriage of Lacy and Rose presents itself as a successful adaptation to new social configuration, it too is revealed to be a more conservative gesture than at first appears. The King upbraids Lincoln who has opposed the marriage of his noble son with the middle-class Rose:

> Dost thou not know that love respects no blood,
> Cares not for difference of birth or state?
> The maid is young, well-born, fair, virtuous,
> A worthy bride for any gentleman.
>
> (V.v.108–11)

The King appeals to love and merit to counter Lincoln's corrosive class-consciousness. "The royal confirmation of the marriage of Rose and Lacy," signals, as the editors of the Revels edition assert, "the final overthrow of class division,"[16] but five lines later almost unnoticed the King firmly reestablishes the very social distinctions that he has just denied, as he knights Lacy:

> As for the honor which he lost in France,
> Thus I redeem it: Lacy, kneel thee down!
> Arise, Sir Rowland Lacy! Tell me now,
> Tell me in earnest, Otley, canst thou chide,
> Seeing thy Rose a lady and a bride.
>
> (V.v.116–20)

Love, perhaps, "cares not for difference of birth or state," but obviously the King, Lincoln, and Otley all do. The comic ending does not subvert social distinctions but reinforces them. Bourgeois desire is gratified by claiming rather than canceling aristocratic privilege.

Again Dekker has it both ways: middle-class desire for social mobility and aristocratic insistence upon social stratification are both accommodated, as when the King releases Eyre from obedience to courtly protocol: "good Lord Mayor, be even as merry / As if thou wert among thy shoemakers" (V.v.13–14). In the presence of the King, Eyre is free to behave as if he *were* among his shoemakers but simultaneously reminded that he is not. The social and ideological contradiction thus becomes itself the term of its resolution, but such resolution can not be other than imaginary.

But the play, after all, is *The Shoemaker's Holiday*, and arguments about the placement of the title's apostrophe seem to miss the central point. The issue is not primarily whether the title refers to a holiday declared for the shoemakers (in which case the title is *The Shoemakers' Holiday*) or a holiday declared by Simon Eyre for all the apprentices of London (in which case the title is *The Shoemaker's Holiday*). Fredson Bowers, in the Cambridge *Dekker,* argues for the former, the Revels editors, Smallwood and Wells, for the latter, but the action of the play itself—and not merely the Shrove Tuesday feast that ends it—is, as I have been arguing, the holiday—a holiday from the historical world of social contradiction and consequence, as the tensions produced by the social realignments of the late sixteenth century are wonderfully resolved in the communal, festive marketplace.

Indeed even the holiday is presented as holiday. The Shrove Tuesday celebration, which Hodge happily predicts "shall continue for ever" (V.ii.213), did continue but not always as a joyful celebration of social coherence and community. John Taylor, the water-poet, describes the Shrove Tuesday that Dekker's audience would have known: "in the morning, the whole kingdome is in quiet, but by that time the clocke strikes eleven, which (by the helpe of a knavish Sexton) is commonly before nine, then there is a bell rung, called The Pancake Bell, the sound whereof makes thousands of people distracted, and forgetfull eyther of manners or humanitie."[17] The holiday was regularly marred by the riots of disgruntled apprentices, who, in 1617,

> to the number of 3 or 4000 committed extreame insolencies; part of this nomber, taking their course for Wapping, did there pull downe to the grownd 4 houses, spoiled all the goods therein, defaced many others, & a Justice of the Peace coming to appease them, while he was reading a Proclamacion, had his head broken with a brick batt. Th' other part, making for Drury Lane, where lately a newe playhouse is erected, they besett the house round, broke in, wounded divers of the players, broke open their trunckes, & whatt apparrell, bookes, or other things they found, they burnt & cutt in peeces; & not content herewith, gott on the top of the house, & untiled it, & had not the Justices of Peace & Sherife levied an aide, & hindred their purpose, they would have laid that house likewise even with the grownd. In this skyrmishe one prentice was slaine, being shott throughe the head with a pistoll, & many other of their fellowes were sore hurt, & such of them as are taken his Majestie hath commaunded shal be executed for example sake.[18]

In actuality, Shrove Tuesday became an occasion for the release of social tension, but in the play what is released is only fellowship and cheer.

As critical response to the play attests, Dekker has fashioned an almost irresistible image of social unity, successfully neutralizing the disintegrative threat of the emerging capitalism and civilizing its dynamism. History is turned into holiday, its tensions refused rather than refuted, recast into an ameliorative fantasy. The play's unnamed King, who should be the aloof and ineffective Henry VI who ruled in 1445 when the historical Simon Eyre was appointed Lord Mayor, is idealized as Henry V, who mingles comfortably with his subjects and promises victories in France.[19] But the impossibility of positively identifying

Dekker's king points to the fact that he is less historical than romantic, a comforting portrait of royal benevolence to guarantee the middle-class energies that are articulated.

The play's prologue spoken before the Queen at court on New Year's Day in 1600, however, suggests a more problematic relation of subject and sovereign. The actors are the Queen's "meanest vassals" who stand before her as "wretches in a storm," fearful and impotent, dependent upon her favor:

> O grant, bright mirror of true chastity,
> From those life-breathing stars, your sun-like eyes,
> One gracious smile: for your celestial breath
> Must send us life, or sentence us to death.
>
> (Prologue 15–18)

If this is conventional flattery of Elizabeth, it is disturbing to discover its echo in Hammon's appeal to Jane: "Say, judge, what is thy sentence? Life or death? / Mercy or cruelty lies in thy breath" (III.iv.55–56). In Hammon's mouth the assertion of weakness blatantly functions as a strategy of manipulation; his conventional petrarchanism articulates and mediates the asymmetry of desire. In the players' prologue, Elizabeth's power is acknowledged and flattered, revealing anxieties produced by an asymmetry of power and belying the play's idealization of the relations between the monarch and his subjects.

In the play, the King's naming of Leadenhall ratifies Eyre's bourgeois energies and establishes the marketplace as both source and symbol of England's health and strength. Its potentially anarchic vitality is effectively contained by collective and patriotic loyalties. But Dekker's strategies of idealization are too blatant to function successfully as instruments of legitimation and social mystification. They declare themselves too openly as wish-fulfillments, and are at odds even with the conditions of their theatrical presentation.

Like the marketplace, the theater was originally a space for the expression of communal energies but in the late sixteenth century it too became an essentially commercial arena. "Man in business," wrote John Hall, lamenting the new, alienating commercial realities, "is but a Theatricall person"[20]; but the reality of the Renaissance stage was that theatrical persons were men in business. "The theatre is your poets' Royal Exchange," writes Dekker in *The Gull's Horn Book*, "upon which their muses—that are now turned to merchants—meeting, barter away that light commodity of words for a lighter ware than words—plaudits and the breath of that great beast which like the threatenings of two cowards, vanish all into air."[21] Dekker's metaphor reflects the existing economic relation of the acting companies and their audiences. An actor might imagine himself an artist whose aristocratic patronage, however complex that relationship was, at least freed him from the commercial logic of exchange, but, as an observer noted in 1615, "howsoever hee pretends to have a royall Master or Mistress, his wages and dependance prove him to be the servant of the people."[22]

And the situation of the playwright was worse still, servant not merely of the audience but also of the acting company that purchased his script. Though praised by Francis Meres in 1598 as one of England's best playwrights, Dekker lived marginally in the London slums—at least when he was not in the London jails for debt, as he was for seven years. The enormous theatrical profits, that made Shakespeare, Alleyn, and Burbage rich, were made by sharers in the acting companies, not by their playwrights. "With mouthing words that better wits have framed," wrote the Cambridge authors of the *Parnassus* plays, "They purchase land, and now Esquiers are made" (*2 Return from Parnassus*, 1927–28). The playwrights, however, were poorly paid piece-workers. A play might command six pounds. Dekker received only three for *The Shoemaker's Holiday,* and in 1598 he was paid by Henslowe a total of thirty pounds for his work on sixteen plays. Art became a commodity to be bought cheap and resold for profits that never reached its maker.

The play—any play—was, then, part of a complex set of social and economic relations that exploited some and enriched (a few) others. The theater might present itself as a green world of fantasy that audiences enter, like Rosalind and Orlando, to be free of the tensions of the real world, but in fact, like the green worlds of Shakespeare's comedies, the restraints and contradictions of the real world are merely disguised rather than discharged. "O happy work" (IV.i.14), Hammon gushes, watching Jane sew in the seamster's shop, but, though Dekker idealizes work in *The Shoemaker's Holiday,* the idealization takes place in a commercial theatrical environment that itself exposes the fantasy. The reality is that, for Dekker, the play is work, as for his characters work is play. *The Shoemaker's Holiday* presents commerce as comedy, converting the work place into a play space, but it does so in a playhouse that is fundamentally a workshop where such idealization can be no more and no less than a utopian compensation for the alienation and fragmentation of Dekker's London.

Notes

1. See, for example, Patricia Thompson, "The Old Way and the New Way in Dekker and Massinger," *MLR* 51 (1956), 168–78; H. E. Toliver, "*The Shoemaker's Holiday:* Theme and Image," *Boston University Studies in English* 5 (1961),

208–18; Joel H. Kaplan, "Virtue's Holiday: Thomas Dekker and Simon Eyre," *Renaissance Drama* 2 (1969), 103–22. Peter Mortenson, "The Economics of Joy in *The Shoemakers' Holiday*," *SEL* 16 (1976), 241–52, has offered a counter-argument, focusing on the play's commercial ethos: "Dekker creates a grim world and encourages us to pretend that it is a green one" (252). See also the provocative essay of Lawrence Venuti, "Transformation of City Comedy: A Symptomatic Reading," *Assays* 3 (1985), 99–134, which recognizes the "darker side" of the comedy as well as the "implausible resolutions" that conclude it.

2. Kaplan, "Virtue's Holiday," 117.

3. *Tudor Economic Documents*, eds. R. H. Tawney and Eileen Power (London: Longmans, Green and Co., 1924), 309–10.

4. Valerie Pearl, *London and the Outbreak of the Puritan Revolution* (London: Oxford University Press, 1961), 25.

5. Peter H. Ramsey, ed., *The Price Revolution in Sixteenth-Century England* (London: Methuen, 1971), 14–15.

6. George Unwin, *The Gilds and Companies of London* (1908; rpt. London: Frank Cass, 1963), 250.

7. See Penry Williams, *The Tudor Regime* (Oxford: Clarendon Press, 1979), 175–215; and Paul Slack, "Poverty and Social Regulation in Elizabethan England," *The Reign of Elizabeth I*, ed. Christopher Haigh (Athens, Georgia: University of Georgia Press, 1985), 221–42.

8. *The Non-Dramatic Works of Thomas Dekker*, ed. Alexander B. Grosart (London: The Huth Library, 1889), 2, 174.

9. Quoted in E. Lipson, *The Economic History of England* (London: Adam and Charles Black, 1931), 3, 357.

10. *The Works of Thomas Deloney*, ed. Francis Oscar Mann (Oxford: Clarendon Press, 1912), 112.

11. Quoted in L. C. Knights, *Drama and Society in the Age of Jonson* (London: Chatto & Windus, 1937), 120.

12. In *Tudor Economic Documents*, 3, 395, 394.

13. Thomas Fuller, *The Holy State* (1642, facs. ed. New York: Columbia University Press, 1938), 2, 113.

14. Lindsay Boynton, *The Elizabethan Militia, 1558–1638* (London: Routledge and Kegan Paul, 1967), 198–206.

15. *The Letters of John Chamberlain*, ed. Norman Egbert McLure (Philadelphia: The American Philosophical Society, 1939), 1, 78.

16. R. L. Smallwood and Stanley Wells, eds., *The Shoemaker's Holiday* (Manchester: Manchester University Press, 1979), 42.

17. John Taylor, *Jack a Lent, His Beginning and Entertainment* (London, 1630), 12.

18. Quoted in G. E. Bentley, *The Jacobean and Caroline Stage* (Oxford: Clarendon Press, 1968), 6, 54.

19. See W. K. Chandler, "The Source of the Characters in *The Shoemaker's Holiday*," *MP* 27 (1929), 175–82; and Michael Manheim, "The King in Dekker's *The Shoemakers' Holiday*," *N & Q* (new series) 4 (1957), 432.

20. John Hall, *The Advancement of Learning* (1649), ed. A. K. Croston (Liverpool: Liverpool University Press, 1953), 37.

21. *Thomas Dekker: Selected Prose Writings,* ed. E. D. Pendry (London: Edward Arnold, 1968), 98.

22. Quoted in *The Elizabethan Stage,* ed. E. K. Chambers (Oxford: Clarendon Press, 1923), 4, 256.

16

Ben Jonson and the Publicke Riot
BEN JONSON'S COMEDIES

Peggy Knapp

Ben Jonson saw his world quite clearly, but he liked almost nothing in what he saw. He was aware of his obligation as a poet to portray that world without idealizing or sentimentalizing it and without turning away from it toward the exotic or the romantic for his material. Yet he held that poetry is never merely an account of history; it is Fable:

> Poet never credit gain'd
> By writing truths, but things (like truths) well faign'd.[1]

The true poet's fable embodies both nature as local reality (such language as men use) and as natural law (enduring patterns of causality)[2] so that the second may expose the defects of the first and reform the age. Nearly everything in society needed reformation; to Jonson's eyes the commonwealth had degenerated into "the publicke riot."[3]

Yet it is not easy to discover from the plays what Jonson would have regarded as an ideal, or even an acceptable, mode of life. *Volpone, Epicoene, The Alchemist,* and *Bartholomew Fair,* the plays I will be discussing, depict little behavior to admire and much to castigate. To find Jonson's ideal social world described fully and without corrosive irony, we might try the non-dramatic poetry. His poem about the Sidney estate, "To Penshurst," is especially useful for its social inclusiveness; the related subjects of economics, family life, social hierarchy, and moral duty are all treated. In treating them Jonson could write with more candor than he could for either the public theater with its crowds to please or the private audiences of his masques with their demands for courtly tact. The Sidneys may have received a draft of the poem before it was printed in *The Forest,* but this is not certain since there is no manuscript copy at Penshurst, in fact none extant (Herford and Simpson, VIII, 8). But even if it was intended as a compliment, Jonson might have made that compliment in many other ways; those things he chose to praise reflect his own social views.

Jonson values the house itself, not because it presents a striking show, but for the opposite reason—it coalesces with nature so completely that the nature gods and sprites think it their home too. Of special worth is its antiquity and congruence with time-honored traditions. The workmen who built the house gave their work freely and did not groan as slaves in forced labor would. The fish and game know their place in the chain of being and willingly give themselves to nourish man because it is the order of things. The harmony between the family's way of life and the order of nature means that nature's own abundance is available for hospitality, and the generosity of the family means that plenty will be offered to the prince and the poor poet alike. For children who grow up at Penshurst lessons in civilization are taught daily by the life that is lived daily.

These ideals describe almost nothing that happens in any of the four plays I will discuss. What they do describe is English social theory in the Middle Ages. Based on a predominantly agricultural experience and the theory of divinely instituted hierarchies, medieval English social and economic expectations were modestly confined to subsistence rather than sudden wealth and self-containment rather than expansion (except in the wool trade). Land tenure was passed on by inheritance and what rights were enjoyed by serf, freedman, and lord were also largely inherited. There were changes and dislocations, but they came slowly and were regarded as aberrant. Even the more urban trades that formed guilds accepted subsistence as their usual aim. They were theoretically (and often in recorded practice) interested in fair dealing with customers, maintaining the standards of the craft, looking after unfortunate members and their families in adverse circumstances, and upholding the morals of apprentices and journeymen.[4]

Where did that England go, just before Jonson arrived to celebrate it? Between 1500 and 1650 prices trebled, and wages and rents could not keep pace. Gold from the Americas swelled the supply of precious metals and stimulated capital investment in England, as well as in the rest of Europe. Elizabeth's parsimony kept the worst effects of this long inflation from undermining her government disastrously, but James, inheriting the problem, blundered into catastrophic policies, which ushered in "the period of perhaps the greatest economic confusion" in England's history.[5] Large-scale land selling disrupted the inheritance of land and of the rights that accompanied the land. Governmental attempts to regulate the economy were hindered by the ministers' lack of skill in mathematics, and often by their dishonesty, but the greatest barrier to intelligent intervention was simply that no one knew any-thing about economies.[6] The medieval proscription on lending at inter-est (usury) could no longer be enforced, or even argued convincingly—Bacon himself said, "It is vanity to conceive that there would be ordi-nary borrowing without profit"[7]—but that proscription was about all the Middle Ages had to offer in the way of economic theory.

This fiscal anarchy created a truly new social situation. Great num-bers had known poverty and disaster under the medieval order, of course, but these calamities had been regarded as natural visitations—crop failures, plagues—as in large measure they had been. The new poverty was man's invention. A corresponding development was the man-made luxury of the ascendent class. From the conservative stand-point, the speculator did not function as the feudal lord had, either in his inherited (and divinely sanctioned) right or in his duty to protect and provide for his folk. King James's policy of creating large numbers of peers (nearly twice as many as Elizabeth had), many of them "up-starts" from the vantage point of the landed gentry, and some who had bribed or blackmailed their way to titles,[8] meant that money, now necessary for subsistence, was also sufficient for status and power. This situation runs exactly counter to everything Jonson praises in "To Penshurst." The social order there is enduring, predictable, and based on a version of the great chain of being. Goods are produced in order to provide for the people. Everyone has a place and knows what it is. Authority merits the respect it commands. And it is quiet.

In an age of faith, some alleviation, if only as economic idealism, would be expected from the church, but the church had troubles of its own. Catholics generally looked to Thomas Aquinas for social doc-trine, and Ignatius Loyola made use of enthusiasm for religious struggle rather than social amelioration.[9] Luther never abandoned his agrarian, non-acquisitive social ethic, nor did other continental reformers, except Calvin.[10] He alone based his vision of society on a commercial rather than an agricultural model, and his followers became, as a result, the only major religious force to exert a steady influence on the increasingly commercial scene.

Jonson constructed his massive fables, *Volpone, Epicoene, The Al-chemist,* and *Bartholomew Fair,* to expose and attempt to arrest this social deterioration. In these plays he assigned the old way of life (or rather, the ideals of it) the force of natural law, what should by nature occur. The new scene is debased nature synonymous with local reality, the passing scene, Vanity Fair—nature because it exists in the world, but an aberration just the same. The four plays use four different but related metaphors for the contrast between the old way and the new. Although all the metaphors are present in all four plays, each play has a dominant image cluster. In *Volpone* the old way involves people begetting children, the new way gold begetting gold; in *Epicoene* the old way is quiet, the new noisy; in *The Alchemist* the old way is having a calling, the new is having a face; in *Bartholomew Fair* the old way is authority chastening vice, the new is vice chastening authority. The controlling idea dominating all four plays is the contrast between industry which aims at provision ("To Penshurst") and industry which aims at market: there is no legacy, no silent wife, no philosopher's stone, but there are markets for all these things.

To use the stage to speak for the old and chastise the new way would be straightforward didacticism—the catch here is that the stage itself is gold, noise, flux, and marketing. To castigate the "publicke riot" caused by capitalism Jonson is forced to use the public theater, which is, like all economic entities, dependent on commercial enterprise and shares some of its chaos. The problem is a real-life version of Hamlet's when he vows in Act I, scene ii that he "knows not seems" and in Act I, scene v that he will "put an antic disposition on."

Edward Partridge finds the central image in *Volpone* to be that of feeding—man feeding on man, symbolizing greed.[11] An equally strong image-cluster in the play, though, and one related to chaos in provision, is that of begetting. Volpone's game is to let his wealth attract suitors who give him presents to advance their claims as his heirs, literally making the gold he has produce more gold. The note of bringing forth progeny is struck in Volpone's first speech. He addresses gold as the "son of Sol, but brighter than thy father," creator of a joy transcending that of "children, parents, friends," and a male so potent that, had he mated with Venus, "twenty-thousand cupids" would have been born. Yet the very next speech lays bare the narcissism in Volpone's love affair with gold—the glad possession (metaphorically the sexual union) is less to him than the cunning purchase (courtship). The trick he is playing on his "clients" is based on the fact that money rather than semen will be allowed to determine inheritance. His household confirms the sense of sexual perversion, in that, whether Volpone has engendered Nano, Androgyno, and Castrone in the usual way or bought them, they are, as Mosca claims, his bastards. He has certainly bought Mosca.

The image of gold begetting gold is contrasted in the first scene with the ways people usually provide for themselves. While Volpone's first long speech describes the way he has substituted gold for God (the Son) and nature (the sun), his next concentrates on the way his greed has perverted his role in society. This negatively phrased list of economic projects has often been read by critics as an exposure of harsh renaissance economic practice. The reference seems to me much subtler. In the first place, the occupations Volpone mentions are the basis of any economic life—we must use plowshares (though it may wound the earth), fatten beasts for slaughter, expose ships to sea dangers, and the rest. Not to do so is to ignore God's injunction about sweating for subsistence after man's fall from grace. This sense of Volpone's words is linked with his later assertion that gold allows one to "live free"; he means free from work and control, but he is also freeing himself from the whole moral and economic order. In the second place, Volpone is stating a self-congratulatory illusion: the capital investor is in reality as responsible for the earth's wounds and the widow's tears as any other participant in the economic system, often more reprehensibly because he does not have to follow the plow or wield the scourge himself. Volpone's particular brand of exuberant wit appears in the way he mixes the honorable human endeavors with abuses: grinding corn is one thing, grinding men another.[12] The point of the Volpone-Mosca list, with its poignant depiction of the plight of the most unfortunate workers, rests mainly on the exposure of Volpone's self-deluding or hypocritical aloofness from normal economic life, and even his pathos for those he pretends to be too delicate to wound reflects ugly things about his mind.

The first scene of the play traces the genealogy of the "world's soul"—gold—to the sun; the second traces the fool's soul to Apollo, the sun-god. Later Volpone as Scoto of Mantua will trace the powder with which French ladies color their hair, and which Volpone is using as a counter in his plot to seduce Celia, to the gift given Venus by Apollo (II.ii.220–45). These three mutability speeches, of course, point out the surprising changes, almost always degradations, things undergo; they also link the idea of gold with folly, deception, and change.

If people believe that gold is the world's soul, they imitate its qualities. Gold does not care whom it belongs to, and it is valued as the economy dictates. Volpone tricks all of his gulls into accepting themselves on those terms. Corvino violates his jealousy and sells his wife; Corbaccio calls his son "a stranger to his loins," repudiating his own past sexual activity as well as the continuity of his line; Voltore sells out the law and his talent for advocacy; Lady Would-be exposes her stupidity where she had bid for sophistication and learning. The key to all this is disguise. Volpone must disguise himself to take the others in, and he is tirelessly willing to do so. A healthy man playing sick, a virile man playing impotent, a rich man playing street-huckster, a live man playing dead, a lawbreaker playing *commendatore*—Volpone is nothing but roles.

Mosca's limberness—he could "skip out of his skin"—and his fantasy of being "dropt from aboue" (III.i.5–9) reveal the deep moral level of both his and his master's pride, the first and deadliest of the deadly sins. Volpone and Mosca were not born like other men (which is the other half of the fact that they do not beget like others), but like the gold they worship are heaven-born, not fixed to a place or calling in the social world, but "free" or endlessly shape-shifting, even contending with Proteus in his own wat'ry element (III.vii.152–3). A man without his own shape or place is outside the great chain of being; he is, in fact, a denier of the great chain of being, a satanic challenger to both God's order and society's.[13]

Volpone's challenge goes very far toward being successful. He has taught Mosca his way, or found an already-proficient Mosca, and stripped away the surface pieties and civilized habits from those he dupes to show them fiercely avaricious and proud. He meets resistance only in Celia and Bonario; they remain, like the lord at Penshurst, centered selves.[14] In the seduction scene, Volpone's speeches are addressed to his own needs, not Celia's. She doesn't see the fun in the constant mutation he claims he could provide, but he reveals that his fantasies of infinite pleasure must be accompanied by infinite variety, disguise, and adornment. No wonder he is gladder of the success of his con game than he would have been of possessing her—she is merely herself and will not change. And Volpone's really shocking image of counting the love-pleasures he and Celia will share while onlookers are frustrated in their tallies, reminds us that his only serious values are acquisitive and competitive. In his world sex has a countable value and can be bought (as Lollia Paulina was), but it is not so valuable that it can dispense with the embellishments and disguises that wealth can provide.

Celia's responses are not so silly as some critics have made out. They only seem silly because they are in this play, and this play has a presiding genius in duplicity, disguise, and devious rhetoric. I would not claim that Jonson has created in Celia a woman both honorable and interesting, like Shakespeare's Desdemona or Beatrice, but I would argue that to regard Celia as the satiric target here is to lose the force of the seduction scene. Our sympathies in this scene are painfully divided. It is funny that Volpone should leap unexpectedly out of bed, but frightening that Celia should stand truly vulnerable to his disgusting imagination. The laughter at Bonario's Dudley Do-Right stance should be a release from this uneasy tension.

The same complexity is present in the trial sequences, both of them. Critics have stressed the corruptness of the judges too much, I think, for the power of these scenes to come through. It is true that one of them, thinking Mosca the rich heir, has designs on him as a husband for his daughter. But how do any of these judges know that Mosca and Volpone are lying? In this world of appearances and disguises, how can they tell that Celia and Bonario aren't spouting pious cant to save their lives? The frightening thing about the new way is that it *is* convincing, it *has* contravened the old loyalties between husband and wife, father and son, professional man and his calling. The trial scene could be read as suggesting the possibility that such a courtroom performance might deceive reasonably honest men instead of exposing the venality of judges already corrupt. If Celia is really threatened and the judges really taken in, we have an appalling fable of the new way.

A word about the subplot. Sir Politic Would-be is new and bad at the disguise game, but he explains the theory of it to Peregrine very well, and he links his less demonic version of it to some topical abuses of King James's reign: projecting, bribery, and buying knighthoods. As the wholly comic embodiment of the new way, and a loser at its strategems, Would-be diverts the horror we might feel at Volpone's success to laughter at Sir Politic's would-be success. The disguise theme is inverted as Lady Would-be takes Peregrine for a disguised whore— she sees plotting everywhere except where it is—and Would-be's desperate and ludicrous interim as a turtle is much like Volpone's end— a disguise which becomes the real thing.

Where in *Volpone* the intrusion of money into the realm of begetting distorted both Volpone's loves and the family lives of his dupes, in *Epicoene* money distorts affection by tempting Morose to conceive a child in order to withhold his fortune from Dauphine. Spending semen in order to divert money is a fairly bizarre idea in itself, though not one which lacks fictional representation in England, where primogeniture was practiced for so long. And that bizarre idea spreads its imagery over all the characters and relationships in the play; as Partridge has pointed out, everybody in the play is epicoene.[15]

There is another image-cluster just as important—noise. Morose hates noise. This hatred means several things at once. As Ray L. Heffner has pointed out, it is a rejection of vanity, hypocrisy, and affectation, especially connected with women and with the court, and a symbol of Morose's contempt for the outside world, "as well as his complete dominance over all the members of his family."[16] In addition Morose's aversion to noise is likely to indicate a quite literal hatred of the noises of increased building and traffic in London (his reason for living on a street too narrow for vehicles), a result of the new way of capitalism.[17] London's population grew from 200,000 to 500,000 in the course of the seventeenth century, a boom that was well underway in 1609 when *Epicoene* was first enacted.[18] More important and only slightly less literal was the growth in consumer industries and industrial projects which a money economy necessarily entailed. Instead of the old, fairly reliable link between a person's work and the provisions it brought him, the Jacobean economy was prone to fluctuations which could offer all kinds of strange new things through money, things not known or needed before. On a small scale this meant the buying of spices or trinkets, on a large scale the buying of social status. Through such connections the literal noise of London's expansion in size and luxury is related to vanity and pretension. This new way also weakened the patriarchal dominance (or dominion, in the medieval term) which was due the master of a manor house like Penshurst as a matter of course. As Lawrence Stone points out, the new economy ruined many such, though it raised the fortunes of some others.[19] The relevant fact is, however, that the self-contained manor *as an economic system* was more and more difficult to maintain, and some kind of integration with the larger national or international economies became a greater and greater temptation to these latter-day feudal lords. Thus the man whose life could be spent "dwelling," like the lord of Penshurst, or exercising his strengths "in his own bosom and at home"[20] is rarer and rarer.

Morose wanted and expected to be such a man, but by the time the play opens he is already bitterly deprived of what in former times he could have taken for granted, and tragically mistaken that he can regain ground by sheer, willful hatred. His opponent, the new man Dauphine, contributes no serious thought for anything beyond his comfort and a talent for the gentleman's version of the con game. *Epicoene* is a "comedy of affliction" (II.iv.145), and both camps are afflicted, Morose's with society-excluding crabbedness, Dauphine's with society-dependent self-indulgence.[21] The intellectual power of Jonson's themes here is made very clear when we consider that all the other characters are Morose's antagonists (even if they don't all realize it) by being addicted to modern social customs, and yet Morose, by the fierceness of his disorder and the power of his prose, balances all of them. The whole busy universe of fools by inheritance, fools who would be scholars, hen-pecked husbands, social-climbing citizens' wives, fashionable ladies living apart from their husbands, conspiratorial barbers, seeming-quiet wives, and town wits is balanced against a madman in a nest of nightcaps sitting over a cross-beam in his attic.

The mode of the play is hurry and extravagance, and every position is pushed to a nearly intolerable extreme. Discussion quickly becomes tirade. On the subject of women's beauty Truewit is moderate in suggesting a little conscious art: "If she have . . . good legs, [let her] wear short clothes" (I.i.97–8), but the extreme is soon to appear in Otter's hilarious exposure of his wife's grotesque artificiality, requiring the lady to be put together "like a great German clock" (IV.ii.94). Captain Otter's diatribe is matched by his wife's harangue on the familial prerogatives given her by her independent fortune (III.i.24–42). Truewit's incredible anti-feminist tirade to Morose is matched by Morose's bitter account of Dauphine as Rake's Progress. La Foole gets carried away stating his genealogy as a fool, and the Latin of the last scenes is not a sprinkling but a torrent.

But scarcely noticed, near the beginning and the end of the play, its two major antagonists take serious and reasonable positions. Truewit discourses to Clerimont in the first scene, passionately:

> O, Clerimont, this time, because it is an
> incorporeall thing and not subject to sense, we
> mocke our selues the fineliest out of it, with
> vanitie and miserie indeede, not seeking an end of
> wretchednesse, but onely changing the matter
> still. . . . With what iustice can wee complain that
> great men will not looke vpon us . . . when wee will
> neuer doe it to our selues: nor hear nor regard
> our selues.
>
> (I.i.51–61)

We have few hints about how Morose had lived the earlier part of his life, but his one calm speech tells us what he had hoped to be like:

> My father, in my education, was wont to aduise mee
> that I should alwayes collect, and contayne my
> mind, not suffring it to flow loosely; that I
> should looke to what things were necessary to the
> carriage of my life, and what not: embracing the
> one and eschewing the other. . . . not that I neglect
> those things that make for the dignitie of the
> common-wealth, but for the meere auoiding of
> clamors, and the impertinencies of Orators, that
> know not how to be silent.
>
> (V.iii.48–59)

Both of these sober statements defend the stoical stance Jonson himself so loved to praise in his non-dramatic poetry. One is the utterance of a young puppy afraid he'll miss some fun by heeding his own dignified words too soon, and the other the somewhat resigned speech of an old man who had taken the ideal too literally and was too insistent on its acceptance by others. Truewit's ability to live this life is merely potential—he has been as deeply immersed in the vanity-loving scene as anybody in the play—and Morose's time has passed—as he finally recognizes by giving up the legacy to Dauphine.

Comedy usually rests on a reestablished hope for future good, for a new household, but the ending of *Epicoene* gives that hope too little nourishment. Jonson could easily have included a true love and a recognition speech for Dauphine, as the 1925 adaptation by Marcel Achard shows.[22] I think Jonson's interest was in a deeper and sadder question. The "arts," industries, and strategems of the new way *are* an affront to a stoical person's values, a waste of life, mere noise; and yet his response to these vanities must not be allowed to encase the thinking man in self-righteous isolation. "Language is the instrument of Society," Jonson said in *Discoveries* (ll.1881–2030), and bitter Morose wanted control over all of it for himself. He is defeated because "Society" must include more than one person.

In *The Alchemist,* a normative vision is even more difficult to locate; pure but helpless Celia and that parody of stoicism Morose are absent, and Surly, though undeceived, gets no noble speeches and no comic victory over deceit. Yet the imagery consistently shows how Jonson's links between money and religion, medicine, government, and sex expose the "venture tripartite" as a travesty of right order.[23] The key idea in this play is the substitution of a face for a calling.

The tracts on usury (aimed, of course, at capital investment) often brought against it that it disrupted the natural order in which every member of the commonwealth "doth live contentedly and proportionally in his vocation."[24] A man's continuance in his calling was seen as both a social necessity and a religious piety. Furthermore, the Christian conception of a social world superintended by God meshed for Jonson with a classical ideal of order, and both fit into the notion of a great chain of being. A person who is a face only, one who can be anything, is nowhere in the chain that binds the world. In claiming all identities, he forfeits the one true one he might have had. The exposure of Face, therefore, is not alone the exposure of a local fraud with unusual talent[25]; it is the exposure of the growing tendency of Jonson's age toward dissolving the chain of being and turning social life into publicke riot. And Lovewit's acceptance of Face's ill-gotten money, goods, and widow is the complicity of a decadent aristocracy in the process of dissolution.

In a certain sense the alchemy in the play merely reveals venalities the dupes had in them to begin with. There is surprisingly little hard work for the con artists to do. But from a slightly different angle, the vulnerability of all the characters could be seen as the result of social arrangements which prevent people from acting rightly. Jonson knew that everybody is *potentially* evil or foolish and that, presumably, most would be better or wiser were conditions right. Without sentimentalizing the cozeners overmuch, we might begin by linking the graphic description of Subtle's poverty—his pinched-horn nose taking in its meal of steam at Pie-corner—and Face's dependency—living with rats on chippings and dole beer—with the very real pauperization of large numbers of dispossessed peasants who swelled London's population early in the century, bringing no urban vocations with them. Right-minded as it would have been for these to follow their callings, they were not responsible for their failure to do so. Unemployment, land enclosure, and long-term inflation were.[26] Our three venturers first become corrupt and then study how to corrupt others.

Poor stupid Dapper has a respect for beauty and fantasy which in less sordid circumstances would have been moved by art or nature; Drugger's simple desire for order might have led him to plain dealing. In other times Kastril would have stayed home and looked after his pliant sister properly. Puritan morality, even the naive variety of it Ananias practices, might have exposed and resisted the alchemical assault, had it not been for the polished sophistry and personal force of Tribulation Wholesome. Through him Puritanism is shown to be a willing partner in the capitalist venture, welcoming all economic means, however tainted.

Sir Epicure Mammon has status and he has imagination—he even has a flickering interest in the public good. Potentially such a knight, wise at other times (Surely says) should be erecting monuments like Penshurst and superintending family and neighborhood, but the alchemy of the social change toward capitalism is too much for him. His soaring fantasies fly only slightly higher than the real extravagance of Jacobean luxury: "the wines of Spain, of France, of the Rhine, of the Levant, and of the Islands: the raisins of Spain, the currants of the Levant, the lawns and cambrics of Hannault and the Netherlands, the silks of Italy, the sugars and tobacco of the West Indies, the spices of the East Indies."[27] Such international trade contrasts sharply with the locally grown supplies brought to Penshurst by friendly tenants or offered freely on the estate by nature herself.

Because Mammon's is the highest place in this cross-section of society, the scope of his avarice is the greatest; he will be able to release Surly from the necessity of the hollow die and the frail card by virtue of his much greater swindle of nature with the stone. His desires swing widely from the magnanimous (curing the plague, rejuvenating the old, founding colleges, streaming rich milk to the children of the poor) to the tainted (making love to succubae, castrating town gallants, feasting on the "swelling unctuous paps of a fat, pregnant sow"). Both kinds of wishing are to be frustrated, of course, because the stone is a fraud, but both are features of the renaissance belief that money could turn England into a real-world land of Cockaine. Francis Bacon deplored "the idolatry that is generally committed in these degenerate times to money, as if it could do all things public and private."[28] Mammon's fantasies may embrace both the most generous and the most bestial in renaissance hopes, but the nearest he comes to fulfilling them is to converse with a whore thinking her a scholar and a baron's daughter.

One of the funniest exchanges in the play is that between Subtle and Surly on alchemical theory: chickens resemble eggs even less than metals resemble each other:

> *Surly:* The egg's ordain'd by nature to that end
> And is a chicken *in potentia.*
> *Subtle:* The same we say of lead and other mettalls,
> Which would be gold, if they had time.
> (II.iii.131–34)

Under the right social circumstances all the assorted victims of the play would be right-minded citizens—none is deeply vicious. The public riot which produced the alchemist's studio (and which the studio symbolizes) did not merely unmask these people, it corrupted them as well. They might have been gold had they had time and a place in the great chain of being. But they were attracted by a Face rather than inspired to a calling.[29]

Bartholomew Fair includes all the aforementioned enormities in its teeming panorama. Although it is a small-time operation, gold begets gold in Smithfield, noise and confusion are everywhere, and all the Fair people (not to mention several of the visitors) are faces. The Fair itself is a medieval institution completely taken over by the lowest elements of the money economy. Its dominating image is the contrast between a normative society (never seen) in which authority chastens vice and the new way in which vice chastens authority. The three figures which represent, albeit in comic and distorted ways, the pillars of renaissance order—law, religion, and education—Justice Overdo, Rabbi Busy, and Tutor Waspe—find themselves together in the stocks while Ursula the pig-woman, not unreliably described by Busy as the world, the flesh, and the devil, presides over the play. An upside down world *is* funny, but the geniality of this sprawling play has been overestimated in a good many critical accounts. For here Jonson is asking once again Voltore's question to the Scrutineo: "Which of you/ Are safe, my honored fathers?" Every age knows vice; Jonson is accusing his own of having lost the judgment and force to check it.

Overdo's "law" is limited by his cavernous naivete, Busy's by his hypocrisy, Waspe's by his ill-temper, and all of theirs by a niggling legalism which has lost sight of the right spirit of lawfulness. This broad comic point is based on a real social fact, the sudden rise of lawyers as a class to a position of enormous importance in national affairs, usually on the side of the rights of private money and property—in Jonson's view, on the side of chaos.[30]

The voice of Adam Overdo sounds through the scenes of the play like a refrain. Overdo takes his calling seriously, enduring his various humiliations and beatings with the patience of the wise, who "for no particular disaster ought to abandon a publike good designe" (III.iii.25–26). He understands his obligations to the law and his susceptibility to false impressions, which is why he undertakes his investigation of the Fair himself and in disguise. And he is given the fine stoical speech of the play, the grandness of which even the comic context cannot undercut:

> In the mid'st of this tumult I will yet be the
> Author of mine owne rest, and not minding their
> fury, sit in the stockes in that calme as shall be
> able to trouble a Triumph.
> (IV.i.43–46)

It would be hard to phrase a passage closer to Jonson's own ideals, and the phrasing, "Author of mine owne rest," links Overdo's role as public servant with Jonson's own. Why, then, is Overdo so thoroughly comic and so roughly used in the play? Most obviously, because he has so little good sense and worldly wisdom that he exactly reverses the cases he observes. Second, the law he upholds is a rigid and inappropriate semblance of Old Testament harshness. The more flexible and perceptive New Covenant of Christ has little place—compassion, says Overdo, though it may become a justice, is "a weaknesse neerer a vice, then a virtue" (IV.i.83–85). Third, Overdo's law, with its theological overtones, has little power to distinguish the committed crime from the pastimes which lead to it—his thundering tirades are against the "terrible taint poetry," and the tawny weed tobacco, which the alligartha may have pissed on (II.vi.27). And finally, there is such a strong strain of self-regard in Overdo's attention to his duties, so many classical heroes and statesmen whose behavior he thinks he emulates, that we are uneasy at the idea of *his* branding enormity in the last scene and relieved when he is relieved of that duty.

Zeal-of-the-Land Busy, although he lodges a protest against Overdo's Latin quotations and nearly precipitates a quarrel among the Authorities, bears his humiliation and discomfort because they are testimony to his calling, his "extraordinary calling." He has a sharp eye out for his reward in heaven (his "surer standing hereafter"), but his zeal may be self-delusion rather than, like Dame Purecraft's, unmitigated hypocrisy. Also like Overdo, Busy says a good many true things, though his flamboyant style and doctrinal narrowness veil their appeal. It is the plot that denies Busy any comic victory: he produces a quibble which allows him to go to the Fair—the pig may "be eaten with a reformed mouth" (I.vi.69), and a quibble defeats him at the puppet show—the puppet-actors have no sex and Busy is "confuted." The trouble with Busy's authority as a man of religion is located just there—his theology is a legalistic, word-centered construction and therefore without the real ethical force necessary to reform the Foul called the Fair. This situation is just what Thomas Greene sees as the paralysis which prevented the religious movements of the renaissance from alleviating the social crisis of the age. The reformation sects (except Calvin's) became almost pietistic, while the Jesuits and Puritans initiated a militant, disciplined following bent on winning a quasi-military victory. "Thus both major parties to the religious quarrel basically rejected the Humanist path of willed metamorphosis through intellectual discipline,"[31] which path Jonson defended.

The classical or Ciceronian ideals of the humanists depended heavily on education for their achievement.[32] Waspe seems ill-fitted for even a comic version of Erasmus or Bacon. But perhaps his thin-skinned, scatological, nearly despairing attempts to make Cokes and the others see their foolishness reminds us of these features of Jonson's own long career as an educator of the public (as well as his brief tenure as a private tutor). Waspe supplies a worldly sharpness of observation both Busy and Overdo lack and provides himself a real-life escape from the stocks rather than a philosphical consolation for his suffering. Yet, like the other authorities, he fails to perform his duties. Also like them he is stripped of his authority and forced to acknowledge his errors: "I must think no longer to reign, my government is at an end. He that will correct another must want fault in himselfe" (V.iv.99–100). Not only are all three Authorities in the stocks, the audience is forced to agree that they all in some sense belong there.

I have described a harsh reading of all four plays. My *Volpone* would be hard for a director to produce and painful for an audience to watch. Whose side are we supposed to be on? Celia and Bonario escape conviction and the judges misprison, but it could easily have been otherwise. The new way produces excellent disguises and no correspondingly good detective methods. But here is the real point: the tools of the new man—disguise and rhetoric—are also the tools of the theater which Jonson is using to condemn them. Celia is not a distressed innocent, but a young boy dressed in women's clothes, speaking lines someone has written for him. The theater audience has watched and been moved by a mere appearance. The tense uncertainty of the seduction and trial scenes arises from the playwright's having given us no place to stand: the new way is evil, the old way is gone. This situation exactly mirrors the artistic problem Jonson faced: the playwright himself had no place to stand, his only weapons against disguise and flux being the deceitful and fluctuating stage. Gold begets gold in the play; the gold of the shareholding company, the King's Men, buys the costumes to create the illusion which is *Volpone,* and the performances of the play bring in more gold. It is no wonder, then, that the world of positive value is not clear in the play, that unresolved tensions remain after the plot has run its course. The same tensions are evident in the other three plays.

As Jonson's own public statements show, a man whose ideal world is disappearing can say some very harsh things about the usurping values. How different is Morose's "All discourses but mine own afflict mee" (II.i.4) from Jonson's own, "Come leave the loathed stage,/ And the more loathsome age" ("Ode to Himself")? The problem for the two men is much the same: Morose, if he is to curb the license of the new generation represented by Dauphine and connected with noise, must marry and beget a child, which will involve linking himself with that notoriously loud creature, a wife; Jonson, if he is to castigate the capitalistic new way, must write plays for the notoriously undependable and itself capitalistic public stage. And the comic point of *The Alchemist,* which works against disguise and fast talk, is made when an audience watches a covey of actors bustling around in front of painted scenery creating an illusion.

The world of *Bartholomew Fair* consists of ingenious, vigorous Fair people (minor capitalists), fools from the middle class, failed authority figures, and indulgent gentlemen who can afford to wait for a favorable outcome. Except for Grace Wellborn. Grace shares the self-contained dignity of Overdo's stoicism without sharing his stupidity. Her name is the name of what Christians believe God sends when man cannot raise himself. Is hers the centered self which represents the connection between Christian and classical values? Why, then, is she handed around a circle of unworthy men to be bid on for marriage? Is the point that in *Bartholomew Fair* Jonson represents his age as so depraved that Grace itself is to be traded for Purecraft and the loser not angry? No wonder Knockem says, "hee may neitheer laugh, nor hope, in this company" (IV.iv.126–27). Indeed the communal feast is reduced to a meal in Ursula's tent, the theater to a scurvy puppet show, the emblematic last-act marriage to the results of a lottery. If this is to be Jonson's riotous real world, it is clear why he is not happy about it. Luckily, as the Stage-keeper tells us ahead of time, it is only a play.

Notes

1. *Epicoene,* Second Prologue, 119–20.

2. Jonson uses "nature" to mean social reality in such passages as this one from *Discoveries:* "The true Artificer will not run away from nature, as hee were afraid of her: or depart from life, and the likeness of Truth; but speake to the capacity of his hearers" (ll.772–75). He is referring to nature's consistent patterns in: "I cannot thinke Nature is so spent, and decay'd, that she can bring forth nothing worth her former yeares. She is alwayes the same, like her self: And when she collects her strength, is abler still. Men are decay'd, and studies: Shee is not" (11.124–28). *Ben Jonson's Works,* C. H. Herford and Percy and Evelyn Simpson, eds., 12 vols. (Oxford: Clarendon Press, 1925–52), Vol. VIII.

3. The phrase is from *Discoveries,* 1.956.

4. L. C. Knights, *Drama and Society in the Age of Jonson* (London: Chatto and Windus, 1951), pp. 15–29.

5. F. H. Durham, quoted by Knights, *Drama and Society,* p. 5.

6. Knights, *Drama and Society,* pp. 30–139. See also Brian Gibbons, *Jacobean City Comedy* (Cambridge, Mass.: Harvard Univ. Press, 1968), pp. 32–49.

7. *Essays,* "Of Usury."

8. Maurice Ashley, *England in the Seventeenth Century, 1603–1714* (Harmondsworth: Penguin, 1960), p. 17.

9. Thomas M. Greene, "The Flexibility of the Self in Renaissance Literature," in *The Disciplines of Criticism,* Peter Demetz, Thomas M. Greene, and Lowrey Nelson, eds. (New Haven: Yale Univ. Press, 1968), p. 243.

10. R. H. Tawney, *Religion and the Rise of Capitalism* (New York: Harcourt, Brace, and Company, 1926).

11. Edward Partridge, *The Broken Compass* (New York: Columbia Univ. Press, 1958), pp. 105–10.

12. Donne does something similar in Holy Sonnet VII:

    > All whom war, dearth, age, agues, tyrannies,
    > Despair, *law,* chance hath slain . . .

13. Charles H. Hallett, "The Satanic Nature of Volpone," *Philological Quarterly* 49 (1970), 41–55, makes a similar, but more specifically theological point.

14. The term is Thomas M. Greene's, "Ben Jonson and the Centered Self," *Studies in English Literature* 10 (1970).

15. Partridge, *The Broken Compass,* chapter VII.

16. Ray L. Heffner, Jr., "Unifying Symbols in the Comedy of Ben Jonson," in *Ben Jonson: A Collection of Critical Essays,* Jonas A. Barish, ed. (Englewood Cliffs, New Jersey: Prentice-Hall, 1963), pp. 137–8.

17. F. J. Fisher, "The Development of London as a Centre of Conspicuous Consumption in the Sixteenth and Seventeenth Centuries," *Transactions of the Royal Historical Society,* 4th series, 30 (1948).

18. Ashley, *England in the Seventeenth Century,* p. 12.

19. *The Crisis of the Aristocracy 1558–1641* (Oxford: Clarendon Press, 1965), pp. 7–15.

20. Jonson, "To the World: A Farewell for a Gentlewoman, Virtuous and Noble," 11.66–7.

21. Calvin G. Thayer claims that the plot invites us to contrast "the private, inverted, obsessive world of Morose and the gallant, free, open world of Dauphine," *Ben Jonson: Studies in the Plays* (Norman, Oklahoma: Univ. of Oklahoma Press, 1963), p. 67. Edward Partridge in the Introduction to *The Yale Ben Jonson: Epicoene* speaks of the "aerial quality" of the play (p. 5). I find both these views a misreading of tone.

22. Jonas Barish, *Ben Jonson and the Language of Prose Comedy* (Cambridge, Mass.: Harvard Univ. Press, 1960), p. 81–85.

23. Partridge, *The Broken Compass*, p. 159.

24. Quoted in Knights, *Drama and Society*, p. 146.

25. Dr. John Dee, who was consulted by "half the fashionable people of London," and Edward Kelly, who had enlisted his alchemical services in helping finance the British navy are the nearest topical targets of the play; see Knights, *Drama and Society*, p. 207.

26. Knights, *Drama and Society*, pp. 132–33.

27. E. Misselden, *Free Trade or the Means to Make Trade Flourish* (1622), p. 11–12, quoted in Knights, *Drama and Society*, p. 121.

28. Knights, *Drama and Society*, p. 123.

29. Jonson praises the idea of a calling in a commendatory poem from the 1632 edition of Richard Brome's *The Northern Lass* (Herford and Simpson, VIII, 409–10).

30. Gibbons, *City Comedy*, p. 53.

31. Greene, "Flexibility of Self," p. 257.

32. Greene, "Flexibility of Self," p. 249.

17

City Talk:
Women and Commodification
EPICOENE (1609)

Karen Newman

In the liveliest London streets, the shops press one
against the other, shops which flaunt behind their
hollow eyes of glass all the riches of the world, Indian
cashmeres, American revolvers, Chinese porcelains,
French corsets, Russian furs and tropical spices; but all
these things promising the pleasures of the world bear
those deadly white labels on their fronts on which are
engraved arabic numerals with laconic characters—£, s,
d (pound sterling, shilling, pence). This is the image of
commodities as they appear in circulation.[1]

Against his great house in the Strand, the enterprising Earl of Salisbury opened "Britain's Burse" in 1609; within the year Jonson's *Epicoene* was first produced. With its galleries and arcades lined with
shops licensed to carry luxury goods, and its upper rooms available
for meeting and conversation, the New Exchange, as it came to be
called, was immediately a place of both erotic and economic exchange.
Already in 1619, a contemporary observer remarked that "thy shops
with prettie wenches swarm, / Which for thy custome are a kind of
charme / To idle gallants."[2] There, and in the nascent West End, as
Stow's great *Survey of London* reminds us,

> Their shops made a very gay Shew, by the various foreign Commodi-
> ties they were furnished with; and, by the Purchasing of them, the
> People of *London*, and of other Parts of *England*, began to spend
> extravagantly; whereof great Complaints were made among the
> graver Sort. There were but a few of these Milliners Shops in the
> Reign of King *Edward the Sixth*, not above a Dozen in all *London;*
> but within forty Years after, about the Year 1580, from the City of
> *Westminster* along to *London*, every Street became full of them. Some
> of the Wares sold by these Shop-keepers were, Gloves made in *France*
> or *Spain*, Kersies of *Flanders* Dye, *French* cloth or Frizado, Owches;
> Brooches, Agglets made in *Venice* or *Milan*, Daggers, Swords, Knives,
> Girdles of the *Spanish* Make, Spurs made at *Milan, French* or *Milan*
> caps, Glasses, painted Cruses, Dials, Tables, Cards, Balls, Puppets,
> Penners, Inkhorns, Toothpicks, Silk-Bottoms and Silver-Bottoms, fine

> earthen Pots, Pins and Points, Hawks-Bells, Saltcellars, Spoons, Dishes of Tin. Which made such a Shew in the Passengers Eyes, that they could not but gaze on them, and buy some of the knicknacks, though to no Purpose necessary.[3]

Stow's sketch of mercantile London in the early seventeenth century bears an uncanny resemblance to Marx's description of the British metropolis almost two hundred fifty years later. Immediately striking is the sheer proliferation of goods, their variety in kind and provenance, and their mode of presentation as spectacle. Commodities offer the buyer access to a larger world, from the far-flung cities of Europe which were early modern England's access to the east, to the American cowboys and Russian winters of Marx's sketch of nineteenth-century London. Both suggest prodigious excess and the demise of the rare, in short, commodification. And for both, the series—the list of substantives with their respective qualifiers, cosmopolitan or colonial—offers the reader-*cum*-buyer the consumer pleasures Stow and Marx describe.

But there are also, of course, striking differences. Whereas the Stow account bears witness to England's expanding maritime power after 1588 and to growing mercantile relations with Europe, Marx's list of goods testifies to Britain's imperial conquests and world power in the mid-nineteenth century and alludes at least to mass production and the development of manufacturing. The *Survey* is characteristically conservative in its solidarity with the "graver Sort" and its critique of London's growth as a center of "conspicuous consumption" where shoppers buy "knicknacks, though to no purpose necessary." The enumeration of Stow's series tends to trivialize the goods named whereas Marx aggrandizes what he describes—they are "all the pleasures of the world"—but his cosmic tribute is deflated by his ironic periphrasis on "deadly" price tickets that reduce variety to identity— from Russia, America, to the Orient, these goods are all for sale. Consumption in Marx is revealed to be a function of production rather than access to cosmic expanse and pleasure. Abundance and desire are revealed as scarcity and lack.[4]

Work in political economy has sometimes idealized pre-industrial cultures, posing them as versions of economic pastoral, golden ages of household production and self-sufficiency before commodification. Recently that nostalgic cliché has been challenged as scholars have begun to study the changing world of goods in early modern Europe: not only the quantity and ownership of objects, but their character, how they were acquired and displayed—objects as representations of a culture and its codes, and ownership not merely as a material fact, but fashioned by conventions.[5] Historians have recognized increasingly the role taste and cultural innovation have played in the development of international trade and patterns of economic growth.[6] Such changes in the early modern material environment were both produced by and had enormous impact on social relations.

Women's relation to the processes of commodification has been situated in a variety of ways. In the modern period, we have been targeted as the primary consumers of proliferating goods, and advertising directed at creating markets has been frequently addressed at us. Women have been represented not only as consumers, but as goods themselves, and inversely, goods are often feminized. Baudrillard writes of what he terms the feminization of objects, the object-as-woman as the privileged myth of consumer persuasion: "Tous les objets se fonts femmes pour être achetés."[7] Marx often conceptualized commodity exchange in terms of the object-as-women in *Capital* where, he uses imagery first of seduction, then rape, to define commodity relations:

> Commodities cannot themselves go to market and perform exchanges in their own right. We must, therefore, have recourse to their guardians, who are the possessors of commodities. Commodities are things, and therefore lack the power to resist man. If they are unwilling, he can use force; in other words, he can take possession of them.[8]

Marx glosses this analysis of commodities with a note that reveals the intersection of commodification, women, and, interestingly, literary representation:

> In the twelfth-century, so renowned for its piety, very delicate things often appear among these commodities. Thus a French poet of the period enumerates among the commodities to be found in the fair at Lendit, alongside clothing, shoes, leather, implements of cultivation, skins, etc., also *femmes folles de leurs corps*.

In equating women and things, Marx betrays a certain anxiety, evinced in his choice of a poetic authority, his euphemism for describing prostitutes, and his lapse into French. Women's relation to commodities is multiple, even extravagant—we are at once goods, sellers of goods, and consumers of goods, and significantly, in Marx's formulation, the object-as-woman is defined in terms of lack. Goods "lack the power to resist man."

The proliferation of goods described in the *Survey* and their availability for sale in the London exchanges and growing West End represent an early episode in the process of commodification under capitalism. Goods from the continent and from more exotic lands were for the first time available in numbers in England: tobacco, porcelain, imported textiles, metalwork.[9] In the early seventeenth century, woman became the target for contemporary ambivalence toward that process. She is represented in the discourses of Jacobean London as at once consumer and consumed—her supposed desire for goods is linked to her sexual availability.

Marriage sermons, conduct books, popular forms such as plays, ballads, and jest books—in short, the discourses which managed and produced femininity in the late sixteenth and early seventeenth centuries—all conflate the sexual and the economic when representing feminine desire. Bullinger's popular handbook, *The Christian State of Matrimony*, translated in England by Myles Cloverdale, includes a lively dramatic dialogue in which the whore ridicules her client, "No more money, no more love."[10] Thomas Becon complained that women were moved to every kind of sexual dishonesty for as little as a "morsel of bread or a potte of bear."[11] Though examples of this conflation could be considerably multiplied, more important for my purpose is the synecdochic representation of feminine desire—sexual or acquisitive— as an open mouth. Becon inveighs against the whore who is never satisfied "but is like as one that goeth by the way and is thirsty; even so does she open her mouth and drink of everye next water, that she may get. By every hedge she sits down, and opes her quiver against every arow."[12] The slippage from the whore's thirsty mouth to her insatiable genitals is a commonplace. The talking woman is everywhere equated with a voracious sexuality that in turn abets her avid consumerism: scolds were regularly accused of both extravagance and adultery.

Talk in women then is dangerous because it is perceived as a usurpation of multiple forms of authority, a threat to order and male sovereignty, to masculine control of commodity exchange, to a desired hegemonic male sexuality. The extent of this perceived threat may be gauged by the strict delegation of the talking woman to the carefully defined and delimited spheres of private and domestic life in which the husband was exhorted to rule. In the Renaissance, as many commentators have pointed out, even those humanists most progressive in their advocacy of women's worth insisted vehemently that rhetoric and public speaking were anathema to women.[13] Whenever women's talk is removed to public spaces, it became a threat; when it burst out of the house and into the streets or village, town or city, or when it took place in the church or alehouse, it became dangerous, even seditious. Traditionally excluded from public life, from government affairs, law courts, the pulpit, women enter the public sphere of early seventeenth-century London by going to market, both to buy and to sell.[14]

Jonson's *Epicoene* is peopled with talkative women whom he portrays as monstrous precisely because they gallivant about the city streets spending breath as well as money.[15] His talking women are not merely the butts of satire, but represented as monstrously unnatural because they threaten masculine authority. Not domestic gossips who meet at home, the women of Jonson's play are

> ladies that call themselves the Collegiates, an order between
> courtiers and country-madams, that live from their husbands
> and give entertainment to all the Wits and Braveries o' the
> time, as they call'em, cry down or up what they like or dislike
> in a brain or a fashion with most masculine or rather
> hermaphroditical authority, and every day gain to their college
> some new probationer.
>
> (I, i, 68–74).[16]

Their college apes contemporary educational institutions and associations for men,[17] and they perform the activities of their "foundation" before an audience—the Wits and Braveries; significantly, it is the voicing of their critical opinions abroad ("down or up") that makes them monstrous.

In the main plot when the silent woman begins at last to speak, Morose wails "O immodesty! A manifest woman" (III, iv, 37). Speech makes her sex immediately, if ironically, apparent to Morose and witnesses her usurpation of masculine authority within the family, that seventeenth-century "little commonwealth": "I'll have none of this coacted, unnatural dumbness in my house, in a family where I govern" (47–9), she explains, to which Morose responds, "She is my regent already! I have married a Penthesilea, a Semiramis, sold my liberty to a distaff" (50–1). Morose figures the talking woman as Amazonian, as a warrior queen, and Epicoene bears out his fears in the next scene when she commands that the door be left open to her friends and promises to "see him that dares move his eyes toward it" (III, v, 31). Morose also immediately assumes that her speech indicates sexual transgression: "I have married his [Cutbeard's] cittern, that's common to all men" (54–5).

Morose's fear of noise, which is presented as generalized at the outset of the play, becomes increasingly gender specific. In Act I we learn that he hates hawking fishwives and orange women, chimney sweeps and broom men, metal workers, braziers, armorers, pewterers, and the "waits" or wind instrumentalists maintained at public expense to play on holidays or other special occasions in the city streets. His house lies on a street "so narrow at both ends that it will receive no coaches" (I, i, 150–1), a status symbol Epicoene promises to buy instantly on her marriage. The "perpetuity of ringing"—the bells that marked the hours and tasks of daily life and also knelled deaths in plague time—drives him to a padded cell: "a room with double walls and trebel ceilings, the windows close shut and calked" (I, ii, 166–8). But as the plot unfolds, Morose's early universal fear of noise is identified specifically with women. Woman becomes the overdetermined locus of noise, the screen on which Morose's agoraphobia is projected: "he has employed a fellow this half year all over England to harken him out a dumb woman. . . . Her silence is dowery enough" (21–3). The city woman tropes urban vices—the noise, the crowd, sexuality, and consumerism. Even her oneiric life is bound up with the city: Mrs. Otter, when she recounts her dream to Clerimont, says "anything I do but dream o' the city" (III, ii, 57).

Jonson presents in luxuriant detail the attractions of London for ladies. In Truewit's attempt to dissuade Morose from marriage, he details the pastimes of city women's lives, their infinite consuming desires: "she must have that rich gown for such a great day, a new one for the next, a richer for the third; be served in silver; have the chamber filled with a succession of grooms, footmen, ushers and other messengers, besides embroiderers, jewelers, tire-women, sempsters, feathermen, perfumers" (II, ii, 87–92). She comes to the city seeking to "be a stateswoman" (95–6), a satiric coinage, as the Yale editor notes. Truewit's modern city woman enjoys public affairs, must "know all the news," and evidently reads widely "so she may censure poets and authors and styles and compare 'em, Daniel with Spenser, Jonson with t'other youth" (97–9). The ladies complain that Morose's "nuptials want all marks of solemnity. . . . No gloves? No garters? No scarves? No epithalamium? No masque? (III, vi, 74–5, 80). These women are consumate consumers—of poems and plays in the same breath as gloves and garters. They frequent the court, tiltings, public shows and feasts, playhouses, even church to show off their clothes, "to see and to be seen" (VI, i, 54).

Favorite haunts of the collegiates are the Strand, which teemed with shops; the china houses; and the New Exchange, a Renaissance shopping mall. Truewit admonishes Morose against marriage by inveighing against woman as consumer in a conventional metaphor often repeated in the early seventeenth century: "she feels not how the land drops away, nor the acres melt, nor forsees the change when the mercer has your woods for her velvets" (II, ii, 92–4). Men and the traditional landed values of the elite are pitted against a burgeoning consumer culture Jonson and his contemporaries identify as feminine. In 1632, Donald Lupton complained of the exchanges:

Here are usually more Coaches attendent, then at Church doores: The Merchants should keep their wives from visiting the Upper Roomes too often, least they tire their purses, by attyring themselves.... There's many Gentle-women come hither, that to help their faces and Complexions, breakes their husbands backs, who play foule in the Country with Their Land, to be faire; and play false in the City.[18]

Epicoene promises to join the ladies in their shopping sprees and promenades "three or four days hence . . . when I have got me a coach and horses" (IV, vi, 1506), a powerful emblem of late sixteenth- and early seventeenth-century urban life and status. Consumption is presented as a female preoccupation and pastime in the discourses of Jacobean England, and women are both consumers and commodities:[19] Otter slanders his wife by exclaiming in a parodic blazon that her "teeth were made i' the Blackfriars, both her eyebrows i' the Strand, and her hair in Silver Street. Every part o' the town owns a piece of her" (IV, ii, 88–90). Women's "pieced beauty" (I, i, 77) is demystified, revealed as goods that are bought and sold in the shopping streets of the city.[20]

In *Epicoene,* the talking woman represents the city *and* what in large part motivated the growth of the city—mercantilism and colonial expansion. Consumption, like female talk, is presented as at once stereotypical (women all do it) and as unnatural (women who do it are masculine, hermaphroditical, monstrous). Critics of *Epicoene* typically discuss its female characters in terms of the opposition between the hermaphroditical, monstrous epicene women and the cultural norm— women who were chaste, silent, and obedient. The play's satire depends on shared, if unrepresented, assumptions about behavior appropriate to women that position the audience to perceive the collegiates' activities as reprehensible. Such readings join Jonson in his censure by assuming the implicit norm as positive and "natural" rather than culturally produced. In Jonson, woman is the focus of cultural ambivalence toward social mobility, urbanization, and colonialism; she is the site of systems of exchange that constituted capitalism, the absolutist state and English colonial power. Mrs. Otter, after all, owes to the China trade the fortune that enables her both to rule Captain Otter as his "Princess" (III, i), and to aspire to a more prestigious class position.[21]

Epicoene dramatizes the discursive slippage between women's talk, women's wealth, and a perceived threat to male authority. But this intersection of woman, the city, and consumerism was not only a literary phenomenon—contemporary observers of early Stuart London from the King himself to men like John Chamberlain witnessed it as well. Whereas Elizabeth, to curb the growth of London, issued proclamations and statutes against building, dividing houses, and an excess of apprentices, James directed his anxiety about the city's growth against women as consumers.[22] In June, 1608, perhaps six months to a year before *Epicoene* was first performed, the King railed at "those swarms of gentry who, through the instigation of their wives and to new model and fashion their daughters (who, if they were unmarried, marred their reputations, and if married, lost them) did neglect their country hospitality, and cumber the city, a general nuisance to the kingdom."[23] The pursuit of London fashion in James's formulation leads not only to over-population, but apparently to sexual transgression, since gentry daughters lose their reputations in their eager migration to the metropolis. The King often reiterated such proclamations: in a major speech before the Star Chamber in 1616, James opined that "one of the greatest causes of all gentlemens desire, that haue no calling or errand, to dwell in London, is apparently the pride of women. For if they be wiues, then their husbands; and if they be maydes, then their fathers must bring them up to London because the new fashion is to bee had no where but in London."[24] John Chamberlain reports that "even upon Christmas eve came foorth another proclamation, for their wives and families and widowes to be gon likewise, and that henceforward gentlemen should remain here during termes only or other busines, without bringing their wives and families, which is *durus sermo* to the women."[25] In Jacobean London, women were held accountable for urban ills.

But I want to look not only at historical and cultural formations, but at the linguistic economies Jonson deploys to represent the relation of women and consumption, that is, at his *means* of representing women and goods. Jonson's comedies might be characterized generally by a fondness for *copia* enacted through the grammatical series. In the reverse *blazon* quoted earlier, or Truewit's enumeration of the evils of marriage, Jonson betrays a penchant for the list. In his study of Shaw's style, Richard Ohmann analyzes Shavian modes of order, particularly in the series. In a series, Ohmann shows, equivalences are set up that typically end with a summation—an "in short" or other phrase that subsumes and extends what precedes it.[26] Even without such summative devices, the grammatical construction of a series implies an equivalence relationship, and particularly "when the series ends with 'and so forth' 'and the like,' or 'etc.' " Such phrases invite the reader to continue, "to extrapolate the class in the direction pointed by the given portion of the extension. . . . [the reader] must have grasped the rubric under which members are alike." The Shavian series, Ohmann claims, typically "does not exhaust the class it defines," but stops short, demanding "that the reader infer similarity."[27] Though Ohmann's concern is similarity, more important to my argument is the productive power of the series, its demand on the reader or audience. The series, seemingly excessive and extravagant, paradoxically produces lack or scarcity and the desire for more.

In *Epicoene,* the series is most often used to describe women, to set up invidious equivalences that stop short but position the audience to produce more. After marriage is defined by a long series detailing increasingly perverse ways of committing suicide, Jonson sums them up with "any way rather than to follow this goblin Matrimony" (II, ii, 27). After marrying, Truewit threatens, a man's wife may run away "with a vaulter, or the Frenchman that walks upon ropes, or him that dances the jig, or a fencer for his skill at his weapon" (50–2), a short series that does a great deal of cultural work with its bawdy innuendo and its class prejudice. Women's behavior as consumers is then represented in the torrential series quoted from above which equates female consumption and sexual misconduct. It ends with Truewit's summative "one thing more, which I had most forget" in which Jonson links sexual transgression and economic power: the woman "whom you are to marry, may have made a conveyance of her virginity aforehand, as your wise widows do of their states, before they marry, in trust of some friend" (119–20). Typically in *Epicoene,* the Jonsonian series enumerates a list of female activities or behaviors, but stops short leaving the audience not with a feeling of completion or abundance, but of lack.

In Jonson's series, or the list of goods from Stow's *Survey* with which I began, the series suggests abundance, profusion, availability. But as Marx's description reminds us, the proliferation of goods and serial multiplicity systematically produce want, a dialectic of scarcity. Commodity pleasures—the more you have, the more you want. On a psychoanalytic axis, consumption figures not possession, but lack, the woman's part. The series seems to democratize things—separated only by commas or the semi-colon, the items of a series hurtle along pell-mell seemingly without distinctions, enacting a sort of grammatical commodification; but instead of erasing differences, the grammatical series, like commodification itself, systematizes privilege and difference. In Jonson, sexual difference is the axis along which commodification is plotted, with privilege or class as a destabilizing variant: the aspiring Mrs. Otter is of a decidedly lower status than the collegiates, but the relation of all the women to commodification is represented as alike, which tends to level class differences; in Marx, class is the constant, but sexual difference is the variable that problematizes his class analysis of commodification.

I would like to end with an episode in what I would term cultural politics rather than cultural poetics, a look at the earliest stage history of *Epicoene,* that takes me back as well to the establishment of the New Exchange with which I began. The historian Thomas Wilson, Salisbury's agent, tells the story, recorded in the State Papers Domestic, that the Earl had first proposed to call his new mercantile enterprise, "Armabell" as a compliment to a lady.[28] That lady is said to have been Arbella Stuart whose complaint about a supposed allusion to her person led to the play's suppression after its first or an early performance. Daughter of James's uncle Charles Stewart, great granddaughter of Henry VIII's sister Margaret Tudor, related as well to Bess of Hardwick, learned lady and dedicatee of Aemilia Lanier, Arbella Stuart was next in line to the English throne after James and believed by some, because of her English upbringing, better qualified than he. Had she been, in Portia's words, "accomplished / With that we lack" (*Merchant of Venice,* III, iv, 61–2) she might well have succeeded. Elizabeth kept her under house arrest for years, fearing her marriage and plots against the throne; James's first diplomatic instructions to the Scottish ambassador in London after his mother's execution were to secure a declaration from Elizabeth that James was the rightful heir and to engage "that the Lady Arbella be not given in marriage without the King's special advice and consent."[29] The Venetian ambassador Nicolo Molin sent the following account of Arbella Stuart to his government in 1607:

> The nearest relative the King has is Madame Arabella, descended from Margaret, daughter of Henry VII, which makes her cousin to the King. She is twenty-eight; not very beautiful, but highly accomplished, for besides being of most refined manners she speaks fluently Latin, Italian, French, Spanish, reads Greek and Hebrew, and is always studying. She is not very rich, for the late Queen was jealous of everyone, and especially of those who had a claim on the throne, and so she took from her the larger part of her income, and the poor lady cannot live as magnificently nor reward her attendants as liberally as she would. The King professes to love her and hold her in high esteem. She is allowed to come to Court, and the King promised when he ascended the throne, that he would restore her property, but he has not done so yet, saying that she shall have it all and more on her marriage, but so far the husband has not been found, and she remains without mate and without estate.[30]

Deprived of her ancestral estates and income, Arbella Stuart nevertheless spent lavishly in accordance with her position at court and was continually in debt; Chamberlain describes her as rivaling the queen in dress and jewels.[31] In the months preceding the production of *Epicoene,*

Arbella Stuart was the subject of rumor at Court. Called to account
before the Council, she disputed claims that she had been converted to
Catholicism or planned to marry without the King's consent; she
complained forcefully of the failed restoration of her patrimony and
of her poverty, and succeeded in winning some relief from James. But
throughout this period she was surreptitiously engaged in a courtship
that issued in her clandestine marriage to William Seymour in 1611.
When the King learned of their marriage, Arbella Stuart was again
arrested and given into the custody of the Bishop of York. In a daring
escape reminiscent of the plots of countless Renaissance comedies and
romances, Arbella herself played an epicene part. Disguised as a boy,
she managed to elude her jailor and fled, chased by the King's authorities, across the channel to meet her husband of seventeen days in
Ostend where she was finally apprehended. The solicitor general who
presided at the subsequent trial figured her transgression as childish
disobedience, chiding her for

> transacting the most weighty and binding part and action of her life,
> which is marriage, without acquainting his Majesty, which had been
> a neglect even to a mean parent.[32]

Imprisoned in the Tower, she died in 1615. According to modern
commentators, she died insane, but contemporaries were more
sceptical of the reports that she was mad. In 1613, Chamberlain wrote
twice to friends that the "Lady Arbella is saide to be distracted which
(yf yt be so) comes well to passe for somebody whom they say she hath
neerly touched."[33] Chamberlain realized the threat she posed the King.
    The relation of Arbella Stuart to Jonson's *Epicoene* is more than an
episode in stage history. The play attacks "hermaphroditical" talking
women, women who transgress the culturally constructed codes of
behavior believed appropriate to them in early modern England. Arbella Stuart, "a regular termagant,"[34] often refused to stay at court,
preferring to live independently and often writing to friends of her
wish for time with her books. Contemporaries always mention her
propensity for study and claimed it made her melancholic, a common
result, according to Renaissance humors theory, of too much study
and learning. The melancholic, of course, was said to favor solitude
and to be prone to distraction. The frequently repeated claims that
Arbella Stuart died mad figures her political transgression in private
terms, within the medical discourse of female hysteria. The judgment,
"died insane," safely categorizes women who transgress their culture's
sex/gender codes by studying, marrying without their "parent's" consent, spending extravagantly, in bed or in shops. Arbella Stuart suffered

for transgressing cultural norms, and for a brief moment, she made Jonson's *Epicoene* suffer with her.

The discourses around Arbella Stuart in State Papers, Foreign and Domestic, are remarkably consistent with the major themes and preoccupations of Jacobean city comedy, and particularly *Epicoene*—the topoi of the shrew and the learned lady, the problems of marriage and inheritance, the political aspirations of women, the position of women as consumers. But as with the comparison of Marx and Stow with which I began, there are also important differences. Arbella Stuart's marriage, her spending and debt, are part of an aristocratic ethos of status and degree foreign to the aspirations of Stuart London's "middling sort." To ally the story of Arbella Stuart to city comedy occludes the status-differentiated histories of seventeenth-century women even as it recognizes a shared position in the Jacobean sex/gender system.

But my telling of Arbella Stuart's story cannot stand unremarked at the end of my argument: the historical anecdote has become notorious, impugned by opposing camps in literary studies. Insofar as it has been used to ground literary interpretation in the so-called "facts" of history, the critique of the new historicist anecdote is justified; but insofar as that critique, mounted either by the literary critic deferential to an imagined scienticity of history, or by the historian claiming for history an archival high ground of "Truth," that critique represents a refusal of the challenges posed by theories of reading and poststructuralism. Stories are fields of struggle, as Lynn Hunt has recently phrased it,[35] hermeneutic arenas in which we contend not for a material ground that is not language, but for meaning and its effects. How we read Arbella Stuart's story determines a whole series of categories and critical questions: how we understand elite and bourgeois women's lives and the management of femininity in early modern England; how we understand Elizabethan and Jacobean political history; how we analyze the relation of playwright to contemporary culture; how we conceive and represent female subjectivity.

In *Reading Capital*, Althusser theorizes a practice of reading by analyzing Marx's commentary on nineteenth-century political economy. In what Althusser calls a *first reading*, Marx reads his predecessors' discourse through his own showing what they discovered and what they missed: he redresses the balance by seeing their oversights or *bévues*.[36] But Althusser argues that this stage of reading remains locked in "the mirror myth of knowledge" since it depends on vision, on sight and oversight, presences and absences. He goes on to demonstrate that in Marx's reading of political economy there is a "*second quite different reading*" not limited to "objects that can be seen so long as one's eyes are clear":

What political economy does not see is not a pre-existing object which it could have seen but did not see—but an object which it produced itself in its operation of knowledge. . . . Through the lacunary terms of its new answer political economy produced a new question, but *"unwittingly."* It made "*a complete change in the terms of the* original *problem,*" and thereby produced a new problem, but without knowing it. . . . it remained convinced that it was still on the terrain of the old problem, whereas it has *"unwittingly changed terrain."*[37]

My reading of *Epicoene* willfully shifts its focus away from Morose and the gallants, away from Jonsonian satire and classical allusion, away from the exclusively literary, and gestures toward, in Althusser's terms, the production of a different theoretical *problematic*. On such a terrain of reading, it is not simply a question of *seeing* the woman, of putting "woman" into discursive circulation, but of changing the terms of reading by mobilizing stories from Marx, Stow, Baudrillard, Jonson, James I, the Venetians, to name only a few. Such intercourse threatens both the customarily literary and the traditionally historical by insisting on shifting relations rather than fixed categories.

Notes

1. "Zur Kritik der Politischen Ökonomie," Karl Marx and Friedrich Engels, *Werke* (Berlin: Dietz Verlag, 1961), vol. 13, 69; thanks to William Crossgrove for advice in translating.

2. Pasquin's *Palinodia* (1619), quoted in Lawrence Stone, "Inigo Jones and the New Exchange," *Archeological Journal*, 114 (1957), 120.

3. John Stow, "The Temporal Government of London, The Haberdashers," *A Survey of the cities of London and Westminster* (London, 1755): 11, 4Aᵛ. Stow's *Survey* appeared in a number of editions in the early seventeenth and eighteenth centuries, each editor adding material from local archives and records. This passage does not appear in the earliest edition, but dates the description directly ("within forty years after, about the Year 1580") and by lexical evidence: the OED cites late sixteenth- and early seventeenth-century uses of *agglet,* points or tags for threading eyelets, but by late in the century the word required definition in glossaries as archaic; similarly, *frizado,* silk plush, was by the eighteenth century a clear indication of the outdated and old fashioned.

4. Herbert Marcuse, *One Dimensional Man* (Boston: Beacon, 1964); and Stewart Ewen, *Captains of Consciousness* (New York: McGraw-Hill, 1976) develop most forcefully lack or scarcity as a consequence of consumption.

5. For a discussion of consumption as a symbolic activity, see Mary Douglas and Baron Isherwood, *The World of Goods* (New York: Basic, 1979).

6. On the world of goods in early modern Europe, see among others, Lawrence Stone, cited above; Joan Thirsk, *Economic Policy and Projects: The Development of Consumer Society in Early Modern England* (Oxford: Clarendon, 1978); Chandra Mukerji, *From Graven Images: Patterns of Modern Materialism* (New York:

Columbia U P, 1983); and most recently, Simon Schama, *The Embarrassment of Riches: An Interpretation of Dutch Culture* (Cambridge: Harvard U P, 1987).

7. Jean Baudrillard, *Le système des objets* (Paris: Gallimard, 1968), 98.

8. Karl Marx, *Capital*, I, ii. Quoted in Rachel Bowlby, *Just Looking: Consumer Culture in Dreiser, Gissing and Zola* (London: Methuen, 1985), 25.

9. For discussion of consumption in early modern London, see F. J. Fisher, "The Development of London as a Centre of Conspicuous Consumption in the Sixteenth and Seventeenth Centuries," *Transactions of the Royal Historical Society,* 4th series, 30 (1948), 37–40; Joan Thirsk and Chandra Mukerji, cited above.

10. Heinrich Bullinger, *The Christian State of Matrimony,* trans. Myles Cloverdale (London, 1575), 34ᵛ.

11. Thomas Becon, "Catechisme," *Workes* (London, 1564), xxiiᵛ.

12. *Ibid.,* xiiᵛ.

13. See, for example, Constance Jordan, "Feminism and the Humanists: The Case of Sir Thomas Elyot's *Defence of Good Women,*" *Renaissance Quarterly,* 36 (1983), 181–201.

14. Though I am looking at the woman primarily as consumer, there are numerous examples of women as sellers in the period, from Heywood's *Faire Maide of the Exchange* in which the middle-class heroine withstands the blandishments of a higher ranking seducer, to *Tell-Trothes New Yeares Gift* (1593) in which merchants are chastised for marrying "suche matchless paragons as are for neatnesse not to be mated in a countrey" to set them "in their shoppes to tole in customers" with only the proviso that "they keepe them out of their mony boxes and closecubberds" (18).

15. For a general discussion of Jonson's metropolitan topicality that does not address issues of gender, see Leo Salingar, "Farce and Fashion in *The Silent Woman,*" *Essays and Studies,* 20 (1967), 29–46; Susan Wells argues that Jonson represents a transitional moment when the marketplace is no longer a communal gathering place, but simply a location of exchange and profit in "Jacobean City Comedy and the Ideology of the City," *ELH,* 48 (1981), 38.

16. Ben Jonson, *Epicoene,* ed. Edward Partridge (New Haven: Yale U P, 1971). All references are to this edition.

17. Margaret Ezell shows that in the early seventeenth century, women began to participate in such educational associations in *The Patriarch's Wife* (Chapel Hill: U of North Carolina P, 1986).

18. *London and the Countrey Carbanadoed,* 25–6, quoted by Fran C. Chalfant, *Ben Jonson's London* (Athens: U of Georgia P, 1978), 72.

19. Fops like Amourous La Foole do not, in my view, argue against the claim for the feminization of consumption since they are notoriously feminized in Jacobean comedy—identified with women in their pursuits, rarely successful in their seductions, and the object of similar satire. A related male character type, the prodigal, is deployed in plots of repentance and salvation not available to female characters.

20. Jonas Barish observes that though Jonson's presentation of cosmetics is based on Ovid's *Ars amatoria,* Ovid emphasizes the factitious rather than the natural in "Ovid, Juvenal, and *The Silent Woman,*" *PMLA,* 71 (1956), 213–24. Whereas in Ovid cosmetics are represented as concoctions of natural ingredients—milk and honey—Jonson's metaphors are taken from metalwork: women are gilders whose

finished products are likened to statues and canvases all painted and burnished. On the economics of the *blazon,* see Patricia Parker, *Literary Fat Ladies* (London: Methuen, 1987), 126 ff.

21. By the Restoration Mrs. Otter is no longer remembered for her fortune or her social aspirations, but merely as a type of the domineering wife and "Tom Otter" as the henpecked husband. Pepys reports that Charles II said of his brother James that he "would go no more abroad with this Tom Otter and his wife. Tom Killigrew, being by, answered, 'Sir, pray which is the best for a man, to be a Tom Otter to his wife or to his mistress?' meaning the King's being so to Lady Castlemayne," J. F. Bradley and J. A. Adams, *The Jonson Allusion Book* (New Haven: Yale U P, 1922), 336.

22. See Norman Brett-James, *The Growth of Stuart London* (London: Allen & Unwin, 1935) and F. J. Fisher, cited above. For a discussion of James's urban policy and Jonson's middle masques, see Leah Marcus, " 'Present Occasions' and the Shaping of Ben Jonson's Masques," *ELH,* 45 (1978), 201–25.

23. I. Disraeli, *The Curiosities of Literature* (1849) III, 402, quoted by Fisher, "Development of London," 45.

24. C. H. McIlwain, *The Political Works of James I* (Cambridge: Harvard U P, 1918), 343–4.

25. John Chamberlain, *The Letters of John Chamberlain,* ed. Norman E. McClure (Philadelphia: American Philological Society, 1939), II, 475.

26. Richard Ohmann, "Modes of Order," *Linguistics and Literary Style,* ed. Donald C. Freeman (New York: Holt, Rinehart and Winston, 1970), 213.

27. Ohmann, "Modes of Order," 215.

28. P. M. Hanover, *Arbella Stuart* (London: Eyre and Spottiswoode, 1957), 243.

29. Hanover, *Arbella Stuart,* 75.

30. Horatio F. Brown, ed., *Calendar of State Papers and Manuscripts, Venice* (London: Eyre and Spottiswoode, 1900), X, 54.

31. Chamberlain, *Letters,* I, 253.

32. Elizabeth Cooper, *The Life and Letters of Lady Arabella Stuart* (London: Hurst and Blackett, 1866), vol. II, 296–97.

33. Chamberlain, *Letters,* I, 434, 437.

34. *Calendar of State Papers and Manuscripts, Venice,* IX, 42.

35. Lynn Hunt, "History as Gesture," presented at the English Institute, 1988.

36. Louis Althusser, et al., *Reading Capital,* trans. Ben Brewster (London: New Left Books, 1970), 18. I am grateful to Ellen Rooney whose recent presentation on Althusser at the Pembroke seminar provoked this discussion.

37. Althusser, *Reading Capital,* 19.

18

Pastimes and the Purging of Theater
BARTHOLOMEW FAIR (1614)

Leah S. Marcus

"And never rebel was to arts a friend," John Dryden observed in *Absalom and Achitophel.* That notion is, of course, untenable: one wonders what John Milton would have made of it. But it was a common perception in seventeenth-century England, at least in certain circles. Traditional pastimes and the theater were parallel cultural forms in that they held the same ambivalent status, outside the rules of ordinary life, yet integrally bound up with it. They tended to happen together, masques, plays, and traditional games all being particularly rife at holiday times and enjoyed in the same places—at court and, in the London area, in the no-man's-land of the liberties, outside the City's legal jurisdiction and under the protection of the crown. Queen Elizabeth I had been an avid, if frugal, supporter of the drama, and the "precise people" who had ventured to condemn plays and players during her reign had sometimes acknowledged warily that they were opposing a group "privileged by a Prince."[1] Under the Stuarts, however, defense of the drama came to be much more closely tied to defense of the monarchy. As in the case of the *Book of Sports,* James I deliberately forced the issue. He made the theater a royal monopoly— a branch of his prerogative—so that anyone attacking the drama was assailing an aspect of his power.

Enemies of the stage regularly charged that plays rested on lies and hypocrisy, reminding their readers that the Greek word *hypocrite* had meant both actor and pretender. But defenders of the drama were quick to return the charge. Those who muttered against plays and masques were "open Saints and secret varlets" who concealed their true natures for nefarious ends.[2] In *Love Restored,* when Robin Goodfellow is accused of hypocrisy, he answers, "We are all masquers sometimes." The joke operates on a number of levels. Robin is in fact a member of the theatrical company The King's Men, playing the part of Robin Goodfellow, a spirit of country jollity, who, in turn, has attempted to pass himself off as a hypocritical Puritan feather-maker—disguise upon disguise upon disguise. But his challenger is also an actor and therefore also a "hypocrite," a player of roles. The need to act, mime, and take pleasure in such functions, Robin implies, is a natural human trait. It can either uplift or debase, depending on the degree to which it is acknowledged and therefore made open to regulation and refinement. This is a standard Jacobean argument for the drama, as for other traditional customs. By extension, it is an argument for the royal monopoly. By claiming the power to "license" and regulate it, James was ensuring that the human needs it met would be channeled to the betterment of the nation. Otherwise, the argument went, those needs were likely to be driven underground, twisted toward evil and seditious ends.

Bartholomew Fair is pervasively grounded in contemporary controversy over theatrical arts and traditional pastimes and trenchant in its commentary upon those Plutuses—Puritan or otherwise—who made it their "lawful" calling to challenge the authority of the king. The play has inspired fine commentary from a number of perceptive critics. But opinion has divided sharply over whether it is (to use one of its own recurrent puns) a foul play or a fair one—a dark indictment of human irrationality and moral decay or a celebration of the rejuvenating energies of folly and festival disorder.[3] A study of its "occasion" will demonstrate that Jonson fully intended to have it both ways. He immerses his audience in the seamy squalor of Smithfield and exposes the vice and blasphemy which can lurk behind noble ideals like law and religion and education. The shabby, tinsel world of Bartholomew Fair seems to slough off higher cultural forms as irreconcilable with its nature. But Jonson's fair is not all foulness, and those who would have it so must reckon with some awkward incongruities.

In the Prologue to the king, Jonson warns James not to expect too much from his fair but nevertheless promises "sport" and, for a "fairing," the gift traditionally offered by those returned from a fair, "true delight."[4] James would presumably have been amused by the fair's grotesques and, beyond that, would have found rare "sport" in the play's unmasking of what he habitually identified as two major species of rebel against his authority: the Puritan who uses religion as a cloak for personal aggrandizement and the judge who argues for the supremacy of law, meaning by that the supremacy of himself. But the true delight Jonson proposes is a wider pleasure than the sport of seeing one's enemies exposed. The play carries too many echoes from contemporary defense of public mirth, echoes even from the Anglican liturgy for the Feast of Saint Bartholomew, an official holiday of the

Church, for its "fair" festival side to be discounted. Unlike some of his sons, Jonson was seldom one to romanticize popular sports—he does not allow his audience to lose contact with their raucous, gritty earthiness. There is considerable tension in the play between the "fair" and the "foul" levels of its argument. But in *Bartholomew Fair* the author's ambivalence, or at least some of it, is channeled into defense of the king. The "fairing" offered King James is the "true delight" of seeing one's cherished beliefs about the potential functioning of plays and pastimes reflected in the uncommon looking glass of a play about plays and pastimes.

In both the Induction to the Hope audience and the Prologue to King James, Jonson adamantly denies that *Bartholomew Fair* is meant to satirize individuals. In the Induction he wards off any "state-decipherer, or politic picklock of the scene" so "solemnly ridiculous as to search out" models for the personalities who wander his fair, and in the Prologue to James he again protests that he writes "without particular wrong, / Or just complaint of any private man / Who of himself or shall think well or can" (*Fair,* 23, 33). This formulation effectively shields *Bartholomew Fair* against accusations of slander. If any individual is so rash as to protest that he has been singled out for reflection in the unflattering mirror of the play, it will be because he cannot think well of himself. His protest will be motivated (according to the standard theory) by secret recognition of his own culpability and will therefore amount to a confession that he needs the play's tart correctives. And yet Jonson's pious caveats against politic picklocking have the effect of whetting our curiosity for precisely the activity he warns us against. Several modern critics, suspecting that the poet doth protest too much, have set out to identify historical figures as the butts of Jonson's satire and found striking parallels among his contemporaries. The Lord Mayor of London in the year 1614, like Adam Overdo, ferreted out dens of iniquity through spies and went "himself in disguise to divers of them"; he also seasoned his discourse with references to classical authors, much in Overdo's style. The famous Banbury Puritan William Whately, known as the "roaring boy of Banbury," habitually preached at fairs, as Zeal-of-the-Land Busy does, to gather a "fairing of souls" for God. Bartholomew Fair was a favorite time for Puritan invective against the drama because the crowds of fairgoers visiting London filled the playhouses to overflowing.[5]

Jonson almost certainly expected a similar picklocking on the part of his contemporary audience, but that does not mean that his warnings against it are entirely disingenuous. When the poet steers us away from attempts at specific identification he is not denying that parallels with contemporaries can be found, but advising us not to dwell on them at the expense of larger issues. Many Puritans preached at fairs; several Lord Mayors played detective. Overdo's bustling in search of "enormities" and his grave distress over the corrosive effects of puppetry and poetry also recapture the attitudes of a number of contemporary Justices of the Peace, whose court records are full of similar opinions and long lists of "notable outrages." There are even intriguing parallels between Overdo and Chief Justice Edward Coke, the king's principal opponent in issues of royal prerogative.[6] But we are not encouraged to stray in search of particulars. Jonson's characters are composites, representative of contemporary anti-court attitudes and argumentative styles; his play analyzes tendencies they have in common, especially their worship of law.

For a play about holiday license, *Bartholomew Fair* is curiously permeated with legalisms. Before it even gets underway, the Hope audience is invited to accept a formal contract granting them lawful right to criticize the work in proportion to the price of their tickets; they are authorized to sit in judgment on their "bench" like justices of the King's Bench (*Fair*, 31). The play itself teems with legal authorities: Busy, Overdo, Wasp, and Littlewit all see themselves as lawgivers in their respective realms of religion, secular government, education, and poetry. There is much talk in the play of licenses and warrants—proofs of legitimacy without which little can be accomplished. At the height of the fair's swirling madness, Trouble-all requires legal sanction even for the act of losing a cloak or downing a pint of ale. There is also much talk of license in the opposite sense of freedom from the authority of law—a liberty which the fair's hostile observers find licentious. Words like *liberty, law, license,* and *judgment* seem forever to be sliding out of meaning in the chaos of Smithfield, so that our sense of what *is* lawful is seriously impaired. Most of those making it their business to enforce some legal system end up in the stocks, like common transgressors of law; the legal documents juggled at the fair finally authorize actions contrary to what they first specified as lawful. One of the play's overriding themes is the *tu quoque*—let him who is without sin cast the first stone. Taken literally, this precept would undo all human capacity to penalize breaches of law.

Bartholomew Fair's emphasis on legalisms has struck a number of readers, but we have failed to recognize how Jonson's *tu quoque* applied to contemporary circumstances.[7] *Law, license,* and *liberty* were loaded words in 1614, as thick in the air about London as they are in the vapors of Bartholomew Fair. Jonson deliberately clouds the atmosphere of his play with legalistic obscurities in order to undercut what he saw as a contemporary tendency to worship legal authority. His target is not the law itself, but the abuse of law. Beneath its surface of folly and obfuscation, *Bartholomew Fair* is a lucid and elegant defense of royal prerogative, particularly the king's power to "license" plays and pastimes, against those contemporaries who grounded their opposition to such "licentious enormities" in the doctrine of the supremacy of law.

The play is aimed specifically at two parallel areas of contemporary dispute over law and license: the drama, under the authority of the king, and the pleasure fair of St. Bartholomew, under the authority of the London Corporation. In his Induction to the Hope audience, Jonson playfully establishes the identity of two things: his play, performed under license by the king's Master of Revels in the newly opened Hope Theater, Bankside, on the night of 31 October 1614 and the fair of St. Bartholomew, allowed by royal charter and proclaimed annually in Smithfield by the Lord Mayor of London from the twenty-fourth to the twenty-sixth of August. Jonson acknowledges that some of his more literal-minded viewers may, like the Hope stage keeper, object to the play's lack of such fine fixtures of the fair as the juggler and "well-educated ape"; nonetheless, Jonson assures us, his "ware" is precisely the same. He has even observed a "special decorum" as regards unity of place, the Hope Theater "being as dirty as Smithfield, and as stinking every whit" (*Fair*, 34). This "special decorum" serves an important rhetorical function. It forces us to see the similarities between the two and therefore points out the inconsistency of those contemporaries, particularly in London, who damned the "license" of the king's theater on all sorts of high moral grounds but managed to tolerate their own fair. The *tu quoque* of *Bartholomew Fair* is aimed especially at them.

For decades, as any student of theatrical history knows, the City fathers had opposed virtually all dramatic activity in and about London, as the king's old enemies, the Kirk, had in Edinburgh and for many of the same reasons. But the patents issued by James I to his own acting companies specifically exempted them from local restrictions. Although privy council records for the period have not survived, we know from numerous other sources that the years just before 1614 were a time of tug of war between the king and his privy council on one hand, and the Mayor and the City Corporation on the other. The king claimed power to license plays and players in and around London, and to override local ordinances against them; the City claimed the right to curb the royal monopoly within its liberties through enforcement of its own and parliamentary ordinances.[8] But what the City fathers condemned when it produced revenue for the king, they found considerably less objectionable when it produced revenue for themselves. Bartholomew Fair had two parts and it is important that we keep them straight. There was, first of all, the cloth fair, mostly business, which took place within the walls of St. Bartholomew Priory; its revenues went to Lord Rich, owner of the priory. Secondly, there was the pleasure fair outside the priory walls; Jonson's play deals almost exclusively with the pleasure fair, whose profits went to the London Corporation.[9] The area of the pleasure fair had not become part of the liberties of London until 1608. In that year, reportedly in return for funds to build a new Banqueting House, the king offered the city a new charter which specified that the "circuit, bounds, liberties, franchises, and jurisdictions" of London be extended to include the area around the priory, noteworthy for its annual fair, and Blackfriars and Whitefriars, noted for their theatrical connections.[10] Just as he was asserting royal control over the culturally marginal institution of the theater, he invited the City to try its hand at coping with the fair. However, while City fathers applied their new authority over Blackfriars and Whitefriars to curb the drama as much as they could, they showed less zeal in Smithfield. There was a notable "reform" in 1614: the muddy swamp of the fairgrounds was paved at City expense and made a "clean and spacious walk." The impetus for this improvement came from the king, who sent a letter to the Lord Mayor ordering it done. The Lord Mayor obeyed only after considerable protest.[11]

It is easy to see how these inconsistencies could be viewed by unsympathetic observers. So long as the City Corporation allowed in their fair the same liberties they condemned in the theaters, their high-sounding arguments about law and morality could appear purely self-serving. We need not, of course, agree with this prejudiced assessment. The king was acting as much in his interest as Londoners were in theirs. But the king's supporters would have drawn additional ammunition from the subsequent history of the fair. Bartholomew Fair was not suppressed during the Interregnum. When plays and traditional holiday pastimes had been banished from all of Britain by act of Parliament, similar frivolities were still allowed at the fair. Even its puppet theater, with its plays of "patient Grisel," "fair Rosamond," and Suzanna survived, as diaries and pamphlets from 1648, 1651, and 1655 record.[12]

Jonson's equation between fair and play therefore functions as an indictment of the king's London opposition, but an indictment tempered with mercy. He advises its grave citizens and judges not to carry on about the "enormities" of the royal monopoly of the drama until they have curbed the "enormities" of their own fair. In the process, they will come to recognize that they themselves participate in the imperfection for which they castigate others. At the end of the Induction, Jonson asks his viewers to judge the "ware" of his play by precisely the same standards that they would the wares of the fair; otherwise, the poet will "justly suspect that he that is so loth to look on a baby or an hobbyhorse here, would be glad to take up a commodity of them, at any laughter, or loss, in another place" (*Fair*, 34). That "other place" is Smithfield. Sober sorts who shrink from the vanities of the playhouse while allowing themselves to profit from the vanities of the fair are counseled to look to their motives.

If Jonson's case against the City of London is to gain conviction, however, he must demonstrate his proposition that the "ware" of the play and the "ware" of the fair are in fact the same. On the most obvious level, he accomplished this by making the two events coterminous. The fair is the play and the play, except for its opening scenes, is the fair. Any objection to the scurrility of one is at once an admission of the foulness of the other since the two are indistinguishable. Both are episodic in structure: the Induction enumerates the "sights" of the play as though they were a succession of spectacles at a fair, and the visitors to the fair watch its changing scene as they would the scenes of a play. Like a play, the fair has its "prologue" of a cutpurse and "five acts," its "orations" and its "tragical conclusions," and a player (Wasp) who is "Overparted" (*Fair*, 91, 96, 100). But Jonson is considerably wittier than that; the landscape of the fair symbolically recapitulates aspects of the Hope Theater, particularly those features its enemies found most reprehensible.

The poet sets us along the path of interpreting his work by pointing out a first element of correspondence between the two—their foulness—Smithfield and the Hope being equally "dirty" and "as stinking every whit" (*Fair*, 34). But the two locations have other physical features in common. The stage at the Hope was not the usual fixed platform, but a movable scaffold resembling the street stages used at fairs.[13] A major contribution to the Hope's stench was that it also served as a Bear Garden and the animals were stabled nearby. On alternate days its scaffold stage was removed and bearbaiting took the place of plays. After 1616 the theater was given over exclusively to bearbaiting, another monopoly of the king's and a frequent form of entertainment at court. City authorities opposed the sport as a danger to public order. In 1583 when a Paris Garden scaffold had collapsed during a Sabbath baiting, the Lord Mayor and other authorities had attributed the catastrophe to the wrathful hand of God, and the sport was not permitted in London.[14] But the City's own fair nevertheless boasts its own holiday bearbaiting: Ursula, the gargantuan brawling "enormity" at the heart of it, has a name signifying *little bear* and she is forever being baited by the other characters. Knockem calls her "my she-bear" and she disdains the "lion-chap" with which he snaps at her (lions did in fact bait bears—a variation on the sport introduced by King James himself). But her encounter with Knockem is a mere opening skirmish. When Quarlous and Winwife enter her booth, the baiting begins in earnest. They snap at the "she-bear," seeking to wear her down with wit, and she roars back with epithets which turn them into her dogs: "dog's-head" and mongrel "trendle-tail" (*Fair*, 80). She begins to tire, but after a brief mêlée and a scalding, she emerges the wounded but triumphant "Ursa major," as bears against dogs generally did.

Jackson Cope has pointed out that Jonson associates Ursula with the standard symbols of Ate, goddess of mischief and discord.[15] However Londoners may rail against royal bearbaiting as a source of riot and disorder, they harbor an equivalent manifestation of the Goddess Discordia in the center of their own fair. Just as the Hope Theater, in the Liberty of the Clink and safely out of their jurisdiction, was transformed into a bear ring every other night, so the "theater" of the fair becomes a ground for the baiting of Ursula. We know that puppet plays were sometimes performed after the baitings at Paris Garden, and the same custom was probably continued at its successor, the Hope. If, as some critics have suggested, Ursula's booth was either adjacent to or actually transformed into the puppet theater for act 5, then the imitative sequence is even closer. The scene of the fair becomes in turn a bear garden and then a puppet stage, as the Hope Theater did in 1614.[16]

Once Jonson's symbolic equivalence is established, it is easy to recognize how the particular types of foulness which surface in his fair parallel the vices City fathers berated in the theater. They condemned plays as the "occasyon of frayes and quarrelles" and argued that tolerance for the theater had brought the fall of Rome,[17] but their fair harbors equal disorder. In act 4, with its complicated and pervasive wrangling, any remaining semblance of social coherence breaks down into lawlessness. They complained that the theaters were a favorite resort of cutpurses and suppressed the jigs at the end of plays ostensibly for that reason in 1612, but at Bartholomew Fair cutpurses do a thriving business under the very noses of the authorities. They condemned plays as "very hurtfull in corruption of youth with incontinence and lewdness" and the "alleurynge of maides" into debauchery,[18] but their fair is equally rife with sexual laxity and in a more organized form. Even upstanding citizens like Win and Mrs. Overdo are easily enlisted among "my Lord Mayor's green women" (*Fair*, 146).

Plays, according to City authorities, were reprehensible even when they did not spawn worse forms of vice because such mere tinsel and trifles foolishly wasted "the time and thrift of many poore people."

The fair is also crowded with cheap allurements and the promise that drums and rattles can transform a life. "What do you lack?", its vendors cry to all comers, and Bartholomew Cokes, a young person notably poor in judgment, heeds their cry, loading himself up with baubles more obviously superfluous than anything he would find at the theater. As Jonson may have known, Bartholomew Fair had been founded by a notable trifler, the court jester of King Henry I.[19] For Jonson's most unsympathetic contemporaries, plays were nothing less than madness: "What else is the whole action of Playes, but *well personated vanity*, artificiall folly, or a lesse Bedlam frenzie?"[20] Yet the madness of the stage yields nothing to the "frenzie" of the fair, which boasts its traditional resident maniac Arthur O'Bradley, which teems with fools natural and "artificiall," and where the very notion of sanity threatens to dissolve altogether.

Jonson's portrait of the fair also speaks to anti-theatrical arguments of an overtly Puritan stamp. Extremists among the Puritans likened playhouses to hell itself, calling them "devil chappels" and evoking lurid visions of the actions on stage as the machinations of demons, half-hidden in the stychian smoke of tobacco.[21] The same can be said of the fair. It is shrouded in noxious "vapors" and its center, Ursula's booth, is its bottomless inferno, belching forth fire and fumes. "Hell's a kind of cold cellar to't, a very fine vault" (*Fair*, 65), or if not Hell itself, then the hellish fires of paganism. Some of the most avid play-scourgers condemned drama on account of its heathen origins and its association with Roman fertility rituals and sacrifices, an argument which receives satiric short shrift in Jonson's own "*Execration upon Vulcan*" when he describes Puritan reaction to the burning of the Globe Theater in 1613:

> The Brethren, they streight nois'd it out for Newes,
> 'Twas verily some Relique of the Stewes:
> And this a Sparkle of that fire let loose
> That was rak'd up in the *Winchestrian* Goose
> Bred on the *Banck*, in time of Poperie,
> When *Venus* there maintain'd the Misterie.
>
> (*Jonson*, 8:209)

But as Jonson and other contemporary classicists knew, fairs, festivals, plays, (and even brothels), had been closely related cultural forms in classical times, found together as part of the same ceremonial structures. Jonson steeps his fair in paganism. It has its resident deities and heroes, an "Orpheus among the beasts," a "Ceres selling her daughter's picture in ginger-work," its Neptune and its Mercury, its "oracle of the pig's head," its overlay of fertility symbols and blessings for increase, its leafy pagan bowers (the fair booths), and its ritual sacrifices with fire "o' juniper and rosemary branches" (*Fair*, 76, 93). Eugene Waith suggests that the staging of the play may have been designed to emphasize the fair's connection with medieval and classical conventions: "The booths recall the mansions of the old mysteries, and more dimly, the houses of Plautus and Terence" (*Fair*, 217).

But Jonson's strongest argument for the hypocrisy of City authorities comes from the fact that all the dramatic arts they declaim against when supervised by the king, they permit in debased form as major attractions of the fair. The Smithfield area had lingering theatrical associations of its own. The royal office of the revels, which prepared masques and plays for court, had until 1607 been located near Smithfield, and Inigo Jones himself had been born in Saint Bartholomew Parish. Jonson certainly had this fact in mind, despite his disclaimers, when he created the character of Lanthorn Leatherhead, whose booth peddles the debased shards of masquing—puppets and tinsel baubles.[22] But the only masque contemplated at the fair is the forty-shilling wedding masque for Bartholomew Cokes—a travesty of the noble spectacles at court—to be scrapped together out of Leatherhead's fiddles and toys, Nightengale's doggerel, and Joan Trash's gingerbread. Smithfield was also associated with plays. The old interludes performed at Skinner's Well, some of them probably in connection with the Feast of St. Bartholomew, the patron saint of Skinners, had died out— perhaps as late as the 1580s[23]—but puppet plays, some of them with religious themes, were allowed at the fair. Near Smithfield there was also a theater, the notorious Red Bull, derided by contemporaries for catering to the lowest citizen tastes and noted from time to time for its attempts to stage opposition plays.[24] Appropriately, then, the reigning dramatic authority at the fair is John Littlewit, who stands upon the supremacy of law (his own) in the kingdom of wit. His wife is as well dressed as any of the wives of the players, and the local Justices of the Peace are on his side. While those "pretenders to wit," the "Three Cranes, Mitre, and Mermaid men," are dependent on "places" at court for their livelihood, he can "start up a justice of wit out of six-shillings beer, and give the law to all the poets and poet-suckers i' town" (*Fair*, 37).

But Littlewit's "dainty device" of a bawdy puppet play stands up rather poorly alongside the work of his rivals, the "Three Cranes, Mitre, and Mermaid men." His puppet play has all the external trappings of a regular stage play: "motions" and other visual effects, elaborate costumes, and an audience with the usual complement of dimwits who fail to understand the nature of dramatic illusion. In

206 / Leah S. Marcus

Littlewit's play, however, there is precious little *but* scurrility and illusion. Through the puppet play, Jonson cleverly exposes Smithfield theatrical tastes, which ran from empty spectacle to simplified rehash of the classics.[25] As Leatherhead explains, to play by the "printed book" would be "too learned and poetical for our audience" (*Fair*, 164). City moralists were tireless in condemning the "license" of the great theaters about London, yet allowed puppet plays at the fair—a drama deprived of noble essence and shabbily jumbled together like baubles from Leatherhead's stand.

Bartholomew Fair does have its would-be correctors: Humphrey Wasp, who buzzes against it out of some secret and incomprehensible wrath; Adam Overdo who tolerates the fair in theory but seeks to curb its enormities in the name of civic zeal; and Zeal-of-the-Land Busy, who declaims against plays, fairs, toys, and every sort of sport on grounds of Puritan principle. On the face of it, this acknowledgment of reforming efforts by contemporary magistrates and religious leaders would seem to blunt the force of Jonson's indictment. If the opponents of the king's public mirth were simultaneously working to redress kindred evils under their jurisdiction, then they were not easily accused of hypocrisy. But they all fail. At the end of the play, they have been disarmed and silenced while the fair continues unabated. And they all fail for the same basic reason: they are so blinded by their own unrecognized faults that they cannot discover what lies beyond. In the mirror of Jonson's play (which is simultaneously the fair) they unwittingly see themselves and their own secret vice. Each learns that the *tu quoque* applies to him.

Notes

1. E. K. Chambers, *The Elizabethan Stage* (Oxford: Clarendon, 1923), 1:129–30; and William Rankins, *A Mirrour of Monsters: Wherein is plainely described the manifold vices . . . caused by the infectious sight of Playes . . .* (London, 1587), fol. 2. The Dryden quotation is from *Absalom and Achitophel*, line 873.

2. See the commendatory poems to Heywood's *Apology*, especially Richard Perkins's, fols. 22ᵛ–23ʳ; William Prynne, *Histrio-Mastix* (London, 1633), 160; and Ian Donaldson, *The World Upside-Down: Comedy from Jonson to Fielding* (Oxford: Clarendon Press, 1970), 66–69.

3. I have tried to be exhaustive in my reading of *Bartholomew Fair* criticism and have gleaned some insight from nearly every piece I have read. I cannot hope to be exhaustive here; I mention only those works to which my own discussion is most greatly indebted. These include, among the "fair" critics, Jonas Barish, *Language of Prose Comedy* (Cambridge, Mass.: Harvard Univ. Press, 1960), 230–39; Joel H. Kaplan, "Dramatic and Moral Energy in Ben Jonson's *Bartholomew Fair*," *Renaissance Drama*, n.s. 3 (1970): 137–56; Richard Levin, "The Structure of *Bartholomew Fair*," *PMLA* 80 (1965): 172–79; Michael McCanles, "Festival in

Jonsonian Comedy," *Renaissance Drama*, n.s. 8 (1977): 203–19; C. G. Thayer, *Ben Jonson: Studies in the Plays* (Norman, Oklahoma: Univ. of Oklahoma Press, 1963), especially his discussion of Jonson's use of classical motifs; Eugene M. Waith's introduction to *Ben Jonson: Bartholomew Fair* (New Haven: Yale Univ. Press, 1963), 1–22; and above all, Ian Donaldson's stimulating discussion in *World Upside-Down*, 46–77 (note 2 above); and Susan Wells, "Jacobean City Comedy and the Ideology of the City," *ELH* 48 (1981): 37–60.

Among critics who emphasize the foulness of the fair, I am especially indebted to Jackson Cope, "*Bartholomew Fair* as Blasphemy," *Renaissance Drama* 8 (1965): 127–52; and Guy Hamel, "Order and Judgment in *Bartholomew Fair*," *University of Toronto Quarterly* 42–43 (Fall 1973): 48–67. In "Infantile Sexuality, Adult Critics, and *Bartholomew Fair*," *Literature and Psychology* 24 (1974): 124–32, Judith Kegan Gardiner sorts out various critical responses to the play in terms of its distinctive atmosphere of sexual regression. One of the best studies of the play's historical and economic context is Jonathan Haynes, "Festivity and the Dramatic Economy of Jonson's *Bartholomew Fair*," *English Literary History* 51 (1984): 645–68. L. C. Knights, whose studies of the contemporary context in *Drama and Society in the Age of Jonson* (London: Chatto & Windus, 1937) are otherwise most helpful, does not discuss *Bartholomew Fair* at all. In his essay "Ben Jonson, Dramatist" in Boris Ford, ed., *The New Pelican Guide to Literature 2: The Age of Shakespeare* (1955; reprinted, New York: Penguin, 1982), he claims that the play's "fun is divorced from any rich significance" (p. 416). My thanks also to Michael Shapiro, who generously allowed me to read his manuscript on the play.

4. Ben Jonson, *Bartholomew Fair*, 23.

5. For the activities of Lord Mayors, see Marchette Chute, *Ben Jonson of Westminster* (New York: Dutton, 1953), 215–16; E. A. Horsman, ed., *Bartholomew Fair* (Cambridge, Mass.: Harvard Univ. Press, 1960), xx–xxi; and David McPherson, "The Origins of Overdo: A Study in Jonsonian Invention," *Modern Language Quarterly* 37 (1976): 221–33. The 1613 Lord Mayor's Show had depicted just such activities as Overdo claims to engage in as laudable, so that Jonson's play can be seen on one level as an undoing of the previous year's pageant, just as *Love Restored* "undoes" the pageant for 1611. See David M. Bergeron, "Middleton's Moral Landscape: *A Chaste Maid in Cheapside* and *The Triumphs of Truth*," in *"Accompaninge the Players": Essays Celebrating Thomas Middleton, 1580–1980*, ed. Kenneth Friedenreich (New York: AMS Press, 1983), 133–46. For the Puritans see also the *Dictionary of National Biography* for Whatley; Henry Morley, *Memoirs of Bartholomew Fair*, 4th ed. (London: George Routledge & Sons, 1892), 140–41; the prefatory biography of William Whatley in his *Prototypes, or the Primarie Precedent . . . Practically applied to our Information and Reformation* (London, 1640); and W[illiam] D[urham], *The Life and Death of that Judicious Divine, and Accomplish'd PREACHER, ROBERT HARRIS, DD.* (London, 1660), 25. John Stockwood's *A sermon Preached at Paules Crosse on Barthelmew day, being the 24. of August 1578* (London, 1578) is a splendid example of an attack on the theater made in connection with the fair.

6. Like Overdo, Coke was an "upstart" judge, had a loose and meddling wife, and was "silenced" by being removed from his post of Chief Justice of the Common Pleas to the post of Chief Justice of the King's Bench on 25 October 1613, a year before the premiere of Jonson's play. See Thayer, *Ben Jonson*, 144; and Catherine Drinker Bowen, *The Lion and the Throne: The Life and Times of Sir Edward Coke* (Boston: Little Brown, 1951), 125–26, 313–50.

7. See especially Donaldson, *World Upside-Down*, 50–59; and Wells, "Jacobean City," who has shown the play's engagement with issues relating to royal licensing. I am also indebted to Steven Mullaney's work on the ideology of theatrical marginality, in *The Place of the Stage: License, Play, and Power in Renaissance England* (Chicago: Univ. of Chicago Press, 1988).

8. In the absence of Privy Council records, elements of the conflict must be pieced together from other sources. For the general conflicts between the king and the City or town corporations during these years, see Chambers, *Elizabethan Stage*, I:337–38 and 4:249 (which describes an inflammatory 1608 sermon by William Crashaw that may have touched off a renewal of the old controversies in London); and Virginia Cocheron Gildersleeve, *Government Regulation of the Elizabethan Drama* (New York: Columbia University Press, 1908), 44–214. For an account of the controversy as carried out through pamphlet warfare, see Elbert N. S. Thompson, *The Controversy Between the Puritans and the Stage* (1903; rpt New York: Russell & Russell, 1966), 134–42; Richard H. Parkinson, ed., *An Apology for Actors (1612) by Thomas Heywood, A Refutation of the Apology for Actors (1615) by I. G.* (New York: Scholars' Facsimiles & Reprints, 1941); and for individual literary works which argue one side or the other, Robert Tailor, *The Hogge Hath Lost His Pearl* (printed in 1614), a play performed illegally by apprentices in 1613 and popularly taken to be about the controversy between the Lord Chamberlain and the Lord Mayor (a proof of the strength of the controversy in the public mind, since the work itself seems to carry only scattered references); *Hogge* is reprinted in Robert Dodsley, *A Select Collection of Old English Plays*, ed. W. Carew Hazlitt, vol. 11, 4th ed. (1875; reprint, New York: B. Blom, 1975), 423–99. See also the dedicatory poems to Heywood's *Apology;* the contemporary sermons and characters cited in Chambers, *Elizabethan Stage*, 4:254–59; and the skirmishes recorded in G. E. Bentley, *The Profession of Dramatist in Shakespeare's Time: 1590–1642* (Princeton: Princeton Univ. Press, 1971), 175–76. Coke himself had argued that local magistrates had the power to suppress the "abuse of *Stage Players*" at least in some cases. See *The Lord Coke His Speech and Charge . . .* (London, 1607), sig. H2ʳ.

9. Morley, *Memoirs*, 80–114.

10. Morley, *Memoirs*, 112; Chambers, *Elizabethan Stage*, 2:480. For an account of some of the limitations of the charter, see also Valerie Pearl, *London and the Outbreak of the Puritan Revolution: City Government and National Politics, 1625–43* (London: Oxford Univ. Press, 1961), 27–33.

11. Morley, *Memoirs*, 114; and for continuing pressure, *Analytical Index to . . . the Remembrancia . . . AD 1579–1664* (London: E. J. Francis, 1878), 471.

12. Morley, *Memoirs*, 172–81.

13. C. W. Hodges, *The Globe Restored: A Study of the Elizabethan Theatre*, 2d ed. (London: Oxford Univ. Press, 1968), 63.

14. Chambers, *Elizabethan Stage*, 2:453–54, 470–71; Gildersleeve, *Government Regulation*, 165.

15. Cope, "*Bartholomew Fair* as Blasphemy," 143–44.

16. See Hamel, "Order and Judgment," 63; William A. Armstrong, "Ben Jonson and Jacobean Stagecraft," in *Stratford-Upon-Avon Studies I, Jacobean Theatre* (London: Arnold, 1960), 54; the discussion of staging in *Fair*, 205–17; and Elliott Averett Dennison's excellent "Jonson's *Bartholomew Fair* and the Jacobean Stage," Ph.D. diss., Univ. of Michigan, 1970, 49.

17. Gildersleeve, *Government Regulation,* 156; and for later recapitulation of the same arguments, the anti-theatrical sources cited in note 8 above.

18. Quoted in Gildersleeve, *Government Regulation,* 164 and 156.

19. Gildersleeve, *Government Regulation,* 164; and Morley, *Memoirs,* 1–19.

20. Prynne, *Histrio-Mastix,* 174.

21. The most colorful example I have found is William Rankins's *Mirrour of Monsters* cited in note 1 above. Rankins later fell into the very vice he declaimed against and applied his fertile imagination to the writing of plays. See Elbert N. S. Thompson, *The Controversy between the Puritans and the Stage* (New York: Holt, 1903), 89.

22. Chambers, *Elizabethan Stage,* 1:102–3; and for the early life of Inigo Jones, Peter Cunningham, *Inigo Jones: A Life of the Architect* (London: Shakespeare Society, 1848), 1–4. Cunningham points out that Jones's father was a clothworker who lived in the clothworkers' area and is therefore certain to have had very close connections with the Smithfield cloth fair.

23. See Chambers, *Elizabethan Stage,* 2:119; Heywood, *Apology,* sig. G3ʳ; and John Stow, *A Survey of London,* ed. C. L. Kingsford (Oxford: Clarendon Press, 1908), 1:16, 104. Morley (*Memoirs,* 65–67) speculates that religious plays may have survived in the Smithfield area even into Ben Jonson's adulthood.

24. On the reputation of the Red Bull, see G. E. Bentley, *The Jacobean and Caroline Stage* (Oxford: Clarendon, 1968), 6:238–47; on the staging of opposition plays, Margot Heinemann, *Puritanism and Theatre* (Cambridge: Cambridge Univ. Press, 1980), 231–32; and on the unlicensed theater, Chambers, *Elizabethan Stage,* 4:327. Thomas Dekker's *If This Be Not a Good Play, the Devil Is in It,* a nearly contemporary opposition play, was, according to its 1612 title page, acted at the Red Bull. See also Martin Butler, *Theatre and Crisis 1632–1642* (Cambridge: Cambridge Univ. Press, 1984), 181–250.

25. Jonson may have had in mind works like Thomas Heywood's four plays in badly rhymed couplets on the golden, silver, bronze, and iron ages; they had been acted at the Red Bull and were published in London between 1611 and 1613.

19

Reading the Body and the Jacobean Theater of Consumption
THE REVENGER'S TRAGEDY (1606)

Peter Stallybrass

In *The Revenger's Tragedy,* the reordering of social boundaries and the construction of genealogies through marriage is displaced by the ordering/disordering of eating and of the kiss. Into the physical gesture of the kiss are condensed the contradictory readings of the body that the play presents. On the one hand, the kiss symbolizes the unification of souls, but a unification here that is imagined as the securing of the enclosure of the family against all "foreign matter." As Gratiana repents her role as go-between, Vindice says:

> Nay I'll kiss you now; kiss her, brother,
> Let's marry her to our souls, wherein's no lust,
> And honourably love her.
>
> > (4.4.56–58)

And Castiza says to her mother:

> Oh mother let me twine about your neck
> And kiss you till my soul melt on your lips.
> > (4.4.146–47)

The kiss is imagined as the vanishing point of the body, where the family turns in upon itself in a spiritual marriage which is socially incestuous while being devoid of lust. But the kiss is also imagined as the grossest of bodily contacts. Where Castiza melts her *soul* in a kiss, the usurer's son would "[m]elt all his patrimony" so as to buy Gloriana's lips. The kiss in this second interpretation is emblematic of every contaminating touch.

In his "Three Essays on the Theory of Sexuality," Freud suggests the symbolic ambivalence of the kiss. "The kiss," he writes, "between the mucous membrane of the lips of the two people concerned, is held in high esteem among many nations . . . , in spite of the fact that the parts of the body involved do not form part of the sexual apparatus but constitute the entrance to the digestive tract" (62). Petrarchan and Neoplatonic discourse, of course, depend precisely upon the suppression of the digestive tract. The displacement upward from the genitals and the anus to the mouth is read as the melting away of the body into the breath of the soul. But the sublimating rituals of romance are always vulnerable to violent reversals. *Othello* hinges upon such a reversal. As Iago watches the elaborate courtesies of Cassio to Desdemona, he notes how Cassio kisses his own fingers: "your fingers to your lips? Would they were clyster-pipes for your sake!" (2.1.176–77). What Iago accomplishes is the violent tracing of Petrarchan sublimations back down the axis of the body to the digestive tract. The lips, rather than being the point where flesh is transformed into the airy nothingness of spirit, are metonymically associated with the anus.

Vindice oscillates between the sublimated kiss which marries his mother to his and his brother's souls and the poisonous kiss between Gloriana and the Duke, a kiss which begins "in a perfumed mist" (3.5.142) and ends with the "eating" of the Duke's mouth: "My teeth are eaten out. . . . Then those that did eat are eaten" (3.5.159–60). The splitting of the kiss into the sign of transcendent immateriality and the sign of corrupting flesh parallels the ambivalence of consumption itself. For in the play, consumption points both toward the consuming away of the body and toward its grotesque increase. Within a Freudian model, this obsession with eating/being eaten would be given a sexual genealogy. But such a model is often taken to imply a one-directional, transhistorical theory of displacement. Having opened up the whole question of sexuality by the inclusion of the mouth and the anus as sexual domains, psychoanalysis (at least in many of its forms) retreats to a teleological reading which insistently returns to the privileged domain of the phallus. Such a reading effaces the specific historical structuring of what Allon White and I have elsewhere called the gradients of displacement—the hierarchical arrangement of domains and discourses such that "displacements may occur in one direction and not in another, or alternatively . . . may encounter kinds of social resistance which they would not if flowing in the contrary direction" (Stallybrass and White, 196).

It is, indeed, striking how frequently within Renaissance discourses of the body the gradient of displacement is *from* the "sexual"/genital *to* the digestive/excretory. In, for instance, "the Church-Porch," which provides the moral gateway into *The Temple,* George Herbert devotes three stanzas to lust which "doth pollute and foul," but they serve as a relatively mild introduction to the four stanzas denouncing drunkenness and the three on boasting and swearing, sins which turn the mouth into an "open sluce." At one level, Herbert's emphasis upon the mouth simply recapitulates the centrality of eating and drinking within Christianity, a centrality recently emphasized by Caroline Walker Bynum in her fine study of the religious significance of food to medieval women, *Holy Feast and Holy Fast*. As the Flemish mystic Hadewijch wrote, "[L]ove's most intimate union / Is through eating, tasting, and seeing interiorly," and John Tauler preached in the fourteenth century that "[t]here is no kind of matter which is so close to a man and becomes so much a part of him as the food and drink he puts into his mouth" (qtd. in Bynum 4). Christ was, after all, born in a *manger*—he was born to be eaten in the sacraments of bread and wine. "You must sit down, sayes Love, and taste my meat: / So I did sit and eat" (Herbert, "Love III"; 189). And the corollary of the sacramental nature of eating was a heightened disgust at the mouth's "perversions": "[i]t was the desire of food," wrote Abbot Nilus, "that spawned disobedience; it was the pleasure of taste that drove us from Paradise. Luxury in food delights the gullet, but it breeds the worm of license that sleepeth not." And Gregory of Nyssa declared that taste was "the mother of all vice" (qtd. in Bynum 36, 38). If through eating the communicant was "oned" with God, in eating, humans could equally be perceived as sinking to the level of dogs. Thus Joseph Hall wrote in *Virgidemiarum*:

> O lawlesse paunch the cause of much despight,
> Through raunging of a currish appetite.
> (bk. 4, satire 4; 62)

I do not mean to suggest that there is any simple separation of the "sexual" from the oral: any such opposition would fall back into the forms of categorization from which Freud rightly tried to free sexuality. But it is important to note how often Vindice, like Herbert, fixates upon the mouth.

Vindice, indeed, stages a sustained meditation, both macabre and playful, upon the eater and the eaten. Hence, the mouth is foregrounded at crucial moments in the play. At his death, the Duke eats poison which eats out his teeth (his own instruments of eating). He is then forced to watch the kissing of his wife and his illegitimate son, an "incest of their lips" (3.5.179), before they exit to "feast" (3.5.213–14); as Vindice previously told Lussurioso, Spurio "like strong poison eats / Into the duke your father's forehead" (2.2.163–64). And the final masque of death is staged after "a furnished table" (5.3.s.d.) has been brought forth for the banquet to celebrate Lussurioso's accession.

It is also of interest that Vindice, in disguise as the corrupt agent of Lussurioso, adopts the name of Piato, which Florio defines as a "dish" or "course" served "at any feast" (qtd. in Tourneur 3). This suggests both his debasement into the food that Lussurioso consumes and the method by which, like Gloriana's skull, he will infect the court. For again and again, eating is transformed into an act of purging, a vomiting out of the poisoned and poisonous body.

This food loathing is one which Julia Kristeva has brilliantly depicted in her description of the abject:

> Loathing an item of food, a piece of filth, waste, or dung. The spasms and vomiting that protects me. The repugnance, the retching that thrusts me to the side and turns me away from defilement, sewage, and muck. The shame of compromise, of being in the middle of treachery. The fascinated start that leads me toward and separates me from them. (Kristeva 2)

But for Kristeva, "food loathing" (such a marked feature of Elizabethan and Jacobean tragedy) is "elementary" and "archaic." As a result, she is forced to misread Mary Douglas's work, upon which her own *Powers of Horror* is so dependent. For Douglas, bodily disgust is never simply an "archaic" given. On the contrary, the processes of attraction and repulsion which Kristeva analyzes are invariably treated by Douglas as *social* processes (which is not for a moment to imply that they are not psychic processes "as well"):

> We cannot possibly interpret rituals concerning excreta, breast milk, saliva and the rest unless we are prepared to see in the body a symbol of society, and to see the powers and dangers credited to social structure reproduced on the human body. (Douglas 115)

The body then is a social map, not the determinant of eternal psychic structure. Yet psychoanalysis is right to emphasize the orifices of the body, even if it is wrong to treat these openings and exits in isolation from other social thresholds.

One alternative account of the body is that provided by Mikhail Bakhtin. Bakhtin defines two competing models of the body: the classical and the grotesque. The classical represents the body as far as possible without orifices: "the opaque surface and the body's 'valleys' acquire an essential meaning as the border of an enclosed individuality that does not merge with other bodies and the world" (320). The grotesque, on the contrary, emphasizes those parts of the body "that are open to the outside world," "the open mouth, the genital organs, the breasts, the phallus, the potbelly, the nose" (26). According to Bakhtin, the grotesque interrogates and subverts the classical, rejecting "all the forms of inhuman necessity that direct the prevailing concept of the world" (49). For Bakhtin, then, the body can only be imagined within specific social representations. Yet he too tends to work within an essentialist problematic, one in which the "classical" always mirrors the dominant classes and the "grotesque" the subordinated.

But in most Renaissance interrogations of the court, as in *The Revenger's Tragedy*, it is the *dominant* which is conceptualized within the canons of the grotesque body: the malcontent or the revenger plays out his transformations within a grotesque aesthetic, while insistently referring to an ideal of the enclosed body which he sets in opposition to the court. Vindice, for instance, characterizes the court above all in terms of the "illegitimate" circulation of organs and orifices: adultery is attributed not only to the Duke but also to Lussurioso, Spurio, and the Duchess, who "will do with the devil" (1.1.4). In other words, *The Revenger's Tragedy* inverts the relations which Bakhtin posits between the two canons of the body. Here, the "classical" body is that of the dispossessed, the "grotesque" body that of the dispossessing elite. But as the relation of dominance between the two canons is inverted, so is the significance of the canons themselves. The "classical" no longer stands in for the haughty separation of the elite from the "vulgar"; on the contrary, it comes to signify a purely defensive posture. Not to be eaten, not to be entered: these are the tropes of negation which organize Vindice's resistance to the court.

The closed body, then, represents the negation of "conversation," that most Janus-faced of Renaissance terms, pointing at once to the supposedly civilizing powers of rhetoric and toward its powers of corruption, and above all of sexual corruption. Words, food, sex, money: all circulate out from the court, all are aimed at the entry, the "poisoning," of the chaste woman. "Chaste" speech, if it exists at all, is imagined as taking place between the living and the dead in the one-sided conversation of Vindice with Gloriana. But in the land of the living, the "starving" Vindice is displaced by his own adopted role as go-between, the bearer of words, money, sexuality which "enter" the enclosure of his own family. Most critics have seen this transformation in terms of Vindice's moral corruption. But if we bracket the question of character, a different perspective becomes possible in which the central issue is the impossibility (both socially and epistemologically) of any enclosed space for the subordinated.

If such a space remains as a phantasy within the play, it is increasingly replaced by the question of whether it is possible to reverse the direction of "gifts": i.e., while the theater of power uses Vindice as the go-between for its "offerings," he attempts to use the power of theater to proffer in return his own poisoned gifts of words and sex. Yet this return is imagined not through any powers of his own, but rather through his mediating role in relation to the body of Gloriana and Castiza. "His" gift, in other words, is the body of another, the body of a woman. But this gift, can only secure his own position if it fulfills two contradictory demands: that it "become" his body and his words (Gloriana) while remaining the opposite of his own entered body and ventriloquized words (Castiza). In the process, woman is split, on the one hand into the very opposite of the phallic tongue, and, on the other, into the poisoning mouth itself. Yet to secure Vindice's role, all knowledge of this split must itself be erased: hence, on the one hand, the disappearance of Gloriana from the script after act 3, and on the other, the securing of Castiza's "integrity." Theatricality, previously inextricably related to women's supposedly protean transformations, is rewritten as the revenger's own ingenuity, a story which can be told and boasted of only on condition of the erasure of the women who initiated that story.

How are we to understand this movement from the foregrounding to the erasure of woman's body? It is inscribed, I would argue, within the ambivalent figure of the tongue (see Simmons). For the tongue stands in for the arts of rhetoric, which are conceptualized both in terms of female seduction and excess and in terms of phallic domination. These two formulations are brought together in the central scene, where the trope of the female seducer, impersonated by a tongueless skull, inseminates the Duke with poison. In this inversion of sexual and social hierarchy, the silent mouth of woman transfixes the tongue of masculine authority. And as the Duke lies, speechless, with a dagger through his tongue, he is forced to watch his Duchess replace his own tail/tale with that of his bastard son. The nailing of the Duke's tongue, in other words, suggests his impotence to prevent his insertion into an "illegitimate" narrative in which he will become, as Othello fears,

> The fixed figures for the time of scorn
> To point his slow unmoving finger at!
> (4.2.54–55)

It is, of course, just such an "illegitimate" narrative (in which the poisonous/unruly woman dismembers the tales of masculine authority) which Vindice stages. Yet Vindice is himself consumed by a narrative aimed at the "illegitimation" of his own family. "Entered" by Lussur- ioso's money (1.3.111), he becomes a mere relay of another's workings: "I must suit my tongue to his desires" (4.2.10). As a consequence, the "enclosed" family will come to play the roles of corrupted sexuality, Vindice as pimp, Gratiana as bawd, and Castiza, in her final appearance, as prostitute. We witness nothing less than the hysteria of negation. Jonas Barish is certainly right to point toward the difficulties of displaying virtue dramatically, and he views Vindice's interrogation of his family's honor as the adoption of "the time-honoured device of the formal test. . . . [V]irtue can be *goaded* into displaying itself" ("True and False Families" 147). But while this view may help to account for dramatic motive, it tends to ignore dramatic effect. For what is displayed, with whatever ironic reservation, is the endless mirroring of the tropes of court corruption. It is not, of course, that we are supposed to suspect Castiza's virtue, but that the familial narrative is constructed out of a negation which can *never* be adequately displayed, because the staging of that display inevitably points back to the insertion of the language, money, and sexuality of the court into Vindice, which he in turn inserts into the family.

Vindice tirelessly seeks to find in woman's body the privileged container of an impermeable honor. But his own role as go-between foregrounds the process of violation by "foreign bodies." He himself is the hole in the familial cell, contaminating his own ideal. But he displaces the social processes of corruption, processes controlled by the elite's ownership and manipulation of power, money, and language, onto the abjectified body of woman, conceptualized as the immutably permeable: "Women are apt you know to take false money" (1.1.103); "Tell but some woman a secret over night, / Your doctor may find it in the urinal i' the morning" (1.3.83–84); "That woman is all male whom none can enter" (2.1.111). What is at stake in this displacement is, of course, the erasure of his *own* permeability: "This Indian devil / Will quickly enter any man" (1.3.86–87); "I've eaten noble poison" (1.3.170); "we are both made bawds" (2.2.16). Castiza, indeed, is the emblematic token of an impermeability which no courtier can attain, and she suggests an inversion of the *topos* to make it read: "That male is all woman whom none can enter." What is demanded of woman is both her obedience and subjection and, at the same time, her assertion of a separateness and self-enclosure foreclosed to the courtier, who is dependent upon the circulation of patronage.

But while one script is organized around the securing of the chaste body, another is played out in the constant oscillation between two sites of contamination: the prince and his corrupted agents, the phantasized body of permeable and permeating woman. As corrupted agent himself, Vindice attempts to transform his own role from that of permeable to that of permeating "woman"—i.e., from the poisoned to the poisoning Gloriana. Yet through his regendering of the ungendered skull, he is able to disown his own oscillations, projecting them into an image of woman's theatrical metamorphoses.

This refiguration of metamorphosis as purely female, though, is never completed. For while such a refiguration would separate Vindice from the imagined scene of contamination, it would also separate him from the scene of power. This is not only because his revenge is mediated through the bodies of Gloriana and Castiza, but also because the carnivalization of discourse, a strategy attributed to the demonized female grotesque, is also *his* strategy. Indeed, it is his precisely for the reasons which would render a female protagonist "grotesque": it is an act of liberation, at least discursively, from any given genealogy. We may say, indeed, that Vindice is split between two genealogical modes. In the first, the demand for purity is so great that it leads to social incest (the "marriage" of Vindice and Hippolito to their mother and sister); in the second, Vindice is so distant from any given genealogy that it is

As if another man had been sent whole
Into the world and none wist how he came.
(1.3.2–3)

The contradiction between these two modes is at its most intense in act 4. There the absorption of Vindice into a fixed essence (i.e., his attainment to a "crystal tower" as impermeable as Castiza's "virgin honour" [4.4.152–53]) is dramatically juxtaposed to his further trans-formation. In the first scene Hippolito tells him that "disguise must off" so that he may resume his "own shape" (57–58), and scene 2 begins with Hippolito's "So, so, all's as it should be, y'are yourself." Yet Vindice imagines this "return" as no more than a move to catch Lussurioso in a "quainter fallacy" (4.2.5). His "own shape," indeed, acts as an incitement to "appear in fashion different": "You must change tongue" (4.2.22,26), as Hippolito says. This self-transforma-tion contrasts ironically with Vindice's accusation in scene 4 that Gratiana is an "unnatural parent" who "usurps" the title of mother "by fraud" (3,9). In the first scene in the play, the prelude to his own protean dissemination was the demise of patriarchal authority ("Our lord and father" [3.5.166]), after which, he claims, "My life's unnatural to me" (1.1.119). But in act 4, scene 4, as always when confronted by female metamorphosis, he adopts the position of the forensic pursuer of a "truth" which he has imagined as leaking out of women like urine. Yet as the analyst of female virtue, Vindice moves from his role as self-conscious protean, only to be split between the positions of judging father and hysterical son ("I'm in doubt / Whether I'm myself or no"

[4.4.24–25]). Only after the "remarriage" of the siblings to each other
and to their mother is sealed by their kisses does Vindice finally turn
away from the familial script to his own self-wrought tale. Variability
of form, shape, conversation, and role: all define the assigned position
of the Renaissance actor, all define the role which Vindice simultaneously plays and repudiates—repudiates, ironically, because he is *only*
playing, as if "behind" the part his "heart" remained his own, as chaste
and unsullied as Castiza's body.

Yet it is precisely this notion of a "behind" which Renaissance
drama, like its enemies, so rigorously interrogated. What could there
possibly be "behind" Gloriana's skull? Not the "deep" signs of a pre-
given sexuality, but rather the shifting constructions of the body's
boundaries, boundaries which, as Mary Douglas argues, are always
social boundaries. So, in Vindice's overvaluation of and disgust at
woman's body, we should find the symbolic burden that women are
forced to bear (as well as the semiotic power with which they are
invested) when they are conceptualized as mapping both an ideal enclosure and its impossibility, both the negation of and the figures for
eating/being eaten, corrupter/corrupted.

When Phillip Stubbes, in his anti-theatrical writing, conceptualized
a politics of conduct, he emphasized the priority of the visual (that
which was "opposite to the eye" and "visible to the sight"). Spectacle
determined essence. But woman and actor alike threatened the legibility
of that spectacle. Consequently both required unmasking, the stripping
away of false faces and false costumes. Yet the notion of "unmasking"
could only make sense if one posited a truth that lay behind the mask.
And it is such a "truth" which, upon the Jacobean stage, the figure of
the woman (Gloriana, Castiza) and of the protean (Vindice) puts into
circulation. In the process, conduct becomes illegible, a series of maskings and unmaskings for which there can be no final stopping point or
destination. Even the theater's anti-theatrical desire to *halt* that process
could lead only to the ambivalent spectacle of Castiza impersonating
the courtesan, Vindice impersonating the bawd, and Gloriana (the
name not only of Vindice's beloved but also of the nostalgic idealization
of Elizabeth I) impersonating the poisonous prostitute. The very attempt to produce a single, "purified" identity (the reduction of woman's body to a skull) becomes the spur to the representation of a
heterogeneity which unsettles bodily decorum and the social inscrip-
tions of status and gender.

This heterogeneity was encoded above all through what I believe
was the dominant phantasy of the body's topography upon the Jaco-

bean stage: the phantasy of the gendered mouth. The mouth: a gaping hole, an absence through which presence is formed and dissolved; the lips, sealed in denial of all circulation or open to seal the marriage of "our souls" (4.4.57) or to eat "noble poison" (1.3.170); the poisoned or poisoning tongue; the teeth which eat but which also are "eaten out" (3.5.159). The mouth of fame, the mouth of abjection. A gendered mouth. In 1607, a play called *Lingua: Or, The Combat of the Tongue, and the Five Senses for Superiority* was published. In it, the five senses (Auditus, Tactus, Olfactus, Visus, Gustus) are all male; Lingua alone, who claims the position of the sixth sense, is female. Yet for all Auditus's desire to "pluck that nimble instrument" from "thy feeble sexe," Lingua's tongue is the spectacle that the play stages. A spectacle of renown and order: "How many Rebells have I reclaymed when [Psyche's] sacred authority was little regarded . . . her will unperformed, her illustrious deedes unrenouned had not the silver sound of my trumpet filled the whole circuit of the Universe with her deserved fame" (3.5, F2v). A spectacle of the vanishing point of all renown and order: "she's a common whore and lets every one lie with her"; "shee railes on men in Authority depraving their Honours"; "shee lends wives weapons to fight against their husbands"; "shee's a Woman in every respect and for these causes not to bee admitted to the dignitie of a Sense" (3.5, F3v). In *The Revenger's Tragedy*, though, the tongue is not just the ambivalent sign of woman. It is, after all, the *male* courtier, Vindice, who is transformed into his patron's "smooth enchanting tongue" (1.3.111); it is he who confesses: "I must suit my tongue to his desires" (4.2.10). To say that the mouth is gendered upon the Jacobean stage is not to suggest that it represents a stable (and demonized) femininity but that it is the mark both of courtship and courtiership alike. But if the mouth is the mark of the oppressed's submission to the words of their oppressors, it is also the instrument through which the narratives of the elite are consumed, deformed, and parodied by woman and malcontent alike.

Works Cited

Bakhtin, Mikhail. *Rabelais and His World.* Trans. Helène Iswolsky. Cambridge, Mass.: MIT Press, 1968.

Barish, Jonas A. "The True and False Families of *The Revenger's Tragedy.*" *English Renaissance Essays in Honor of Madeleine Doran and Mark Eccles.* Ed. S. Henning, R. Kimbrough, and R. Knowles. Carbondale: Southern Illinois UP, 1976. 142–54.

Bynum, Caroline Walker. *Holy Feast and Holy Fast: The Religious Significance of Food to Medieval Women.* Berkeley: U of California P, 1987.

Crewe, Jonathan A. "The Theatre of the Idols: Marlowe, Rankins, and Theatrical Images." *Theatre Journal* 36 (1984): 321–33.

Douglas, Mary. *Purity and Danger: An Analysis of the Concepts of Pollution and Taboo.* London: Routledge, 1970.

Freud, Sigmund. "Three Essays on the Theory of Sexuality." In *On Sexuality.* Trans. James Strachey. Ed. Angela Richards. Pelican Freud Library, vol. 7. Harmondsworth, Eng.: Penguin, 1977.

Hall, Joseph. *The Poems of Joseph Hall.* Ed. Arnold Davenport. Liverpool: Liverpool UP, 1969.

Herbert, George. *The Works of George Herbert.* Ed. F. E. Hutchinson. Oxford: Oxford UP, 1941.

Kristeva, Julia. *Powers of Horror: An Essay on Abjection.* Trans. Leon S. Roudiez. New York: Columbia UP, 1982.

Lingua: Or, The Combat of the Tongue, and the Five Senses for Superiority. London, 1607.

Shakespeare, William. *Othello.* Ed. M. R. Ridley. Arden edition. London: Methuen, 1965.

Simmons, J. L. "The Tongue and its Office in *The Revenger's Tragedy.*" *PMLA* 92 (1977): 56–68.

Stallybrass, Peter, and Allon White. *The Politics and Poetics of Transgression.* Ithaca: Cornell UP, 1986.

Stubbes, Phillip. *The Anatomie of Abuses.* Ed. F. J. Furnivall. The New Shakespeare Society. 2 vols. London: Trubner, 1877–79.

Tourneur, Cyril. *The Revenger's Tragedy.* Ed. Brian Gibbons. New York: Hill, 1967.

20

The Logic of the Transvestite
THE ROARING GIRL (1608)

Marjorie Garber

Bottom. I will aggravate my voice so that I will roar
you as gently as any sucking dove; I will roar you and
'twere any nightingale.
(Midsummer Night's Dream 1.2.76–78)

The phenomenology that emerges from analytic
experience is certainly of a kind to demonstrate in
desire the paradoxical, deviant, erratic, eccentric, even
scandalous character by which it is distinguished from
need.[1]

Materialist and historicist feminist critics have tended, recently, to
read Middleton and Dekker's play *The Roaring Girl* thematically as a
play about the economic injustices of the sex-gender system. These
critics see female cross-dressing as a metaphor for the changing condition of women. As we will see, the play's anxiety about clothing
and fashion, which is omnipresent, is indeed conjoined with a related
anxiety about sexuality, but that anxiety is not so much based upon
women's emancipatory strategies as upon the sexual inadequacies of
men. In an effort to explore the relationship between transvestism and
desire, then, let us look at *The Roaring Girl,* a less readily allegorized
text than cross-dressing plays like *As You Like It* or *Twelfth Night,*
with its urban setting, canter's slang, and biographical subtext, the
"real-life" story of Mary Frith. For in this play the historical figure
herself functions as an unmasterable excess, and thus opens the question of transvestism's relationship to the embodiment of desire.

Born in 1584, Mary Frith, better known as Moll Cutpurse, was a
notorious London figure, who dressed in men's clothes throughout her
long life (she died at 75, after a career that spanned professions from
pickpocketing to prostitution and bawdry, and ultimately—long after
the play—to tavernkeeping). Her predilection for male attire, and the
angry resistance of Jacobean society to women in men's clothing, is
strongly attested to in *The Consistory of London Correction Book,*
where dressing as a man is one of the offenses with which the historical
Moll was charged.[2]

Moll had appeared on the stage in a scandal of self-display, unseemly
for women of any class but the aristocracy—in this case, the public

stage of the Fortune Theater, where, according to court records, she
"sat there upon the stage in the publique viewe of all the people there
p[rese]nte in mans apparrell and playd upon her lute & sange a songe."[3]
The Epilogue to the play seems to promise a return of this spectacle,
dissolving the artifice of the false or fictive Moll in the anticipation
of the "real" one: if the writers and actors have disappointed the
expectations of the audience, "The Roaring Girl herself, some few days
hence, / Shall on this stage give larger recompense." Yet this is as likely
to be a sly glance backward at the first scandalous appearance as a
genuine offer to display Moll's body again for public delectation. The
lute playing incident may also be behind the episode of Moll's singing
and playing upon a viol in 4.1. where jokes are made upon her taking
down the gentleman's instrument and playing upon it, and reference
is made to censorious dames who think the viol "an unmannerly
instrument for a woman." In any case, the play is clearly grounded in
social history as well as literary and formal precedent. Like David
Hwang's *M. Butterfly,* which capitalized on the real story of a French
diplomat's love affair with a Chinese "woman" who turned out to be
a man,[4] *The Roaring Girl* was produced at a time when the cultural
referent, the "real" Moll, was in the news; as Mary Beth Rose notes,
it is probable that Middleton and Dekker were "attempting to benefit
from the *au courant* notoriety of the actual Moll in the timing of their
play."[5]

That the play itself is concerned with clothing, and with the commu-
tability of class and gender as categories capable of anxious social
disruption, is manifest not only from its titular heroine but also from
Middleton's note to the "Comic Play-Readers" in the 1611 Quarto:

> The fashion of play-making I can properly compare to nothing so
> naturally as the alteration in apparel; for in the time of the great crop-
> doublet, your huge bombasted plays, quilted with mighty words to
> lean purpose, was only then in fashion; and as the doublet fell, neater
> inventions began to set up. Now, in the time of spruceness, our plays
> follow the niceness of our garments; single plots, quaint conceits,
> lecherous jests, dressed up in hanging sleeves; and those are fit for
> the times and the termers. Such a kind of light-colored summer stuff,
> mingled with divers colors, you shall find this published comedy;
> . . . Venus, being a woman, passes through the play in doublet and
> breeches; a brave disguise and a safe one, if the statute untie not her
> codpiece point.[6]

The "statute" referred to in this last phrase is of course the code of
sumptuary laws that prohibited both cross-dressing and sartorial class-
jumping from one station to another.[7] *Should* the statute untie her

codpiece point, of course, the audience would see more than it had perhaps bargained for, since the wearer of the codpiece, the player dressed as Moll the roaring girl, would have been a boy actor. Venus in doublet and breeches might have suggested the goddess's cross-dressed appearance in the *Aeneid,* where her buskins, quiver, and tucked up gown made her resemble a huntress, a Spartan or Thracian girl, one of the followers, not of Venus, but of Diana, an Amazon *in potentia,* and a mortal rather than a goddess—a class distinction of some moment. But not to her son. That Aeneas reads beneath the disguise, does not interpret the clothes except as a ruse, is itself some indication of Middleton's take on the pervasive, indeed obsessive, concern with clothing in this play. The sense of this passage is that bulky clothing styles and bulky, weighty plays are likewise out of fashion. "The alteration in apparel" is made deliberately analogous to other alterations in public taste; anxiety about clothing, as well as anxiety about *sexual* alteration (sexual identity and sexual performance) will predominate throughout the play.

Thus Mary Fitzallard, daughter of Sir Guy and beloved of the young hero, Sebastian Wengrave, makes her initial appearance (and the first appearance of any actor in the play) "disguised like a sempster," or seamstress, carrying a case of "falling bands," or flat collars, a style that had replaced the ruff. "Sempster" is immediately glossed as "needle-woman" by Sebastian's servant, (1.1.51), presumably with a glance at the phallic woman who is the boy actor playing Mary Fitzallard. As for "falling bands," a sartorial joke is made on them, too, since "bands" are also "bonds" and "banns"; face to face with Sebastian, Mary reproves him for his neglect of their "bond fast sealed"; "Is this bond canceled? Have you forgot me?" (1.1.57–60)—in effect, she accuses him of the "falling bands" that she has emblematically chosen as her wares. Later in the play Mary Fitzallard will appear in another disguise, that of a page, the traditional Renaissance stage role for the woman-dressed-as-a-man; in 4.1. Mary, Sebastian, and Moll Cutpurse are *all* dressed as men, and as Sebastian kisses Mary, Moll comments drily that it seems strange for one man to kiss another. The homoerotic subtext here, like the encoding of sartorial/class consciousness, is not merely thematic or illustrative, but intrinsic to the inner dynamics of the play, to what might be called the play's "unconscious."

What else is in the play's unconscious? What does it know?

The Roaring Girl is a play about the circulation of parts, about women with penises and testicles and men who lack them. Thus, for example, when in Act 2 scene 2 Sir Alexander overhears a tailor designing a costume for Moll, he realizes that the design is not only for a pair of breeches, but, in effect, for a phallus, one that will stand round and full (if somewhat stiffly) between the legs (2.2.80–100). Moll is to be a "codpiece daughter." No wonder he is disconcerted; this is what has always been feared about women who wear the pants. "Normalized" or tamed by a dramatic genre which seems reassuringly realistic and socio-economic (the emergent middle class, the male and female shopkeepers of the City, the moneyed urban aristocracy with their conservative mores, the tavern underclass, and, in this context, the woman who rebels against social and economic constraints) this play, looked at hard, discloses a dangerous, carnivalized fantasia of dislocation, in which the fetishization of commodities is the cover for the fetishization of body parts. It is a play that theorizes the construct-edness of gender in a disconcertingly literal way through the construc-tion of bodies—and of clothes. The tailor makes the man (and the tail); but the tailor also wields the shears.

Consider the character of the suggestively named Laxton. Laxton is described by Rose as a "lecherous, misogynistic gallant" (380), and by Jean Howard as a "gentleman rake,"[8] but a joke as broad as the one about Moll's extra "yard" of cloth in the tailor scene ("yard" of course is also slang for penis) is made by Sir Alexander the first time he appears onstage:

> Sir Alexander.   furnish Master Laxton
> With what he wants, a stone—a stool, I would say,
> A stool.
> Laxton.   I had rather stand sir.
> Sir Alexander.   I know you had, good Master Laxton.
>   (1.2.56–60)

Laxton is in fact "lack-stone," the fellow without testicles, who would stand if he could, but may not be capable of doing so. Sir Alexander's parapraxis (Laxton "wants," that is both *lacks* and desires, a *stone*) suggests his estimate of his companion's virility. "Stone" as testicle recurs throughout the play—a stallion is a "stone-horse" (2.1.86) (something Moll tells Laxton derisively that she knows how to ride), and the dandies in the feather shop are informed by no less an authority than Mistress Tiltyard that certain feathers are "most worn and most in fashion / Among the beaver gallants, the stone riders, / The private stage's audience" (2.1.156–59). (Beaver hats were notoriously expensive—Stubbes in the *Anatomie of Abuses* cites prices of 20, 30, and 40 shillings[9]—and were worn at one time by both men and women; it seems possible that the modern slang meaning of "beaver" may also be anticipated here, especially since a "beaver" is a hat.[10])

It may be worth noting that the New Mermaid editor, Andor Gomme, looks resolutely away from this reading of Laxton's sexual etymology, preferring an entirely different onomastic code; Laxton's name, he says, "suggests that . . . all his lands are sold."[11] This is in the context wholly reasonable, since, as we will see, the marriage/ property system in this play is located in, and exists as a sign for, the register of the symbolic (one of the play's merchant aristocrats is named "Lord Noland"). Laxton's name foregrounds him as a figure of "lack," and the recognition of this lack permits or requires his entry into the socio-economic world of patriarchy and commerce. But to deny or repress the specific sexual elements of "lack" in Laxton by regarding these passages as merely general proofs that "Middleton is a master of . . . sexual innuendo"[12] is like labeling the dirty jokes as "bawdy" or "obscene punning" and leaving them at that. In a similar way Gomme (whose own name means "eraser") comments on Moll's assertion, upon the appearance of Mary Fitzallard as Sebastian's true bride "thank me for't; I'd a forefinger in't" (5.2.169) that "despite Moll's skill with instruments we should probably resist a sexual innuendo here." His decision to register this resistance in a footnote is more interesting than the "innuendo" itself. In short, *The Roaring Girl*'s omnipresent references to castration, emasculation, penises and testicles worn (like clothing; extra "yards," "codpieces," "trinkets") by women rather than men tell a story—a story somewhat different from the progressivist narrative of economic and cultural reconfiguration urged by both modern British editors and modern American feminists.

Nor is Laxton the only ambivalent (or ambivalently named) male figure in the play: the gallants are named Jack Dapper, Sir Beauteous Ganymede, and Sir Thomas Long—this last yet another familiar reference to the penis yet again (cf. *Lady Chatterley's* "John Thomas"; Sir Thomas—Sir Thomas *Long*—would seem to be a walking penis), while the interest of the men in fashion (Dapper, Beauteous) is related by the text to their questionable (bi)sexuality. Jack Dapper's father, who jokes in a complex pun (based on the name of a law court and debtors' prison, the "Counter") that he will make his son a "counter-tenor" (equating castration with loss of economic power [3.3.81]) laments further that "when his purse jingles, / Roaring boys follow at's tail, fencers and ningles" (3.3.67). Ningles, or ingles, are homosexual boy-favorites, whose attractiveness as love-objects offers a strong homo-erotic subtext. In the beginning of Act 4 Moll sees Sebastian kissing Mary Fitzallard when Mary is dressed as a page boy (Gomme, apparently uncomfortable with the implications of this scene, describes it as a "dubiously suggestive piece of something near perversity"[13]). Moll herself notes wryly that it's strange to see one man kissing another (she of course is also dressed as a man in that scene, and both women's parts are played by men).

The anxiety of lack and the circulation of simulacra are, for Jacques Lacan, the very insignia of human sexuality. Because the human being is a *speaking* being, he or she must articulate desire and identity in language, must have recourse to the dimension of the Other in the constitution of a self. Thus, body parts take on the value of signifiers and can enter into circulation in multiple, figurative, displaced forms. The system of desire is organized around the phallus, which is neither a phantasy nor an organ but "a signifier . . . intended to designate as a whole the effects of the signified . . . . It can play its role only when veiled, that is to say, as itself a sign of the latency with which any signifiable is struck when it is raised . . . to the function of signifier."[14] In learning that the mother does not have the phallus (that is, in interpreting the difference between the sexes in terms of lack), the subject, according to Lacan, gains access to the desire of the Other ("designating by the Other the very locus evoked by the recourse to speech"). Lacan goes on:

> One may, simply by reference to the function of the phallus, indi-cate the structures that will govern the relations between the sexes.
>
> Let us say that these relations will turn around a "to be" and a "to have," which, by referring to a signifier, the phallus, have the opposed effect, on the one hand, of giving reality to the subject in this signifier, and, on the other, of derealizing the relations to be signified.
>
> This is brought about by the intervention of a "to seem" that replaces the "to have," in order to protect it on the one side, and to mask its lack in the other, and which has the effect of projecting in their entirety the ideal or typical manifestations of the behaviour of each sex, including the act of copulation itself, into comedy. (289)

In other words, there is a profound connection between theatricality and sexuality, between having, being, and "seeming." Once "seeming" enters the picture, it is capable of coming to substitute for all other terms, and everything is "derealized"; anything can be a simulacrum, a "comedy." Lacan makes the theatricality of sexuality even more explicit in what follows:

> Paradoxical as this formulation may seem, I am saying that it is in order to be the phallus, that is to say, the signifier of the desire of the Other, that a woman will reject an essential part of femininity, namely, all her attributes in the masquerade . . . . (290)
>
> The fact that femininity finds its refuge in this mask, by virtue of the fact of the *Verdrangung* [repression] inherent in the phallic mark of

desire, has the curious consequence of making virile display in the human being itself seem feminine. (291)

"Having" and "being" the phallus are alike conditions of lack. It is that lack which constitutes desire, and which calls into play the "masquerade." In *The Roaring Girl* the lack is multiply overdetermined, in the masquerade of Moll Cutpurse in male attire (even her name), in Laxton's multiple lacks and *his* emblematic name, in the dandyism of Laxton and the other gallants, Dapper, Ganymede, and so on, whose displays of virility (in the feather shop, in the sempstresses', in swordplay with Moll) precisely "has the curious consequence of making virile display in the human being itself seem feminine."

As the play has been trying to tell us all along ("yard," "stones," "trinkets," "stiff," "stand," at tiresome length), Moll is the phallus. The mark of desire in the Symbolic. The signifier that is constituted by, and in, a split.

Over and over again *The Roaring Girl* draws attention to the fact that its two heroines have the same name: Mary. Moll says that she pitied Mary Fitzallard "for name's sake, that a Moll / Should be so crossed in love" and therefore arranged for her to dress (*cross*-dress) as a page: "My tailor fitted her; how like you his work?" (4.1.68–71). Sir Alexander, convinced by his son's stratagem that Sebastian wants to marry Moll Frith (rather than Mary Fitzallard), remonstrates that "Methinks her very name should fright thee from her":

> *Sebastian.* Why is the name of Moll so fatal, sir?
> *Sir Alexander.* Mary, one, sir, where suspect is entered;
> For seek all London from one end to t'other,
> More whores of that name than of any ten other.
> (2.2.156–61)

Marylebone Park, called here (as if for emphasis) "Marybone," is the dubious district where, Laxton instructs his coachman, they are likely to find Moll Frith.[15] The name of the district, derived from "Mary le bon" (originally a reference to the Virgin) ironically incorporates both "good" and "bad" Maries (as well as the vexed question of virginity itself, and the contiguity of madonna and whore as object types of male desire[16]). In a play in which, as we have already seen, names take on a humorous or allegorical significance (Lack-stone, Dapper, Beauteous Ganymede), this doubling of Moll and Mary Fitzallard (both Mary Fs) extends the range of the psychoanalytic reading suggested by Laxton's lack and the phallicized Moll. The figure of the transvestite, in dream-logic terms already a figure *for*—as well as *of*—overdetermination, here becomes split into the apparently marginal and separable, and the apparently central. But it does so, again, in an insidious and disturbing way, by substitution and replacement. Sebastian wants one girl, and so pretends to want the other; he substitutes Moll for Mary in order to get Mary. But what he gets may be a Mary who is no longer separable—if she ever was—from Moll.

Let us see how this works within the text. The play begins, and ends, with Mary Fitzallard's betrothal to Sebastian; in the opening scene it is covert and contested, opposed by Sir Alexander in his role as patriarch; in the last scene Mary and Sebastian are openly reunited, with Mary publicly welcomed as young Wengrave's "wife" and "bride." In between these two scenes comes Sebastian's subterfuge (he pretends to be in love with Moll in order to make his father see how much better off he would be with Mary), Moll's arrangement with her tailor for a new pair of breeches and her (offstage) employment of that same tailor to dress Mary in a page's costume, and the denouement in which Moll appears in her role as Sebastian's fiancée dressed as a man, is greeted with horror by Sir Alexander because of her clothes ("Is that your wedding gown?" [5.2.101] he asks, and his friend Goshawk, with a gesture toward the homoerotic subtext of the boy actor, replies: "No priest will marry her, sir, for a woman/Whiles that shape's on; and it was never known/ Two men were married and conjoined in one./ Your son hath made some shift to love another" [106–109]) and is finally replaced in the wedding tableau by Mary Fitzallard. Sir Alexander, who could be said to represent the stereotypical male gaze throughout the play, now asks her pardon for his misreading:

> Forgive me, worthy gentlewoman; 'twas my blindness:
> When I rejected thee, I saw thee not.
>
> (5.2.192–193)

But Sir Alexander's apology, though gracious, is misdirected. He *did* see Mary Fitzallard when he looked at the cross-dressed Moll Frith; the conflation of the two figures, as in dream logic, tells its own suggestive truth about who and what Sebastian is marrying. (We might here remember that other Sebastian, in Shakespeare's *Twelfth Night,* who was also "betrothed unto a maid and man"). Both Rose and Jean Howard read Mary Fitzallard as a much more conventional, female character than Moll; Howard remarks that though Moll sees marriage as a straightjacket for herself, she nonetheless promotes it for Mary, "and if comedy demands a marriage, it gets the marriage of Mary Fitzallard and Sebastian, but not the marriage of Moll" (Howard, 438–

39). Rose recognizes a strategy of displacement, but locates it on the level of conscious choice and dramatic convention: Moll, she claims, takes on the social and psychological freedom of the traditional disguised heroine "without providing the corresponding reassurance implicit in that heroine's eventual erotic transformation. These functions are instead displaced onto Mary Fitzallard, who, disguised as a page, joyously sheds the disguise to take her place as Sebastian's wife in the final scene. Moll, on the other hand, having served as the instrument who brings about the happy ending, is nonetheless excluded from the renewed comic society" (Rose, 389).

In effect, these feminist historicist readings, despite themselves, reinstate the patriarchal aesthetics of closure, by separating (or keeping separated) the figures of Moll and Mary. But I would contend that in doing so they reinscribe the politics the play deconstructs. If Moll *is* Mary, if the similarity of their names indicates that one is a projection of the other, then Moll is not so much a role model as a recognition and a phantom, not a sign of the road not taken or a metaphor for the aspirations of early modern feminists but a sign of the double division of the concept of the "roaring girl" (female/male; Mary/Moll). Not either/or but both/and. The *in*divisibility of the subject-as-object, the female transvestite as that which puts in question the traditional gender divisions, is present not only in Moll, the liminal, lower-class outsider who outspokenly dismisses marriage as social enslavement, but also, and already, in the apparently more conventional Mary Fitzallard, whose desire for marriage compels her, through the play's logic, to cross-dress.

The scene in which Moll, Mary, and Sebastian all appear onstage in men's clothes is, in one sense, the exposure of the transvestite theatrical structure and its homoerotics (Moll: "How strange this shows, one man to kiss another?" Sebastian: "I'd kiss such men to choose, Moll, / Methinks a woman's lip tastes well in a doublet" [4.1.47–49]), but in another sense it is the navel of the dream, the *mise en abyme*, the place where "truth" is disclosed—or "disclothed." The play splits the figure of the "roaring girl" into acceptable and less acceptable, social integrated and outlaw, upper class and lower, Mary-the-good and Mary-the-not-so-good. But, as in a dream, this split is a defensive acknowledgment of what is not so readily separated in waking life, or in history, or in any other configurations of the self-designated "real." However assured Sir Alexander may be to the contrary, Sebastian does marry Moll Frith, as surely as he does kiss a man.

Thus the conception of Moll-as-politically-correct-marginal is a construct that reinscribes what it purports to challenge. The point is not that Moll represents a brave but legible and separable element of the play's populace, one whose self-avowed chastity (in contrast with the historical Moll's prostitution) protects against promiscuity in the past and self-replication in the future, but rather than in getting Mary Sebastian gets Moll, too—and in getting Moll (as heroine, as role model, as proto-feminist) the reader or audience gets Mary, the monogamous heterosexual woman who cross-dresses—in a way frequently recorded in historical cases from the period[17]—in order to be with her man.

The editor of the New Mermaid edition of Dekker and Middleton's play commented as recently as 1974 that "the revival of interest in Jacobean comedy has largely passed *The Roaring Girl* by."[18] Despite approving comments by Swinburne and T.S. Eliot, wrote Andor Gomme at that time, "*The Roaring Girl* has dropped back into obscurity." Yet ten years afterward the play was already enjoying a new vogue.[19] In the manner of such things, it has now become the one cross-dressing play (other than Shakespeare's) most students of the period study. I can't help but think that that is at least in part because of the positive-role-model-challenge-to-the-sex-gender-system-disruption-of-the-old-verities view of the play. Moll Cutpurse is indeed, as is often noted, a cross-dresser who differs from Rosalind and others in that she is not in disguise; she is what sexologists today would call a (relatively) continuous or constant cross-dresser, rather than an episodic one,[20] though she does not cross-dress to pass (everyone onstage knows she is a woman—although everyone offstage, presumably, also knew she was played by a boy). She has been extensively cleaned up from the original, "historical" Moll, as is also noted; her virginity—in fact, a fairly common choice on the part of female-to-male cross-dressers in the early modern period[21]—and the fact that she gives back stolen money make her an attractive rogue heroine of the Robin Hood (or Paladin) type. She is not really anti-social or disturbingly transgressive to a modern reader, though she stands as a placeholder for the energies of transgression. By looking backward at Moll's place in "history," contemporary readers can look forward to their own struggles with sex-gender inequalities, and also (though this sounds trivial) to their own struggles with gender-inflected dress codes. The female professor in pants, the female undergraduate in blue jeans, finds in Moll (and even in Mary) an attractively innovative predecessor.

Furthermore, *The Roaring Girl* occupies a position in the Elizabethan-Jacobean canon quite analogous to the position occupied by Moll within the play. Like her it is marginal, a kind of outsider, hard to contextualize and integrate into the old rules (in this case, the conventional rules of comedy), doubled (the "shared authorship" question: which part is by Dekker and which by Middleton? do they represent distinct literary, cultural, and class interests, and if so can their contributions to the text be separated from one another?), but finally not disruptive to the canon itself. Again like Moll, it is the exception that proves the rule.

Even the play's fathers, patriarchal and phallocentric arbiters of the law, show the lack which is common to New Comedy, as Sir Alexander tries in vain to forbid his son's marriage to Mary, and thereby invites all the subterfuge that follows. Sebastian's "courtship" of Moll Cutpurse, the several maskings and unmaskings of the final scene (which is the bride? Moll or Mary? the one in pants or the one dressed like a woman?) all stem from this paternal repression, which is (needless to say) only an externalization of repressions that could as well be located within Sebastian—or within seventeenth-century London—or within the "sex-gender" system. The phallus is the mark of desire, and the sign of the entry into the Symbolic (the world of commerce, of land, of law, of marriage contract). Its lack, or the consciousness of its lack, is what motors the play. And if, as I have already suggested, the transvestite, specifically here the female transvestite, is the complexly overdetermined marker of that lack—is, in fact, a sign of overdetermination *itself*, as well as itself an overdetermined sign—then the play's appropriation of the locally celebrated story of Moll Frith makes *literary* sense, interpretive sense, not only sense as a historical reminder of shifting class and gender roles and *their* attendant anxieties. The anxiety here is not—or not only—about the rising power of women and the middle class, the breakdown of legible cultural distinctions as signified in dress codes governing class and gender decorum, but about something that underlies those specific cultural anxieties: an anxiety about the ownership of desire.

Critics of *The Roaring Girl* emphasize that Moll is not in disguise. Whether in pants or her frieze jerkin and black safeguard she is always read as a woman, unlike Rosalind/Ganymede, or Viola/Cesario, or any of the dozens of female pages who turn up in the cross-dressing plays of the period. What this means is that she does not, will not, cannot disappear into the fictively "real" identity of the "woman" she is supposed to be, her transvestite "other" going underground, or becoming incorporated into the dominant fiction of womanhood (femininity, object of desire). Mary Beth Rose notes that Moll "is human and will not disappear from social life" (Rose, 389). Unlike Ganymede, the transvestite who "vanishes," or who "escapes," Moll remains. She is not a figure but a subject.

Moll's existence on the "outside" or fold of the text of *The Roaring Girl* is thus a strong argument against the domestication or taming of transvestism as metaphor. "Enter Moll like a man," says the stage direction to Act 3 scene 1. The force of the theatrical moment comes from 1) the audience's awareness that this is *not* a man (i.e., is Moll), 2) the audience's awareness that this *is* a man (i.e., is a boy actor), 3) the audience's awareness that Laxton will likely be deceived, at first, by her disguise (he has just said, with sublime self-confidence, "I see none yet dressed like her; I must look for a shag ruff, a frieze jerkin, a short sword, and a safeguard"), 4) the audience's awareness that there *is* (or *was*) a cross-dressed historical personage of this same name who walked the London streets, and 5) the audience's awareness that this "Moll" is *not* that Moll, is a representation. That the play's Moll is cross-dressed, but not in disguise—that her recognizable, semi-legendary identity (in London, in literary and cultural history) as "Moll Cutpurse" is indivisible from her men's clothing—that Moll "unmasked" (SD 5.2.142) is Moll in transvestite garb suggests that the appropriation of "transvestite" and "masquerade" as enabling figures for women—for feminist critics as well as for female spectators[22]—is itself an act of phallogocentric mastery. The pleasurable tease of being a woman in masquerade, a "transvestite" in imagination, still refers back to the male as norm and hence is still itself a hegemonic move. The question is whether, in calling Moll the "phallus," we ourselves have escaped that move.

Notes

1. Jacques Lacan, "The Signification of the Phallus," in *Ecrits: A Selection,* trans. Alan Sheridan (New York: W. W. Norton, 1977), p. 286.
2. P. A. Mulholland, "The Date of *The Roaring Girl,*" *Review of English Studies* 28 (1977), 20–21, 30–31.
3. Mulholland, "The Date of *The Roaring Girl,*" 22, 30–31.
4. See "The Occidental Tourist," in Marjorie Garber, *Vested Interests: Cross-Dressing and Cultural Anxiety* (Routledge, forthcoming) for an extensive discussion of Hwang's play.
5. Mary Beth Rose, "Women in Men's Clothing: Apparel and Social Stability in *The Roaring Girl,*" *ELR* 14 (1984), 379.
6. Thomas Middleton, "To the Comic Play-Readers, Venery and Laughter." Cited from Russell A. Fraser and Norman Rabkin, *Drama of the English Renaissance, II: The Stuart Period* (New York: Macmillan, 1976). All references to *The Roaring Girl* are from this edition.
7. See, for example, Frances Elizabeth Baldwin, *Sumptuary legislation and personal*

Regulation in England (Baltimore: Johns Hopkins University Press, 1926), and Wilfred Hooper, "The Tudor Sumptuary Laws," English Historical Review 20 (1915), 433–39.

8. Jean E. Howard, "Crossdressing, The Theatre, and Gender Struggle in Early Modern England," Shakespeare Quarterly 39:4 (Winter, 1988), 437.

9. Andor Gomme, ed., The Roaring Girl (London: Ernest Benn, Ltd. 1976), p. 32.

10. See Sigmund Freud, Interpretation of Dreams, Standard Edition (London: Hogarth Press, 1901), 5:360–62.

11. Gomme, Roaring Girl, p. xxviii.

12. Gomme, Roaring Girl, p. xxx. Christopher Ricks, "The Moral and Poetic Structure of The Changeling," Essays in Criticism X (July 1960), 291.

13. Gomme, Roaring Girl, p. xxiv.

14. Lacan, "The Signification of the Phallus," p. 288.

15. Gomme's note reads: "Until 1611 Marlybone Manor was crown property: the gardens (ultimately incorporated into Regent's Park) were said in A Fair Quarrel (IV.iv.217ff.) to be suitable as a burial ground for whores and panders because it was near Tyburn. The point of Laxton's quip, however, is enriched by the linking of a pun on Marybone (=marrow bone [popularly thought of as an aphrodisiac]) and park in the sense of 'the female body as a domain where the lover may freely roam' (Shakespeare's Bawdy, 163; cf. Venus and Adonis 231ff.)."

16. See Sigmund Freud, "A Special Type of Choice of Object made by Men," SE 11:165–175.

17. Rudolf M. Dekker and Lotte C. van der Pol, The Tradition of Female Transvestism in Early Modern Europe (London: Macmillan, 1988), pp. 27–30. Under the heading of "Romantic Motives" Dekker and van der Pol report the cases of numerous women who cross-dressed as sailors, marines, or soldiers in order not to be separated from their lovers or husbands. They summarize this section with a matter-of-fact statement that registers the extraordinary difficulty of interpreting cross-dressing, even in a given historical period, as "meaning" something rather than its opposite: "In short, for the women whom we know to have been married, transvestism appears to have been either a means to remain with their husbands, or escape from them" (30).

18. Gomme, Roaring Girl, p. xix. The "Acknowledgments" to Gomme's edition carry a date of November, 1974, which is why I give that date (rather than the publication date of 1976) as the time frame for his opinion here.

19. See not only Rose and Howard, but also Linda Woodbridge, Women and the English Renaissance (Urbana: University of Illinois Press, 1986), and an excellent essay by Jonathan Dollimore, "Subjectivity, Sexuality, and Transgression: The Jacobean Connection," in Renaissance Drama 17, Renaissance Drama and Cultural Change, ed. Mary Beth Rose (Evanston: Northwestern University Press, 1986), pp. 53–81.

20. John Money, Gay, Straight, and In-Between: The Sexology of Erotic Orientation. (New York: Oxford University Press, 1988), p. 85.

21. Dekker and van der Pol, Tradition of Female Transvestism pp. 35–39. They observe that, even though many of their cases are derived from judicial archives, and would therefore present the stories of cross-dressing criminals, a documentable criminal subculture did exist in Dutch cities in the seventeenth and eighteenth centuries, in

which cross-dressing women did play a prominent role. Male disguises, pseud-
onyms, and nicknames were obviously good cover, but Dekker and van der Pol
suggest that both cross-dressers and criminals are already disposed to violate social
norms. "For women who had already crossed one fundamental social boundary,
that between men and women, it must have been relatively simple to set aside other
norms. On the other hand, women who had already attempted criminal paths felt
less intensely the social pressure which impelled individuals to behave in a way
consistent with their sexes, and they must have found it relatively easy to make the
decision to begin cross-dressing." The data generated by Dekker and van der Pol's
research is fascinating, and gives an invaluable sense of the frequency and variety
of female-to-male transvestism in the period. Nonetheless, I remain somewhat
skeptical about the elements of "must have been" and "must have found" that go
into this analysis, and indeed about any easy "psychologizing" of tendencies among
cross-dressers, in the early modern period as in the modern (or post-modern) one.

22. For transvestism as metaphor in film theory see Mary Ann Doane, "Film and the
Masquerade: theorizing the Female Spectator," *Screen* 22, nos. 3–4 (September–
October 1982), 81. Laura Mulvey, "Afterthoughts . . . inspired by *Duel in the
Sun,*" *Framework* 6, nos. 15–17 (Summer, 1981), 13. Joan Riviere, "Womanliness
as a Masquerade," in *Formations of Fantasy,* ed. Victor Burgin and Cora Kaplan
(New York: Methuen, 1986) is a key founding text for these film theorists, and
for their deployment of "transvestism" as a figure. I regard the relegation of
"transvestism" and "transvestite" to the status of a metaphor or an analogy as an
appropriation. It is striking that materialist feminists and film theorists both ar-
rive—from such different directions—at this point, of utilizing transvestism as
a metaphor, rather than confronting its transgressive power to destabilize and
reconfigure.

21

The Spectre of Resistance
THE TRAGEDY OF MARIAM (1613)

Margaret W. Ferguson

She was the only child of a rich lawyer; she was precociously bright but not beautiful; she was married at fifteen to an aristocrat who wanted an heiress's dowry. He was Protestant, as were her parents; she converted secretly to Catholicism in the early years of what proved a stormy marriage. Most of what we know about this female contemporary of Shakespeare (she was born around 1585 and died in 1639) comes from a biography written (anonymously) by one of her daughters who became a Catholic nun in France. This daughter does not however mention the fact about her mother that contributes most to her (still slim) claim on the attention of modern literary critics, namely that she was evidently the first of her sex in England to write an original published play. Her name was Elizabeth Cary and her play, printed in London in 1613, was entitled *The Tragedie of Mariam, Faire Queene of Jewry*. Mary Sidney Countess of Pembroke had translated Robert Garnier's *Marc Antoine* in 1592, and Cary's play is clearly indebted to that aristocratic experiment in Senecan closet drama.[1] But Cary's interest in the drama and in women's relation to that genre goes far beyond that of any female English writer we know before Aphra Behn. According to her daughter, Cary "loved plays extremely" and for a time at least managed to go occasionally to the London theater.[2] Her authorship of *Mariam*, along with an early play now lost and a later one on the history of Edward II, makes her the first woman in England to attempt substantial original work in the drama, a genre socially coded as off-bounds to women, authors and actresses alike.[3]

Cary's play was never performed on stage, and whether or not it was published with her permission, much less at her active request, is a question I wish I or anyone could answer.[4] Having that information would make it considerably easier than it is now to accomplish one of my chief aims in this essay, which is to prepare the ground for assessing the political significance of this play, both in its own time and in ours. Access to more empirical information about the circumstances of the play's publication would be useful because the question of a woman's right to assume a "public" voice is both central to the drama and unanswered within it. That unanswered question, which is, moreover, central not only to the play but also to Renaissance debates about the nature and proper behavior of womankind, underlies the lack of consensus among the play's (few) readers about its ideological statement. *Mariam* seems at times to mount a radical attack on the Renaissance concept of the wife as the "property" of her husband; but the play also seems—or has seemed to some of its readers, both feminist and non-feminist—to justify, even to advocate, a highly conservative doctrine of female obedience to male authority.[5] I don't intend to make a case for or against either of these interpretations. I hope, rather, to show how, and to begin to show why, the play's ideological statement is so mixed, so contradictory.

The Tragedie of Mariam tells the story of the marriage between King Herod and his second wife, the royal-blooded Jewish maiden Mariam. Like many other Renaissance dramas about this ill-fated match, *Mariam* is based on a narrative in Josephus's *Jewish Antiquities* (ca. 93 A.D.), which was published in an English translation by Thomas Lodge in 1602.[6] Evidently following Lodge's Josephus quite closely, the author nonetheless revises her source significantly. She compresses, amplifies, and transposes material in order to observe the dramatic unities, and she alters the characterization of the heroine and other female figures, as well as the portrait of the troubled marriage between Mariam and Herod, in ways that are both more extensive and more ideologically charged than critics have noted.[7]

The play opens at the moment in Josephus's narrative when Herod has been summoned to Rome by Caesar to answer for his earlier political association with Mark Antony, who had helped him acquire Judea. Having overthrown Antony, Caesar is likely to punish Herod, and indeed a rumor of his execution reaches Jerusalem, bringing joy to many who had suffered under his tyranny and bringing relief mixed with sorrow to his wife. Her ambivalent reactions to the news of Herod's death become even more complex when she learns from Sohemus, the man charged by Herod to guard her during his absence, that orders had been given that she should be killed in the event of Herod's death. Outraged by Sohemus's revelation of her husband's jealous possessiveness, and grieving still for the brother and grandfather Herod had murdered in order to secure his claim to the Judean throne (as Mariam's mother Alexandra continually reminds her), Mariam is unable to rejoice when Herod does unexpectedly return from

Rome at the beginning of Act 4. His sister Salome, who hates being placed in a subordinate position both by Mariam and by the Jewish marriage laws which prevent women from suing for divorce, schemes to get rid of her husband Constabarus and Mariam too. Fanning Herod's anger at his unresponsive wife by "proving" that Mariam is engaging in adultery with Sohemus and is at the same time plotting to poison Herod, Salome convinces the still-infatuated king to order Mariam's death by beheading. After the execution, which is described by a messenger, Herod spends most of the final act regretting, as Othello does, the loss of his "jewell."[8] Unlike Othello, however, this jealous husband created by a female playwright laments not only his innocent wife's death but, specifically, the loss of her too lately valued powers of speech.[9]

At the beginning of the play, Mariam is torn between the demands of wifely duty, which coincide at least intermittently with her feelings of love for Herod, and the demands of her conscience, which are initially defined in terms of family loyalty and voiced through the figure of Mariam's mother Alexandra. The nature of Mariam's dilemma shifts, however, as the play progresses, partly because her long soliloquies, like Hamlet's, work to dissolve binary oppositions. Also like *Hamlet,* Cary's play gives us, at the level of character, dramatic foils who mirror certain aspects, and unrealizable potentials, of the central figure. At first glance, Cary's two major foils seem to come from a medieval morality play: on the one hand there is Salome, who works, Vice-like, to plot Mariam's death; on the other, there is Graphina, a slave girl loved by Herod's younger brother Pheroras. Virtuous, humble, obedient, she seems to embody the ideal of womanhood prescribed in Renaissance conduct books.[10]

The ethical opposition symbolized by these two characters, an opposition which emerges, specifically, as one of different modes of speech, is however also shot through with complexities. Salome's structural resemblance to the morality Vice figure is partly occluded when she is made to speak crudely but eloquently against the injustice of Jewish law which gives (rich) men but not women the right to divorce (1.4); and Graphina—the only character whose name is not found in Josephus's text or in Lodge's translation of it—becomes more opaque the more one studies her brief appearance in Cary's text (2.1).[11] She is strongly associated with the feminine virtue of modest silence, but the dramatic presentation prevents us from conceiving of that virtue as a simple alternative to the "vice" of female speech, either Salome's or Mariam's. Pheroras tells Graphina that he prefers her to the bride Herod had designated for him because that "baby" has an "Infant tongue" which can scarcely distinguish her name "to anothers eare"

(2.1.562–63); the "silent" Graphina evidently has won her lover's admiration for her powers of speech: "move thy tongue," he says, "For Silence is a signe of discontent" (2.1.588). She obeys. The strange little scene queries the logic of the "chaste, silent, and obedient" topos first by suggesting that womanly "silence" may function just as erotically as speech in a non-marital relation (the conduct books never consider this possibility); and second, by suggesting that a certain kind of speech signifies the same thing that "silence" does in the discourse of wifely duty, that is, compliance with the man's wishes: Graphina tells her lover only what he wants to hear, when he wants to hear it. She may therefore be said to figure a mode of "safe" speech, *private* speech that neither aims at nor produces offense. Cary's invented name for this character might, on this line of interpretation, be significant: the name evidently plays on the Greek word for writing, *graphesis*.

If the figure of Graphina represents for Cary both the possibility of a non-transgressive mode of discourse (like private writing?) and the possibility of a mutually satisfying love relation, neither of those possibilities is available to the play's heroine. The first words Mariam speaks, which are also the play's first words, epitomize the problem:

> How oft have I with publike voice run on?
> To censure Rome's last Hero for deceit:
> Because he wept when Pompeis life was gone,
> Yet when he liv'd, hee thought his Name too great.

These lines, which are spoken in soliloquy and initiate a complex parallel between Mariam's situation and that of Julius Caesar,[12] link the theme of female public voice immediately with the idea of transgression ("run on") and the idea of "censure." The question mark after the first line seems at first merely an oddity of seventeenth-century "rhetorical" punctuation. But the question itself, voiced at the play's threshold moment by a female character whose "unbridled speech" eventually plays a major role in her husband's decision to censor her voice definitively, is not by any means simply rhetorical. It is, we might say, complexly rhetorical—for several reasons. First, to make it the kind of question that obviously requires the affirmative answer "very often," the reader must "run on" over the line's end and its punctuation. The structure of the verse creates for the reader a slight but significant tension between pausing—to respect the seemingly self-contained formal and semantic unit of the first line—and proceeding, according to the dictates of the syntactic logic which retrospectively reveals the first line to have been part of a larger unit. The verse thereby works to fashion a counterpoint between formal and semantic strains. We pause on the theme of "running on," we run on to encounter the theme of censure (as "censorship" and "critical judgment" both). The lines work not only to anticipate the drama to come (deploying the strategy of the "pregnant" opening most famously used in *Hamlet*), but also to mark the play, for Cary herself and perhaps for her first "private" readers, with something we might call the woman author's *signature*.

That signature consists not of a name but of a Chinese box set of questions about the logic of the Pauline injunction against female public speech and the cultural rule of chastity that injunction ostensibly supported. Like a lawyer presenting ambiguous fact situations to a judge, Cary invites us to consider whether the play text itself is "covered" by the law: Is *writing* a form of "public voice"? Is a *drama* not necessarily intended for performance on the public stage a legitimate form of female verbal production? Is a *soliloquy*—by theatrical convention, a "private" speech overheard (overread?) by an audience—legitimate? In short, the play opens in a way that seems designed to test, but not overtly to disobey, the rule proscribing "public voice" for women. Here we have a written representation of a female character soliloquizing, as if in private, about a prior event of (ambiguously) culpable public speech—ambiguously culpable because the comparison with Caesar's speech "degenders" Mariam's prior speech act, although the issue of gender, and a potential male audience's response to the speaker's gender, is clearly on the heroine's (and the author's) mind. Mariam goes on to transform the figure of Caesar from an (imperfect) model for a speaker to an authoritative model for an audience or judge. She suddenly apostrophizes the "Roman lord" with an aggressively defensive apology for exhibiting a fault (rash judgment) commonly ascribed to the daughters of Eve, but also characteristic of many male rulers including Caesar (who died when he failed to heed Portia's dream–inspired warnings against a public appearance):

> But now I doe recant, and Roman Lord
> Excuse too rash a judgment in a woman:
> My sexe pleads pardon, pardon then afford,
> Mistaking is with us, but too too common.
> (1.1.5–8)

Mariam's opening lines arguably address a problem that has to do not only with female speech in general but with the play's own mode of material existence, indeed, its *right* to exist in the world. The act of writing, for oneself or for an audience of family and friends, would seem—like the dramatic form of the soliloquy—to occupy a shady territory between private and public verbal production. Because of the ambiguous status of writing, Cary could in one sense have applied Mariam's opening question to herself and answered it with a decorum the fictional character lacks. "How oft have I with publike voice run on?" "Never." But that answer would not have satisfied the culturally constructed censoring power that the play text ascribes chiefly to the figure of the tyrant-husband but also to the Chorus, and, at certain moments, to the heroine herself, speaking, evidently, for an aspect of the author's own conscience or superego.[13]

According to her daughter, Cary "did always much disapprove the practice of satisfying oneself with their conscience being free from fault, not forbearing all that might have the least show or suspicion of uncomeliness or unfitness; what she thought to be required in this she expressed in this motto (which she caused to be inscribed in her daughter's wedding ring): *Be and seem*" (*Life*, 16). This passage, which attributes to Cary a rule of spiritual and social conduct as fraught with problems as the rules Hamlet formulates for himself, might be paraphrased as follows: never be satisfied that you really are as virtuous as you may seem to yourself—but always be what you seem. The difficulty of putting such a principle into practice is dramatized, in Cary's play, by the fact that the Chorus formulates one version of this rule in order to condemn Mariam for following (and articulating) another version of it.

At the end of Act 3, just after Mariam learns, through her guardian Sohemus, that Herod is still alive, she swears that she will never disguise her true feelings through hypocritical speech (3.3.1168–69) and she vows also to abandon her husband's bed (3.3.1136). Interestingly, Sohemus chastizes her, after she has left the stage, for her verbal intransigence but not for her refusal to pay her sexual "marriage debt":

> Poor guiltles Queene! Oh that my wish might place
> A little temper now about thy heart:
> Unbridled speech is Mariam's worst disgrace,
> And will indanger her without desart.
>
> (3.3.1184–87)

His lines anticipate the Chorus's criticism of her in a long speech which virtually equates female speech—and the *will* to utterance—with unbridled sexual behavior:

> Tis not enough for one that is a wife
> To keep her spotles from an act of ill:
> But from suspition she should free her life,
> And bare her selfe of power as well as will.
> Tis not so glorious for her to be free,
> As by her proper selfe restrain'd to bee.

When she hath spatious ground to walke upon,
Why on the ridge should she desire to goe?
It is no glory to forbeare alone,
Those things that may her honour overthrowe.
But tis thanke-worthy, if she will not take
All lawfull liberties for honours sake.

That wife her hand against her fame doth reare,
That more then to her Lord alone will give
A private word to any second eare,
And though she may with reputation live.
Yet though most chast, she doth her glory blot,
And wounds her honour, though she killes it not.

When to their Husbands they themselves doe bind,
Doe they not wholy give themselves away?
Or give they but their body not their mind,
Reserving that though best, for others pray?
No sure, their thoughts no more can be their owne,
And therefore should to none but one be knowne.

Then she usurpes upon anothers right,
That seekes to be by publike language grac't:
And though her thoughts reflect with purest light,
Her mind if not peculiar [i.e., "private"] is not chast.
For in a wife it is no worse to finde,
A common body, then a common minde.

And every mind though free from thought of ill,
That out of glory seekes a worth to show:
When any's eares but one therewith they fill,
Doth in a sort her purenes overthrow.
Now Mariam had, (but that to this she bent)
Beene free from feare, as well as innocent.

                                        (3.3.1219–54)

    In this remarkable speech, Cary's Chorus offers contradictory statements about the precise nature of the error Mariam has committed. According to the second stanza, the error involves indulging in, rather than refraining from, something that is characterized as "lawfull" liberty. When the Chorus goes on to specify the error as a fault of *speech,* however, its "lawfull" status seems to disappear. By stanza five, the error is the distinctly illegitimate political one of "usurping upon anothers right." And there is a corresponding contradiction in the Chorus's views of the "virtue" it is advocating. In the third stanza, which stresses the duty of relinquishing desires for speech and fame, the virtue being advocated is quite distinct from the possession of physical chastity: the woman may be "most chast" even if she does grant a "private word" to someone other than her husband. By stanza five, however, chastity has evidently been redefined as a figurative property pertaining to the mind, which is "not chast" if it's "not peculiar" (in the old sense of "private property" given by the OED). Which formulation are we to take as authoritative?

Interpreting the Chorus's speech becomes even more difficult when we try to read it in its dramatic context, as an ethical prescription for this particular heroine. The final lines seem to suggest that Mariam's tragic fate could have been averted had she refrained from speaking her mind to anyone other than her husband. But the play's subsequent development makes this notion absurd: it is precisely because Mariam speaks her mind not only to others but also, and above all, to her husband that she loses her life. Transgressive speech, defined as non-hypocritical speech, when Mariam says "I cannot frame disguise, nor never taught / My face a looke dissenting from my thought" (4.3.1407–8), is, however, not the whole problem: Mariam also contributes to her downfall by refusing to sleep with Herod. She censors the wrong thing: his phallus rather than her tongue.[14]

The problem of her sexual withholding is addressed by the Chorus only obliquely, in the form of the (apparently) rhetorical question, "When to their Husbands they themselves doe bind, / Doe they not wholy give themselves away?" By the end of its speech, the Chorus has evidently suppressed altogether the crucial issue of Mariam's denial of Herod's property rights to her body. The strange logic of the speech anticipates that of Herod's later accusation of Mariam: "shee's un-chaste, / Her mouth will ope to ev'ry strangers eare" (4.7.1704–5). The equation of physical unchastity with verbal license, expressed through the provocative image of the woman's mouth opening to a man's ear, alludes, perhaps, not only to the common Renaissance trope of the female tongue as a substitute penis but also to anti-Catholic propaganda against Jesuit priests as Satanic corrupters of women and of the institution of the confession, where male "strangers" received women's secrets. The image of a female mouth promiscuously opening to a male ear rewrites Mariam's fault as one of double excess or "openness," whereas what the play actually shows is that Mariam's verbal openness is a sign of sexual closure. Her behavior entails a property crime in certain ways more threatening than adultery is to the dominant ideological conception of marriage: this crime takes to a logical extreme, and deploys against the husband, the paradoxical ideal of wifely chastity elaborated by so many (mostly Protestant) Renaissance writers.

Neither the Chorus nor any other character in the play can clearly articulate this central problem in Mariam's behavior. The Chorus concludes by asserting that Mariam would have been "free from feare, as well as innocent" if only she had been willing to forbear filling "any's ears but one" with her words. The pronoun *one* evidently refers here, as it does in the earlier phrase "none but one," to the husband. Since the play makes it hard to give a simple "yes" to the Chorus's question about whether women should give themselves "wholly" away in marriage, however, we need to ask whether the shifter *one* might alternatively refer to God or, as Catherine Belsey suggests, to the wife herself.[15] Mariam is after all in danger because she speaks to her husband, and perhaps Cary's point, if not the Chorus's, is that if a wife has such thoughts she "would be wiser to keep them to herself, precisely because in marriage they are no longer her own" (Belsey, pp. 173–74). Salome, who successfully manipulates her husband and brother and other male characters by *never* telling them what she really thinks, offers an intriguing counterpoint to Mariam in the sphere of female verbal politics. Indeed, as Martha Slowe has cogently argued, "while Mariam who is chaste arouses suspicions by her open speech, Salome, who takes sexual and discursive liberties, preserves her reputation by guarding her speech and appearing to confine it to patriarchal limits."[16] Moreover, the play seems obliquely to ratify Salome's tactics of feigning by leaving her unpunished at the end; as Betty Travitsky has observed, the play confounds conventional moral and generic expectations by failing to expose Salome's villainy, for she is guilty of numerous crimes including that of husband murder—the felony which Renaissance jurists called petty treason and regarded as much more heinous than wife murder, since the former unlike the latter involved an offense against the very concept of "degree."[17]

The very real possibility that Mariam should have followed Salome's stark model of "private vice, public virtue" rather than the Chorus's more conventional (but very confused) prescriptions is countered, however, by the fact that verbal hypocrisy, had she adopted it, would *not* have worked to save her (married) life unless it were accompanied by sexual surrender of a kind Salome is never required to undergo. In any event, the Chorus's ethical precepts begin to look at best incoherent, at worst cynically similar to Salome's dark twisting of the "be and seem" motto into a rationalization for wives to seem as others think that they should be.

This Chorus is the moment in the drama where Cary most directly interrogates her play's own right to exist. However we construe the injunction that wives should reveal their thoughts to "none but one," it is clear that the Chorus draws around the wife a circle of privacy so small that she would err by *circulating* a manuscript, much less by publishing it. Had Cary obeyed the rule of privacy set forth by her Chorus, she might have written a play, but we would not be reading it. The play offers, however—in addition to the fascinating example of Salome's powerfully amoral and apparently successful verbal exploits—an equally problematic but more theologically sanctioned model for female disobedience to masculine authority. Behind the figure of the non-compliant Mariam lies, I would suggest, a cultural discursive construction that we might label "minority religious dissent" and trace in both Catholic and Protestant writings on the Christian subject's and/or wife's right to disobey a prince, magistrate or husband on those (few) occasions when his commands conflicted with the dictates of Christian conscience.[18] Protestant discussions of this (limited) right of dissent are well known, but Catholic teachings, which of course often portray an individual conscience disobeying ungodly authority on the advice of a Jesuit priest, are less frequently cited by modern students of English Renaissance literature.[19] If, however, historians are right in finding a distinct gender assymmetry in English recusant culture (more women than men adhered to the pre–Reformation dogmas and rituals), a passage like the following, from the Jesuit Henry Garnet's *Treatise on Christian Renunciation* (158?), would seem an important subtext for Cary's play (and her life too, as reported by her daughter): "your husbands over your soul have no authority," the treatise advises its female readers, "and over your bodies but limited power."[20]

The language Mariam uses to justify her resistance to a husband who is also a king clearly belongs to this discursive tradition of minority religious dissent, a tradition that drove a wedge into the apparently hegemonic social rule linking female chastity with silence and obedience: "They can but my life destroy, / My soule is free from adversaries power" (4.8.183–84), Mariam says after Herod has accepted Salome's false charge of adultery and proclaimed his intention to kill his wife.[21] Although the Chorus continues to argue that Mariam should have submitted to Herod's authority, thereby paying her marital "debt" and winning, through submission, the "long famous life" denied her as an object of writerly ambition (4.8.1939), Elaine Beilin rightly argues that the play's final act reconceives, and simplifies, the ideological conflict between the Chorus's perspective on wifely duty and Mariam's by presenting her death as an allegorical version of Christ's crucifixion.[22] Josephus had shown Mariam meeting her death with noble fortitude, but Cary adds numerous details that give Mariam a specifically Christological aura: the butler of Cary's play, for instance, suborned by Salome to accuse Mariam of seeking to poison Herod, hangs himself from a tree, as Judas does, in remorse for his betrayal; in Josephus, there is no mention of the butler's death.

Cary further revives her source by specifying the mode or Mariam's death; Josephus simply says that Herod ordered her executed, whereas in Cary's play, there is considerable emphasis on the "fact" that she is beheaded. This detail, unremarked by Cary's critics so far as I know, seems an overdetermined and historically volatile allusion: it conjures up the ghost of Mary Queen of Scots, whose son ruled England when Cary wrote her play and who was in the eyes of many English Catholics a victim of Protestant tyranny; it also links Mariam with the figure of Christ's harbinger John the Baptist, beheaded by Herod's servants at Salome's request. Finally, the detail implies a possible similarity between Mariam and Anne Boleyn, killed by a royal husband who had broken with the Catholic church to divorce his first wife and who was explicitly likened to the tyrant Herod by some of his disapproving subjects.[23] Infused with rich but obscurely coded theological and political meanings, Cary's play surrounds Mariam's death with an aura of sanctification altogether absent from Josephus's narrative.

There is however a price for such sanctification, with its uncannily proleptic justification of the rebellious path Cary herself would follow when she converted publically to Catholicism in the mid-1620's, enraging and embarrassing both her father and her husband, who was then Lord Deputy of Ireland. In the play's final act, Mariam is not only absent from the stage but also represented, through the messenger's account of her last moments, as a woman who has somehow learned to bridle her tongue. On the way to her scafford, she is cruelly taunted by her mother, who, after having urged Mariam throughout the play to despise Herod, now suddenly and cravenly condemns Mariam for "wronging" princely authority (5.1.1968). Enraged at this report of Alexandra's behavior, Herod asks Mariam's response and learns, from the messenger, that "she made no answere" (5.1.1992); she died, he adds, after saying "some silent prayer" and "as if she were content" (2026–27). The wickedness associated with the female tongue and with women in general (according to Constabarus's misogynist tirade against Salome's sex [4.6.1578–1619]), is here symbolically transferred from Mariam to her mother, who takes Mariam's place as the object of Herod's censoring wrath: "Why stopt you not her mouth? where had she words / to darke that, that Heaven made so brighte?" (5.1.1979–80), he asks the messenger, and we remember that Herod has just exercised his power to stop Mariam's mouth. Once he has done so, in what seems the play's most complex and ambivalent irony, he suddenly starts to value Mariam's words with passionate desire: "But what sweet tune did this faire dying Swan / Afford thine eare: tell all, omit no letter," he exclaims (5.1.2008–9); and again, in an exchange that seems designed to effect a wishful revenge on the tyrannical

censorious husband, he asks for the "food" of her words, nourishment
he all too belatedly craves.

Cary imagines Herod coming to value Mariam's voice at the moment
when the disputed property of her body is absent both from the stage
and from the narrative "present": "Her body is divided from her
head," the messenger announces, and the graphic image of the dead
and sundered woman (which appears nowhere in Josephus's account)
allows us further to gauge the price Mariam must pay for her freedom
of conscience. The price includes not only a symbolic acceptance of a
lesson of female silence, now, however, seen as a virtue enjoined by
God rather than by social authority; the price also includes the female
saint's earthly body. To assess what that loss figured as a sacrifice
might mean for the symbolic and real economies of Cary's upper-class
culture, insofar as we can infer them, or for our own critical and erotic
economies (but who is this "we" I'm hypostasizing?) would be a task
as intriguing as it is beyond the scope of the present essay. I shall
conclude, however, by simply stating my strong suspicion that intellectuals in modern western societies have by no means shrugged off
the burdensome ideological legacy of Cary's play, in which a female
subject's desires for spoken, written, or printed words are seen as
somehow inimical to her desires for life, much less for bodily pleasure.

Notes

For invaluable help in the preparation of this article I would like to thank Elaine
Beilin, David Kastan, Mary Nyquist, Mary Poovey, and David Simpson. I would
also, and above all, like to thank my mother Mary Anne Ferguson, in whose honor
this essay was originally written, in a longer version to be published in *Tradition
and the Talents of Women,* ed. Florence Howe (Champaign-Urbana: Univ. of
Illinois Press, 1991).

1. First published as *Antonius* for William Ponsonby in 1592, the work was reprinted
   by Ponsonby in 1595 as *The Tragedie of Antonie Doone into English by the
   Countesse of Pembroke.* STC 11623. Reel no. 243. Rpt. "Countess of Pembroke's
   Antonie." Ed. Alice Luce. In *Literarische Forschungenen,* 3 (Weimar: Verlag von
   Emil Felber, 1897). For useful comments on Mary Sidney's translation and its
   influence on various dramatists including Cary, see Betty Travitsky, ed., *The
   Paradise of Women: Writings by Englishwomen of the Renaissance* (1981, rpt.
   New York: Columbia Univ. Press, 1989), pp. 116, 216.

2. The quotation about loving plays is from *The Lady Falkland: Her Life,* ed. Richard
   Simpson (London: Catholic Publishing & Bookselling Co., 1861), p. 54. The *Life,*
   by one of the four of Cary's daughters who became nuns, exists in a single
   manuscript found in the English Benedictine convent in Cambray and now in the
   Archives of the Department of the North, at Lille. Subsequent references to this
   work will be given in the body of the essay.

3. For useful discussions of Cary's life, writings (many of which are evidently lost),

and status as the first Englishwoman to publish an original play, see Nancy Cotton Pearse, "Elizabeth Cary, Renaissance Playwright," *Texas Studies in Language and Literature* 18 (1977), 601–08; Sandra K. Fischer, "Elizabeth Cary and Tyranny, Domestic and Religious," in *Silent But for the Word: Tudor Women as Patrons, Translators, and Writers of Religious Works,* ed. Margaret P. Hannay (Kent, Ohio: Kent State Univ. Press, 1985), pp. 225–237; Elaine Beilin, "Elizabeth Cary and *The Tragedy of Mariam,"* *Papers on Language and Literature* 16 (Winter 1980), 45–64 (rpt. in *Redeeming Eve: Women Writers of the English Renaissance* [Princeton: Princeton Univ. Press, 1987]); and Betty Travitsky, "The *Feme Covert* in Elizabeth Cary's *Mariam"* in *Ambiguous Realities: Women in the Middle Ages and Renaissance,* ed. Carole Levin and Jeanie Watson (Detroit: Wayne State Univ. Press, 1987), pp. 184–96. See also the introductory material to the selections from Cary's works in *The Paradise of Women,* ed. Betty Travitsky, pp. 209–12; in *The Female Spectator,* ed. Mary R. Mahl and Helene Koon (Bloomington: Indiana Univ. Press, 1977), pp. 99–102; and in *Kissing the Rod: An Anthology of Seventeenth-Century Women's Verse,* ed. Germaine Greer et al. (New York: Farrar, Straus, Giroux, 1988), pp. 54–55. In a paper entitled "To Seem, to Be, Elizabeth Tanfield Cary: A Woman's Self-Fashioning" and circulated to members of the seminar on "Renaissance Women as Readers and Writers" at the 1990 Shakespeare Association of America meeting, Donald W. Foster offers a cogent analysis of Cary's entire writing life.

4. The fact that the play was entered in the Stationers' Register (Dec. 1612) and licensed by the Master of Revels leads its modern editor A. C. Dunstan to surmise that it "can hardly have been printed without the author's knowledge and at least acquiescence" (*The Tragedie of Mariam,* 1613; Malone Society Reprints [Oxford: Horace Hart for the University Press, 1914], p. ix).

5. Angeline Goreau, who takes Cary's Chorus as unequivocally representing the author's opinions, sees the play as an ideologically conservative text in "Two English women in the seventeenth century: notes for an anatomy of feminine desire," in *Western Sexuality: Practice and Precept in Past and Present Times,* ed. Philippe Aries and André Bejin, trans. Anthony Forster (Oxford: Blackwell, 1985), pp. 104–05; and in her introduction to *The Whole Duty of a Woman: Female Writers in Seventeenth-Century England* (Garden City: Doubleday, 1985), p. 13. In *The Tragedies of Herod and Mariamne* (New York: Columbia Univ. Press, 1940), p. 90, Maurice Valency states that "the author sides throughout with Herod," having "a low opinion of women in general."

6. For persuasive evidence of Cary's reliance on Lodge, whose conversion to Catholicism in the late 1590s may have sparked Cary's interest in his work, see A. C. Dunstan's introduction to *Mariam,* pp. v–ix. See Valency, *Tragedies,* and also Gordon Braden, *Renaissance Tragedy and the Senecan Tradition* (New Haven: Yale Univ. Press, 1985), for information about other versions of the Herod and Mariam story on the Renaissance stage.

7. To study Cary's revisions of Josephus, which are more complex than this essay can indicate, I have used both the Loeb Classical Library bilingual edition of the *Antiquities of the Jews* (Book 15 is in vol. 8 of the Loeb *Josephus,* trans. Ralph Marcus, ed. and completed by Allen Wikgren [Cambridge, Mass.: Harvard Univ. Press, 1963]) and Thomas Lodge, *The Famous and Memorable Works of Josephus* (London: Peter Short, 1602; copy in the Beinecke Library, Yale University).

8. Quoted from Dunstan's edition of *Mariam,* Act 5, scene 1, line 2061. All subsequent quotations of *Mariam*—referenced by act, scene, and line number only, there being

no page numbers—are from this edition, which is full of textual problems I have not sought to correct (though I have silently emended "i" to "j" and "v" to "u"). A new, annotated edition, prepared by Barry Weller and me, is forthcoming from the Univ. of California Press.

9. For brief discussions of the verbal and structural parallels between *Mariam* and *Othello* see Margaret W. Ferguson, "A Room Not Their Own: Renaissance Women as Readers and Writers," in *The Comparative Perspective on Literature*, ed. Clayton Koelb and Susan Noakes (Ithaca: Cornell Univ. Press, 1988), pp. 93–116 and Gordon Braden, *Renaissance Tragedy*, pp. 167 and 128, note 11. The long history, and cultural significance, of metaphorically equating a wife with a private property, a valuable "treasure," or jewel in need of strict guarding, is discussed by Patricia Parker, *Literary Fat Ladies* (London: Routledge, 1987), pp. 126–54.

10. For discussions of the ideals of female behavior prescribed by conduct books, educational treatises, and other Renaissance texts, see Suzanne W. Hull, *Chaste, Silent & Obedient: English Books for Women 1475–1640* (San Marino: Huntington Library, 1984); Angeline Goreau, *The Whole Duty of a Woman*; Peter Stallybrass, "Patriarchal Territories: The Body Enclosed," in *Rewriting the Renaissance*, ed. Margaret W. Ferguson, Maureen Quilligan, and Nancy Vickers (Chicago: Univ. of Chicago Press, 1986), pp. 123–42; Margaret W. Ferguson, "A Room Not Their Own," pp. 96–103; and Ann R. Jones, *The Currency of Eros: Women's Love Lyric in Europe, 1540–1621* (Bloomington: Indiana Univ. Press, 1990), pp. 1–18.

11. "With one exception," as Dunstan notes in his Introduction to *Mariam* (p. xii), "the names of all the characters are taken from Josephus." The exception is the name of the slave woman loved by Pheroras. Josephus and Lodge mention a "Glaphyra," wife to a certain Alexander, near the part of the narrative in which Pheroras's story appears; even if, as Dunstan surmises, Cary's "Graphina" was suggested by "Glaphyra," the coinage is nonetheless more purposive, I think, than critics have allowed.

12. As Germaine Greer notes (*Kissing the Rod*, p. 56), Cary alludes here to Plutarch's account of Caesar weeping when he learned of his popular rival Pompey's death. The anecdote, which appears both in the "Life of Caesar" and in that of Pompey, ironizes Caesar's grief: he had after all ardently desired and indirectly engineered Pompey's murder. Cary's analogy works to imply that Mariam is Herod's political rival and also that her desires somehow *caused* his (supposed) death in Rome, where he has gone, ironically enough, to answer to Julius Caesar for using murder as a means to the throne.

13. For evidence of Cary's own husband's conventional views on women's duty as "private" beings see, for instance, Sir Henry's letter of 5 April 1626 complaining of his "apostate" wife's "over-busy nature" and lamenting that she refuses to retire "quietly" to her mother's country house. On other Renaissance women who challenged the cultural definition of women as private beings, see Merry E. Wiesner, "Women's Defense of Their Public Role," in *Women in the Middle Ages and Renaissance: Literary and Historical Perspectives*, ed. Mary Beth Rose (Syracuse: Syracuse Univ. Press, 1986), pp. 1–27.

14. In *Still Harping on Daughters: Women and Drama in the Age of Shakespeare* (1983; rpt. New York: Columbia Univ. Press, 1989), pp. 121–23, Lisa Jardine discusses numerous texts, among them *The Taming of the Shrew* and *Othello*, which bawdily deploy the common Renaissance tropes on the tongue as a woman's "weapon" and as her substitute penis. Cary's plays on female tongues as (illicitly)

phallic should be read with reference to the ideologically charged semantic field in which female tongues operate in English Renaissance culture. See, for instance, Catherine Belsey's discussion of the anonymous but often reprinted play *Lingua* (1607), in which the heroine is imprisoned in a phallic tower and guarded by thirty watchmen "to keep her from wagging abroad" (*The Subject of Tragedy: Identity and Difference in Renaissance Drama* [London and New York: Methuen, 1985], p. 181).

15. Belsey, *The Subject of Tragedy*, p. 173. There is a fascinating nearly contemporary analogue for Cary's formulation—corroborating readings of either "God" or "one-self" for Cary's "none but one"—in Lady Mary Wroth's *Pamphilia to Amphilanthus* (1621); Sonnet 36 of this sequence suggests that the woman writer-lover's testimony should be hid "From all save only one" (*The Poems of Lady Mary Wroth*, ed. Josephine A. Roberts [Baton Rouge: Louisiana State Univ. Press, 1983]). I am indebted to Margreta de Grazia for this reference, discussed in the paper she wrote for the 1990 Shakespeare Association of America seminar on Renaissance Women and entitled: "The Body of Lady Mary Wroth's Writing in *Pamphilia to Amphilanthus.*"

16. Slowe, "Speech Crimes in *The Tragedy of Mariam*," p. 5; this is also a paper done for the 1990 Shakespeare Association of America seminar on Renaissance Women.

17. See Travitsky, "Husband Murder and Petty Treason in English Renaissance Tragedy," a paper for the 1990 Shakespeare Association of America seminar on Renaissance Women.

18. The notion of a Christian subject's right to "passive resistance" on the grounds of conscience has a long history but becomes a vexed political issue in the Reformation, as Quentin Skinner has shown (*The Foundations of Modern Political Thought*, vol. 2 [Cambridge: Cambridge Univ. Press, 1978], pp. 12–19) and as Constance Jordan remarks, citing Skinner, in *Renaissance Feminism: Literary Texts and Political Models* (Ithaca: Cornell Univ. Press, 1990), p. 24, note 25. See her discussion of the common analogy between "the political status of the woman vis à vis the male head of the family and of the subject vis à vis the magistrate" (pp. 23–24) and her more detailed discussion of "exceptions" to the rule of wifely obedience allowed in some Protestant treatises on marriage (pp. 214–20).

19. Valuable exceptions to this generalization are Sandra K. Fischer's essay on Cary in *Silent But For the Word* (cited in note 3, above) and Marta Straznicky's paper on Cary in the context of the English Catholic community, "Rewriting the Source: The Work of Elizabeth Cary and Authoritative Female Discourse in the Renaissance," a paper circulated for the 1990 Shakespeare Association of America seminar on Renaissance Women.

20. The quoted passage, from Henry Garnet, *Treatise on Christian Renunciation,* is cited in Marie Bowlands, "Recusant Women 1560–1640," in *Women in English Society 1500–1800*, ed. Mary Prior (London and New York: Methuen, 1985), p. 165. For useful general discussions of the key role of Catholic wives of both Protestant and recusant landowners in maintaining "a subversive, underground religion" (Straznicky, p. 4), see also John Bossy, *The English Catholic Community 1570–1850* (London: Darton, Longman and Todd, 1975), ch. 7 and Retha M. Warnicke, *Women of the English Renaissance and Reformation* (Westport, CT: Greenwood Press, 1983), pp. 164–85.

21. Compare Mariam's assertion of spiritual freedom with the statement by the Lady in Milton's *A Masque* (1637): "Thou canst not touch the freedom of my mind /

With all thy charms, although this corporal rind / Thou hast immanacl'd, while Heav'n sees good"; quoted from John Milton, *The Complete Shorter Poems*, ed. John Carey (London: Longman, 1971), p. 209; and see also the similar proclamation by the heroine of the anonymous play of 1620, *Swetnam the Woman Hater Arraigned by Women*, 2.1.97 (in *"Swetnam the Woman Hater": The Controversy and the Play*, ed. Coryl Crandall [Purdue: Purdue Univ. Press, 1969], p. 73).

22. See Beilin, "Elizabeth Cary," pp. 58–60 and also Sandra K. Fischer, "Elizabeth Cary and Tyranny," esp. pp. 235–37.

23. I am still working through the complex evidence, in literary sources and in polemical, religious and political tracts, for an overdetermined topical allegory in *Mariam*, an allegory toward which I can only gesture in this essay. I am grateful to Peter Rudnytsky for helping me trace allusions to Henry VIII in Cary's text. The evidence suggests that many English Catholics criticized Henry VIII by figuring him as a type of Herod-the-tyrant, a composite character which, like his morality play predecessor, often conflated the identities of three different biblical Herods— Herod the Great, slaughterer of the innocents; Herod Antipas, who judged Christ and ordered John the Baptist's death; and Herod Agrippa. I'm indebted for this information to Rebecca W. Bushnell's fine summary of scholarship on the medieval Herod figure, and her analyses of various humanist Herod plays, in *Tragedies of Tyrants: Political Thought and Theater in the English Renaissance* (Ithaca: Cornell Univ. Press, 1990), ch. 3.

Further support for my hypothesis of a complex topical allegory, rooted in Catholic writings in the years after the "Anglican Schism," lies in a 16th-century report that Robert Garnier represented Mary Stuart in his characterization of Cleopatra in *Marc Antoine*. See Gillian Jondorf, *Robert Garnier and the Themes of Political Tragedy in the Sixteenth Century* (Cambridge: Cambridge Univ. Press, 1969), p. 29.

22

Italians and Others
THE WHITE DEVIL (1612)

Ann Rosalind Jones

The Italy of English playwrights from the 1580s on was not a geographer's record but a fantasy setting for dramas of passion, Machiavellian politics, and revenge—a landscape of the mind. What kind of landscape and whose mind? Historically, Italy was a collection of city states, each with a civic identity defined by local sovereigns or councils and conflicting political interests, each also a collection of monuments and social customs observable by English tourists. But what Italy mainly signified in Renaissance England was another country, a country of others, constructed through a lens of voyeuristic curiosity through which writers and their audiences explored what was forbidden in their own culture.[1]

One way of coming at the unstable mixture of admiration and loathing mobilized by Italy as a cultural construct is to read two contemporary texts in relation to each other: the book in which the travel writer Thomas Coryat represented Venice, which he visited in 1608 and described as the climax of the first part of his *Crudities,* published in London in 1611, and John Webster's tragedy *The White Devil,* first printed in 1612. Like Jacobean drama, Coryat's travelogue was aimed at a mixed audience: sensation-seekers eager for news from exotic places and educated gentlemen willing to decipher his many Latin citations, from Roman poetry to Continental tombstones. Felix Raab's comment about the English reception of the texts and the myth of Machiavelli applies as well to the versions of Italy produced by Coryat and his playhouse contemporaries for the audiences of the 1610s: they "horrified them, instructed them, entertained them—in fact [they] affected them over the whole attraction/repulsion spectrum" (67). Coryat writes with a double agenda: to thrill his readers and to protect their morals, to sell his book with the promise of titillation and to dignify it by setting his ethical seriousness as an Englishman against the variety of "Ethnicke" types he encounters. This set of conflicting purposes sets up rhetorical tensions and tensions about rhetoric that link the travel writer's genre to the mixed tragic-satiric mode of plays such as Webster's *The White Devil.*

Coryat begins his "Observations of Venice" with a modest demurral, but his hesitation rapidly gives way to his citation of a standard formula through which Venetians themselves praised their city:

> I ingenuously confesse mine owne insufficiency and unworthiness, as being the unworthiest of ten thousand to describe so beautifull, so renowned, so glorious a Virgin (for by that title doth the world most deservedly stile her).
>
> [I, 302]

A certain paradox underlies this sentence, however. According to the gender ideologies through which early modern Europe consigned virtuous women to the private domestic realm, a proper virgin would not usually be known or praised by ten thousand admirers. And Coryat goes on to personify the city in a curiously familiar way, suggesting that he has enjoyed as intimate a welcome by Venice as Ulysses did on the islands of Calypso and Circe. Coryat's countryman Roger Ascham had denounced Italy in *The Schoolmaster* as "Circe's court," teeming with "wanton and dallying" Calypsos and Sirens (62–4), but Coryat represents himself as a Ulysses landed in an urban paradise. He represents Venice as an insistently feminine landscape, which he praises in the vocabulary of courtly compliment ("this thrice worthie city: the fairest Lady, yea the richest Paragon and Queene of Christendome"), but he also introduces the city as a beautiful seductress whose sexuality is insistently offered for sale by its men. This ambivalence is clear in his description of a playhouse in which he saw a comedy performed. On the one hand, the Venetian theater reinforces his sense of national superiority: it strikes him as "very beggarly and base in comparison of our stately play-houses in England" (386). But he is also impressed by the presence of women actors, who, he concedes, perform "with as good a grace, action, gesture and whatever convenient for a Player, as ever I saw [in] any masculine Actor." In a symptomatic association of ideas, he moves from this instance of feminine self-display to a first description of the courtesans for which Venice was famous: masked and veiled at the theater, they are protected by their pimps, their *ruffiani,* against prying eyes—eyes which he warns could be his own or his countrymen's: "If any man should be so resolute to unmaske one of them but in merriment only to see their faces, it is said that . . .

he should be cut in pieces before he should come forth of the roome, especially if he were a stranger" (387).

The interplay of pleasure and danger becomes more explicit in Coryat's description of courtesans at work, a description framed by conflicting strategies of representation. He begins his account of his visit to Margarita Emiliana, a famous courtesan, by announcing that he has included a portrait of himself and her together, an obvious attempt to add erotic visual appeal to his book: she greets him with bare breasts and an eager, come-hither gesture of the hand. The frontispiece to the book multiplies the association of countries with women, although in a more grotesque style than that of the double portrait. Coryat's bust, in a oval frame or roundel, is surrounded by three female figures, labeled as "Gallia, Germania, Italia." To the right Italia, dressed in a Venetian courtesan's gown, gazes ecstatically upward. On the left, a woman in French court dress holds a shell, possibly representing Fontainebleau, where Coryat saw the scallop shell, the emblem of the royal mistress, Diane de Poitiers, repeated in sculpture and stucco. In the middle, Germania, set above Coryat and coiffed with the great wine cask of Heidelberg, typifies her countrymen's reputation for drunkenness by vomiting down onto Coryat's head. This transformation of the survey of states into a grotesque spectacle of eros, which is made explicit in the "Panegyrick Verses" with which the book opens, is set in tension with Coryat's purifying pedagogical purpose. This tension demands contradictory responses as Coryat leads his reader, implicitly male, through the narration of an encounter with a courtesan. Like the courtesan herself, the writer lures his client on, enumerates the delights she offers, links her erotic power to the splendor of her city. But then he breaks off the seduction by denouncing the sexual enticements he has been cataloguing: "yet if thou shalt rightly weigh them in the scales of a mature judgment, thou wilt say with the wise man . . . that they are like a golden ring in a swines snout" (404–5). Whatever didactic justification might be claimed for this alternation of hot and cold prose, in practice it makes Coryat an accomplice to the courtesan's "allurements." In order to inoculate his readers against the dangers of Venice, he acts as a go-between before he admonishes the lustful. But he denies this role by projecting it onto the courtesan herself: *she* is the speaker who fascinates through language:

Also thou wilt finde the Venetian Cortezan . . . a good Rhetorician, and a most elegant discourser, so that if she cannot move thee with all these aforesaid delights, shee will assay thy constancy with her Rhetoricall tongue.

(405)

In Coryat's version, then, the courtesan combines skillful manipulation of her person and her surroundings with verbal enticement; she is a "super-subtle Venetian," as Iago says of Desdemona (*Othello*, I, ii, 357), the feminine counterpart of the politic Machiavel, a dazzling and frightening figure at once. Italianate through and through, she sums up the oppositions through which Coryat constructs the repellent fascination of her homeland. Like Italy as a whole in the English system of representation, Venice is built of fascinating contradictions: she is a virgin city ("most glorious, peerlesse, and mayden . . . : I call it mayden, because it was never conquered," 301), famous for her unconquerability as a state but also for the sexual accessibility of one class of her female citizens. That is, her political autonomy coexists with sexual commodification. The splendor of the city is condensed into the exotic costumes and surroundings of its courtesans: magnificence coexists with, indeed, is intentionally allied with temptation. And Venetian discourse is typified by the hyper-civilized rhetoric of its courtesans and by the deviousness and violence of their male cohorts. Coryat's complicity in this vision of irresistible corruption is evident throughout his text, in its gendered personifications, its allusions to literary fellow travelers, its acknowledgment of men's vulnerability to the artifices of courtesanship—and in its deliberate blindness to its own participation in rhetorical seduction. "I must denounce you," says the Englishman to Italy; "only in that way can I sustain my pleasure in being obsessed with you."

Irresistible others

The White Devil shares the paradoxes generated by English suspicion of Italian "policy," of the stratagems of language and power for which Italians were more often blamed than praised. But in Webster's play, the hierarchy is reversed: intricate devising is given the upper hand. Four amoral conspirators produce the dramatic plot: Vittoria Corombona, who obliquely persuades her lover to murder her husband; Flamineo, the scheming malcontent; Francisco, the politic hero; Ludovico, his ingeniously murderous sidekick. And the play deploys a new discourse about enemy others: the sensational appeal of Venetian intrigue is set in opposition not to a lofty Anglo-Saxon ethic but to the primitive violence attributed to another set of significant others for the English, the wild Irish—who are linked, in the case of Zanche, Vittoria's servant, to Moors and women as well. The allure of Venice is condensed into the figure of Vittoria herself and into the revengers, the inventors of a series of fascinating horrors for which the play provides no stable counter-position. Webster's Rome is Coryat's Venice minus the moral certainties of English admonition yet intensified by another maneuver of cultural self-consolidation: mockery of England's others to the West.

One of the changes Webster made in his source materials was to change Vittoria Accoramboni from a noblewoman of Gubbio to a Venetian prostitute.[2] The publisher's 1612 title page to the play claims a documentary reality for its heroine: "The Life and Death of Vittoria Corombona the famous Venetian Curtizan." Cardinal Monticelso uses similar terms to accuse Vittoria in the trial scene: "You were born in Venice, honourably descended/ From the Vitelli; . . . You came from thence a most notorious strumpet,/ And so have you continued" (II, ii, 233–4, 242–3). Yet the allure of the woman, like the homeland to which the play assigns her, is paradoxically made more brilliant for the corruption implicit in both. Vittoria conspires to murder Camillo, but she also defends herself through spectacular public eloquence. In his dedication to the Prince of Wales, Coryat describes Venice as "that most glorious, renowned . . . Citie, . . . that Diamond set in the ring of the Adriatique gulfe, and the most resplendent mirrour of Europe" (2). This language of inviolate brilliance is exactly what Vittoria invokes as she faces down her persecutors in the trial scene: "know that all your strict combined heads,/ Which strike against this mine of diamonds,/ Shall prove but glassen hammers, they shall break" (III, ii, 141–3).

Another revision Webster made in his sources was to shift Vittoria's place of banishment from a nunnery to a house of convertites, a grimly guarded penitentiary for reformed prostitutes. But as his heroine leaves for her imprisonment there, she defies Monticelso with a challenge built on an antithesis that draws again upon the image of Venice as enduring treasure:

> It shall not be a house of convertites.
> My mind shall make it honester to me
> Than the Pope's palace . . .
> Know this, and let it somewhat raise your spite,
> Through darkness diamonds spread their richest light.
> (III, ii, 287–292)

In the scene of her escape, Webster mobilizes Vittoria to transform a heavily policed workhouse into a place of assignation with Brachiano, where their erotic reconciliation leads to their romantic flight: more like the fantasy of Venice as city than like any one of its repentant prostitutes, Vittoria regains her freedom. And even in her final lines, she associates herself with the magnificent corruption of her surroundings as the source of her downfall: "O happy they that never saw the court,/ *Nor ever knew great men but by report*" (V, vi, 258–9). Like the white devil of the title, Vittoria sums up the impossible paradox of Venice: luxurious delicacy and the claim to unassailable autonomy are intertwined, in the city as emblem and in the dramatic heroine, and both are linked to scandalous impropriety.

No wonder that, like the city, the glamorous rhetoric of Webster's heroine has attracted and repulsed Anglo-Saxon critics for centuries. Those who condemn Vittoria often do so in terms that reveal their own ambivalence toward Italy. John Addington Symonds, for example, registered a Victorian horror at Webster's exemplar of feminine *virtù:* "Hard as adamant, uncompromising, ruthless, Vittoria follows ambition as the load star of her life" (174). His praise for Webster reproduces the cultural bias that he interprets as the playwright's realism: "That mysterious man of genius had explored the dark and devious paths of Renaissance vice, and had penetrated the secrets of Italian wickedness with truly appalling lucidity." Similarly, F. L. Lucas sees Vittoria as an emblem of Italian seduction and danger, "the incarnation" of the "burning beauty and haunting call" of the South as seen by the North; he links her immediately to the stereotypically villainous figures of Machiavelli and Lucrezia Borgia (2: 98). In contrast, critics who admire Vittoria often attribute the intensity of her effect as a character to the contradictions she presents. Muriel Bradbrook is uneasy about these contradictions; first she normalizes Vittoria as a "reconciliation of opposites," then goes on to imply that as a character she falls short of realist psychology: "Supreme beauty and glamour are mixed with lust and selfishness. In either case Vittoria remains a splendid figure-piece rather than a natural character" (190). More recent critics have read Vittoria-as-contradiction more positively. Travis Bogard suggests that Webster constructed her in order to "baffle ordinary moral judgment" (97). Jonathan Dollimore argues convincingly that her problematic character makes a smooth ethical foreclosing of the play's meaning impossible (238); Catherine Belsey uses her to typify "the radically discontinuous subject-positions" which constitute the representation of femininity in Jacobean drama (163). In my view, if Vittoria comes across as "less" (or indeed more) than "a natural woman," it is because as a literary construction she distills English fantasies of Italianate excesses into an unstable personification of Venetian vice and allure. Psychic contradiction is maintained in a constant state of play by the political and sexual systems of representation that produced both Coryat's portrait of Margarita Emiliana and Webster's dramatic heroine.

But unlike Venice as a republic, Vittoria as a woman is vulnerable to attack. As she falls victim to the treachery of the Roman faction, she becomes the target for a simpler xenophobic discourse of abuse that circulates throughout the play: she is associated with the undercivilized behavior of the Irish.[3] When Brachiano intercepts the love letter sent to her by Francisco, he turns on her with an insult through which he distances himself from her in two ways, categorizing her both as a duplicitous whore and as one of the savages whose barbarity was regularly invoked by Webster's countrymen to justify their righteousness as colonizers. Brachiano accuses Vittoria of faking the keening of Irish mourners: "Procure but ten of thy dissembling trade,/ Ye'ld furnish all the Irish funerals/ With howling, past wild Irish" (IV, ii, 92–4). Thus, he draws upon two available although contradictory vocabularies of contempt: misogyny's suspicion of feminine insincerity and English disdain for the unbridled emotionality of the Irish.

This second alien population is invoked elsewhere in the play as a foil, an instance of sub-political primitivism, whenever the Roman plotters celebrate their own vengeful "policy." Not surprisingly, Webster's revengers resemble Coryat in their construction of a positive identity through opposition to a frequently invoked other, in this case the brutish others of English colonial discourse. At the beginning of his book, Coryat announces that his travelogue will open with praises written "in the best and most learned languages of the world" (20). He includes "the Welch and the Irish" in the list but then rejects them with a footnote signaling his use of "Ironia" in setting these primitive dialects alongside Greek and Latin. In a similar move, Francisco invokes the simpleminded betrayals of the Irish in order to affirm his superior skill as a punisher of evildoers. He says that the informers who provided the information in Monticelso's black book, his "catalogue of knaves," handed over the names of their fellows "As th'Irish rebels were wont to sell heads" (IV, i, 80), that is, as they sold their fellows for English pay. The difference between these Irish Italians and himself, Francisco implies, is that he can manipulate their venality for his own ends: he reads the book of names to spur himself on to calculating revenge. The scene ends with a second reference to Irish headhunting, toward which Francisco adopts the exploitative familiarity of the ethnologist temporarily gone native. He will cut off the head of his sister's killer as fiercely as the Irish decapitate each other:

> Brachiano, I am now fit for thy encounter.
> Like the wild Irish I'll ne'er think thee dead
> Till I can play at football with thy head:
> (IV, i, 135–7)

But lest Francisco seem to have sunk to the level of his cultural inferiors, Webster assigns him, as a last word, a Virgilian tag that dignifies his murderous purpose by citing a precedent for it in one of the "best and most learned languages" of his time. Invoking Juno's oath of vengeance against the Trojans in *Aeneid VII,* the avenging hero aligns himself with a culturally privileged text and thereby raises himself through it above any merely brutish Irish violence: "Flectere si nequeo superos, Acheronta movebo" (If I cannot prevail upon the gods above, I will move the depths of hell). Classicizing humanism here reinscribes Francisco's "Irishness" as one of the ethnological fantasies of the cultural sophisticate.

Francisco uses anti-Irish cliché to affirm his superiority again in the scene in which he and Ludovico confront Zanche, Vittoria's Moorish maid, in order to elicit what she knows about Brachiano's murder of Isabella. The scene positions Zanche as a triply gullible figure: as a Moor, she is taken in by Francisco's disguise as a Moorish prince; as a servant, she is induced to reveal the secrets of her mistress; as a woman who makes advances to the prince, she is the object of sexual mockery. Francisco tells her lewdly that he has dreamed he put an Irish mantle on her—that is, a rough blanket under which, English colonizers claimed, Irish men wore nothing and Irish women hid their illegitimate pregnancies. Edmund Spencer's Irenius, for example, in *A View of the Present State of Ireland* (1598), condemns the mantle as a "coverlet" for the Irishwoman's "lewd exercise": "when she hath filled her vessel, under it she can hide both her burden and her blame" (53).[4] Francisco's rhetoric of seduction positions Zanche, like the Irish, as a lustful dupe, all too easily fooled by her betters. Adding class bias to available categories of ethnic contempt, Ludovico links Zanche's folly to her blackness in an aside that associates physical labor with filth: "Mark her, I prithee, she simpers like the suds/ A collier hath been washed in" (V, ii, 238–9). This simile, like Francisco's use of the connotations of the Irish mantle as tribal emblem, places Zanche at the absolute bottom of interlocking cultural, racial, gender, and class hierarchies. Because these hierarchies define her as sexually and socially presumptuous (aggressive toward the man who attracts her, aiming above her station), and because she is permanently rather than like Francisco cosmetically black, she can be mocked according to the plotters' logic, then disposed of according to their purposes. (The pattern of verbal and physical violence is repeated in the final scene of the play when Ludovico's accomplice calls her a "black fury" before he stabs her to death.) The language of the scene sets her up as a comic dupe and elevates the two plotters by defining their canny manipulations *against* the naive overreaching of the Irish Mooress. Zanche, the most culturally overdetermined Other in the play, finally functions to shore up the revengers' identity as experts in finding out evil and as artists of retribution.

No heroic or English ideal is explicitly defined in *The White Devil*, but in its practice as plot, the most effective mode of behavior is located between Italian hyper-subtlety of concept and Irish "wildness" in action. Vittoria is accused of the first, Zanche of the second; the male revengers prevail by setting each mode of performance against the other. The play's linking of hyper-conscious villainy with the art of tragedy is affirmed in Ludovico's chillingly unrepentant final speech. Webster as dramatist might be heard speaking in these lines:

> . . . I do glory yet
> That I can call this act mine own. . . .
> . . . here's my rest:
> I limb'd this night-piece and it was my best.
> (V,vi,290–3)

Others re-ordered

I have been suggesting in this inter-reading of two English uses of Italy that both Coryat and Webster exploit oppositional thinking about cultures through manipulations of genre that assure them literary profit. Both writers, by drawing on stereotypes of the hyper-civilized Italian, the savage Irish, and the "Ethnicke" Moor, provide their audiences with pleasures more complex than those officially sanctioned by the genres they use. At the same time that Coryat claims to inform his readers, to tell them something new, he appeals to predictable curiosities, to the desire to hear about foreign evils already presented in earlier English versions of Italy. Less guardedly, the dedicatory verses to the *Crudities* expose the erotic sensationalism that Coryat's role as edifying travel writer conceals. Similarly, the convention of sensationally corrupt Italian courts permits Webster to de-moralize tragedy as genre, to intermix the rise and fall of a "notorious strumpet" with a series of ethically unstable but spectacular plots and counterplots. Rome and Venice as settings multiply representations of vice rather than provide a centered *de casibus* pattern of hubris followed by punishment and contrition. The Ulysses of 1611 titillates armchair tourists with his sensuously and cartographically specific description of Venice; the dramatist excites his audience by assembling a horde of Italian types: the courtesan, the Machiavel, the corrupt pope, the criminal thug. Thus the foreign Other can be denounced as a source of corruption at the same time that s/he frees the travel writer and the tragedian from strict obedience to the didactic assignments built into English travelogue and tragedy.

Recent work on colonialist discourse emphasizes the self-interest at work in any society's presumed knowledge of other cultures.[5] First, such claims to knowledge are always motivated by the will to legitimate one's own culture. Coryat's pedagogical patriotism confirms what Barbara Johnson writes in a study of Zora Neale Hurston: "Difference disliked is identity affirmed" (284). Second, and perhaps more relevant, the dislike itself, as Edward Said's study of Europe's sexualization of the Orient reveals, permits its opposite: the nourishing of a fantasy of irresistible evil, imaginable at length because it is located elsewhere: across the Channel, west of the border, below the equator. For the English, Italy provided one such field of fantasy. As a construction saturated with contradictions, the peninsula afforded Coryat a credible itinerary of seduction and correction; for Webster, it provided an exhilaratingly lawless framework for tumult irreducible to fixed ethical categories. In both texts, references to Irish primitivism are briefer, more pervasive, and simpler, perhaps because more was immediately at stake. Italy was a territory mainly of literary exploitation, but the wild Irish were seen to need taming there and then. They could, as Webster's play shows, be invoked even to make Italian super-subtlety look good—although without the immediate political effect derived from their representation as savages in statesmen's reports written to justify the violence of Tudor and Stuart "diplomacy." Either way, "Englishness" required its supplements, its sinister outsiders and sites of banishment for threats to the imperialist policy that consolidated, from the center, the self-representations of that "green and pleasant" land. But at the same time, those supplements threatened, at least in the work of Webster, to throw off balance the concepts of legitimacy and self-identity which nationalist discourse sought to establish.

Notes

1. Mario Praz, in his early study of English views of Italy, argued that English playwrights' versions of Italy combined the sensational violence of Senecan tragedy with second- and third-hand condemnations of Machiavelli. This analysis of sources is challenged (or at least augmented) by G. K. Hunter's recent studies of English representations of foreigners in general and of Italy in particular. He argues that Italy was a rich field of fantasy for the English precisely because they had so little direct (i.e., military or mercantile) contact with it: "The ambivalence in relation to travel, the simultaneously held desire to know, and fear of knowing, operated at maximum pressure in relation to Italy, for here there was a plethora of imaginative material and very little of that practical experience which might have limited its use" ("Elizabethans and Foreigners," 22). He also argues that Jacobean uses of Italy for dramatic settings followed on Englishmen's Realpolitical reading of Guicciardini's *Storia d'Italia*, which posed contradictions, in drama, to the persistent structure and moral judgments of medieval morality plays ("English Folly"). I am indebted to the members of the Shakespeare Association of America's

1986 seminar on "The Italianate Englishman and Shakespearean Drama," especially Jonathan Crewe and Frank Whigham, for a thought-provoking discussion and useful references; and, as always, to Peter Stallybrass for his merciless scrutiny of earlier versions of this paper.

.2   See Elizabeth Brennan's summary of Gunnar Boklund's *The Sources of* The White Devil (Uppsala, 1957), ix–xvi. Curiously, the Revels edition of *The White Devil* reproduces Coryat's engraving of himself with Margarita Emiliana on the cover, without comment: the 1960 choice of image silently reinforces the 1612 association between Venice as city and Vittoria as problematic heroine.

3.   For a study of Elizabethan representations of the Irish, see Quinn and Canny. Canny cites Barnabe Rich in a typical formulation: Rich claimed that the Irish wanted "to live like beastes, voide of lawe and all good order," and characterized them as "more uncivill, more uncleanly, more barbarous and more brutish in their customes and demeanures, than in any other part of the world that is known" (127). For an analysis of Jacobean versions of the Irish as typified in Ben Jonson, see Lindley.

4.   See Lindley for several references to the Irish mantle as a symbol of cultural inferiority, and his citation of Sir John Davies's expectation that the Irish would demonstrate their willingness to conform to English civility by "convert[ing] their mantles into cloaks" (333n15).

5.   My obvious theoretical points of reference are Said's *Orientalism* and the "Race,' Writing and Difference" issue of *Critical Inquiry* (Autumn, 1985).

Works Cited

Ascham, Roger. *The Schoolmaster* (London, 1570). Folger Documents of Tudor and Stuart Civilization. Ed. Lawrence Ryan. Ithaca: Cornell UP, 1967.

Belsey, Catherine. *The Subject of Tragedy*. London: Methuen, 1985.

Bogard, Travis. *The Tragic Satire of John Webster*. Berkeley: U of California P, 1955.

Bradbrook, M. C. *Themes and Conventions of Elizabethan Tragedy*. Cambridge: Cambridge UP, 1935, rpt. 1973.

Brennan, Elizabeth. Introduction to *The White Devil*. New Mermaid Series. New York: Hill and Wang, 1966.

Canny, Nicholas. *The Elizabethan Conquest of Ireland: The Pattern Established 1565–76*. Hassocks, Sussex: Harvester, 1976.

Coryat, Thomas. *Coryat's Crudities* (London, 1611). Glasgow: James MacLehose, 1905. 2 vols.

Dollimore, Jonathan. *Radical Tragedy*. Chicago: U of Chicago P, 1984.

Hunter, G. K. "Elizabethans and Foreigners." *Dramatic Identities and Cultural Tradition: Studies in Shakespeare and his Contemporaries*. Liverpool: Liverpool UP, 1978. 10–26.

———— . "English Folly and Italian Vice: The Moral Landscape of John Marston." *Dramatic Identities*. 110–8.

Johnson, Barbara. "Thresholds of Difference: Structures of Address in Zora Neale Hurston." *Critical Inquiry* 12 (1985): 278–89; rpt. in *"Race," Writing, and Difference*, ed. Henry Louis Gates, Jr. Chicago: Chicago UP, 1986.

Lindley, David. "Embarrassing Ben: The Masques for Frances Howard." *English Literary Renaissance* 16 (1986): 343–59.

Lucas, F. L. *The Complete Works of John Webster*. London: Chatto & Windus, 1927. 4 vols.

Pocock, J. G. "Giannotti and Contarini: Venice as Concept and Myth." *The Machiavellian Moment: Florentine Political Thought and the Atlantic Republican Tradition*. Princeton: Princeton UP, 1975. 272–330.

Praz, Mario. " 'The Politic Brain': Machiavelli and the Elizabethans." *The Flaming Heart*. Gloucester, Mass.: Peter Smith, 1966. 91–135.

Quinn, David Beers. *The Elizabethans and the Irish*. Ithaca: Cornell UP, 1966.

Raab, Felix. *The English Face of Machiavelli*. London: Routledge and Kegan Paul, 1964.

Said, Edward. *Orientalism*. New York: Vintage, 1979.

Spenser, Edmund. *A View of the Present State of Ireland* (London, 1598). Ed. W. L. Renwick. London: Oxford UP, 1970.

Symonds, John Addington. "Vittoria Accoramboni and the Tragedy of Webster." *Italian Byways*. London: Smith and Elder, 1883. 156–78.

Webster, John. *The White Devil*. Revels Plays. Ed. John Russell Brown. London: Methuen, 1960. Rpt. Manchester: Manchester UP, 1977.

23

Incest and Ideology
THE DUCHESS OF MALFI (1614)
Frank Whigham

"The real subject is not primarily sexual
lewdness at all, but 'social lewdness'
mythically expressed in sexual terms."—
(Kenneth Burke on *Venus* and *Adonis*)

Most readings of *The Duchess of Malfi* have applied two kinds of
analysis: psychological inquiry (what are Ferdinand's motives?) and
moral evaluation (what is the status of the duchess's marriage to
Antonio?) But prior questions can be asked. *Why* does Webster give
us a wandering duchess? An incestuous brother? And why are these
figures in the play together? How are their features and actions linked?
Correlations between incest and promiscuity, ascribed and achieved
status, community and alienation, can help us chart this sprawling yet
impacted play by situating it in Jacobean culture. Such analysis would
align the play with many other efforts, from those of James I to those
of Hobbes, to articulate and construe the friction between the dominant
social order and emergent pressures toward social change. I will thus
read the noble brother and sister in light of anthropological notions of
incest, seeking Webster's interrogation of the highly charged boundary
phenomena of a stratified but changing society.

During the last fifty years anthropologists have developed an extensive body of theory about incest. Debate continues regarding many
issues,[1] but a basic outline is now visible. A narrowly psychological—
that is to say, universal—explanation of incest (via, for instance, "in-
stinctive repulsion") is stymied by the diverse data available from non-
western cultures. Jack Goody shows that the object of the defining
"horror" that incest supposedly "inevitably arouses" varies greatly.
Sometimes intercourse with blood relatives arouses the repulsion; on
other occasions only relatives by marriage are forbidden (32, 35–42,
46). Moreover, as Kenneth Burke notes, "psychoanalysis too often
conceals . . . the nature of exclusive social relations behind inclusive
[i.e., universal] terms for sexual relations (*Rhetoric*, 279–80).[2] A vocabulary of "human nature" obscures crucial variations specific to differ-

ent social formations. To deal with these we need to reconceive such "givens" of human psychology as *social products.*

Anthropologists propose two general sets of social explanation for the incest taboo: arguments from factors *internal* to the nuclear family (such as competition among males for females), and from factors *external* to it. It is the argument from the larger social situation that construes Webster's play. It specifies, in Talcott Parsons's words, that

> it is not so much the prohibition of incest in its negative aspect which is important as the positive obligation to perform functions for the subunit and the larger society by marrying out. Incest is a withdrawal from this obligation to contribute to the formation and maintenance of supra-familial bonds on which major economic, political and religious functions of the society are dependent. (19)[3]

This notion of public determination of private social structure is quite flexible, as Raymond Firth noted long ago.

> I am prepared to see it shown that the incest situation varies according to the social structure of each community, that it has little to do with the prevention of sex relations as such, but that its real correlation is to be found in the maintenance of institutional forms in the society as a whole, and of the specific interest of groups in particular. (340)

This powerful account also explains exceptions to the rule, such as those of ancient Egypt or Hawaii (and, as we will see, exceptions of individual inclination such as Ferdinand's). "Where interest of rank or property steps in," says Firth, "the incest prohibition is likely to melt away" (340).[4] Both the taboo and its infringements are thus seen as social products, determined by the pressures and limits of particular social formations.

The model so far presented derives from traditional societies, where intermarriage is the most important device for ordering "the interpenetration of memberships among the different elements in the structural network" (Parsons, 18). Jacobean England, though differentiated in many ways, exhibits some structural relations of traditional society. Lawrence Stone judges that "in the sixteenth century, kin groupings remained powerful in politics, [and] much of the political in-fighting of the century revolved around certain kinship rivalries. . . . In local affairs, kin ties undoubtedly continue to be important well into the eighteenth century" (*Family*, 126, 128).[5] Aberle and his colleagues generalize the notion:

For the bulk of pre-industrial complex societies, the functions of the incest taboo in its extended form remain important at the community level. There, the regulation of affairs is not impersonal and legal. . . . The nexus of social life and cooperation continues to be based on kinship to a significant degree, until societies with well-developed market-economies appear. (18)

Such politics of kinship thus continued in importance among the hereditary aristocracy throughout the Jacobean period.

With the development of a differentiated class structure there arises a new sort of pressure which, contrary to the pressure in traditional societies toward intermarriage, tends to limit exogamy. In its movement from traditional toward differentiated structure, Jacobean England was marked by this new constraint. Among other ideological pressures, according to Stone,

the custom of the dowry, according to which brides from all ranks of the propertied classes were expected to contribute a cash sum, together with the great sensitivity to status and rank, meant that there was a very high degree of social and economic endogamy [i.e., required marriage within the group, here defined in terms of class]. Since marriage involved an exchange of cash by the father of the bride for the settlement of property by the father of the groom for the maintenance of the couple and a pension for the widow, it was inevitable that the great majority of marriages should take place between spouses from families with similar economic resources. . . . The fact that most [elite] families aspired to maintain status and enlarge connections through marriage meant that in most cases like would marry like. (*Family*, 60–61)

These limits to intermarriage were further stressed in aristocratic consciousness by that gradual contamination of the ruling elite by invasion from below which Stone has described in *The Crisis of the Aristocracy*. Although the elite responded with hegemonic contempt to most of these penetrations, public fascination with the issue testifies to its continuing potency. Castiglione's *Book of the Courtier* was functionally a prolonged sneer at what Sir Thomas Hoby translates as those "many untowardly Asseheades, that through malapartnesse thinke to purchase them the name of a good Courtier" (29).[6] And Shakespeare explores the problem repeatedly, from Bottom to Bassanio and Edmund and Othello. This problem of mobility of identity is palpably at the center of the cultural consciousness, certainly in London, nowhere more than in the theater. In *The Duchess of Malfi* the class-endogamy pressure specifies an outer frontier of licit marriage, which the duchess trespasses, just as the incest taboo marks the inner wilderness, where Ferdinand longs to dwell.[7] But to grasp the significance of these symmetrical vectors of social force, we must mark the details of the play.

First, though, a glance at the critical history of Ferdinand's incestuous desires. F. L. Lucas first addressed the possibility, though he thought it dubious (II, 23–24); Clifford Leech presented the view fully, in *John Webster* (100ff.). Leech's argument occasioned resistance, from, for instance, J. R. Mulryne, as implying too readily "the desire to consummate the passion" (223). In response Leech itemized his evidence in *Webster:*

> The grossness of his language to her in Act I, the continued violence of his response to the situation, his holding back from identifying her husband and, when that identity is established, from killing him until the Duchess is dead, his momentary identification of himself with her first husband, his necrophily in Act V—all these things . . . seem to point in one direction. (57)[8]

These items have been widely accepted as suggesting incestuous desires, but they do not address Mulryne's doubts, nor do they clearly relate the incest theme to other elements in the play. The anthropological view of incest, which emphasizes not sex relations but the maintenance of institutional forms, allows us to add to Leech's evidence, make a virtue of Mulryne's objection, and integrate Ferdinand's behavior with the otherwise all-embracing issue of social mobility.

The core of this hypothesis can be briefly stated. I view Ferdinand as a threatened aristocrat, frightened by the contamination of his ascriptive social rank, and obsessively preoccupied with its defense. This view, when coupled with Leech's evidence, suggests that Ferdinand's incestuous inclination toward his sister is a *social posture,* of hysterical compensation—a desperate expression of the desire to evade degrading association with inferiors. Declining Muriel Bradbrook's substitute view that the notion of Ferdinand's incest "can satisfactorily compensate for inaccessible Jacobean theological or social moods" (144), I propose to retrieve the social mood, and read the two explanations as one, through an understanding of the ideological function of the incest taboo. The taboo enjoins transfamilial bonding: when Ferdinand flouts the taboo he violently refuses such relations. His categorical pride drives him to a defiant extreme: he narrows his kind from class to family, and affirms it as absolutely superior, ideally alienated from the infections of interactive social life. The duchess then becomes a symbol, flooded with affect, of his own radical purity. In reaching for her he aspires to the old heroic tag *par sibi*, to be like only himself, excelling, transcendent, other.[9]

This obsession is made clear by, and accounts for, many small touches early in the play. Webster's initial presentation stresses Ferdinand's elaborately maintained alienation from these below. When Castruchio, making small talk, avers that the prince should not go to war in person, but rather "do it by a deputy," Ferdinand replies "Why should he not as well sleep, or eat, by a deputy? This might take idle, offensive and base office from him, whereas the other deprives him of honour" (1.1.99–102). While this hallowed pursuit of distinction warrants personal participation, Ferdinand otherwise enacts his alienation precisely by eschewing participation and employing prosthetic agents: "He speaks with others' tongues, and hears men's suits / With others' ears . . . dooms men to death by information, / Rewards by hearsay" (1.1.173–74, 176–77). His courtiers are to be his creatures, will-less, without spontaneity: "Methinks you that are courtiers should be my touch-wood, take fire, when I give fire; that is, laugh when I laugh" (1.1.122–24). (It is common to describe this behavior as usual for flatterers and ambitious men; for the prince to require it publicly involves a different emphasis altogether.) Ferdinand especially enjoys the distancing trick of surprise: "He will seem to sleep o'th'bench / Only to entrap offenders in their answers" (1.1.174–75). Nicholas Brooke emphasizes how Ferdinand's courtly appearance constitutes an "absolute spectacle" ("laugh when I laugh," "The Lord Ferdinand / Is going to bed" [3.1.37–38], "the Lord Ferdinand laughs" [3.3.54]) (Brooke, 52, 54, 61). Bosola's criticism suggests that this may be an intentional effect. "You / Are your own chronicle too much; and grossly / Flatter yourself" (3.1.87–89). This pattern of distancing objectifies those below Ferdinand, as mere reflective witnesses to his absolute surpassing. His embattled sense of excellence insists on ontological separation from those below, but his frenetic iteration of this motif suggests its ongoing failure. For there is an inherent contradiction in this device, as in Hegel's Master-Slave relationship:

> The master was actually dependent on the slave for his status as master; both in the general society and in the eyes of the slave, the master was recognized as such only because he controlled slaves. What is worse, the master could not achieve the recognition he originally fought for in this relationship because he was recognized only by a slave, by someone he regards as sub-human . . . He needed an autonomous person to recognize his desire as human, but instead of free recognition, he received only the servile, dependent recognition of the slave. (13)[10]

Self-defeated, Ferdinand also fails his subjects: instead of acting as the traditional fount of identity to them, he generates the loss of their identity, striving to become more himself by reducing others. His strategy of domination reduces them to tools, to things.

Ferdinand's fascination with his sister is equally strategic. His leering assurances to her that all of her most private thoughts and actions will come to light marks the invasive urge to control of the authoritarian voyeur.[11] The news of the duchess's liaison brings the social element firmly into view, for Ferdinand's fantasy leaps to the assumption of class disparity. He imagines "some strong thigh'd bargeman; / Or one o'th'wood-yard, that can quoit the sledge, / Or toss the bar, or else some lovely squire / That carries coals up to her privy lodgings" (2.5.42–45). (When he actually discovers Antonio's identity, he describes him as "A slave, that only smell'd of ink and counters, / And ne'er in's life look'd like a gentleman, / But in the audit-time" [3.3.72–74].) This anger specifies *cross-class* rivalry, and the debasement by occupation marks the intensity of the aversion.[12] For him invaders are mere laborers, well-equipped with poles and bars, false, and potent; by coupling with the duchess they couple with him and contaminate him, taking his place. His contrary desire is for exclusiveness, which he pursues not by intercourse but by blockage. Mulryne is right, I think, to doubt the urge to physical consummation: for Ferdinand the passion's fruit is in denial, closed and whole in his preemptive possession. To use Firth's terms, the point of Ferdinand's incestuous rage is not the achievement of sexual relations, but the denial of institutional slippage via contaminating relation. Just as the taboo is cast as a denial but functions as a positive pressure outward, so Ferdinand's infringing attitude looks like a desire but functions as a hostile withdrawal inward. As James Nohrnberg has suggested in another context, "incest has some claim to being a kind of intentional chastity" (432).

This formulation helps decipher another recalcitrant fact. Firth notes that "in general the harmony of group interests is maintained" by the taboo; "the 'horror of incest' then falls into place as one of those supernatural sanctions, the aura of which gives weight to so many useful social attitudes." But in some cases the reverse is true: "Where [group interests] demand it for the preservation of their privileges, the union permitted between kin may be the closest possible" (340). If Ferdinand's incestuous impulse is determined by class paranoia, then he might well feel a cognate but reversed horror for the out-marriage which contravenes what he needs to believe about social absolutes. Firth frames just this affective reversal in terms of racial rather than class out-marriage.

> The attitude toward incest has something in common with a popular, uninformed view about union of the sexes in the "colour problem." Here one meets with a comparable repugnance to the idea, the same tendency to put the objection of a "natural" or "instinctive" foundation. Close family sentiment is even invoked as the clinching argument in favor of the impossibility of the admission of such unions—in the well-known formula, "Would you like to see your sister marry. . . ." Here, as in the case of the prohibition of the union of very close kin, is an irrational emotional attitude, developing from a set of powerful complex social institutions. (341)

Hamlet is horrified that his own mother would "post with such dexterity to incestuous sheets." Ferdinand's horror is quite equally aroused by posting and dexterity, but instead of incest the referent is the duchess's horrifying out-marriage.[13]

Her action is also threatening to Ferdinand because it suggests that the supposedly ontological class categories are brittle, and will fall to the powers of flexible self-determination exhibited by the duchess and her base lover. This rewriting of the rules threatens to impose an awareness beyond his tolerance, of the human origin, and thus the mutability, of the ultimate elevation upon which he rests himself. The suggestion is even more frightening in view of its source—one of his own kind, become heretic, apostate. His cruel execution of the duchess may thus have several overlapping motives. To destroy her is to destroy the necessarily potent source of doubt, and the process of destruction reconstitutes them both: she is now the felon, the outlaw; he, the transcendent judge. His imprisonment of her re-isolates her, puts her in her place, and so restores her status as untouchable, in a private realm which only he may enter. And if her murder counts as a kind of rape, a consummate possessing, he typically employs an agent, a debased and dehumanized prosthesis used teasingly, like the dead man's hand. (The modern phrase "object rape" seems extremely appropriate here.) So Ferdinand maintains the style of alienation we have seen on the bench (or, for that matter, in the voyeuristic boudoir scene). Such devices allow his forbidden conduct while punishing hers, and then allow him to deny his implication in them. This final evasion is couched in revealing terms, for he returns to the issue of disparity in rank when interrogating Bosola for what has now become an unauthorized murder: "Let me but examine well the cause: / What was the meanness of her match to me?" (4.2.281–82). Her marriage was for him an adulteration which his own fantasy of possession was designed to occlude. He now averts his eyes from his aversion, and so alienates himself from himself.

This usurping investment in denial can only be maintained by increasingly radical devotion to the task, a surgical practice degenerating toward ultimate alienation: the solipism of insanity.[14] Ferdinand had already long contracted his ground of being to the two of them; when, gazing upon her corpse, he sees that he has accomplished his revenge for her divisive betrayal, he reveals (at 4.2.267) the striking fact that they are (were) twins, restoring a lost unity between them even as her death makes him singular. The enormous condensation at work here may be partially untwisted with the aid of Pausanias's alternative version of the Narcissus fable (the Ovidian version having been pertinent all along). Narcissus in fact had a beloved twin sister.

> Upon her death, he is said to have come to a fountain alone, and suffering from desire, gazed upon his own image there. But although that seemed somewhat of a solace, he at length perished with great desire, or as is more pleasing to others, threw himself into the fountain and perished.[15]

When Ferdinand looks down into his dead sister's dazzling eyes he seems himself, faces his own death too.[16] The circle shrinks again, becoming more and more rapidly only his own. When asked why he is so solitary, he replies that the noble eagle flies alone: "they are crows, daws, and starlings that flock together" (5.2.30–31). Next he tries to divest himself of his shadow, attacking even this inherent multiplicity (5.2.31ff.). His lycanthropia, unitary wolf at last, brings him to his logical end in total isolation. Walled in alone, not in a secret garden but an inward hair shirt,[17] he is finally *sui generis*, unique, a peerless class of one—a final entropic apotheosis of the superb Renaissance hero.

My analysis has sought to reclaim Ferdinand for understanding (if not sympathy) by reading his motives as the absolute and finally self-destructive core of a frightened nobility's collective project for dominance and self-protection. Ferdinand's savage gestures strip the skin from the soothing discourse of reciprocity. To the incantations of this discourse the play is addressed as a disruptive symbolic act, the reverse of Burkean Prayer—and an Imprecation.[18]

Notes

1. For a summary of the debate see Aberle et al.

2. However, see Marotti's approach to this problem, esp. 486.

3. As has often been observed, this account slurs the distinction between the incest taboo (on sexual relations within the group) and the injunction to exogamy (prohibiting marriage within the group). But for the purposes of this study the gap may be collapsed, given the link between prohibitions of sex and of marriage within a

descent group. "If therefore the rule of exogamy is to be related to the external value of the marriage alliance . . . then the intra-group prohibition on intercourse cannot be dissociated from it. The rejection of temporary sexuality within the group is in part a reflection of the rejection of permanent sexuality, and the latter is related to the importance of establishing inter-group relations by the exchange of rights in women" (Goody, 44). In the case of incest with blood relatives (as in Webster) the explanations of the incest taboo and exogamy thus tend to be congruent. The situation of incest with relations by marriage (what Goody calls "group-wife adultery" [33]) is more obscure: this infringement cannot be an exogamic crime, for the women are by definition marriageable. In any case, Goody connects this different offense with *internal* explanations of the taboo and so suggests a different way of dealing with, say *Hamlet* or *The Revenger's Tragedy,* where the incest takes place through the "group-wife."

4. It is no surprise to find this open formulation in a pioneering study of Polynesia, a region famous (among anthropologists, anyway) for incest. This passage is quoted by way of conclusion in Middleton's "A Deviant Case," a strong argument for the non-universality of the incest taboo based on Egyptian exceptions, especially in the middle class.

5. This book has received severe strictures in reviews, but it is generally agreed that Stone is reliable on the aristocracy, my subject here.

6. For a detailed study of these matters, see Whigham, *Ambition and Privilege.*

7. A confrontation between these inner and outer boundaries is present in the normative patterns of cuckoldry in Jacobean city comedy, where an older member of the merchant rank with a young wife is often cuckolded by an active young gentry figure. Sexual interaction between members of different generations (as here between husband and wife) has been called "metaphorical incest" by Levi-Strauss (10)—witness our modern exclamation, "he's old enough to be her father"—so both boundaries may be entangled somehow.

8. The issues of restraint seem to be adapted from Ernest Jones's famous account of Hamlet's delay.

9. On the general issue of "degree" compare Selzer, "Merit and Degree," a study which overlaps in some way with my own. Selzer, however, utilizes a reified moral concept of "degree" which addresses neither the role of the concept in the period's ideological workings, nor the growing body of work in the sociology and anthropology of Renaissance culture which would ground the term in the social context to which it refers.

   Selzer does deserve credit for one of only two linkings I have seen of the incest motif to the question of isolated social grouping in *The Duchess of Malfi.* He observes in passing that Ferdinand's "tendency toward incest" is "rooted in an obsession with rank" (74). Empson's earlier comment is also somewhat better grounded. In a review of Leech's *Webster* he says that "Elizabethans believed that Lucrezia Borgia went to bed with her brothers because, owing to her intense family pride, which was like that of the Pharoahs, she could find no fit mate elsewhere" (85). Empson reports in correspondence that he cannot recall the documentary source for this suggestive claim, nor have I located it. The notion may well derive from gloating reports of rumors which circulated in Italy when Lucrezia's father, Pope Alexander VI, dissolved her marriage to Giovanni Pesaro: her husband claimed that Alexander wanted her for himself, and public opinion soon extended the idea to her brothers. I have not located any English Renaissance texts expressing this view, which modern historians regarded as the sheerest propaganda.

On *par sibi* see Price.

A word as to the status of Ferdinand's action. I take it that family relations are not static structures but *activities,* pursued in the mode specified by Bourdieu, who prefers "to treat kin relationships as something people *make,* and with which they *do* something . . . they are the product of strategies (conscious and unconscious) oriented towards the satisfaction of material and symbolic interests and organized by reference to a determinate set of economic and social conditions" (35–36). Bourdieu's analysis of parallel-cousin marriage, "a sort of quasi-incest" strategically deployed (40), offers an extended test of this view (see 307–71).

At this point I should also mention Bob Hodge's interesting article on false consciousness in Webster, which covers some of the same ground this essay addresses. (Hodge's piece appeared when this study was largely complete.) I will not attempt here a point-by-point comparison of views, aside from marking the significantly different final valuations of Webster and Bosola. It is, though, worth noting that Hodge shares something like Bradbrook's sense of the separateness of the sexual and social strands of the play: "Ferdinand in *The Duchess* is the only main protagonist who is concerned about class or status, but his incestuous obsession with his sister's purity is a stronger motive than his concern for Antonio's lowly status. It is as though the dramatist had conceived his plays from two totally unrelated points of view" (106). Again, I hope, by construing these ingredients very differently, to demonstrate their deep interdependence. Nonetheless, I recommend Hodge's piece to readers interested in the social freight of Webster's play.

10. This is Poster's useful report of Kojève's presentation of Hegel; for Hegel's argument see the Miller translation, 111–19, esp. 117 (where the terms appear as "lordship" and "bondage"). See also Sartre's discussion of the Look, 340–400. The notion fits neatly with the social situation of the Renaissance court. Further analysis might suggest that Brooke's "absolute spectacle" is an attempt to dominate the Look, to appropriate its freedom; according to Sartre this attempt would be doomed to fail (see 494–534).

11. Hunter observes of the related "disguised prince" motif that one usually finds both "the desire to participate" and "the desire to condemn and withdraw" (101). Other relevant materials for this courtly *concupiscentia oculis* are Auden and Whigham.

12. That we are still responsive to such shocks, though perhaps along different axes, may be seen by reference to Billy Wilder's *Sunset Boulevard* (1950), where we respond with a similar shudder to the news that Erich von Stroheim, Gloria Swanson's butler, is her former husband. Then as now these are categories difficult to mix.

13. This argument revalues the status, as evidence of incest, of Ferdinand's turbulent response to his sister's marriage. It also reflects on the formulation that he responds as a cuckold rather than a wounded brother (proposed by Brennan, 493). Whether these arguments are alternatives I don't know.

14. Williams points out (29) that the term "alienation" could literally mean "insanity" (as in "alienation of the faculties") at this time. See also *OED* "alienation" 4. The common sense of alienation from God is also relevant here.

15. I cite Nohrnberg's translation of Comes's Renaissance version from the *Mythologiae,* which details the death (see 433n); for Pausanias see *Description,* IX, 31.78.

16. Sartre's moving discussion of sadistic torture is worth comparing to Ferdinand's

final reaction. Sartre says that one who loves wants to be chosen both freely (contingently, from among others) and absolutely (to be the unique occasion of the total limitation of the beloved's capacity to choose) (479). The sadist fastens on this latter aspect of the irrevocably contradictory desire, seeking to appropriate the other's freedom, to steal and own it: "this is why the moment of pleasure for the torturer is that in which the victim betrays or humiliates himself" (523). But the victim always *chooses* the moment to yield, and so retains his freedom and denies it to the sadist, Sartre argues (523). When the duchess says, "Dispose my breath how please you" (4.2.228), she chooses her death and retains her freedom unbroken, frustrating Ferdinand's desire for ownership. The result is that "the sadist discovers his error when the victim *looks* at him; that is, when the sadist experiences the absolute alienation of his being in the Other's freedom . . . The sadist discovers that it was *that freedom* which he wished to enslave, and at the same time he realizes the futility of his efforts" (525–27). Maybe this is why Ferdinand says "Cover her face." In any case, the immediate imputation of the crime to Bosola may be the displacement of failure.

17. I owe this striking and obviously authorial view of the internal hair to Baker (350).

18. For a much fuller version of this essay, dealing also at length with the duchess, Antonio, and Bosola, see "Sexual and Social Mobility in *The Duchess of Malfi*," *PMLA* 100 (1985): 167–86.

Works Cited

Aberle, David F., et al. "The Incest Taboo and the Mating Patterns of Animals." *Marriage, Family and Residence.* Ed. Paul Bohannon and John Middleton. Garden City: Natural History, 1968, 3–19.

Auden, W. H. "The Joker in the Pack." *The Dyer's Hand.* New York: Vintage, 1968. 246–72.

Baker, Susan C. "The Static Protagonist in *The Duchess of Malfi*." *Texas Studies in Literature and Language* 22 (1980): 33–57.

Bourdieu, Pierre. *Outline of a Theory of Practice.* Trans. Richard Nice. Cambridge: Cambridge UP, 1977.

Bradbrook, Muriel C. *John Webster, Citizen and Dramatist.* New York: Columbia UP, 1980.

Brennan, Elizabeth M. "The Relationship between Brother and Sister in the Plays of John Webster." *Modern Language Review* 58 (1963): 488–94.

Brooke, Nicholas. *Horrid Laughter in Jacobean Tragedy.* New York: Harper, 1979.

Burke, Kenneth. *A Rhetoric of Motives.* 1950; rpt. Berkeley: U of California P. 1969.

Castiglione, Baldassare. *The Book of the Courtier* (1528). Trans. Thomas Hoby (1561). New York: Everyman: Dutton, 1966.

Empson, William. "Mine Eyes Dazzle." *Essays in Criticism* 14 (1964): 80–86.

Firth, Raymond. *We, the Tikopia: A Sociological Study of Kinship in Primitive Polynesia,* New York: American, 1936.

Goody, Jack. "A Comparative Approach to Incest and Adultery." *Marriage, Family and Residence,* Ed. Paul Bohannon and John Middleton. Garden City: Natural History, 1968. 21–46.

Hegel, Georg. *Phenomenology of Spirit.* Trans. A. V. Miller. Oxford: Clarendon, 1977.

Hodge, Bob. "Mine Eyes Dazzle: False Consciousness in Webster's Plays. *Literature, Language and Society in England, 1580–1680.* By David Aers, Bob Hodge, and Gunther Kress. Totowa, N.J.: Barnes and Noble, 1981. 100–21.

Hunter, G. K. "English Folly and Italian Vice: The Moral Landscape of John Marston." *Jacobean Theatre.* Ed. John Russell Brown and Bernard Harris. New York: capricorn, 10960: 85–111.

Jones, Ernest. *Hamlet and Oedipus.* 1949. Garden City: Anchor-Doubleday, 195.

Leech, Clifford. *Webster: The Duchess of Malfi.* Studies in English Literature 8. London: Edward Arnold, 1963.

Lévi-Strauss, Claude. *The Elementary Structures of Kinship.* Trans. James Harle Bell, John Richard von Sturmer, and Rodney Needham. Boston: Beacon, 1969.

Lucas, F. L. ed. *The Complete Works of John Webster.* 4 vols. London: Chatto, 1927.

Marotti, Arthur F. "Countertransference, the Communication Process, and the Dimensions of Psychoanalytic Criticism." *Critical Inquiry* 4 (1978): 71–89.

Middleton, Russell. "A Deviant Case: Brother-Sister and Father-Daughter Marriage in Ancient Egypt." *American Sociological Review* 27 (1962): 603–11.

Mulryne, J. R. "*The White Devil* and *The Duchess of Malfi.*" *Jacobean Theatre.* Ed. John Russell Brown and Bernard Harris. New York: Capricorn, 1960: 201–35.

Nohrnberg, James: *The Analogy of* The Faerie Queene. Princeton: Princeton UP, 1976.

Parsons, Talcott. "The Incest Taboo in Relation to Social Structure." *The Family: Its Structures and Functions.* Ed. Rose Laub Coser. New York: St. Martin's, 1974.

Pausanias. *Description of Greece (Descriptio Graeciae).* Trans. W. H. S. Jones. London: W. Heinemann, 1918.

Poster, Mark. *Existential Marxism in Postwar France: From Sartre to Althusser.* Princeton: Princeton UP, 1975.

Price, Hereward T. "Like Himself." *Review of English Studies* 16 (1940): 178–81.

Sartre, Jean-Paul. *Being and Nothingness.* Trans. Hazel Barnes. New York: Pocket Books, 1966.

Selzer, John L. "Merit and Degree in Webster's *The Duchess of Malfi.*" *English Literary Renaissance* 11 (1981): 70–80.

Stone, Lawrence. *The Family, Sex and Marriage in England, 1500–1800.* London: Weidenfeld, 1977.

Whigham, Frank. *Ambition and Privilege: The Social Tropes of Elizabethan Courtesy.* Berkeley: U of California P, 1984.

Williams, Raymond. *Keywords: A Vocabulary of Culture and Society.* New York: Oxford UP, 1976.

24

Beatrice-Joanna and the Rhetoric of Love

THE CHANGELING (1622)

Sara Eaton

Forsooth, if we are to hear of no wickedness, history must be done away with. So those comedies should be prized which condemn the vices which they bring to our ears, especially when the life of impure women ends in an unhappy death.

—*Scaliger*

Scaliger's prized deaths of "impure women" suggest the seriousness of Renaissance attitudes toward femininity. Conventionalized in Courtly Love literature and under scrutiny in Puritan sermons and the popular press, femininity was considered especially in terms of modes of appearance, whether physical or theatrical. As Tuke explained in his *A Treatise Against Painting,* "It is not enough to be good, but she that is good, must seem good: she that is chast, must seem chast."[1] This distinction between feminine being and seeming pervaded dominant Renaissance ideologies concerning and defining the wickedness of women. Implicit in the Courtly Love and edenic ideologies, for instance, is the assumption that women may be what they are, but that their gender does not allow them to seem so. Such logic allowed for a woman who failed to seem pure to be thought impure.

Complicating these Renaissance notions of feminine "seeming" is the fact that their source was male. Edenic and Courtly Love representations of women focus on female figures whose apparent purity is undercut by their failure to fulfill male expectations of their behavior. These notions of femininity subjected woman to a double-bind of either being pure but not seeming so or seeming so but not according to male conventions. Middleton and Rowley, I will suggest, locate the "frightful pleasure" of *The Changeling* in this double-bind. By linking the male problem of knowing women, the confusion of being and seeming, to the rhetoric of Courtly Love and edenic longing, the play displays its linguistic exchanges as a drama of sexual revenge leaving the deaths of impure women to be "prized."

Throughout *The Changeling,* Beatrice-Joanna succeeds all too well in her attempts to be as she is perceived. On the one side of Courtly

Love's polarities, she portrays Alsemero's idealization of her. On the other side, she personifies DeFlores's view of self-degradation. Her rhetoric merely reproducing theirs, Beatrice-Joanna becomes an apparently harmonious representation of their conflicting desires. As a woman capable of seeming to be as they perceive her, she comes to perceive herself as an image of both idealized and degraded femininity—as a fallen Eve. Not autonomous in her actions, Beatrice-Joanna internalizes and reflects the inherent contradictions in male perceptions of women, especially as couched in the rhetoric of Courtly Love. Through Beatrice-Joanna's representation of the effects of Courtly Love, *The Changeling* indicts courtly rhetoric in its historical personification as unhappy death.

If it is not surprising that Middleton and Rowley use Courtly Love rhetoric to expose its contradictions, it is surprising how many critics, like Scaliger, argue that Beatrice-Joanna is morally culpable in how she is perceived.[2] Such critical arguments repeat the characters' expectations for feminine behavior, that women should be as they seem. From this point of view, Alsemero or DeFlores is seen as the hero of the play, and Beatrice-Joanna, who has concealed her ethical vacuity and fooled the male characters into believing romantic notions about women, gets exactly what she deserves. This perspective does not account for the play's action, which forms in reaction to Beatrice-Joanna's attempts to be equal to the male characters' perceptions. If the critical endeavor accepts the notion that female characters should be merely the vehicles for other characters' moral and aesthetic "pleasures," Beatrice-Joanna's fate is trivialized, the male characters' views are valorized, and the main thrust of Middleton and Rowley's drama is lost.

The question the play asks, then, is what kind of pleasures women can offer. It shifts attention from the revenge tragedy motifs, heroic concerns, to psychological and linguistic ones that can reflect the mechanics of sexual revenge. Although one of *The Changeling's* most obvious dramatic constructs is a tragic exploration of "the lunatic, the lover and the poet," contemporary expectations for Senecan conventions are distinctive in this play's dramatic structure primarily because they matter so little. For example, Alonzo's ghost, instead of either terrorizing the guilty DeFlores and Beatrice-Joanna or urging his brother toward revenge, becomes "some ill thing that haunts the house."[3] His brother, the justified avenger, is frustrated; DeFlores enacts a sexual revenge. Traditional Senecan conventions are trivialized so that the audience must focus on characters who appear in a tragic "moonlight madness," slowly turning into a nightmare that explores the possession of women through the language of Courtly Love.

The dialogue in the first four acts presents polite, courtier-like statements, full of the customary wit and neoplatonic conceits common to wooing in Renaissance drama. But the characters puncture these dialogues with frequent asides that reveal to what extent the public, idealized language masks the characters' other assessments of situations. For example, in Act II, scene i, approximately two-thirds of the first ninety lines are spoken in either soliloquies or asides. Regardless of how this display of "private" language is staged, the audience is aware of these shifts in the play's language. Indeed, most of the dialogue between Beatrice-Joanna and DeFlores is directed toward the audience through asides:

> Bea. [Aside] Again!
> —This ominous ill-faced fellow more disturbs me
> Than all my other passions.
> De F. [Aside] Now't begins again;
> I'll stand this storm of hail though the stones
> pelt me.
> [II. i. 52–54]

Her passionate revulsion and his physical determination are forcefully articulated—to the audience. The content and tone of the asides in themselves introduce a second level of signification in addition to that of the play's public language.[4]

The public and private languages demonstrate both sides of the rhetoric of Courtly Love, the idealized language appropriate to wooing, and the private language reflecting physical corruption. Beatrice-Joanna lives in a world where expectations of "transformations" in love are expressed in one version of Courtly Love rhetoric while the characters' private assessments of their world and each other are expressed in another. In a sense, then, the public dialogues, both in the plot and subplot, are merely a veneer covering other meanings in the play. By Act V, moreover, the asides of the first four acts disappear, as their reflections on the nature of love's transformations prevail and become the primary language. Although *The Changeling* here moves toward a rhetorical unity, I will suggest that this unity is essentially repressive: both the public and private languages hinge on the possession of females. In fact, Beatrice-Joanna's death at the end of the play means the end of her attempts to be rhetorically effective in her own world. The rhetorical unity of the play, then, amounts to the silencing of Beatrice-Joanna.[5]

Beatrice-Joanna's body is the referent of the play's rhetoric; the male characters discuss her as an object to be claimed and possessed. Alsemero views her as the ideal lady in a Courtly Love scheme in which he wants to believe; his language is the most obvious example of *The Changeling's* public discourse. His talk of magic potions and his constant observations of omens reflect his doubts about love while reinforcing his idealized perceptions of Beatrice-Joanna as the perfect woman. His opening declaration, "With man's first creation, the place blest, / And is his right home back, if he achieve it" (I. i. 8–9), closes off Beatrice-Joanna's actual sexual identity by linking it to Eden and the temple where he first sees her. His perception of her sacred sexuality is verified and, from his point of view, realized in his physician's closet. There he keeps his "Book of Experiments Call'd Secrets in Nature" (IV. i. 24–25), the "key that will lead to a pretty secret" (IV. ii. 111)— the secrets of chastity and feminine sexuality. Declaiming that she is "Chaste as the breath of heaven, or morning's womb, / That brings the day forth, thus my love encloses thee" (IV. ii. 149–150), he perceives Beatrice-Joanna as a way back to a sacred and enclosed world through his possession of her. His exalted perception is ironically revealed as an obsessive possessiveness when, in the last act, he forces her into the closet with the macabre threat, "enter my closet; / I'll be your keeper yet" (V. iii. 86–87).

But from the beginning of the play, when Alsemero tells her that "there is scarce a thing but is loved and loathed" (I. i. 126), we are aware that his view includes the underside of the Courtly Love tradition: the woman-as-monster, the Duessa. Alsemero "cannot be too sure" (IV. ii. 126) as he tests her virginity; he is disturbed and uncertain about his role as a courtly lover and distrusts his own judgment (an attitude that Jasperino, his man, aids and abets). Beatrice-Joanna argues that Alsemero is as implicated as she is in the murders, because she has become a "cruel murd'ress" (V. iii. 65) to insure their marriage. He is not affected by this reiteration of the argument used so successfully with Beatrice-Joanna by DeFlores. He ignores any logic or psychological truth in her argument, and instead pronounces his sense of her static, inherently flawed sexuality. Saying "Twas in my fears at first, 'twill have it now: / Oh, thou art all deformed" (V. iii. 76–77), he thinks of the marriage-bed in a crypt, "itself's a charnel, the sheets shrouds" (V. iii. 83), even though the marriage has not been consummated. Conflating sex and death, ignorant of how Beatrice-Joanna, DeFlores, and even Diaphanta have allied to insure his marriage, "this dangerous bridge of blood" (V. iii. 81), Alsemero expects Beatrice-Joanna to be a chimerical representation of female sexuality. She functions as a vaginal pathway back to an edenic world that he would also test in this one.

Alsemero begins the play as a frustrated revenger, and manages to continue in that role as he constantly suspects the "murderer" of his illusions to be one of the characters around him. Beatrice-Joanna becomes the vehicle for his return to a perfect world at the same time that she represents that impossibility. This dream requires a passive Beatrice-Joanna who does not murder, who will remain in the closet of "sweet secrets" as an imagined but frustrated version of female sexuality. When Alsemero forces her into the closet in Act V, his language again stresses love's dual nature: "I'll be your pander now; rehearse again / Your scene of lust, that you may be perfect" (V. iii. 114–115).

Alsemero's actions after this reveal the extent to which he has strengthened his allegiance to Vermandero, Beatrice-Joanna's father, in reaction to his own perceptions of love. His consolation to Vermandero as they view the bodies—"Sir, you have yet a son's duty living" (V. iii. 216)—suggests that "his right home back," the edenic world he has searched for since the opening of the play, is organized around a father who is still living. Alsemero sees himself as replacing Beatrice-Joanna in her father's eyes; he would maintain both his perception of female sexuality, and his identity as a would-be revenger, by acting in an essentially adolescent role that grants him the "father's son" position he has filled throughout the play. But, implicated by his marriage and Beatrice-Joanna's death, his place in this patrilineal system is based on ambivalence: his idealization and denial of Beatrice-Joanna's actions and what they mean.

Alsemero desperately needs to maintain the closet of "sweet secrets," although he never really recognizes the fears and desires projected on the "fallen Eve" locked up in it. He avoids meaningful action, when, for example, he thinks on his marriage: "The bed itself's a charnel, the sheets shrouds / For murdered carcasses; it must ask pause / What I must do in this" (V. iii. 83–85). And he counsels repression when he recommends to Vermandero: "Let it be blotted out; let your heart lose it, / And it can never look you in the face / Nor tell a tale behind the back of life" (V. iii. 182–184). Implied by his language, Alsemero's ambivalence is revealed in his actions—other than bedding Diaphanta and locking first Beatrice-Joanna and then DeFlores in the closet, he does nothing to initiate dramatic action. In the final analysis, Alsemero finds his "right home back" by locking his psyche in a closet of secrets.[6]

The other important male character, DeFlores, speaking in the corrupted private language of the asides, the underside of Courtly Love rhetoric, views Beatrice-Joanna as an "odd feeder" (II. ii. 153). His language and gestures characterize him as driven toward a violent, deadly possession of Beatrice-Joanna, and his view of her character, like Alsemero's, is a projection of his own desires. He would "thrust [his] fingers / Into her sockets" (I. i. 236–237), confusing a vaginal metaphor with, perhaps, a visual reference to her gloves. Anticipating fulfillment of *his* projected erotic intentions, he presents her dead Alonzo's finger with her betrothal ring still on it. Representations of death and sexual possession are further conflated when, after killing the proxy-bride, Diaphanta, he brings her charred body back for Beatrice-Joanna to see. In these incidents, DeFlores implicates Beatrice-Joanna in the murders through her perceptions. That is, he would have her see what he has seen and done for her favors. Description will not suffice. Distrusting the idealized metaphors of Courtly Love—the public language that Beatrice-Joanna espouses—he consistently produces the content, the bodies, that result from her usage of the play's public language. It is thus DeFlores who interprets and reproduces her metaphoric intentions in the flesh, enacting these connections between language and actions. When Beatrice-Joanna and DeFlores are locked into the closet together, Alsemero assumes fornication; instead, in an attempt at ultimate consummation, DeFlores stabs her with his penknife. Finally, stabbing himself and presenting his own body "as a token," he tells the dying Beatrice-Joanna to "make haste"; he would "not go to leave [her] far behind" (V. iii. 175, 177).

In his death speech, DeFlores tells Alsemero of his greedy obsession with Beatrice-Joanna; the taking of her virginity "was so sweet to me / That I have drunk up all, left none behind / For any man to pledge me" (V. iii. 169–171).[7] This is wishful thinking. DeFlores's actions can only be seen as an endless pursuit of absolute consummation, a continuous circling around a deflowered Beatrice-Joanna who by his own definition has been rendered nothing. For this reason, quite literally, he cannot get enough of her. Throughout the play, DeFlores signifies his intentions toward Beatrice-Joanna through violent oral and anal metaphors. He wants to "drink her up," and produces pieces of his murdered victims for her approval.[8] His metaphors indicate an intense egotism that he projects back on Beatrice-Joanna, anticipating that "peace and innocency has turned [her] out / And made [her] one with [him]" (III. iv. 139–140). To DeFlores, as with Alsemero, Beatrice-Joanna is still primarily the imagistic locus for an active psychological exchange of introjected and projected male sexual desires. But if Alsemero creates Courtly Love's version of idealized feminine sexuality, DeFlores designs one for his digestive tract. Beatrice-Joanna's identity remains elusive except in terms of the sexual excitement she generates, one that promises a reunion with Alsemero's and DeFlores's version of the "Other" that is "I."

What Alsemero locks away, DeFlores greedily drinks up. These two male characters would seem to be the play's actual "twins of mischief" (V. iii. 142). Their projections of desire onto Beatrice-Joanna seem to shape the play's rhetoric. Together Alsemero and DeFlores enact two psychological motions involved in the production of Courtly Love rhetoric. In a romance or a single poet's inspirational mode, Alsemero's idealization of Beatrice-Joanna would be complementary to DeFlores's ingestion or internalizing of what she represents as an idealized figure. Split, the two men act out variants of Courtly Love's tragic potential occurring when the source of poetic inspiration may not be as she appears. Frederick Goldin explains that in a harmonious Courtly Love relationship, the lover seeks the "guiding image of his completeness":

> first, that image coincides with the self-image of his class, so that the more he pursues his own desires, the more he is at one with his equal, the more he is part of a community; second, that personal image of his perfection, because it is embodied in the person of the lady, is now capable of responding to him, of loving him and making it possible for him to be at one with the image that guides him. This joy is worth the renunciation of every other joy, for it gives inner peace and certainty. Here now is the perfect dream of love: all the aspects of the Courtly man become harmonious and one.[9]

Alsemero constructs a "self-image of his class" which DeFlores would locate inside the psychological boundaries of his body. Like their characteristic languages, these men are psychological doubles, enacting the implications of their rhetoric.

Alsemero fears Beatrice-Joanna's unworthiness to the same degree that DeFlores defines her as such; conversely, DeFlores fears sharing Beatrice-Joanna with the "community" formed through her idealization to the same extent that Alsemero desires access to it. These characters could find completion in each other, and Beatrice-Joanna would still be the vehicle for expressing their desires. Instead, both characters act as though "knowing" Beatrice-Joanna as the "Other" includes seeing a corruption which must be enclosed, termed nothing, and rendered silent. The metaphors which reveal this knowledge deny her an autonomous identity while disclaiming any responsibility for her murder. What does she do to trigger the violent insistence that she has failed to reflect adequately their expectations of harmonious completeness?

In a play where the men see what they want to see, Beatrice-Joanna says: "Would creation— . . . had formed me man . . . / Oh, tis the soul of freedom. / . . . I should have power / Then to oppose my loathings, nay, remove 'em / For ever from my sight" (II. ii. 107–109, 111–113). Beatrice-Joanna enlists DeFlores as her "man" primarily to dispose of Alonzo, upon whom her "eyes were mistaken" (I. i. 85). Her father is determined to see her married; whether to Alonzo or Alsemero seems to be of little importance so long as the marriage amounts to "the addition of a son" (II. i. 99). She would marry Alsemero, whom she sees "now with the eyes of judgment / And see the way to merit, clearly see it" (II. i. 13–14). In this world, it does not occur to her to act alone; she defines herself through others' perceptions of her, and she is, consequently, powerless "to oppose [her] loathings." She would "see" as the male characters do, but unlike them, she needs an accomplice to turn her dreams into the play's "reality." Accordingly, she always assumes that DeFlores will respond as a courtier to her request for service. The "merit" she sees in Alsemero is his embodiment of the idealized Courtly Love rhetoric; ironically, he becomes her frustrated chivalric lover.

More importantly, she begins to perceive the world around her through male eyes. She becomes the Eve around whom Paradise will collapse. She is initially horrified at DeFlores's serpent-like interpretation of her complicity in Alonzo's murder—she says, "Thy language is so bold and vicious" (III. iv. 123)—but she finally is seduced by her own perceptions of what Alsemero and DeFlores represent. While before her defloration she asks, "Was my creation in the womb so cursed / It must engender with a viper first?" (III. iv. 165–166), she later declaims that "the east [the sunrise] is not more beauteous than [DeFlores's] service" (V. i. 72). She shares with Alsemero the public language that characterizes her perceptions of her world at the same time that she inures herself to the growing heap of bodies around her. Personifying Alsemero's ambivalence, she incorporates the debased concept of self that DeFlores offers.

Beatrice-Joanna's anger and disappointment with Diaphanta's lust in the marriage bed that should be hers, and her insistence to the end that she has been sexually honorable, do not necessarily indicate her villainy, or even her guilt. Rather, she refuses to relinquish what she perceives as her prerogative in the Courtly Love scenario. As DeFlores works out the details for Diaphanta's death, Beatrice-Joanna declares that she is "forced to love [him] now, / 'Cause [he] provid'st so carefully for my honor" (V. i. 47–48). Here, sex, death, love, and honor become equational terms, and the play's meanings behind the private and public languages converge. Still, she relies on DeFlores to implement those meanings, since she "must trust somebody" (V. i. 15) to sustain her power in a patriarchy. Beatrice-Joanna allows DeFlores to realize her dreams, to act on, and thereby define, her perceptions of what constitutes powerful behavior. For Beatrice-Joanna, DeFlores becomes the active equivalent of the asides in the first four acts; he is the agent of her desire to be as she appears.

Thus, Beatrice-Joanna accepts her role as the "fallen Eve" for the male characters. She voices, manipulates, and incorporates the public and private languages of the play, the languages of male projection that comprise the rhetoric of Courtly Love. Her allegiance to their rhetoric is evidenced not only by her refusal to admit adultery, but also by her insistence that DeFlores has done her only "service," as her "honor fell with him," and then her life (V. iii. 158). By perceiving her world as if, by extension, she could have been "formed a man," she has invested in her own destruction.

The transformation in love that Beatrice-Joanna accomplishes is, finally, one of reflection—she sees herself as a mirror reflecting male desires, as a vehicle for their pleasures. She reflects back upon Alsemero and DeFlores their language through her own; she adheres to the Courtly Love discourse whose underside is enacted for her by DeFlores. In this sense, she embodies the language that characterizes her world, and she unifies in one figure what in the previous acts has been rhetorically split. The asides of the first four acts disappear in the fifth because by then Beatrice-Joanna embodies all the possibilities of Courtly Love that the rhetoric of the play can offer.

Yet, we should not be too quick to argue only for patriarchal harmony in *The Changeling*. Beatrice-Joanna is perceived by the others as being "both of sport and wit, / Always a woman striving for the last hit" (V. i. 126–127). Her "sport" and "wit" are enough to reproduce the play's private and public languages and to disturb the perfectly narcissistic image both Alsemero and DeFlores want to have mirrored back to them. Her dream of acquiring male prerogative is expressed, as Stilling suggests, in "the language of female rebellion, shown as an impulse toward evil."[10] Because she insists that she speaks the language of Courtly Love and that both Alsemero's and DeFlores's views of her are equivalent to her own perceptions (for which she has "kissed poison . . . stroked a serpent" [V. iii. 66]), her "sporting" discourse becomes the distorted reason for her destruction.

Beatrice-Joanna dies for the "truth within her," the power of the language she speaks and embodies. Even though she thinks her language includes her in the males' world, her rhetoric becomes the ultimate declaration of "Otherness" that DeFlores and Alsemero would close off in their possession of her. As a screen, as a vehicle of exchange in Courtly Love rhetoric, she actually reflects the opposite of what Alsemero and DeFlores *would* see. She personifies Alsemero's fears that her sexuality will disrupt his tenuous union with Vermandero, his community. To DeFlores she performs his inability to "fill himself up" with another human being, his sense of being alone in his physicality and not part of the male community he serves.[11] Both men define their community, then, in terms of other men: for Alsemero, it is Vermandero, for DeFlores, the men who cannot "pledge" him. Whereas Beatrice-Joanna mirrors what these characters would not see, she is like her counterpart in the subplot, Isabella, who reveals her suitors' folly in pursuing her love by reflecting back to them the roles they have presented to her. But Beatrice-Joanna assumes that her ability to mime, to speak the play's language of love, includes choosing how she will be perceived and possessed.

She does not "see," as Nancy Chodorow puts it, that

> feminine roles are less public or "social," that they exhibit less linguistic and institutional differentiation. . . . Women's roles are thus based on what are seen as personal rather than "social" or "cultural" ties. The corollary to this is that women's roles typically tend to involve the exercise of influence in face-to-face, personal contexts rather than legitimized power in contexts which are categorical and defined by authority. Finally, women's roles, and the biological symbolism attached to them, share a concern with the crossing of boundaries: Women mediate between the social and cultural concerns which men have defined; they bridge the gap and make transitions—especially in their role as socializer and mother—between nature and culture.[12]

Beatrice-Joanna mimes the rhetoric's failure to make the connection between "nature" and "culture," between DeFlores and Alsemero in these terms. But for the male characters, as an image of corrupted nature and failed culture, she also demonstrates the deadly possibilities of their conjunction that must be denied.

Such disintegration and disorder, moreover, threaten *The Changeling* from its first act; the characters are preoccupied with their world's outward symbols of stability—Vermandero's castle and Alibius's madhouse. Guarded against strangers, Vermandero explains that "our citadels / Are placed conspicuous to outward view, / On promonts' tops, but within are secrets" (I. i. 167–169). The bridegroom Alonzo's obvious curiosity and his pleasure at finally seeing the "most spacious and impregnable fort" (III. i. 4) the day before his wedding ironically leads him to his death. Nicholas Brooke comments that:

> The Castle and the House are derived from their medieval and renaissance significance as emblems of both the world and the human body. The peculiar imaginative power of DeFlores' leading Alonzo through the dark passages is that the suggestive language long established for him is sustained there; it is also a journey through the organs of a female body to an anal death, *and* a descent into hell.[13]

Vermandero supports this analysis when he says: "An host of enemies entered my citadel / Could not amaze like this: Joanna! Beatrice-Joanna!" (V. iii. 147–148), followed by "We are all there, [hell] circumscribes us here" (V. iii. 164). The analogies between Vermandero's castle and Beatrice-Joanna's body are further reinforced by Beatrice-Joanna's last assertion that her blood is Vermandero's, and that the "common sewer take it from distinction" (V. iii. 153), as though she is merely waste. Seen as the source of their language, Beatrice-Joanna has been kept "secret" as a body to be found out, defended against, and purged—in her father's castle, in Alsemero's physician's closet, and in DeFlores's body—just as Isabella has been locked in her husband's madhouse to save him from cuckoldry. But where Isabella articulates the illusions in the male characters' perceptions ("I have no beauty now, / Nor never had, but what was in my garments" (IV. iii. 135–136]), Beatrice-Joanna is deluded into believing that her language, her garment of speech, corresponds to what the male characters perceive her to be in the flesh.

Beatrice-Joanna's persistent belief in the power of her rhetoric exposes Courtly Love as a linguistic system that must deny women a voice. When the play opens, Beatrice-Joanna's mother is already dead, in "heaven . . . married to joys eternal" (III. iv. 5), and Beatrice-Joanna and Diaphanta join her in deathly silence by the end of the play. In the comic subplot, Alibius, Isabella's husband, interprets Isabella's actions as a reason to "never keep / Scholars . . . wiser than myself" (V. iii. 214–215), not as reason enough to free her from the madhouse. The female characters are consistently forced to the boundaries of the dramatic action, and reduced to what is signified by the male characters. The male characters define the terms of what Chodorow calls social and cultural concerns—language, marriage, and the metaphors that connect them with sexual revenge and death. Beatrice-Joanna particularly disturbs these terms because she doubles, or reproduces and articulates, the pathological connections between Courtly Love and the action of the play. She mediates between those "secrets" of nature and culture which the male characters would not perceive as articulated in their linguistic community. She becomes what Caren Greenberg describes as "the point of intersection between masculine power and pleasure. . . . A sexual battleground important not because of her own intrinsic power, but rather as a mark of the father's power. In this sense, the wife/mother's body fulfills the first requirement of a language system: it marks something other than itself."[14] As the projection of the male characters' illusions, as the "mark" of a language system, Beatrice-Joanna is what she says—a "prophet to the rest" of her world in her destruction (V. iii. 157).

286 / Sara Eaton

The last scene of the play reenacts a psychological stasis that characterizes the entire play and reveals the extent to which Beatrice-Joanna marks something other than herself. Alsemero pledges a "son's duty" to Vermandero, who has wanted all along "the addition of a son." Beatrice-Joanna, reinforcing this patriarchal system, tells her father that she "was blood taken from [him] / For [his] better health; look no more upon't, / But cast it to the ground regardlessly" (V. iii. 150–152). DeFlores presents her with a last dead "token"—himself. None of the characters change psychologically as a result of the dramatic action. The audience senses that this scene replicates previous ones— the death scenes of Beatrice-Joanna's mother before the play opens, and Diaphanta's during it—death scenes vigorously denied as meaningful to the participants. The male characters' language, shaped by the "truth" of Beatrice-Joanna's self-affirmation as "Other" in her discourse, reveals the extent of their emotional investments in their perceptions, not only of her, but of their world. Their language, to quote D. W. Winnicott, is "organized to defend against a repetition of 'unthinkable anxiety' or a return to the acute confusional state that belongs to disintegration."[15] The characters employ Courtly Love as a language of power to defend against internal psychological disorder.

Beatrice-Joanna is as "blind" as the other characters. She becomes the "point of intersection" for locating meanings in the play because she represents a dramatic and rhetorical unity that is split in its practice. The asides, which originally were directed towards the audience, become lodged inside the dramatic action—inside Beatrice-Joanna, as her name implies. As Beatrice, she is Courtly Love's Lady; as Joanna, she is a pun, perhaps, on Gehenna, hell.[16] Her name symbolizes the play's rhetorical intensions to signify a spiritual hell. She becomes the focus of the dramatic action, organized to get her off the stage, because she is designated this hell's source.

The transformation in the language of love that does occur, the movement of the asides from the outside to the inside of the play's action, reveals the extent to which Beatrice-Joanna is both outside and inside of her own world. She marks the limits of the play's rhetoric as she embodies it. The tragedy occurs, not because Middleton and Rowley want to point out the depravity inherent in beautiful women, but because Beatrice-Joanna cannot successfully "mediate between the social and cultural categories which men have defined" as inward and outward symbolic experiences; she cannot "bridge the gap and make transitions" between being and seeming in relation to her appearance. Possessing no voice, she marks off the cultural boundaries. Her body is defined as a fortress and her language exposes the "gap," the locus of a societal "hell," that a cultural psychology has built upon the "secrets" of the female body, and then used as the referent for its language of love.

Middleton and Rowley point toward this interpretation through Alibius's description of the *danse macabre* his madmen will present to Beatrice-Joanna on her wedding night:

> Only an unexpected passage over
> To make a frightful pleasure, that is all,
> But not the all I aim at; could we so act it,
> To teach it in a wild distracted measure,
> Though out of form and figure, breaking time's head,
> It were no matter, 'twould be healed again
> In one age or other, if not in this.
>
> (III. iii. 270–276)

As a "frightful pleasure," Beatrice-Joanna (and Isabella to a greater extent than I have argued here) shapes the dramatic action of the play, and incorporates its meanings in her embodiment of its split rhetoric. Beatrice-Joanna's "unexpected passage" initiates Alsemero's and the other characters' movements toward a "right home back." They all participate in love's blind transformations. Beatrice-Joanna exposes to the audience the gaps in the drama's language even as she embodies its psychological coherence. She functions as an illusory body of text in which the male characters read the "wild distracted measure" of love's dreams turned nightmares, as though she were both the vehicle for dreaming and the origin of its hells.[17] For the audience, Beatrice-Joanna functions as an image which embodies in her designation as "Other" all the possibilities and limitations of the play's tragic language. She shapes everything and, finally, nothing, worth articulating about love's possessive power. Whether a "frightful pleasure" or an "impure woman," Beatrice-Joanna embodies the site of the interpretation of tragedy.

Notes

1. T. Tuke, *A Treatise Against Painting* (London, 1616), p. 10, as quoted by Sandra Clark, *The English Pamphleteers* (East Brunswick, N.J.: Fairleigh Dickinson Press, 1983), p. 178.

2. Fredson Bowers, *Elizabethan Revenge Tragedy, 1587–1642* (1940; rpt. Princeton: Princeton University Press, 1966), p. 204; Christopher Ricks's important study. "The Moral and Poetic Structure of *The Changeling*," *Essays in Criticism*, 10 (1960), p. 295; Roger Stilling, *Love and Death in Renaissance Tragedy* (Baton Rouge: Louisiana State University Press, 1976), pp. 250–56; Lenora Leet Brodwin, *Elizabethan Love Tragedy* (New York: New York University Press, 1971); and

Robert Jordan, "Myth and Psychology in *The Changeling*," *Renaissance Drama,* NS 3 (1970), p. 165.

3. Thomas Middleton and William Rowley, *The Changeling,* in *Drama of the English Renaissance,* Vol. II, ed. Russell A. Fraser and Norman Rabkin (New York: Macmillan, 1976), V. i. 62. All subsequent references from this edition are included in the text.

4. M. C. Bradbrook, *Themes and Conventions of Elizabethan Tragedy* (Cambridge: Cambridge University Press, 1952), p. 124.

5. The *OED* sheds light on both the title of the play and what I have been describing. Contemporary usages of "changeling" suggest: 1) One given to change, fickle or inconsistent person (the most cited explanation of the title); and 2) A person or thing (surreptitiously) put in exchange for another. Besides referring to the bed-switch and nearly every characters' shift in position in the play, the second meaning also would apply to a rhetorical exchange. The *OED* refers, moreover, to Puttenham's description of the rhetorical figure, hypallage, as a "changeling." Etymology suggests, then, that the meanings of the word are variations on exchanges or what one might call metonymic transfers.

6. For further discussion, see Melanie Klein, *Envy and Gratitude and Other Works, 1946–1963* (New York: Dell, 1975), p. 217. Klein's description of the common male pre-Oedipal movement between the love-object and the authority figure (the mother and father) seems to provide an explanation for Alsemero's psychological realignment with Vermandero.

7. This assertion reflects ironically on Alsemero's assumptions that the potion Beatrice-Joanna drank was a "pledge" of her virginity. Alsemero's and DeFlores's perceptions converge metaphorically, leaving Beatrice-Joanna at their center.

8. Melanie Klein, "The Emotional Life of the Infant," *Envy and Gratitude.* Klein's description of the infant's libidinal responses, fixated on oral and anal functions, is useful in understanding DeFlores's preoccupation with drinking and dead bodies. The infant's sense of producing feces for the mother is both a pleasurable and a frequently conflicted psychological response. According to Klein, cathexis with a death-wish towards the self or mother often occurs.

9. Frederick Goldin, "The Array of Perspectives in the Early Courtly Love Lyric," *In Pursuit of Perfection: Courtly Love in Medieval Literature,* eds. Joan Ferrante, George D. Economou, Frederick Goldin, Esther Quinn, Renata Karlin, Saul N. Brody (Port Washington, N.Y.: Kennikat Press, 1975), p. 56. For a discussion of narcissism in Courtly Love, see Goldin's *The Mirror of Narcissus in the Courtly Love Lyric* (Ithaca, N.Y.: Cornell University Press, 1967), pp. 50ff.

10. Stilling, *Love and Death,* p. 254.

11. Lacan's "Le Stade du miroir" underlies my discussion here. Without attempting to paraphrase the subtleties of his argument, I would expand it to include the psychodynamics of speech at work in the play. More suggestive, perhaps, is D. W. Winnicott's argument n "Mirror-role of Mother and Family in Child Development," *Playing and Reality* (New York: Basic Books, 1971). Responding to Lacan, Winnicott argues that "the precursor of the mirror is the mother's face" (p. 111), and expressions mediate "the discovery of meaning in a world of seen things" (p. 113). For Winnicott, as for Lacan, infants' assumptions of union with the mother are necessarily disrupted by their autonomous responses to beliefs that they are identical to, and linked with, her. Healthy development depends on these autono-

mous disruptions of the sense of doubling. In a tragedy like *The Changeling*, where language, plots, and characters double, and "seeing" becomes problematic, the characters might be experiencing "unhealthy" disruptions of the sort Winnicott describes that result in pathological behavior. To the other characters, Beatrice-Joanna may represent the mother's face.

12. Nancy Chodorow, *The Reproduction of Mothering: Psychoanalysis and the Sociology of Gender* (Berkeley: University of California Press, 1978), p. 180.

13. Nicholas Brooke, *Horrid Laughter in Jacobean Tragedy* (London: Open Books, 1979), p. 85.

14. Caren Greenberg, "Reading Reading: Echo's Abduction of Language," *Women and Language in Literature and Society,* ed. Sally McConnell-Ginet, Ruth Borker, Nelly Furman (New York: Praeger, 1980), p. 302.

15. Winnicott, "The Location of Cultural Experience," *Playing and Reality,* p. 97. Winnicott's description of an infant's creation and use of a transitional object, and the emotional investment in it, has influenced my argument here; in the way Beatrice-Joanna mediates between language and culture, she seems to function as a transitional object for the other characters.

16. My thanks to Parker Johnson for suggesting this possibility.

17. Greenberg argues that a "mediating text is female—and dead" (p. 303).

Notes on Contributors

Catherine Belsey teaches at University of Wales College of Cardiff, where she chairs the graduate Centre for Critical and Cultural Theory. Her books include *Critical Practice* (1980), *The Subject of Tragedy* (1985), and *John Milton: Language, Gender, Power* (1988).

Jonathan V. Crewe has taught at the Johns Hopkins University, the University of Tulsa, and, currently, is Professor of English at Dartmouth College. He is the author of *Unredeemed Rhetoric: Thomas Nashe and the Scandal of Authorship* (1982), *Hidden Designs: The Critical Profession an Renaissance Literature* (1986), and *Trials of Authorship: Anterior Forms and Poetic Reconstruction from Wyatt to Shakespeare* (1989).

Jonathan Dollimore is Reader in the School of English and American Studies at the University of Sussex. He is the author of *Radical Tragedy: Religion, Ideology and Power in the Drama of Shakespeare and his Contemporaries* (1984), and joint editor with Alan Sinfield of *Political Shakespeare: New Essays in Cultural Materialism* (1985). He has recently completed *Sexual Dissidence: Augustine to Wilde, Freud to Foucault* (1991).

Sara Eaton teaches at North Central College in Naperville, Illinois. She has published widely on Shakespeare and Renaissance drama and is completing a book on emblem theory and the rhetoric of praise.

Margaret W. Ferguson is Professor of English Literature at the University of Colorado, Boulder. She is the author of *Trials of Desire: Renaissance Defenses of Poetry* (1983), co-editor (with Maureen Quilligan and Nancy J. Vickers) of *Rewriting the Renaissance* (1986), (with Mary Nyquist) of *Re-membering Milton: Essays on the Texts and*

Traditions (1987), and she is completing a book, *Partial Access,* on female literacy and literary production in early modern Europe.

Marjorie Garber is Professor of English and Director of the Center for Literary and Cultural Studies at Harvard University. Her work includes *Dream in Shakespeare* (1974), *Coming of Age in Shakespeare* (1981), *Shakespeare's Ghost Writers: Literature as Uncanny Causality* (1987), and, most recently, *Vested Interests: Cross-Dressing and Cultural Anxiety* (1991).

Jonathan Goldberg is Sir William Osler Professor of English at The Johns Hopkins University. He is the author of *Endlesse Work: Spenser and the Structures of Discourse* (1981), *James I and the Politics of Literature; Jonson, Shakespeare, Donne, and their Contemporaries* (1983), *Voice Terminal Echo: Postmodernism and English Renaissance Texts* (1986), and, most recently, *Writing Matter: From the Hands of the English Renaissance* (1989). He is also joint editor with Stephen Orgel of *Milton* in the Oxford Authors series.

Stephen J. Greenblatt is The Class of 1932 Professor of English Literature at The University of California at Berkeley. He is the author of, among other works, *Renaissance Self-fashioning: From More to Shakespeare* (1980), *Shakespearean Negotiations: The Circulation of Social Energy in Renaissance England* (1988), and *Learning to Curse: Essays in Early Modern Culture* (1990).

Jean E. Howard teaches Renaissance literature at Columbia University. She is the author of *Shakespeare and the Art of Orchestration* (1984), co-editor (with Marion O'Connor) of *Shakespeare Reproduced* (1987), and has recently completed *Discourse of the Theater: Stage and Social Struggle in Early Modern Europe.*

Lisa Jardine is Professor of English at Queen Mary and Westfield College, University of London. She is the author of *Francis Bacon: Discovery and the Art of Discourse* (1975), *Still Harping on Daughters: Women and Drama in the Age of Shakespeare* (1983), and joint author with Anthony Grafton of *From Humanism to the Humanities* (1986) and with Julia Swindells of *What's Left? Women in Culture and the Labour Movement* (1990). She is currently collaborating with Anthony Grafton on a book on reading in the Renaissance.

Ann Rosalind Jones is Professor of Comparative Literature at Smith College. She is the author of *The Currency of Eros: Women's Love Lyrics in Europe 1540–1620* (1990) and the joint editor with Michèle Barrett, Annette Kuhn and Anne Phillips of the Verso series "Questions for Feminism."

David Scott Kastan is Professor of English and Comparative Literature at Columbia University. He is the author of *Shakespeare and the Shapes of Time* (1982), an Associate Editor of the Bantam Shakespeare, and author of the forthcoming *Proud Majesty Made a Subject: Representation and Authority in the Drama of Early Modern England.*

Peggy Knapp is Professor of English at Carnegie Mellon University. She is the editor of *Assays: Critical Approaches to Medieval and Renaissance Texts.* Her own work has appeared in journals such as *PMLA, ELH, Speculum, Philological Quarterly, Criticism,* and *College English.* Most recently she has published *Chaucer and the Social Contest* (1990).

Randall McLeod (Random Cloud), Associate Professor of English at the University of Toronto, has published numerous articles on Shakespeare, textual criticism, and unediting. A recent Guggenheim fellow, he is issuing a collection of his essays, entitled "Material Shakespeare." An extended version of the essay in this volume will be published in George Walton Williams's *Shakespeare's Speech Headings* (1991), and will similarly appear under the name Random Cloud.

Leah S. Marcus is Professor of English at the University of Texas at Austin. She is the author of *Childhood and Cultural Despair: A Theme and Variations in Seventeenth-Century Literature* (1978), *The Politics of Mirth: Jonson, Herrick, Milton, Marvell and the Defense of Old Holiday Pastimes* (1986), and *Puzzling Shakespeare: Local Reading and its Discontents* (1988).

Steven Mullaney teaches English at the University of Michigan, Ann Arbor. He is the author of *The Place of the Stage: License, Play, and Power in Renaissance England* (1988).

Karen Newman is Professor of Comparative Literature and English at Brown University and the Director of the Pembroke Center for Teaching and Research on Women. She is the author of *Shakespeare's Rhetoric of Comic Character* (1985) and *Fashioning Femininity and English Renaissance Drama* (1991).

Stephen Orgel is the Jackson Eli Reynolds Professor of Humanities at Stanford University. He is the author of, among other studies, *The Jonsonian Masque* (1965) and *The Illusion of Power* (1975), and he is the co-author, with Sir Roy Strong, of *Inigo Jones: The Theater of the Stuart Court* (1973). He has edited *The Tempest* (1988) for the Oxford Shakespeare series, and, with Jonathan Goldberg, is the editor of *Milton* in the Oxford Authors series. Presently he is completing a book about the transvestite acting tradition of Renaissance England.

Annabel Patterson is Professor of Literature and English at Duke University. She is the author of *Hermogenes and the Renaissance* (1970), *Marvell and the Civic Crown* (1978), *Censorship and Interpretation* (1984), *Pastoral and Ideology* (1987), *Shakespeare and the Popular Voice* (1989), and *Fables of Power* (1991). She is also the co-editor of *The Journal of Medieval and Renaissance Studies*.

James Shapiro is an Associate Professor of English and Comparative Literature at Columbia University and the Associate Editor of *Medieval and Renaissance Drama in England*. He has recently completed *Rival Playwrights: Marlowe, Jonson, Shakespeare* and is currently at work on a book on the relationships between the theater and daily life in the course of one year: *1599 and the Drama of Shakespeare's England*.

Peter Stallybrass is Professor of English at the University of Pennsylvania. He is the joint author with Allon White of the *The Politics and Poetics of Transgression* (1986), and author of the forthcoming *Embodied Politics: Discourses of Enclosure and Transgression in Renaissance England and Ireland*.

Leonard Tennenhouse is Visiting Professor of Comparative Literature at the University of Minnesota. He is the author of *Power on Display: The Politics of Shakespeare's Genres* (1986), joint editor with Nancy Armstrong of *The Ideology of Conduct: Essays in Literature and the History of Sexuality* (1987) and *The Violence of Representation: Literature and the History of Violence* (1989), and the joint author with Nancy Armstrong of the forthcoming *The Imaginary Puritan: Literature, Intellectual Labor, and the Origins of Personal Life*.

Frank Whigham teaches English at the University of Texas at Austin. He has written widely on Elizabethan culture and literature, including *Ambition and Privilege: The Social Tropes of Elizabethan Courtesy Theory* (1984). He is now completing a book on the tensions existing in status and family structures in the drama of early modern England.